Judith Wells Lindfors

University of Texas, Austin

CHILDREN'S LANGUAGE AND LEARNING

Prentice-Hall, Inc., Englewood Cliffs, New Jersey 07632

Library of Congress Cataloging in Publication Data

Lindfors, Judith Wells.
CHILDREN'S LANGUAGE AND LEARNING.

Bibliography: p.
Includes Index.
1. Language and languages   2. Children—Language.
3. Learning, Psychology of.   I. Title.
P106.L534   401'.9   79-26139
ISBN 0-13-131953-1

**To Mom and Dad,
who talked, listened, and accepted**

PRINTED IN THE UNITED STATES OF AMERICA

10   9   8   7   6   5   4   3   2   1

Prentice-Hall International, Inc., *London*
Prentice-Hall of Australia Pty. Limited, *Sydney*
Prentice-Hall of Canada, Ltd., *Toronto*
Prentice-Hall of India Private Limited, *New Delhi*
Prentice-Hall of Japan, Inc., *Tokyo*
Prentice-Hall of Southeast Asia Pte. Ltd., *Singapore*
Whitehall Books Limited, Wellington, *New Zealand*

ACKNOWLEDGMENTS

Permission to reprint the following is hereby gratefully acknowledged:

Excerpts on pp. 237, 242, 310 from James Britton, *Language and Learning* (Allen Lane The Penguin Press/Pelican Books, 1972) pp. 19, 97, 130 © James Britton, 1970. Reprinted by permission of Penguin Books, Ltd.

Excerpts on pp. 2, 3, 4, 53, 55, 66, 67 from *An Introduction to Language* by Victoria Fromkin and Robert Rodman. Copyright © 1974 by Holt, Rinehart and Winston, Inc. Reprinted by permission of Holt, Rinehart and Winston.

Excerpt on p. 94 from *How Children Learn* by John Holt. Copyright © 1967 by Pitman Publishing Corporation. Reprinted by permission of Fearon-Pitman Publishing, Inc., 6 Davis Drive, Belmont, CA 94002. Pp. 56–57.

Excerpt on pp. 211–212 from *The Open Classroom* by Herbert Kohl. Copyright © 1969 by Herbert Kohl. Reprinted with permission of *The New York Review of Books.*

Excerpts in Chapter 7 from Katherine Nelson, *Structure and Strategy in Learning to Talk.* Chicago: The University of Chicago Press Monographs of The Society for Research in Child Development, Serial No. 149, 1973. © The Society for Research in Child Development at the University of Chicago Press.

Excerpt on pp. 238–39 from Connie and Harold Rosen, *The Language of Primary School Children* (Penguin Education, 1973), pp. 49, 89. © Schools Council Publications.

Excerpt on p. 108 from Dan I. Slobin, "Comments on 'Developmental Psycholinguistics,'" in F. Smith and G. Miller, Eds., *The Genesis of Language* (Cambridge, Mass.: M.I.T. Press, 1966), pp. 87–88. Reprinted by permission of M.I.T. Press.

Excerpt on p. 353 from *The Grapes of Wrath* by John Steinbeck. Copyright 1939, copyright © renewed 1967 by John Steinbeck. Reprinted by permission of Viking Penguin Inc.

Excerpt on p. 23 from "Fern Hill" from Dylan Thomas, *Collected Poems.* Copyright 1946 by New Directions Publishing Corporation. Reprinted by permission of New Directions.

Excerpt on p. 23, copr. © 1950 James Thurber. Copr. © 1978 Helen W. Thurber and Rosemary Thurber Sauers. From *The 13 Clocks,* published by Harcourt Brace Jovanovich.

Contents

Preface and Acknowledgments

This is a book about language, for teachers and prospective teachers. There are other books about language. Many of them are theoretical in nature and are for linguists, not for teachers. And there are other books for teachers. Most of them are pedagogical in nature and, insofar as they deal with language at all, do so superficially or for purposes of presenting possible language activities for children. What I hope this book will do is provide an introduction to fundamental concepts and questions about some important aspects of language, and relate those concepts and questions to classroom concerns. Note that "classroom concerns" does not equal "classroom activities." This is not a language arts methods text, at least not in the traditional sense. You will not find "how to" chapters here on the teaching of spelling, handwriting, and listening skills. The fact is that I could not write such a book, for my belief is that learning to produce and interpret language effectively is not a separate subject area in the curriculum, some delimited body of content, but rather something children and teachers are *doing,* actively engaging in, all day long. My assumption is that by increasing their understanding of language, its acquisition, and its use, teachers can—will—become more aware of the language abilities of their children, and be better able to provide rich classroom environments which will be maximally facilitative of children's continuing language growth.

Further, this book, unlike many traditional language arts textbooks, is more about children learning than it is about adults teaching. In my view, an understanding of how children learn is the only valid starting place for considerations of what teachers might usefully be doing in classrooms. In focusing primarily on children acquiring and using language, this book is in the most important sense, an education textbook.

In order that we not lose sight of real children when the discussion becomes theoretical, I have included real dialogues, language episodes, and exercises involving children wherever possible. They are all "real" in the sense of either being actual language episodes collected by myself, other teachers, other researchers, my former students, or, in the case of the suggested exercises, real in the sense of having been tried and found helpful by many of my former students (pre- and in-service teachers).

Thus this book is an attempt (1) to provide a solid theoretical framework, a well-rooted rationale, in terms of which teachers might view the language aspects of their classrooms more insightfully, and (2) to draw on real classroom situations and interactions with children, that will make the theoretical framework more meaningful. The dual focus—theoretical framework and classroom interaction—is not in equal balance throughout the book. Of necessity, the earlier sections are more heavily weighted toward building a basic understanding of language and its acquisition, whereas the later sections balance the theory/implications goals more equally.

I hope that as you read this book you will "learn" something from it, and yet I feel more confused all the time about what "learning" is. We generally regard "teaching" and "learning" as opposites. Yet it is when I engage in activities that others call "teaching," that I know at my deepest level of knowing, that I am more powerfully engaged in "learning" than at any other time, and certainly that I am learning far more than any of the students who are engaged in an activity we designate as "learning."

But though I do not know what "learning" is exactly, I do know that dialogue is at its core—dialogue with oneself, with an author's written ideas, with friends or fellow-students, with a teacher. My hope is that as you read this book you will engage in dialogue of whatever kind is most in accordance with your own learning (dialoging?) style. Whether you dialogue verbally with other students in formal classes or in small informal sessions, or with yourself or with me in some quiet corner, I hope that you will actively engage in dialogue.

You will quickly recognize that there are different types of material in this book, including at least descriptions of selected current research, extrapolations from that research, descriptions of different and often conflicting theoretical perspectives, anecdotes, examples from child language data collected in natural settings, expression of personal convictions. I have tried to make it clear what kind of material is being presented at each point in the hope that you will consider each type on its own terms, e.g., that you will consider a description of a research study (basically presentation of factual material) differently than you will the suggested extrapolation from it (a more tentative and subjective venture). Be particularly thoughtful and cautious at those points where I express personal convictions about children and their language and their learning. These are convictions forged from my experiences studying about children and their language, observing children and their language, and interacting with children through language. I express these beliefs not as truths to be swallowed whole, but as a point of view to be considered, questioned, challenged, modified, accepted, or rejected as feels right to *you,* as fits in with where you're coming from and with what you hope to become. The teacher you are constantly in process of becoming throughout your teacher training and teaching career will be one which is *you,* which expresses your own convictions, your own style, your own continual growth and change. You can't wear someone else's beliefs any more than you can comfortably wear a dress or shirt that's "OK for somebody else, but it just isn't *me.*" The teaching you do grows from and expresses the beliefs you hold about children, about their language and their learning. Considering someone else's beliefs, as you will do in places in this book, will, I hope, help you focus, clarify, and refine your own beliefs.

Whoever would have guessed that the most recurrent and resistant problem during the writing of this book would be the use of generic *he?* My initial writing, using generic *he* throughout, brought a violent reaction from an early reviewer, a reaction including the citing of research that indicates that the "generic he" isn't so "generic" as some people think, but in fact does suggest maleness. Thinking to remedy the problem, I dutifully changed every generic "he" to "s/he," every generic "him" to "him/her," and every generic "himself" to "himself/herself." The next reviewer's reaction was as violent as the earlier one: "All this s/he, him/her, himself/herself drives me crazy! I've now read four chapters and it doesn't get any better. After all this reading, it's still driving me crazy."

Both views are valid and important. But how to resolve the matter so as to give full consideration to our female students, while achieving the smoothness that readable prose demands? I have dealt with the conflict by using generic *he* and generic *she* in alternating chapters. In odd-numbered chapters, you will find generic *he* throughout; in even-numbered chapters you will find generic *she.*

Some of my cynical colleagues, most of them from fields other than education, tell me that pre- and in-service teachers do not care about building a theoretical language base that will render their teaching practice more insightful and relevant, more responsive to children's ways of understanding their world and expressing their understanding. They tell me, "What teachers really want is a bag of tricks, language activities, 'What-Do-I-Do-Monday'— that sort of thing." My experience in working with pre- and in-service teachers has convinced me that these colleagues are wrong. Though I have met some teachers aptly described by my cynical friends, certainly the best of the teachers I have known and worked with do not fall into this category.

Surely all teachers are concerned, *as they must be,* with what they will do with their twenty-five charges from 8:30 till 3:00 Monday through Friday, week after week. No conscientious human being with such an awesome responsibility could be unconcerned about what kinds of activities might profitably fill that time. But the concern of the many good teachers I know does not end there. They are vitally interested in rooting their classroom activities and interactions with children in a solid knowledge base about language, its acquisition, and its use.

It is all well and good for researchers to be concerned entirely with theory; and it is all well and good for baby sitters to be concerned entirely with entertaining activities. But it is *not* well and good for teachers to reside entirely in either camp. Unfortunately the land between the two often seems a "no man's land," some vague area where we wander and know only what we are not: *not* really a theorist, *not* simply a practitioner.

But that land between theory and practice is not a vacant "no man's land"; it is very much someone's land—ours! We can inhabit it knowing not what we are *not,* but what we *are*—experts in integrating theory and practice into some meaningful whole, so as to provide rich interactive classroom environments for children that will make a difference in their growth in language and learning. I write this book out of my conviction that teachers want to grow in their understanding of children's language, and want to bring that increased understanding to bear on their daily interactions with children. I believe that teachers want to know and feel good about both what they are doing, and why they are doing it. It is for them—for you—that this book is written.

ACKNOWLEDGMENTS

I am grateful to many people who have supported the writing of this book in various ways. Thanks to:

the University Research Institute of the University of Texas at Austin for two small grants;

numerous reviewers somewhere "out there" who remain anonymous, but whose comments were often helpful;

Carole Urzúa who was unfailingly generous with her dissertation data (everyone should have such a publicity agent!);

Beth Driver and David Dillon for reading parts of the manuscript and providing insightful and intelligent feedback;

Carole Edelsky for reading the manuscript in its entirety and dialoging with me about it frequently. This is a much improved book thanks to her input and suggestions—always perceptive, knowledgeable, relevant.

the many students in my early childhood language acquisition classes who have tried many of the project ideas suggested here, who have willingly agreed to let me include excerpts from their projects, and most of all, who have suffered through various portions of this book in earlier versions and have given helpful feedback.

Some debts predate the writing of this book. Two are especially noteworthy. The first is to Noam Chomsky whose profound contribution to the fields of linguistics and psychology heavily influenced my own linguistic training and thus has shaped much of my thinking about language in ways so basic and pervasive that I cannot specifically identify them and thus give the credit that is due. The second is to Professor Andrew Bongiorno who, in my undergraduate days at Oberlin College, taught me through his example what it means to be a learner.

Alita Zaepfel was primarily responsible for transforming barely readable cut and pasted drafts into attractive final copy, all of which she accomplished with unfailing patience and good humor (and an occasional free review).

Many friends were supportive during this entire effort, but none more so than Nancy Richey and Mary Lou Serafine.

My parents and sisters have been a solid support team and fan club ever since I can remember, but never more so than for the duration of this project.

The final and most substantial debt is to my own family: to Brenda, Susan, and Erik who understand "what families are for." And to Ben. For this one there are no words.

Chapter 1

An Overview of Five Dimensions of Language

INTRODUCTION

Language is always and everywhere with us. It pervades every area of our waking lives—our family relationships, our friendships, our working relationships, and even our aloneness. And those of us who carry on lively conversations or write great poetry in our dreams would argue that language pervades our hours of sleep as well as our hours of waking.

With a phenomenon so vast and complex, so pervasive in human experience, it is no wonder that people the world over, throughout the centuries, have been asking questions about language—What is it? How does it work? How did it begin? How does it change? How do we learn it? No wonder, too, that the searching questions have focused on various dimensions of this complex and often elusive and unwieldy "beast."

Remember the story of the blind men and the elephant? According to one version of this tale (Saxe 1968), there were six blind men and each was trying to find out what an elephant was. The first bumped into the elephant's side and concluded that the elephant was "very like a wall." The second,

1

grabbing the elephant's tusk, decided the elephant was "very like a spear." The third, who happened to take hold of the elephant's trunk, thought the elephant "very like a snake." The fourth, feeling about the elephant's knee, assumed the elephant was "very like a tree." The fifth, happening on the elephant's ear, decided the elephant was "very like a fan." And the sixth decided the elephant was "very like a rope" after grabbing the elephant's tail. We smile at the blind men for their naiveté, each one thinking that he had "the truth," that he had grasped the essence of elephantness. But we realize too, that each man had indeed grasped some valid understanding about the kind of beast the elephant is.

As there are many valid perspectives on elephants, each based on different aspects of elephants and each lending significant insights into their nature, so there are many valid perspectives on language, each focusing on particular aspects of language, and each contributing important insights into the complex phenomenon of language. But just as no single perspective on elephants is sufficient to characterize that beast, so no single perspective on language begins to characterize that complex phenomenon adequately.

Is there a teacher anywhere who is unaware that language plays an important role—or rather, *many* important roles—in his classroom? Teaching is fundamentally a human encounter; it is person-to-person, people-to-people contact day after day. Where there are humans encountering other humans, there language lives. The classroom is one such place.

IDENTIFICATION OF
FIVE DIMENSIONS OF LANGUAGE

Below you will find some quotations relating to language. They are divided into five groups or clusters, with the quotations in each cluster focusing on an important aspect of language. Study the five clusters, and for each one try to (1) characterize the dimension of language which is being focused on (it may help to state the common dimension of interest as a question), and (2) describe the relevance of a study of that aspect of language for the classroom teacher. You may find it helpful to discuss these clusters with some friends, and to work together in trying to characterize the language dimensions and their relevance to the classroom. (Please do not go on until you have done this.)

CLUSTER 1

Language is . . . a system by which sounds and meanings are related. (Fromkin and Rodman 1974, p. 2)

We can say . . . that a language consists of all the sounds, words and possible sentences. And when you know a language, you know the sounds, the words, and the rules for their combination. (Fromkin and Rodman 1974, p. 6)

Language ... is a system which relates sounds with meanings, and when you know language, you know this system. (Fromkin and Rodman 1974, p. 12)

CLUSTER 2

All normal children everywhere learn the language of their society. (Fromkin and Rodman 1974, p. 324)

The mental abilities of a little child seem to be rather limited in many ways, yet he masters the exceedingly complex structure of his native language in the course of a short three or four years. (Slobin 1971, p. 40)

It seems that the child extracts regularities from the speech he hears, and that the sentences he produces are more like reconstruction than imitation. (Bellugi 1971, p. 115-116)

... in order to acquire language, the child must attend both to speech and to the contexts in which speech occurs—that is, he must be trying to understand what he hears, and be trying to express the intentions of which he is capable. (Slobin 1973, p. 186)

CLUSTER 3

... language influences our habitual manner of perceiving and thinking. (Robinson 1971, p. 49)

... thinking could not exist as we know it in the absence of language ... we want to know to what extent language may actively shape human thought and action. (Slobin 1971, p. 98)

Clearly, one cannot *equate* thought with either speech or language. But still, language must play an important role in some cognitive processes. (Slobin 1971, p. 102)

... language is a major instrument of thought. (Bruner 1968, P. 104)

... the basic prerequisite of language learning is conceptualization. (Nelson 1973, p. 117)

CLUSTER 4

... everywhere language consists of utterances performing a universal set of communicative functions (such as asserting, denying, requesting, ordering, and so forth) ... (Slobin 1973, p. 179)

... language is put to a multiplicity of purposes, ... (Hymes 1972, p. xxii)

... different uses of language may be seen as realizing different intentions. (Halliday 1973, p. 17)

We know far more about the developmental course of syntax, of phonology, and of semantic systems than we do about the use of speech to express, to inform, or to influence. How is the child able to request, to deny, to promise? (Garvey 1975, p. 41)

CLUSTER 5

... languages do differ in many, often substantial ways. (Postal 1968, p. 283)

All speakers of English can talk to each other and pretty much understand each other. Yet no two speakers speak exactly alike. . . . Thus every speaker of a language has his own "dialect" (called an *idiolect*). . . . Even beyond these individual differences, the language of a group of people may show regular variations from that used by other groups. English spoken in different geographical regions and different social groups shows *systematic* differences. Such groups are said to speak different *dialects* of the same language. (Fromkin and Rodman 1974, p. 252)

Speakers of English, and other languages as well, fall into groups defined by associations of similarities and differences. These groups are called *dialects*. Dialects exist as a function of all forms of linguistic isolation and separation—in space, time, social class, occupation, age, etc. (Postal 1968, p. 284)

DISCUSSION OF
FIVE DIMENSIONS OF LANGUAGE

Cluster 1

Many language scholars, two of them quoted in Cluster 1, have concerned themselves with trying to understand and describe the structure of language: What are the parts of language? How do they interrelate to form that integrated system which every speaker knows and which underlies the many uses he makes of his language? Clearly there must be some set of organizational principles for every language, which enables its speakers both to produce meaningful sentences and to grasp the intended meanings in the sentences of others.

Language has various types of units. Every language has its own set of possible sounds, sound combinations, words, and word combinations; not all selections and combinations of them convey meanings. If you doubt this, write down a straightforward sentence about ten words long. Now read the words in some other order, for example, in reverse. It is clear that there is no randomness in what constitutes the significant parts of any language and the possibilities for their combination. There is structure; some basic set of organizing principles is involved. Without an orderly, nonrandom system of organizational structure, we would not have language, but only a conglomeration of verbal noises. Every language has a structure that serves, in highly complex and abstract ways, to relate verbal sounds with meanings.[1] One way to characterize the language dimension being focused on here (and treated at length in Section One) is with the questions: "What is the structure of language?" "What are the parts of language and how are they organized and related?"

[1] In the case of some handicapped people, other means than verbal expression are employed, for example, sign language for the deaf and mute. However the basic principle is the same —our overt expression system relates to our intended meanings.

Cluster 2

The quotations in Cluster 2 focus on another fascinating and important question about language: How do humans acquire their language(s)? We know that young children are not formally instructed in the abstract complexities of language structure, complexities which trained linguists understand only imperfectly and most parents of young children understand far less. Yet without such instruction, virtually all children master the structure of at least one language system, and do so in a remarkably short time and across a wide range of diverse environments. Whether more or less fortunate intellectually, economically, socially, or physically, children learn the language of their community, and do so at a time when their congnitive functioning in other areas is far less complex than language learning seems to require. How does this happen? We will examine this question in detail in Section Two.

Cluster 3

Studying the quotations of Cluster 3 you may have gotten something of a "which-comes-first-chicken-or-egg" feeling. Is our language shaped by our mental representation of the world, or is our construction of a mental representation of the world shaped by the language that surrounds us in the community we are born into? Some scholars maintain that each language reflects and perpetuates a particular world view; it provides levels for those divisions and relations of various domains of experience which its speakers consider significant. Thus, the argument runs, when a child acquires the language of his community, he also acquires the world view held by its members, the world view expressed in the categories and relationships of the language. However, as scholars grow in their understanding (as they continue to ask more relevant and searching questions), they move away from the more simplistic question, "Does language shape thought or does thought shape language?" toward the richer question, "How do language and thought interact?" This is a movement away from a notion of either-or, one-directional influence toward a consideration of the complex mutual influence of language and cognition. Apparently cognitive growth is crucial to language growth, and language growth supports cognitive development. Each is rooted in and crucially aids the further development of the other. But *how? How* do language and cognition interact? This is the exciting question that faces us in Cluster 3 and is treated in greater depth in Section Three.

Cluster 4

As children grow, they learn much more than language structure. They develop a range of communication styles, each appropriate in certain types of situations. They learn, somehow, to take into account a host of social factors in each communication situation, and to use the appropriate expressive style for that occasion. For example, the age, sex, status, and relationship of the person with whom a child is speaking, and the context in which the communication is taking place, will significantly influence what the child says (or does not say) and how he says it. Sociolinguists, some of whom are quoted in Cluster 4, are concerned with studying language in its social context. They ask, "What are the key aspects of a communication encounter, and how do they influence one another? How do we adapt the language to various social contexts? And how does the language style used affect the social context itself?"

Language is indeed ". . . put to a multiplicity of purposes." The quotations of Cluster 4 suggest a few of these purposes, and several ways of categorizing the array of different functions our language serves. However, the categorizing system we choose for analyzing language functions is largely a matter of personal choice, and matters much less than does the profound realization of the many purposes for which we use our language each day.

Notice that this concern with language use in social contexts is different from the first concern (language structure), yet not unrelated to it. We are not talking here about the actual structure of language, but rather about the vast range of possibilities the structure of language offers for relating expression and meaning. How do speakers select and use those expressive means which are appropriate to the particular social context and purpose of the discourse? What constitutes the "appropriateness" of language within a given social context? How can we explain that young children acquire, without special tutoring, not only the structure of language, but the subtle variations in the social use of language as well? For example, how do they come to know that "Shut up, stupid" is an OK communication to a younger sibling, but not to a visiting grandparent? How does the child come to know that his mother's gentle "Bobby, are you almost ready for bed?" is not simply a question calling for a yes or no answer, but that it also conveys her desire that he move more efficiently toward that goal? In short, what is the meaning provided by the social context of the message, and how does a child learn to recognize it and adapt his language appropriately? That is a major concern of Cluster 4 and of Section Four.

Cluster 5

All natural human languages are similar in important ways. They all involve the association of verbalized sounds to conceptualized meanings; they all provide for making statements, questions, requests, equational propositions; they all include both vowel and consonant sounds. And yet, within the bounds of what constitutes human language, there is a range of diversity which has been a source of fascination for many scholars. We know that an Englishman does not talk like an Iranian; we say they speak different languages. But we know, too, that English people do not talk like Americans, though most would agree that they do speak the same language. And what of the differences between English, a single language, as spoken in Australia, Ireland, and Canada? But we do not even need to go that far. What about the English spoken by a Bostonian, a Texan, a Brooklyner, an Alabaman, a Los Angelean? These dialect differences are geographically based. There are also dialect differences relating to ethnic and social groups—what of the dialects of English spoken by Navajo children in Albuquerque, by Mexican-American children in San Antonio, by black children in Harlem, by Puerto Rican children in Miami? How can we understand and describe the endless richness within any single human language? It is not hard to see why the writers of the quotations of Cluster 5 have long been intrigued with the variations which exist within the bounds of human language possibilities. How is this diversity to be understood and accounted for? These questions face us in Section Five.

We all "have a language." What does that mean? It means, at the very least, that we control the underlying structure of at least one complex language system; that we have had the experience of acquiring this system without special tutoring; that we have a dynamic language system which interacts complexly with our cognition, both influencing and being influenced by our cognitive growth; that we have the ability to use our language structure variously and for many different purposes, automatically adapting our use to givens in the communication context in which we find ourselves, and often changing the nature of the context by altering our language style; and that we understand and have definite attitudes toward language varieties—other dialects, other languages.

THE RELEVANCE OF
FIVE DIMENSIONS
OF LANGUAGE FOR TEACHERS

The five important dimensions of language which we have focused on in our clusters of quotations, and which we will consider in greater depth throughout the remainder of this book, are not God-given categories, nor are they as separate and distinct as this categorization scheme might suggest. They are simply a few important aspects of language, selected for further consideration here because each one is not only of tremendous intrinsic significance and interest, but also because an understanding of each is vitally important to those who teach children.

Why is Knowledge of Language Structure
Important for Teachers?

Educators often speak of the importance of knowing "where the child *is.*" If we really mean this, then we must understand where the child *is* in his control of the structure of his language(s). There is perhaps no greater accomplishment in a child's life than that of learning the structure of language, much of which is accomplished in a remarkably short five or six years. To understand and appreciate the magnitude of the child's accomplishment, we must comprehend the kind of structured system that language is—so complex, so abstract in many ways, so intricate in its design. Mastery of the structure of one's language makes possible a wide range of uses for a mighty cognitive and social tool, the tool, in fact, that teachers are more concerned with than any other.

Children's control of the structure of their language, largely mastered by the time they come to the first grade, is basic to all their learning. Their understanding of what they hear and what they read, and their ability to express what they know in speech and in writing, depend on their knowledge of the relationships between the sounds and the meanings of their language. Much of what we do as teachers involves expansion and further development of cognitive, attitudinal, and social meanings. For example, "pounds," and "ounces," "liberty and justice for all," "less," "sinister," "multiply" may be new meanings for a child, but once he grasps these meanings and their labels, they find a ready home in his total language system. We take it for granted that children will tell us "I multiplied them" but not "I sinistered them." They may talk of "10 pounds" or "6 ounces," but not "10 justices" or "6 sinisters." The child knows, without our telling him, the kind of language unit the new concept/term is, and he readily incorporates it into his well developed existing linguistic framework.

As teachers, we often become so preoccupied with what a child does not know that we fail to recognize and appreciate the tremendous knowledge he does possess. An understanding of the remarkably complex language system the child controls just may, and certainly should, help to renew our respect for children and their abilities. It will also help us to sort out what we are and are *not* teaching. Such knowledge may help us differentiate, for example, between teaching a child his language, and teaching a child to *read* his language, that is, to process the printed symbols representing the language the child already knows. Thus, we will avoid falling into confusions like the following:

> There seems to us to be some evidence for assuming that the period of learning to read is one in which each child *develops an extensive internal and private grammar and phonology* [sound system] *for his language....* Up to the time of learning reading a child is asked only to mimic what he hears. He is *not asked*

to guess or to create . . . prediction is not possible until long after the business of learning to read is completed. Nevertheless this control is a final expression of *the grammar the child begins to construct as he learns to read.* (Reed and Sawyer 1970; italics added)

These authors refer to *"the language being taught"* when the child comes to the reading task, and conclude that reading should be taught ". . . as part of a unified program of instruction in language, in which the patterns of the total language are well understood by the teacher and become at least matters of unconscious knowledge to the learner." If we understand what language structure is, and if we listen to the children we teach, we will recognize that they *have* a "grammar and phonology" when they come to us, that they *do* guess and create with language (and have for a long time), that they do not "begin to construct" their language as they learn to read, and that we do not need to teach them the "patterns of the total language" for many of these they control already. When we teach children to read, we are not teaching them the structure of their language, but rather how that familiar structure is represented in printed symbols.

Further, such knowledge may help us differentiate between a child's learning the structure of a language—the parts and how they go together—and his learning to talk about that structure using agreed on labels: "noun," "verb," "suffix," "phrase." The two are very different.

Most of all, an understanding of the structure of language may help us gain a more accurate perception of our role in furthering the child's language growth. We may come to see that, as teachers, we are mainly engaged in increasing the child's meanings, expanding his range of uses of language (to include persuading, describing, narrating, explaining), and increasing his effectiveness in using language for these various purposes.

Why Is Knowledge of Language Acquisition Important for Teachers?

Extensive recent research in child language acquisition has caused us to rethink some of our most cherished traditional notions about learning, at least as these notions relate to language learning in young children. Though this will be discussed more extensively in Section Two, brief mention of a few of these notions is in order here.

We have traditionally maintained that a child will learn more effectively if we (1) structure the content to be learned so that it moves in a sequence from more simple to more complex items; (2) "reward" correct responses, thus strengthening them, and "punish" incorrect responses (for example, correct them) thus making them less likely to recur; (3) maximize the likelihood of successful responding, so that errors will not occur and be imprinted in the child's responding patterns; and (4) provide ample opportunity for the practice of correct behaviors so that they will be strengthened. But careful study of children acquiring language has made us reconsider the significance of these principles in language learning.

(1) Observing the language that surrounds children and is directed toward them, we see that, although mothers (and some other adults) do simplify their speech to children in somewhat predictable ways, there exists nothing like the carefully structured simple-to-complex sequence that is used to teach subjects like math or reading. And yet without this careful sequencing, far more children are successful in learning to speak a language than are successful in learning to read or multiply.

(2) Substantial research on children learning language in natural situations indicates that adults do not give or withhold reinforcement on the basis of the formal correctness of what children say, but rather on the basis of the truth of the message. Yet without the provision of reinforcement contingent on the correct use of language structure, all children, except those who are extremely handicapped, develop, over time, the ability to create and use sentences which the adult would call grammatically well formed.

(3) As children learn language, they say many sentences that adults would say contain "errors" or "mistakes" in form. Earlier structures like "all gone sticky" and "Where he is going?"; earlier pronuciations like "cwackers" and "twuck"; earlier word forms like "comed" and "goed," "mans" and "sheeps"; and earlier overgeneralized references like "doggie" used to refer to cats, dogs, sheep, and cows alike—are all in time replaced by adult forms. These earlier "errors" are not imprinted in the child's response patterns, but, without any drilling or special direct instruction designed to erradicate them, drop out as the child matures, and are eventually replaced by adult forms.

(4) Language acquisition research demonstrates that children early use correct irregular forms like "went," "came," and "children." However, despite their practice of these correct forms, children later replace them with the incorrect forms "goed," "comed," and "childs" when they become aware of regular patterns for expressing past tense and plural in English (Ervin 1964). The early practice of "correct" behaviors in these (and other similar) instances does *not* strengthen them. Thus sequenced content, reinforcement contingent on correctness of form, error-free responding, and practice of correct forms— whatever their relevance may be for other areas of learning (and some question their importance in any areas of learning)—clearly do not contribute significantly to the child's learning of language in any simple obvious way.

Humans are apparently endowed with innate propensities for processing the language sounds to which they are exposed in meaningful contexts, so as to construct for themselves the complex underlying system by which people in their linguistic community relate those sounds to meanings. The young child actively uses his special language learning abilities to discern regularities in the language he hears, to construct working hypotheses based on them, and to continually revise his earlier hypotheses in the light of conflicts revealed through further language exposure and use. Thus his system over time is continuously revised and refined until it ultimately matches the adult system. It is crucial that we understand the nature of language acquisition in the child —both the developmental sequence involved and the processes that the child employs—in order that we can move with this very strong current rather than interfere with it. This understanding is particularly important in view of the substantial differences we find between the way a child learns his language, and the way we have traditionally maintained that he learns other things. Recent research is beginning to suggest some ways in which we can work with the current, providing optimum environments for the child's language growth; these we certainly need to be aware of.

Though much of the child's language structure is mastered by age five or six, we find that there are typically still some differences between child language and adult language after that age. We hear a lot of "bringed" and "buyed" in first grade classrooms, and Carol Chomsky has found that some syntactic subtleties are not completely mastered by some children until as late as ten (Chomsky 1969). But perhaps more important for preschool, kindergarten, and primary level teachers are the recent findings regarding the meaning that various "school-ish" terms have for children. We have assumed all along that children understand the terms "more," "less," "same," "different," "true," "false," "equals," etc., in the same way we adults do. There is a growing body of research that suggests that this is not the case. We need to know what those terms, which are so basic in our teaching, mean to children (Behr, personal communication; H. Clark 1970; Donaldson and Wales 1970).

Why is Knowledge of the Interaction of Language and Cognition Important for Teachers?

"Is there language without thought?" "Is there thought without language?" Many answer "yes" to the first question, based on their experiences of politicians and cocktail parties. Many answer "yes" to the second, based on their experiences of not being able to "find the words" to express a deeply felt emotion or to describe a visual experience. But to answer "yes" to these questions is not to lessen the fact of the actual composite existence of thought and language in ourselves and in the children we teach. The interdependence of language and cognition is crucial in the child's movement toward what we claim is one of our major goals: maximum development of intellectual capacity. This broad goal necessarily involves the development of meanings (cognition), and the ability to express them through language and to understand others' expression of their meanings through language.

Language acquisition studies focusing on the child two years old and under demonstrate that most of his earliest utterances are attempts to express cognitive understandings, and that the understandings he expresses are precisely those he has developed through his direct physical interaction with the world—for example, utterances based on his recognition of the existence of separate objects in space ("that ball," "see baby"), the nonexistence of expected things or events ("all gone juice"). As the child grows, his language continues to develop as a device for expressing his increasing understanding of experience.

"But of course," you say. "Isn't it obvious that, in order for you to talk about something, you have to have a 'something' to talk about? You have to know something before you can talk about it." I would have thought this perfectly obvious too *if* I had never become a teacher and subsequently worked with other teachers. In classrooms, my own and those I have observed, I have so often seen teachers give children verbal labels that "labelled" nothing, that related to no concept for them.

> *T: (pointing to diagram of earthworm) And what do we call this? (Silence) This part of the earthworm? (Silence) Right here? The cliiiiii (hopefully)* . . .
>
> *C:* Clitellum.
>
> *T:* Right! The clitellum. What can you tell us about the clitellum, Jimmy?
>
> *C:* Every earthworm has one.
>
> *T:* Good. Every earthworm *does* have one.

And these children, because they had mastered the structure of their language so skillfully, were able to manipulate these empty verbal labels convincingly. We need to become aware of when we ourselves are engaging children in such mindless, empty verbal exchanges, for such interactions dangerously mislead children into thinking that meaning has nothing to do with language, and that verbalizing readily substitutes for understanding.

But not only is the child's growing language rooted in his developing meanings; it also contributes to his further development of meaning. Control of language symbols helps the child to move beyond the immediately present situation. Through language the child is able to manipulate concepts in the absence of a direct referent. Aided by linguistic expression, children can fantasize, predict, speculate, and reason about that which has meaning for them. They can go beyond the immediate—the actually present or actually experienced—to new arrangements, combinations, and possibilities. The child may in fact, only have seen one Goodyear blimp in his entire life, and that dull gray. But, aided by language, the child can go beyond this to conceptualizing and describing three Goodyear blimps, one shocking pink, one chartreuse, and one purple-and-white striped, each carrying an elephant and a duck wearing a ruffled collar and ribbons. . . .

Further, the very act of expressing our thought through language often "nails it down" for us. As adults we are all aware of this in our own experience. We understand better, have a better grip on a difficult concept, once we have struggled to put it into words, once we have written a paper about it or tried to explain it to someone else. So for children, giving expression to their developing concepts can help to strengthen those very concepts (as well as make it possible for them to receive feedback relating to those developing concepts —feedback mainly through language, of course).

A better understanding of language and cognition is important to us, then, because children's intellectual development is a major concern of ours as teachers. Cognitive and linguistic factors—both necessarily present and each contributing to the growth of the other—are crucial to that intellectual development. Increasing our understanding in this area gives us a good start on providing experiences for children which are meaning-full (not simply word-full) for them, and in which language expresses, furthers, and is furthered by those expanding meanings.

Why is Knowledge of Language Use Important for Teachers?

It is important to understand the interaction of cognitive and linguistic factors in children's growth in order to help them develop their full intellectual potential. It is no less important to understand the interaction of linguistic and social factors in order to help children toward another important goal—that of developing their full social potential, their ability to interact effectively in a wide range of social contexts.

The classroom is, among other things, a social community, a cohesive group that shares a base of common experiences. It is difficult to think of a setting that offers greater possibilities than the classroom for giving children a diverse range of situations and purposes for communicative interaction. Of course the classroom has this social potential only if we refuse to think of the classroom as a place, and think of it, rather, as people interacting.

We are all aware that we use language differently in different situations: We talk to our spouses differently than we talk to our pupils, and we talk on the phone to our intimate friends differently than we talk to a large PTA audience in the school auditorium. But when we begin to be aware of the array of situational variables that influences our use of language, we can begin to see the tremendous possibilities the classroom can offer for the exploitation of these variables. Who is the child interacting with? Someone much older? A peer? A younger child? A small group? A large group? Someone he knows intimately? A stranger? And what is the purpose of the interaction? Is the child trying to maintain a friendship relation? Trying to get something? Trying to instruct or explain? Trying to gain information? Trying to entertain? Trying to engage another in reliving a shared experience? Once we understand what situational variables affect the use of language in communication encounters, and how diverse the communication purposes of language are, then we can begin to translate these variables into experiences that we can provide for children. We can build into the child's school life opportunities for interacting with a diverse range of people for a diverse range of purposes. And through such richly varied interaction experience, the child's ability to communicate effectively in many social situations, to adapt language for a variety of social purposes, can only increase.

Why is Knowledge of Linguistic Diversity Important for Teachers?

Teachers of linguistically and culturally diverse groups of children are aware that this diversity has implications for what and how they teach. The implications are most obvious in curricular areas focusing directly on communication skills. Much has been written about alternative approaches for developing reading, writing, listening, and speaking abilities in children whose school learning experience includes more than one language or dialect. But since language pervades all of the interactions in our classrooms, the content and methodological implications reach far beyond the confines of "communication skills" into other curricular areas—for example, use of free time, and type of classroom structure. The decisions we make as to how we can best teach our students whose first language or dialect is not (standard) English, are rooted in our assumptions about where these children are in their linguistic, cognitive, and social growth, where they have been, and where they are going. As our assumptions about these children become more accurate, the learning experiences we provide for them will be more appropriate and effective. In short, a better understanding of the various language and life styles our students bring to school with them, can help us improve our assumptions about them and ultimately result in the provision of more relevant learning experiences for them.

But increased understanding of language and cultural diversity is even more important for another reason. The *who* that we teach is always more important than the *what* and the *how*. We tend to be unaware of the subtle but pervasive influence that children's varying language and behavior styles have on our attitudes toward them and on our expectations regarding their intellectual and social potential. Whether we like it or not, different language styles foster different attitudes toward people who use them. Some language styles (dialects, languages or whatever) convey "nice, but not too bright"; others convey "intelligent, but cold"; others "quick, but stuck up or hostile"; others "slow but it's not *his* fault (poor thing)," depending on who we are, what our language and life style happens to be, and what sort of familiarity we have with members of various social and linguistic groups.

Whatever problems we still have in learning to understand, accept, and effectively teach *all* the children in our increasingly diverse classrooms, there are encouraging signs that we are coming to realize that this diversity does not confuse children or contaminate their language, cognitive, and social growth, but rather contributes positively to the rich environment we know is most conducive to that continuing growth. How effectively we capitalize on that richness for children's learning will depend in no small part on how well we understand it.

Our task throughout this book will be to focus on each of the five selected dimensions of language briefly discussed here, in order to understand the specified dimension of language, and better relate our increased insights to classroom interaction. It is not an easy task certainly, but when we are done, we, unlike our blind men, may be closer to having constructed just what every classroom needs: a *whole* elephant—a richer, more comprehensive and more relevant understanding of what language is and how it lives in our classrooms.

Section One

LANGUAGE STRUCTURE

Chapter 2

Native Speaker Abilities

We are concerned in this section with what it means to know the structure of one's language. Put another way, what is it that you know when you "know a language?" What do you know about the parts of that language and the possibilities for their combination? We will begin by exploring some of the amazing abilities that you have as a speaker (or knower) of a language, abilities that you may not have thought about before. As the fish is the last to discover water, so we—always and everywhere surrounded by and participating in human language—may be the last to discover the fascinating complexities of this medium. Exploring some of the language abilities you possess may help you become aware of the knowledge you have that enables you to understand and produce sentences in your language, that same knowledge that every child will develop over time.

RECOGNIZING GRAMMATICAL AND
UNGRAMMATICAL SENTENCES

As a speaker of English, you have the ability to judge which strings of words are acceptable arrangements of appropriate parts, and which strings are not. The kind of "acceptability" we are concerned with here does not have to do with use of polite words rather than rude ones, but rather with the organization of language parts to convey intended meanings. Speakers of any language will judge some strings to be OK organizations of parts, and others not to be. Further, these judgments will, in the vast majority of cases, be the same for all speakers of that language. Here are some examples for you to judge. Put a check mark beside those sentences in the group below that you feel are unacceptable English sentences.

1. Mary married a drunken sailor.
2. It was a drunken sailor that Mary married.
3. It was Mary that married a drunken sailor.
4. That was it Mary married a drunken sailor.
5. It was drunken that Mary married a sailor.
6. It was nice that Mary married a sailor.
7. It was sailor that Mary married a drunk.
8. It was strange that Mary married a drunk.
9. It was a drunk that Mary married strange.
10. It was drunk that Mary married a strange.
11. It was a drunk that strange Mary married.
12. That Mary married a drunken sailor was strange.
13. That Mary married a strange sailor was drunk.
14. That Mary married a drunk was sailor.
15. That Mary married a drunk was inevitable.
16. Mary's marrying a drunken sailor came as a surprise to us.
17. Mary's drunken sailor came to surprise us.
18. Sailor Mary's drunken to surprise us came.
19. What shall Mary do with a drunken sailor?
20. What with a drunken sailor Mary shall do?
21. Shall Mary do drunk with what a sailor?
22. Shall Mary have fun with such a sailor?
23. With what a sailor shall Mary do drunk?

I checked 4, 5, 7, 9, 10, 13, 14, 18, 20, 21, 23, and my guess is that you did too. It would be interesting to take this set of sentences (or better yet, some set of sentences that you make up) and try them out on other speakers of English to see whether their judgments are the same as yours. Chances are they will be similar, if not identical, to your own.

What I am calling your ability to judge the acceptability of sentence strings, many linguists call the ability to judge the grammaticalness of sentences. But we need to be careful of the term "grammatical" here because for many of us this word conveys a notion of "correctness" that contemporary linguists do not intend. Probably most of us had at least one English teacher, usually somewhere between fifth grade and ninth grade, who tried to give us "good grammar" with the same kind of determination and noble intentions with which our parents had earlier tried to give us castor oil or vitamin pills. We labeled words as verbs, adjectives, nouns, interjections; we avoided ending sentences with prepositions (at least during English class); we diagrammed sentences; and we spouted definitions about "name of a person, place, or thing" on demand. Some of our teachers seemed to feel that these activities would make us "educated" and well-rounded as adults; others seemed to feel that such activities would lead us to increased social status and better paying jobs; and still others seemed convinced that these activities would build character, as the endurance of hardship is felt, by some, to do.

But if we are going to use the term "grammar," we need to rid ourselves of our traditional notions—our seventh-grade labels, definitions, shoulds and shouldn'ts of speaking, and our memories of classroom tedium and drudgery. We use "grammar" here as a neutral term, referring simply to what you know intuitively about the basic units of your language and the possibilities for their combination—the structure of your language. To say, then, that you recognize some sentences of your language to be "grammatical" and others to be "ungrammatical," is only to say that you will judge some to be sequences of language elements which are in accordance with your intuitive knowledge of the organizational possibilities of English units, and others not. Notice that your judgment of the grammaticality of a sentence does not depend on whether or not you have ever actually encountered that particular sentence before, but rather on whether you feel that such a sentence is an acceptable possibility for your language. Notice too, that your grammaticality judgments do not depend on your ability to talk about why or how you made them, nor on your ability to label sentence parts.

How do we account for the overwhelming (though not total) agreement among the speakers of a language as to which sentences are and are not grammatically possible in that language? When you know a language, you intuitively know a set of structural possibilities for sentences (possibilities for selection and organization of parts), and you recognize particular sentences as being consistent or inconsistent with that set, even though you are probably not able to actually describe the set of principles against which you are "checking" each sentence. Whatever this set of principles is, it is clearly one you share with other speakers of your language, for they, for the most part, make grammaticality judgments similar to yours, though they—like you—cannot describe the set of organizational principles against which they judge the grammaticality of each sentence.[1]

RECOGNIZING MORE AND LESS GRAMMATICAL SENTENCES

We have considered two extremes: grammatical and ungrammatical. Actually the situation is more complex and far more interesting than this. Some of the sentences we encounter are difficult to categorize simply as grammatical or ungrammatical; we might want to put them in a "well . . . sort of OK" area. Much of poetry and humor live in this middle region where sentences are often structured somewhat deviantly in order to create special effects and convey special meanings. As speakers of English (or any language, of course) there would be considerable agreement among us as to which of several sentences is "more grammatical" and which is less so—that is, which sentences conform more nearly to our notions of what constitutes acceptable arrangements of parts in the sentences of our language. A well-known trio follows, and most speakers of English would rank the three sentences from most to least grammatical as they are ordered here:

> John plays golf.
> Golf plays John.
> John plays symmetrical.

One university student, obviously more concerned about math than about golf, offered this trio as a substitute.

> I'm taking math.
> Math's taking me.
> I'm taking symmetrical.

Whichever set you prefer, you will probably find the first sentence of each straightforward enough; that is, clearly in accordance with the set of principles you have regarding parts of sentences and their possible arrangements. For the third sentence in each set, you probably feel a need to change it in some way to make it a message-carrying structure: For example you might want to change it to "John plays symmetrical*ly*" (we might picture John lining up a

---

[1]It is interesting to study the grammaticality judgments children make, to get an idea of how closely the developing system of children of various ages matches the adult's. Overall, the closer the agreement between your grammaticality judgments and a child's, the closer, we assume, is the match between the child's intuitive set of organizational principles and your own—that set of principles which serves as the basis for these judgments. See suggestion 1 on page 82 for further discussion of how you might plan and execute such a study with children.

course for himself in which both sides were identical, and he played item 1 on one side and then item 1 on the other, etc.), or to "John plays *Symmetrical*" in which "Symmetrical" is the name of a new game that has just come on the market. But the sentence as it stands is simply puzzling. There are a number of things one can "play"—golf, second fiddle, the piano, tricks, Parcheesi, sick, host, Hamlet, hop scotch—but one cannot play "symmetrical." One can take math, a coffee break, a joke, her book, tennis lessons, an aspirin, but one cannot take "symmetrical." We may want to ask, "You're taking symmetrical *what?*" We look for a something to be played or taken, and "symmetrical" alone just will not do.

But what about the middle sentence of each set? Here is where the fun is. We expect some*one* to be playing/taking some*thing*, but we find the reverse —the some*thing* is somehow controlling (playing/taking) the some*one*. It is as if we have attributed human characteristics to golf or math. We might hear John's wife, who knows her husband is not a promising golfer, say, "Golf plays John." We might hear a frustrated university student sigh, "Math's taking me." But notice that the something/someone switch in the second sentence of each set—a switch from one kind of noun to another—is much less drastic than the switch in the third sentence of each set, from a "something" (played or taken) to a descriptor word—from a noun to an adjective.

Some linguists refer to this ability of native speakers as the recognition of "levels of grammaticality." But whatever you choose to call it, the fact is that we realize when sentences violate our structural expectations in interesting ways that still convey meanings (and often add special ones), and when they violate our expectations so drastically that they cease to convey meanings at all. Poets and humorists often use language in deliberately deviant ways in order to achieve special effects. From A. A. Milne's *Winnie-the-Pooh* comes:

> "And how are you?" said Winnie-the-Pooh.
> Eyore shook his head from side to side.
> "Not very how," he said. "I don't seem to have felt at all how for a long time."(Milne 1956, p. 43)

And from James Thurber's *The 13 Clocks:*

> The Duke is lamer than I am old, and I am shorter than he is cold, but it comes to you with some surprise that I am wiser than he is wise. (Thurber 1950, p. 63)

And Dylan Thomas' *Fern Hill:*

> Now as I was young and easy under the apple boughs
> About the lilting house and happy as the grass was green,
> 　　The night above the dingle starry,
> 　　　　Time let me hail and climb
> 　　Golden in the heydays of his eyes, ... (Thomas 1953, p. 178)

Notice again that your ability to rank sentences for grammaticality levels, like your ability to judge clear cases as simply grammatical or ungrammatical, is attributable to your knowledge of a set of possible sentence elements and their possible arrangements to convey meanings in your language.

Would children rank sentences in a set from most to least grammatical in the same way that we would as adults? A reasonable expectation is that as children grow older and their knowledge of language structure comes to match more nearly that of adults, their ordering of sentences for grammaticality will also come to more nearly match that of adults, for this is an ability which is a result of their knowing the organizational principles of their language.[2]

RECOGNIZING RELATIONS WITHIN SENTENCES

A key concept in language, as in any structured system, is that of relatedness —relationships among the parts. For now, we can think of the words of our language as being its major parts (though we will want to modify this later). We know that sentences in our language are not randomly ordered strings of words. If they were, then different arrangements of the same set of words would mean the same thing and there would be no difference in meaning between, for example, "The squirrel was looking for a nut" and "The nut was looking for a squirrel." But in English, as in many languages, the order of words does make a difference in meaning. It is largely in the ordering of the parts in sentences that relationships among the meaning parts are expressed. The following sentences all contain the same set of words, but the differences in the order of words corresponds to differences in relational meanings (and in fact, some orders convey very little if any meaning at all).

> The teacher spanked the rude girl.
> The girl spanked the rude teacher.
> The rude teacher spanked the girl.
> The rude girl spanked the teacher.
> Rude the the spanked teacher girl.
> Spanked the girl the teacher rude.

George Miller has said, "The meaning of an utterance is not a linear sum of the meanings of the words that comprise it" (Miller 1965, p. 18). Much of the meaning of the sentence is relational, and clearly the order of the parts helps to convey those relational meanings. We would all pretty much agree as to what is meant by "girl," "rude," "teacher," "spanked," and "the," but the

[2]This possibility for a small-scale exploratory study is discussed more fully at the end of this section. See suggestion 2 on page 84.

arrangements of these meaning parts convey, in addition, another essential kind of meaning—who is doing the spanking, who is getting the spanking, who is rude. The arrangement of the elements provides the answers: "rude girl" attributes the characteristic of rudeness to the girl; "rude teacher" attributes it to the teacher. The ordering " . . . teacher spanked . . . " makes the teacher the spanker, relating these parts as agent and action, while the order " . . . spanked . . . girl" makes the girl the spankee, relating these parts as action and recipient. Reversal of "teacher" and "girl" in the sentences changes the relationships so that the girl becomes the agent of the spanking and the teacher the receiver. Who is doing what to whom is largely conveyed by the ordering of those parts (words) which name the doer, what is done, and to whom.[3] Miller, attempting to demonstrate that the ordering of words in sequence gives clues to their relationships, once used this example: "A Venetian blind is not the same as a blind Venetian" (Miller 1965, p. 16).

Another way to approach this important point about sentence meaning relating to the arrangement of the individual words in sentences as well as to their individual meanings, is to take the individual word meanings out of a "sentence" and see what kind of meaning (if any) is left. Here is a sentence that contains little in the way of word meaning, but much in the way of relational meaning.

> The blugy chinzels slottled prasily on the flubbish wub. (Campbell and Lindfors 1969, p. 106)

You can ask and answer a number of appropriate questions relating to this sentence without having any meanings at all for the basic "words": "blugy," "chinzels," "slottled," "prasily," "flubbish," and "wub." (Try to make up your own questions and answer them before looking at the questions below.)

1. What did the blugy chinzels do?
2. How did they slottle?
3. Where did they slottle?
4. What kind of chinzels were they?
5. What slottled?
6. What kind of wub did the chinzels slottle on?

What does your ability to ask and answer these questions tell you about your knowledge of the relationships in the sentence? That you can ask and

[3]Notice that the same ordering of the three important words "teacher . . . spanked . . . girl" indicates different relationships—the who is doing what to whom—if we make some additional changes in the sentence, for example "The *teacher* was *spanked* by the *girl.*" Clearly word order is not the only expressive means by which we convey relationships of sentence parts, but it is a major way.

answer questions 1 and 5 indicates that you understand "the blugy chinzels" to be the doers of the action of slottling. Being able to ask and answer question 2 shows that you recognize "prasily" as indicating the way in which the action was carried out. If you can ask and answer question 3, you clearly understand that the phrase "on the flubbish wub" tells where the action occurred. And your ability to ask and answer questions 4 and 6 indicates that you recognize "blugy" to be an attribute of the "chinzels," and "flubbish" to be an attribute of a particular "wub." The relationships of agent-action, action-manner, action-location, attribute-object are indentifiable even in the absence of familiar word meanings. Notice that there are other questions you would *not* have asked about the original sentence, for example: "How did the flubbish blugy?" "Where did the prasily chinzels?" "Where did the slottled wub?" Why not?

The order of the "words" in our nonsense sentence gave you important clues to the relational meanings in the sentence. But you are no doubt aware that it was not *only* the word order that provided clues. Suffixes on some of the words helped you a lot. Can you find all five suffixes that gave you clues to the function various (non)words were serving in the sentence? Two very important ones are the "s" of "chinzels" and the "ed" of "slottled." Many English words which are not plural nouns are written with a final "s" (pronounced like a /z/[4] in "Chinzel*s*") as in goe*s, is,* Marie'*s.* However, the final letter "s" (with different pronunciations as in buss*es* /əz/, truck*s* /s/, and train*s* /z/) often does indicate a plural noun, and in this case you interpreted the "s" in this way. And though there are many English words which we write with "ed" as the last two letters and which are not past tense verbs (*red,* se*ed,* Fr*ed*), many English words that end this way in writing *are* past tense verb forms (with the "ed" variously pronounced as /t/ in hopp*ed,* /d/ in tri*ed,* and /əd/ in want*ed*), and you interpreted "slottled" as a past tense verb form. The "y" of "blugy" and the "ish" of "flubbish" follow adjective suffix patterns familiar to you, and the "ly" of "prasily" doubtless reminded you of this familiar pattern found in a host of manner adverbs you know—briskly, sluggishly, laughingly, aggressively. So, though you had never before encountered the major content words of this sentence and thus had no experiential meanings for them, you were able to glean a considerable amount of information from the arrangements of the parts of the sentence, and from the suffixes of some of the words. The word order and suffixes suggested a familiar organizational framework of sentence relationships to you that we can informally characterize in the diagram at the top of page 27.

Clearly, then, there is far more to your understanding of the possible sentences of your language than the meanings of the individual words that

---

[4]We will use the symbol / / to indicate that we are talking about sounds in words, rather than about spellings. The symbol /ə/ represents the "uh" sound that we often insert as a hesitation in conversation, or the unstressed word "a" in, for example, "They bought *a* new house."

The	blugy	chinzels	slottled	prasily	on	the	flubbish	wub
The	some kind of	somethings	acted	some way	on	the	some kind of	something

something   did something   some way   somewhere

comprise them. In a sentence like, "The teacher spanked the rude girl," it is surely important to know what a teacher is; but it is just as important and necessary to know how "teacher" functions in relation to the other sentence elements.

You might like to have a look at two more nonsense sentences, both of which some university students made up and had children (some six- to eleven-year-olds) answer questions about. Though the six-year-olds either did not answer the questions about the nonsense sentences or else answered by substituting real words for the nonsense ones, all the children seven and older in this small informal sample answered the questions with ease. (You might want to conduct a similar informal study with elementary school age children. See suggestion 4 at the end of this section for fuller discussion of this possibility.) Below are the nonsense sentences and accompanying questions used, and some sample responses to them. Study the sentences, questions, and responses and figure out what the responding children must know about the relationships of sentence parts and the way they are signalled in their language, in order to perform in this way. You may want to discuss this item with fellow students. (Note: The children heard the sentences as many times as they wanted, as this was not a memory test of any kind, but rather an attempt to see what relationships the child understood through word order and suffix signals.)

SENTENCE 1: THE GROK MUFFED THE RUPPLE BLEET WITH HIS MALFOON.

Question: What did the grok do?

Sample Responses: muffed
muffed the bleet
muffed the bleet with his malfoon

Question: What did the grok muff?

Sample Responses: the rupple bleet
the bleet
the bleet (or whatever you call it)

Question: What kind of bleet was it?

Sample Responses: gruppled bleet
rupple
a rupple bleet

Question: How did the grok muff the rupple bleet?

Sample Response: with his malfoon

27

SENTENCE 2: THE PRAT RUGGLED GLINGILY DOWN THE SLAZOO.

Question: What ruggled?

Sample Response: the prat

Question: Where did the prat ruggle?

Sample Responses: slazoo
                    at the kazoo
                    down the slazoo

Question: How did the prat ruggle?

Sample Responses: slingily
                    glingily

Question: What did the prat do?

Sample Responses: ruggled
                    he ruggled

If you were given a straightforward, routine sort of English sentence and asked to divide it into its major parts, there would be considerable agreement among you and your fellow English speakers as to where the major breaks would occur. And there would be virtually total agreement as to where major breaks could not occur. Try these English examples:

1. The little boy was bouncing a red ball.
2. Put your coat in the closet.
3. Joan fled when she saw her mother coming around the corner carrying a heavy sack of groceries.

Most speakers of English would probably see the major divisions of the first sentence as "the little boy," and "was bouncing a red ball," and would probably put a secondary break between "was bouncing" and "a red ball." Asked to describe your reason for dividing the sentence as you did, you would probably say something like "Well, 'the little boy' tells who was doing something, and 'was bouncing the red ball' tells what he was doing, and within that, 'the red ball' tells what it was that he was bouncing." But probably no native English speaker would divide that sentence exactly in the middle, with four words on each side of the break: "The little boy was" and "bouncing a red ball." In explaining this you would say perhaps that "the little boy was" is an incomplete part and does not seem to function as any kind of a sensible unit. Probably no English speaker would have regarded "a little" or "a red" or "bouncing a red" or "boy was bouncing a" as major cohesive sentence parts either.

Of sentence 2 you would perhaps say something like " 'Put' tells you what to do, and 'your coat' tells you what you're going to 'put,' and 'in the closet' tells where you're going to put it." But probably no English speaker would divide the sentence as "Put your" + "coat in" + "the closet."

How about the third sentence now, a considerably longer one? Most English speakers will see this sentence as a combination of parts, each of which is like a sentence itself and thereby potentially divisible into the same kind of parts that we could identify in our first two sentences—doers, things done, locations of things done, things that get done to (recipients of action). Most would agree that one major part of this longer sentence has to do with Joan's fleeing, another with her seeing her mother, another with her mother coming around the corner, and another with her mother carrying a sack of groceries. Thus we get something like:

Joan fled
when she saw her mother
(her mother was) coming around the corner
(her mother was) carrying a heavy sack of groceries.

We need not worry at this point about the repeated "her mother was," which I have put in parentheses. These repeated portions are present in the meaning of each major sentence part. However, English, like most languages, deletes repeated expression of the same meaning elements when shorter sentences are combined into longer ones.

You might well ask, "Yes but don't we all tend to divide the sentences in similar ways because of those teachers we had who drilled us so hard on all that business about subjects and predicates, direct objects and adverb phrases, and because of all those exercises where we had to 'Draw one line under the subject and two lines under the predicate' for endless lists of sentences?" It is a good question, but the answer is "Probably not." Probably you divide the sentences into major parts as you do in spite of, rather than because of, your seventh-grade English teacher's efforts. Your divisions, and your *non*-divisions, reflect your grasp of the important functional units of sentences. You know that certain words cluster and work as a kind of unit in the sentence, and that those units can often be further subdivided into finer relationships among their parts.

It is interesting to note in passing that many early utterances of young children, whatever the language they are acquiring, express the basic relationships that your sentence divisions reflect. Somewhere around two years of age, children go through a period in which many of their sentences are two-word constructions. Here are a few examples of types of early two-word utterances of children, which demonstrate some important basic relationships present in their earliest combinings.

Throw ball   (Meaning "Throw me the ball." Action-object relation)
Doggie chair   (Meaning "My toy dog is on the chair." Object-location relation)
Daddy go   (Meaning "Daddy is going." Agent-action relation)
Go bye-bye   (Meaning "I want to go outside." Action-location relation)

Baby little   (Meaning "The baby is little." Object-attribute relation)
Mommy juice   (Meaning "It's Mommy's juice." Possessor-object relation)

Notice what the child's two-word utterances do *not* include: me the, doggie is, on the, to go. The point is that even at this tender age a child seems to be working with major sentence elements and relations.[5]

It is also interesting to note in passing (and this too will be discussed more fully in Section Two), the way children in this early stage of language development "repeat" longer utterances that are said to them. Here are some examples from a two-year-old:

MODEL	CHILD
I showed you the book.	I show book
It goes in a big box.	Big box
Read the book.	Read book
I am drawing a dog.	Drawing dog
I will read the book.	Read book
I can see a cow.	See cow

(Brown and Fraser 1964, p. 73)

We note again that the child seems to be focusing in on major relational meanings, processing the adult's longer utterance and reproducing her own shorter version, but with important aspects of relational meaning intact. It appears that relations of major sentence parts play a crucial role for the child as she attempts to construct the set of organizational principles of the language of her community, those principles that somehow hold together and account for the diversity of the specific sentences she hears. No seventh-grade English teacher has as yet gotten hold of the two-year-old child and put her through her subject-predicate paces. Our sensitivity to the relationships in the sentences of human language runs much deeper than anything any teacher ever "gave" us. It is more likely that it was our sensitivity to sentence relationships that enabled us to identify "subjects" and "predicates," rather than that our "being taught to" identify subjects and predicates enabled us to grasp relationships within sentences. Our teachers may have given us some labels and they may have brought to a conscious level the relational meanings of our language that we had already grasped intuitively, but they did not put these relational understandings in our heads in the first place. We built those understandings

[5]Brown (1973), Bloom (1970), Bowerman (1973), and others have also indicated early meanings—for example, nomination, nonexistence, recurrence, in Brown's terms—which are an important part of the young child's earliest word combinations. The present discussion of the relational meanings is not meant to exclude this aspect of major meanings as unimportant, but merely defers it until Section Two when language acquisition will be discussed more fully.

for ourselves through our exposure to and interaction through language, and our own figuring out of how it works.

Summing up, we find that we recognize basic parts of sentences and how they are related. We recognize some subparts of sentences as forming clusters, as belonging together as single units that serve some special relational function in the sentence. We get clues to the relationships within sentences from the order or arrangement of the words in sequence, as well as from the particular forms of some of the words. We know that both the meanings of particular words (which we know) *and* the meanings inherent in their forms and in their arrangements in strings are crucial to the total "meaning" of a sentence. That is quite a bit of knowing! And that knowing accounts for our ability to divide sentences of our language into major parts and subparts. But as considerable as that knowledge is, it represents only a small fraction of what we know and what all children learn as native speakers of a language.

RECOGNIZING RELATIONS AMONG SENTENCES

Your knowledge of relationships in language extends beyond your recognition of the interaction of the parts of individual, single sentences. You also recognize some sentences as being what Fromkin and Rodman call "stylistic variants" of other sentences (Fromkin and Rodman 1974). That is, you recognize some sets of sentences as being related in that they represent various ways of expressing virtually the same meaning.

1. John's little sister kicked him in the shins.
2. John's younger female sibling kicked him in the shins.
3. It was John's little sister that kicked him in the shins.
4. What John's little sister did was kick him in the shins.
5. John was kicked in the shins by his little sister.
6. The one who kicked John in the shins was his little sister.

If you examine these sentences you will see that each one contains the same set of propositions, namely that (1) John has a sister, (2) she is younger than John, (3) she kicked him in the shins, (4) it happened at some time in the past. Each sentence in the set, each "stylistic variant," may focus our attention more on one aspect of the message than on another, but they all contain the same basic set of meaning elements and meaning relationships.

What kinds of differences are there among the sentences of the above set? You will see that some sentences include additional words not present in the first sentence, which is the simplest, most direct, and unelaborated version of the message: for example, "It was . . . that," "What . . . did was . . . ," " . . . was . . . by," "The one who . . . was. . . . " You will also notice that in some of the sentences the parts are ordered differently—in sentences 5 and 6 the one kicked (John) is mentioned before the kicker (his little sister). Sentence 2 refers to John's little sister as his "younger female sibling," a phrase which, although slightly different in tone, identifies the same person.

Now here is another set of sentences for you to contrast with the above set. You will see that these are *not* related structurally as was the case with the first set; they are not stylistic variants of one another, describable as having added, rearranged, deleted, or substituted parts, while keeping the original meaning intact.

1. John's little sister kicked him in the shins.
2. John's little sister kicks hard.
3. John dislikes his little sister.
4. John's leg is in a cast.
5. John kicked her back.
6. Little sisters can be dangerous.

Each sentence of the set relates to the original in some important way, but not (as with the earlier set) as a stylistic variant of it. You might want to see if you can characterize in your own words how each of sentences 2 through 6 relates to sentence 1. You will see that each is conveying a new message rather than merely restructuring the elements of the original. You might enjoy following suggestion 3 at the end of this section, to explore to what extent the children you know understand various sentences as being stylistic variants which convey the same message (comprehension), and also to what extent they are able, given a straightforward sentence, to produce another one which "says the same thing a different way" (production).

RECOGNIZING AMBIGUITIES

Knowing that we can express the same message by using different sentence structures is an important part of our knowledge as native speakers of a language. Equally important perhaps, is our knowledge of the reverse—a single sentence structure can convey more than one meaning. It will not be hard for you to find several meanings for each of the following sentences.

1. The bill was large.
2. I walked beside the bank.
3. That's really cool.
4. That movie was far out.

5. They are eating apples.

6. Did you ever see a horse fly?
7. That's a beautiful woman's handbag.
8. Orkin—world's largest pest control company.
9. The astronauts are taking underwear and spices to season their food.

10. His cooking upsets me.
11. Visiting relatives can be a nuisance.
12. Dress optional.

The sentences have been grouped into three sets because, though they all are single sentences that can be interpreted in different ways, the variability of possible interpretation depends on different characteristics for each set. You can see that, in the first set, the sentences are ambiguous (have more than one possible interpretation) because of the various possible meanings of a particular word. What was it that was large? The amount you had to pay for a purchase or service? The denomination of the paper currency you had? The actual size of the paper currency in question? The mouth part of a duck? Or even, in some areas of the country, the front flap of a cap? And did you walk beside a river bank or beside the bank where your money is kept? Does the coolness of the object in sentence 3 refer to its temperature or to how much the speaker admires it? And what about that movie—is it some distance from town, or is it very contemporary and appealing to teen-agers? In these examples, the multiple meanings of the particular words "bill," "bank," "cool," and "far out" account for the ambiguity.

Try this one. What is the crucial word on which the ambiguity hinges in this children's joke from Bennett Cerf's *Book of Laughs?*

> Another day Marvin ran into his house. He let a fly come in.
> Then Marvin ran out of the house.
> He let in another fly.
> Marvin ran into the house again.
> Another fly came in.
> At last his mother said, "Marvin, I wish you would not run in and out of the house. I do not like all of these flies in here."
> Marvin said, "All right, Mother, show me which flies you do not like, and I will make them go out." (Cerf 1959, pp. 6–7)

What is Marvin's meaning of the word "all"? What is his mother's meaning for this same word?

For the sentences of the second group (5 to 9), it is not the meanings of the individual words that make the sentences ambiguous. The crucial question about each of these sentences is: How do the words cluster into phrases and how do the parts relate to each other? Notice that in sentences 5 and 6 you actually say the sentence differently for each of the two possible meanings. Your voice reflects the phrases and relations in the stress and rhythm you use when you say each one. (If you doubt this, try saying each of these two sentences with one of its possible meanings to a friend, to see if you can communicate the meaning you intend just by the way you say it.)

> They   are eating   *apples.*
> They   are   *eating* apples.

The first of this pair could be an appropriate answer to the question, "What are they eating?" The second could be an appropriate answer to the question, "What kind of apples are they?" Now can you describe the differences in the way you say the horse fly sentence, depending on whether you are asking about an insect or whether you are asking about a horse that flies?

Sentence 7 makes us want to ask, "What is it that is beautiful, the handbag or the woman?" That is, what does "beautiful" cluster with or belong with? Is it a beautiful handbag belonging to a woman? Or a handbag belonging to a beautiful woman? There is a relation of attribution here, and the question is, is "beautiful" to be attributed to the woman or to the handbag? The situation is similar in the Orkin sentence: What is it that is the "largest?" What does "largest" cluster with, or what is "largest" an attribute of? Is Orkin the control company for the "world's largest pests"? Or is it the "world's largest company" for controlling any pests, regardless of their size?

In sentence 9 (actually spoken by a newscaster), two organizations or groupings of the words are possible:

> The astronauts are taking underwear   and spices to season their food
>
> The astronauts are taking   underwear and spices   to season their food.

For each of the sentences of the second group then, there are two different possible organizations in the groupings and relations of the sentence parts, and each carries a different meaning.

The special shared characteristic of the sentences of the third group (10, 11, and 12) which makes them all ambiguous, may be harder to detect than that of the first two groups. It helps to understand their special character, I think, if we rephrase these sentences a bit, beginning each one with "something":

10. Something upsets me.
11. Something can be a nuisance.
12. Something is optional.

Now we can ask what the something is in each case. Is it *that* he cooks, or *how* he cooks that upsets me (notice that in the one case my upset is psychological and in the other case probably physical)? Is it relatives *coming* to visit me, or me *going* to visit relatives that can be a nuisance? Is it *how* to dress or *whether* to dress that is optional? In each case we seem to have a reduced version (his cooking, visiting relatives, nothing at all) and we cannot tell what it is a reduced version of; the reduction could have had two possible original sources.

In summary, then, an item might be ambiguous because

1. one word or expression can have several different meanings
2. the sentence can reflect several different relations of the parts
3. there are two different possible original meaning sources for part of the sentence, and it is not clear which one the sentence part is a reduced version of.

Can you find and describe the ambiguities in the following headline and cartoons?

Disappearance
Of Man in Lake
Called Strange

© 1975 Newspaper Enterprise Association, Inc.

© 1974 United Features Syndicate, Inc.

"Why did Mr. Allen say the scenery's nice? I don't see any scenery."

"The Family Circus" by Bil Keane, reprinted courtesy The Register and Tribune Syndicate, Inc.

Usually when we meet ambiguous sentences in our everyday lives, their meaning is clear from the situation in which we encounter them. (I say "usually," remembering the student who told me he vividly recalls, as a child, begging his mother not to buy "toilet water" from a cosmetics saleswoman who came to the door.) But the point that is important for us here is the insight that our understanding of ambiguity can give us into what we know about the structure of our language. We know that certain words in our language have different meanings, and we pretty much agree on what those words and meanings are (though of course no one knows all the words of a language, let alone all the meanings of all the words). But we are also aware of various possible structural organizations which underlie the actual strings of words we say or hear. The structure of our language clearly is not simply words in a string. We know, we have access to and use, some set of principles for relating parts of sentences, and these relationships are not always immediately obvious from the sentence string itself. And finally, our recognition of some ambiguous sentences shows us that we know that certain phrases or parts within sentences could possibly relate to several more fully specified meanings—that they are, in a sense, traceable to more than one original relational meaning source. Our understanding of ambiguity is one reflection of our very complex intuitive understanding of the structure—the parts and putting-togethers—of our language.

But do children understand ambiguities of various types? If they do, what can we suppose that they know about the structure of their language? Think of the children's joke books that abound on public library shelves, and the myriad of jokes that elementary school children tell that hinge on ambiguities. What about, for example, *The King Who Rained* by Fred Gwynne, *Amelia Bedelia* by Peggy Parish, or Bennet Cerf's *Book of Laughs,* great favorites with many children (and many adults)? That children understand and *enjoy* these books that focus on language play tells us not only something about their understanding of the structure of their language, but also that they, like us, can and do have fun with language, based on their intuitive understanding. (Suggestion 4 at the end of this section describes an ambiguity study you might want to do with children across an age range.)

CREATING NOVEL SENTENCES

As remarkable as your abilities are as a native speaker of a language, to recognize grammatical and ungrammatical, and more and less grammatical sentences, to recognize relationships within and among sentences, and to recognize ambiguities of various kinds—these abilities are not nearly as remarkable as another ability which lies right at the heart of human language. You have and use the ability to endlessly create and understand sentences which you have never encountered before. Except for a small set of ritualized kinds of exchanges—such as greetings ("Hi," or "How are ya' "); conversation openers ("Know what?"); leave-takings ("See ya' later," "Take care," "Say 'hi' to your family for me")—you communicate with specific sentences which are entirely novel in your experience, and which are the result of your own creation. Search your memory for five sentences you have said so far today that are repeats of sentences you have heard, spoken, read, or written before. Now search for five sentences that people have said to you so far today, that you have encountered previously. Chances are that, except for the kinds of ritualized exchanges cited above, you will not be able to think of a single sentence you have spoken or heard today, that was not novel to you.

If you find it hard to scan today's communication events so far, just listen to a conversation. To what extent are the participants using sentences they, or you, have encountered before? Yet they understand each other and you understand them, though the sentences of the exchange are completely novel to your experience and theirs. Or list five sentences from this book or from today's newspaper (not including ads), that you have never encountered before in speech or writing. Easy enough. But now list five that you *have* heard, read, written, or spoken before. Impossible.

How does it happen that I can say sentences to you which are new to both of us, and yet you will immediately comprehend my intended meaning and reply with another sentence which is also new to both of us, yet is a sentence which I immediately comprehend? Whatever language *is,* one thing it surely *is not:* It is not some supply or storehouse of specific sentences ready to be pulled out and used on appropriate occasions. The human mind could neither learn nor store such a set. We communicate by creating new sentences, not by pulling old ones out of mothballs. But *how?*

LEVELS OF LANGUAGE STRUCTURE

When you know a language, you know unconsciously, intuitively, the set of possible sounds in that language, the set of possible meanings in that language, and a finite set of abstract principles for relating these meanings and sounds. When you listen to someone speak a language you do not know, all you hear is verbal sounds—noises, babbling. What is lacking for you, a nonknower of that language, but present for the speaker, is an association of those verbal sounds with meanings. It is precisely the existence of these sound-meaning associations that identifies the speaker as a knower of that language, and the absence of these associations for you that identifies you as a nonknower of that language.

In the above example, you were the hearer, and we were thinking in a sound-to-meaning direction. But the reverse is also possible. You may have had the experience of wanting to ask a speaker of another language some question or to make some comment to her, but though you had a clear and simple meaning to convey and knew that that meaning was easily graspable by her, you lacked the knowledge of the sounds associated with that meaning in that person's language—that is, you did not know her language. To "know a language" is to share with others in a speech community a finite set of principles of relating sounds and meanings. Put another way, we know the sounds of our language, the meanings of our language, and how the two are related.

The concept of two levels of structure in language, one level relating to meanings (sometimes called deep structure) and one level relating to the sounds we use to express the meanings (sometimes called surface structure), is an important one. It is easy enough to demonstrate that there are two levels of language structure. Think back over some of our ambiguity examples. We found that for each of the single strings of sounds we had several possible meanings. One representation at the expression level had two (or more) possible representations at the meaning level. In our "stylistic variants" about John and his little sister, we saw the reverse. Here a single representation at the meaning level had various possible representations at the sound level. If there were only a single level of language structure, then a single sound string would have to convey always and only a single meaning.

Further, we can think of many examples of sentences which are very similar, though not identical sentence strings at the surface level, yet which are distinctly different at the meaning level in terms of the relationships they convey.

John is	easy	to please. (N. Chomsky 1964, p. 66)
	eager	

Mary's sisters	begged	
	asked	
	persuaded	her to clean the room.
	told	
	promised	

She	asked	
	told	him what to paint. (Based on C. Chomsky 1969, p. 100)

One word substitution in the string—substituting one adjective or verb for another—results in a radically different relational meaning, a markedly different organization of the entire sentence. Can you describe the differences in relations in the sentences of each group above? For the first, the crucial question is who is doing the pleasing and who is being pleased. Is John pleasing someone else, or is someone else pleasing John? The second involves the question of who it is who is going to clean the room in the "promise" case, as opposed to the other cases: Is it Mary or her sisters who will do the cleaning? And the crucial question for the last sentence pair is who is doing the painting.

Notice here that the changes do involve the substitution of one meaning part for another, for example, "easy" and "eager" are different meanings, as are "begged" and "promised." However, the rest of the sentence in each case remains unchanged in form. Yet the relational meaning of the parts changes drastically for the entire sentence, not just for the meaning of the particular substituted word. By making one seemingly small change, substituting one member of a word class for another member of the same class, we totally change the organizational relations for the entire sentence. Though remarkably similar at the surface level, the sentences in question are vastly different at their deeper level of organization, a further argument for the existence of two levels of language structure.

There is further evidence for your knowledge of two distinct levels of language structure. We often know that a certain meaning is present in a sentence, though there is no actual expression (sound string) directly relating to that meaning. Commands offer the clearest examples here. If I say to you

"Put your shoes on," or "Take the trash out," there is no doubt about who is to perform the action, even though I have not named a doer in the string of sounds I have uttered. The fact that you respond to these commands—that you put your shoes on, or that you angrily shout "Take it out yourself"—indicates that it is clear to you that you are the doer in that sentence. My eighth-grade English teacher used to call this "you understood." Not a bad description, perhaps. Where is that "you"? Clearly not at the level of that sentence as a pronounceable string (surface structure), but just as surely present at the meaning level (deep structure). It is "understood" to be there. We know it is "there" in the deep level of structure.

We also find cases where elements in the sound string are difficult to relate to specific meanings. If someone said to you "It's mine," it would make perfectly good sense to ask "What's yours?" But if someone said to you "It's raining," it would make no sense at all for you to ask, "What's raining?" "It" just has to be there in the surface structure for the sentence to "sound right," to be an OK (grammatical) sentence of English, but it does not correspond to any meaning element. And what about "to" in "I asked him to come"? We would not think of leaving it out, any more than we would think of including it in "I saw him (to) come." It does not really *"mean,"* it just *is* because the sentence sounds like—*is*—an OK English sentence with it, and is not an OK English sentence without it.

Do you begin to get the feeling that language structure, that system which we so take for granted, is a rather complex business? As speakers of a language we know the associations that hold between two levels of structure, and the associations clearly are not reducible to a simple one-to-one matching of a meaning hunk to a pronunciation hunk. Each level has its own structure, its own possibilities and restrictions. As speakers of a language, we know the significant elements and the possibilities for their combination at each level, and we also know how the levels relate to one another—we unconsciously know the structure of our language. And because of this, we are able to recognize grammatical and ungrammatical and more and less grammatical sentences, to recognize relations within and among sentences, to recognize ambiguities and stylistic variants, and most of all, to create and understand sentences which are entirely novel in our experience. This is no simple business.

Chapter 3

Components of Language Structure

INTRODUCTION

One helpful way to describe the structure of a language is to focus on its three major components: (1) the semantic component, which involves the set of meaning elements; (2) the syntactic component, which involves the set of principles or possibilities for combining meaning elements and which accounts for relational meaning; (3) the phonological component, which involves the set of expression principles or possibilities for conveying the meanings in a language. To know a language is to have considerable knowledge of each of these components and their interrelation.

SEMANTIC COMPONENT

Semantic Categories and Labels

A British woman teaching English composition to a class of secondary school Kenya students once asked her class to write a composition about the English language—a "What English Means to Me" composition. The opening sentence of one student's composition was "English is a language which is full of words." And so it is! One of the three major components of native speakers' knowledge of the structure of their language relates to the meaning parts of their language and the words that represent these meaning parts or concepts —their "mental dictionary." This *semantic component* is an important part of the sound-meaning association system which constitutes the structure of a language. One thing the speakers of any language surely know is the way the people of their community view the world, the way they divide reality into significant categories and label them in their language.

No two language-culture communities view reality the same way, and each community's language reflects its world view, what it regards as the significant categories and relations of experience.[1] Though all humans are endowed with the same types of perceptual and cognitive mechanisms, each group represents reality differently, assigning to their experience of the world different significance, groupings, relationships. Examples are legion of different groups dividing and labeling reality differently. The color continuum that English divides into the six categories labeled purple, blue, green, yellow, orange, red, some American Indian languages divide into four labeled categories· and others into only two categories. English speakers regard snow as a single category, but Eskimos have many categories for snow, depending on the kind of snow it is. English speakers see one (singular) and more than one (plural) as significant categories. But many languages differentiate between one (singular), two (dual), and more than two (plural). In English, this and that indicate near and not near spatial divisions. But some languages label spatial areas much more specifically with categories, for example, for "near me but not near you," or "far away from both of us," or "out of sight of both of us," or "near both/all of us." Much of what English categorizes as a "that" (inanimate), some languages categorize as a "who" (animate).

Every human being is born into a community which views reality its own way, and whose language reflects that world view. As a member of that community, the human learns that particular world view as he learns the language which expresses the groupings and relations it labels. Because we live with the categories our language uses, we tend to feel that these categories and labels are somehow God-given or inherently logical in the objects and experiences themselves. But this is clearly not so, for if our categories and labels were inherently logical, then all languages would encode the same categories. As we have seen, they do not. Each culture simply groups diverse objects, experiences, and events so that its members, in a sense, agree to regard some sets of

[1]This is, admittedly, an oversimplified discussion and does not deal with the problems of defining "community" and the diversity of languages and dialects that often exist within a "community" or the effect of contact between "communities." I am simplifying the social aspect here to enable you to focus in greater depth on the linguistic one.

unidentical things which share certain features, as "the same" or equivalent, and to regard other events, experiences, and objects not possessing certain crucial features, as "different," as belonging to different classes or categories. The words of our language convey our categories.

It has been argued by many, Benjamin Whorf chief among them, that one's way of thinking and of viewing the world is determined by the language he learns, for as he learns his language, he is necessarily learning the categories and relations it encodes. The English speaker views (and labels) some things as "red" and others as "orange," some things as animate and others as inanimate, because his language "tells" him through its labels that it is so. Certain features of object shape, or certain spatial divisions, he regards as significant and uses as categorization bases for new items or experiences, because his language expresses categories based on these dimensions. Other potential category bases—those his language does not use (though other languages may)—he does not use as bases for grouping his experiences into categories.

Many, including me, would protest that this deterministic view of the iron control that language has over the way one thinks is too strong. Native speakers of one language are able to learn, to some degree, to think about reality as organized according to some scheme other than the one their own language expresses. We do so, to some extent, every time we learn an additional language. That our thinking is not completely controlled by our language seems clear from the fact that we can, at some intellectual level, consider other possible categorization schemes. And anthropologists do, after all, study cultures other than their own and come to understand, at least to some extent, the world view of the group under study, though never completely. How could this happen if anthropologists were unable to think outside of the framework imposed on them by their own language?

But whether one takes a strongly deterministic Whorfian position or a modified position, it is certain that a very important part of what a native speaker of a language knows is the reality his language encodes: the significant categories and relationships of experience, the significant features of reality for understanding and categorizing new experiences, and how the language labels the significant divisions of reality as the community sees them. Every language represents reality differently; you know the way your language does it.

It is intriguing that our bases for grouping objects into categories are so variable. Those "crucial features" on which we base our particular categorizations are hardly predictable. We categorize now according to one dominant feature, now according to another. All objects which we identify as "round" share a perceptible attribute, a readily recognizable shape. But notice that similarity of appearance is not the dominant feature in categorizing which animals are and are not "dogs." If appearance were crucial to "dogness," how could German shepherds and chihuahuas end up in the same general category "dog," but German shepherds and wolves end up in different categories? We place A,$\mathcal{A}$, a andα, in the same category: They are all "a's" (Or are they all "A's"?"$\mathcal{A}$'s"? or "α's"?), but we insist that "α" and "o" and "c" belong in different categories, as do "b" and "d," though "B," "β," "b", and "b" belong in the same category, and "D,"$\mathcal{D}$," "d" and "d" do also. And of course there is always "G," "$\mathcal{G}$" "g," and "g." Appearance, though an important basis for some categories, is less important for others. A feature of tameness (the result of historical development) is crucial to the dog-wolf distinction, and functional considerations are crucial in the alphabet letter examples. And so, as we categorize, we seem to be focusing now on one important dimension and now on another, sometimes on a perceptible characteristic (shape, size, contour, texture, weight, hue, sound), sometimes on function, sometimes on structural similarity.

Let's summarize for a minute. The speakers of a particular language view reality in similar ways, in terms of categories and the relationships among them. The words of their language reflect their categories (dog, wolf, loud) and relations (bigger, less, because). The speakers of English basically agree on what actions constitute the categories jumping, eating, sleeping. That is, the domain of experience labeled by these words is similar (though not identical) for most speakers of English. English speakers would agree on what it means to "own" something, to "think" something, to "throw" something. They would also basically agree on which items in the world are or are not "lizards," "daughters," "benches," "preferences." They share common meaning associations for "happy," "pretty," "energetic," "sluggish," "slovenly" (though they might disagree as to which particular people should be described as possessing these characteristics). The semantic knowledge of a speaker of a language includes knowledge of how the world of his community is categorized and labeled. These labels constitute his lexicon or mental dictionary. He shares with other speakers the words—lexicon—that are associated with specific, basically agreed upon meanings or domains of experience. A language is indeed "full of words."

The fact that we have dictionaries at the ready and consult them frequently is sufficient evidence that we never learn all the words and all the meanings of all the words in our language, especially since new words are entering our language all the time as a result of new experiences (going to the moon, producing CB radios) and increased contact with other languages from which we borrow lexical items. Also, some lexical domains will be more elaborated for one speaker (tennis terms, legal terms, fishing terms), and different domains more elaborated for another. You have probably had the experience of listening to a specialist (for example, a sportscaster or doctor), who used so many terms you did not have in your lexicon that you wondered whether you and he were speakers of the same language at all. Nevertheless, the lexicons or mental dictionaries of the speakers of any language are significantly similar.

Inflectional Morphemes

Notice that in this semantic component, it is not only total words that convey meaning. Words can also contain smaller elements of meaning of various kinds and this is part of our semantic knowledge also. The words in each of the columns in the accompanying table, although distinctly different in total meaning, share a common element of meaning. Can you identify it?

1	2	3	4	5	6
cupcakes	came	feels	its	bigger	jumping
women	walked	has	Susan's	better	crying
provisions	ran	is	their	prettier	studying
children	went	hopes	person's	friendlier	chewing
jealousies	schemed	says	people's	worse	chewing
people	strutted	supposes	Jack's		waving
glasses	thought	does	the Jones'		wondering
			mine		

It is helpful to think of these words as exemplifying changes from some basic, unmarked word form. Then we can ask, "What is the meaning change or meaning addition in each set?" In the first set, the meaning element "plural" or "more than one" is contained in each word. If we think of the singular as being the basic unmarked form, then we can say that the meaning of plural has been added to each.

The meaning of plural is common to each item in the first group, but notice how variously that meaning can be expressed: as /s/ in cupcakes, as /z/ in jealousies and provisions, as /əz/ in glasses, as /rən/ and a vowel change in children, as two vowel changes in women, and as a totally new sound string in people. And do you ever count sheep to help yourself fall asleep? The meaning of plural is in sheep, but the presence of the meaning plural does not change the basic word form in any way. You could say that it is silent. Of course the idea is not new to you that in language a meaning can be present without having a specific pronounceable item to express it. Remember the "you understood" in commands, where the meaning "you" was present, though not expressed in the sound string?

Is it any wonder that we hear children say "mans" and "sheeps" where we would say men and sheep? Of course not. They recognize that English differentiates between one of something and more than one of it, and that the meaning of more than one is generally expressed by adding /s/ ("cupcakes"), /z/ ("jealousies"), or /əz/ ("glasses") to the basic form. What they have not yet learned, but will in time, is (1) that there are specific cases where the meaning of plural is expressed in some other way, (2) just what those other ways of expressing plural are, and (3) just which words they apply to. All of this is part of the adult English speaker's knowledge of his language, and over time becomes part of the child's knowledge as well. Rather than being struck by children's failure to appropriately express irregular plural forms, we should be impressed that at a tender age, they (1) grasp the notion of plural, and differentiate between one and more than one, (2) know (unconsciously) that the notion of plural is usually expressed as an addition of /s/, /z/, or /əz/ to the base form, and (3) usually select appropriately between the three typical expressions of plural, adding the appropriate ending to a word whose plural form they have not heard before.

The common meaning element expressed in various ways in the words of the second set is the notion of "past." In walked, schemed, and strutted, past is expressed according to the regular pattern of adding /t/ (walk*ed*), /d/ (scheme*d*), or /əd/ (strutt*ed*) to the unmarked form of the verb. But the meaning "past" is expressed by a vowel change in ran and came, and by a totally different form in went and thought. As with the meaning element plural, the meaning element past can be "expressed silently" as in "She put her books in her desk." In view of the variety of expression possibilities for past, it is rather remarkable that young children, without special tutoring, conceptualize a present/past distinction, express that distinction in their speech, discern that the usual way of expressing past is through the addition of /t/, /d/, /əd/ to a base form (as children's "putted," "comed," "goed," "thinked" clearly indicate), and that in time, through continued verbal interaction with others, they come to recognize which verbs are the exceptional cases that do not follow the general pattern for expressing the notion past, and to understand how those idiosyncratic cases work.

The common meaning conveyed in the third group is simply that the subject of each verb is a third person singular (he, she, it, John, or Mary, but not we, they, or you), and that the verb is in the present tense. One cannot help wondering, if "run" is a perfectly OK form to go with "I, you, we, they, John and Mary," why it is not a perfectly OK form to go with "he, she," and other third person singular subjects. But this is idle wondering. The fact is that historically, English has developed in such a way that the information "third person singular subject" is conveyed by a special verb form (as well as by the subject itself). Notice that the usual expression is the addition of /s/ (hope*s*), /z/ (feel*s*), or /əz/ (suppos*es*) to the base form, the same sounds we generally add to nouns to express the meaning element plural. But note again, that the one notion—third person singular—has various representations in addition to the regular set (vowel changes in says and does, substitution of /z/ for /v/ in has, and a special form in is). How surprised would you be to hear a four-year-old say, "He haves a lot of them"? Why?

The familiar /s/, /z/, /əz/ pattern occurs in group 4, this time as the usual expression for the meaning "possession." (Note the /z/ of Susan'*s*, people'*s*, and person'*s*; the /əz/ of the Joneses' and the /s/ of it*s* and Jack'*s*.)

But note again that the common meaning element, possession, can be expressed in other ways as well—mine and their suggesting just two of the possibilities.[2]

The common meaning element in the words of group 5 is sometimes called the "comparative." Again, though that notion is most often expressed by a certain change of a base form (adding "er" to the adjective or preceding it with "more"), irregularities occur, as in better or worse. (Have you ever heard children say "gooder" or "badder"?)

The words in group 6 are striking for their lack of irregularity in expression. The common meaning element contained in all of them you doubtless recognize as what is sometimes called "progressive" or "continuous"—action actually in progress. That meaning is always expressed in English through the addition of /iŋ/ (usually spelled "ing") to the basic verb form. But notice that these forms also require that a form of "be" precede the verb. Not surprisingly, expressions like "I jumping" and "Daddy coming" in which the "be" preceding the verb is missing, are typical at an early stage of language acquisition in children.

Clearly, your mental dictionary or lexicon includes meanings like plural, past, possessive, comparative, third person singular, and continuous, as well as meanings like "goat" and "scratch." The term *morpheme* is helpful here. A morpheme is the smallest meaning unit in language. Thus, in talking about your mental dictionary or lexicon, it is more accurate to say that it includes an inventory of morphemes than to say that it includes an inventory of words, for you understand meanings like past and plural which are not words, as well as meanings like goat and scratch which are. And just as you know how the notion goat or scratch is represented in speech (at the sound level), so you know how the notion past or plural is represented in speech. You understand the words women, ran, supposes, bigger, Bob's, (be) wondering each to be a complex morpheme containing two morphemes or meaning units: woman + plural, run + past, suppose + third person singular subject, big + comparative, Bob + possessive, wonder + continuous.

The six meaning units we considered in the groups above all add some special meaning to a basic form. They all belong to a class of morphemes called *inflectional* morphemes.[3] We inflected the verb "run" for past when we changed it to "ran"—that is, when we added the information *past*. "People" includes the inflectional morpheme *plural*. With inflected forms, an original

[2]Given the /z/ regularity of "They're your*s* (hi*s*/her*s*/our*s*/their*s,*)" is it any wonder we sometimes hear young children say, "They're mine*s*"? This is not a sign of lack of intelligence. Quite the reverse. It is further evidence of children's remarkable ability to discern and utilize regularities in the language.

[3]Do not confuse the present use of the term "inflection" (the adding of meanings to basic morphemes) with another and quite different meaning of the term (the rising and falling of one's voice when speaking).

morpheme has been further refined through the addition of some meaning like possessive, comparative, plural.[4]

Derivational Morphemes

Now let's look at another type of morpheme. The complex morphemes (morpheme combinations) in each of the five groups below all share a common meaning element. Can you find and characterize it?

1	2	3	4	5
teacher	flexible	generosity	waspish	foxy
baker	adaptable	sincerity	impish	wily
singer	replaceable	blindness	foolish	crafty
player	responsible	scarcity	clannish	sneaky
preacher	expendable	messiness		sloppy
	audible	purposefulness		hasty
		foolishness		
		irregularity		
		stupidity		
		kindness		

These complex morphemes include only a few examples of the many simple morphemes called *derivational* (in contrast to the inflectional ones we considered above). These derivational morphemes, which are usually expressed as suffixes added to a base form, most often change the class the word belongs to. "Teach" is a verb, but adding the "er," to convey the meaning "one who does it," changes the original verb form to a noun (teacher) comprised of two morphemes. The addition of "er" *derives* a noun form from what was originally, in its basic unmarked form, a verb. The addition of the derivational suffix "ible/able" changes a verb base form to an adjective; the addition of "ity" or "ness" generally changes an adjective form to a noun, whereas the addition of "ish" does the reverse, generally changing a noun (wasp, fool, imp, clan) to an adjective. The addition of "y" generally changes the original noun to an adjective. You can see, no doubt, that the meanings of derivational morphemes (which change an item from one word class to another) are quite different from

---

[4]Throughout this discussion of morphemes we will try to maintain a distinction between the meaning unit itself (which we are calling a morpheme) and its representation in speech. Thus past is a morpheme, and /əd/ is one possible expression of it; "cat" is a morpheme, and /kæt/ is the expression of it; "cats" is a complex morpheme composed of two simple morphemes, the first represented as /kæt/ and the second represented as /s/, and the new complex morpheme represented as /kæts/. However, in other works, you may encounter the term morpheme used to refer to the meaning *and* its representation or to the representation itself.

inflectional meanings, which do not tamper with the word class of the item in question, but simply provide additional meaning to that item. "Run" is a verb and so is "ran"; "big" is an adjective and so is "bigger"; "jump" is a verb and so is "jumping."

It would be lovely if the distinction between inflectional and derivational were perfect and always held true. But it is not that neat. There is an embarrassing and intriguing set of items generally called derivational morphemes and expressed as prefixes (coming before, rather than after, the base form), which do not change the word class of a base morpheme. These morphemes largely have to do with meanings of recurrence and negation: *re*group, *re*-convene, *re*assert; *in*compatible, *in*escapable, *un*important, *in*edible, *in*comprehensible, *im*possible, *in*complete, *ir*replaceable, *un*scientific; *anti*social, *anti*climactic, *anti*septic, *anti*histamine; *mis*understand, *mis*trust; *dis*trust, *dis*appear.

If inflectional morphemes pose "problems"[5] in the variation of their possible, irregular expressions, just think of all the possible expression "problems" derivational morphemes raise in terms of which ones can go with which basic forms or with which already complex forms. (Remember "antidisestablishmentarianism"?) If someone is lovely, it is her loveliness, not her loveliosity or lovelicity that impresses us. But if she is sincere, it is her sincerity, not her sincereness, that impresses us. I can be hasty or unhasty, but can I be slow or unslow? I can be mindful or unmindful, but can I be wonderful or unwonderful? I can be clear or unclear, but can I be understood or unununderstood (which is different, of course, from being misunderstood). If I am ambitious, I have ambition, not ambitiousness or ambitiosity. If I am generous, I have generosity, but if I am a genius I do not have geniosity.[6] And if someone can be uncouth or incorrigible or unwitting, why can he not also be couth or corrigible or witting? If I can redo or regain things, why can I not relose or refix things? I can like, dislike, or hate someone, but I cannot dishate him. I can unwind or rewind things, but I cannot unfind or refind things.

You know what kinds of morphemes—meanings—can combine to form more complex morphemes; you know what forms of expression they will take in combination; and you also know how they will be ordered: ir-regular-ity, not ity-regular-ir. You use your knowledge of possibilities of morpheme combinations to create and understand new forms. I have heard students describe acquaintances as being "sort of cute-ish" or as having "no couth" or a lot of

---

[5]I put " problems" in quotes here, because, in fact, our learning of this part of our language does not seem to be problematic. We learn it, as we do the rest of our language, with no apparent difficulty or even conscious awareness. It only looks "problematic" when we stand back, as we are now doing (and as children do not do), and see how complex a system we actually have mastered.

[6]I am indebted to Mildred Miran for this example from a university student learning English as his fourth language.

"stick-to-it-ive-ness." Especially interesting are the novel creations of children acquiring their language. Here are some examples, each showing remarkable semantic knowledge on the child's part. Describe what these examples show that the child does know about language.

> A three-and-a-half-year-old, sitting at the table in a booster chair, finished her lunch and wanted to get down from the chair. Unable to push her chair back from the table, she said to her mother, "Mommy, will you unpush me?"
>
> A group of five- to six-year-olds, having decided that they did not like Mark, formed a "Mark un-fan club."
>
> A four-year-old had been put to bed by someone else in her mother's evening absence. In the middle of the night she came to her mother's bed, woke her, and requested that the mother put her to bed properly, saying "I need to get good-nighted."[7]
>
> A six-year-old, looking at a picture in Mercer Mayer's *Bubble Bubble,* got to the page where a fat mouse that had been blown with magic bubbles had suddenly disappeared. He pointed to the visual representation of the poof where the mouse had been, and said, "It's a deblown mouse."[8]
>
> A teacher asked a four-year-old who was sweeping the nursery school floor "Are you mopping?" The child replied, "No, I'm brooming."[9]
>
> A four-and-a-half-year-old was trying to put on his shoes, but could only find one of them. He asked his father, "Where is the other shoe that rhymes with this one?"[10]

James Britton cites these examples from a child of two-and-a-half:.

> I'm spoonfulling it in.
>
> On successfully buttoning her coat she said, "I'm a button-up-er."
>
> Skipping ahead down the road she called, "I'm jumper than you are." (Britton 1973, p. 43)

And from a child close to three years comes this conversation with an adult.

> *Adult:* What are you doing?
>
> *Child:* I'm just zzz-ing about.
>
> *Adult:* And what's Teddy doing? Is he zzz-ing too?
>
> *Child:* No. He's waiting for me to stop zzz-ing. (Britton 1973, p. 43)

These idiosyncratic creations of children as they attempt to discern and apply the complex principles of the language they are learning help us to recognize how vast and complex our own knowledge is. They also may amaze us by

---

[7] I am indebted to Sally Means for this example.
[8] I am indebted to Candy Poland for this example.
[9] I am indebted to Janet Rothschild for this example.
[10] I am indebted to John Henderson for this example.

indicating how much of the complex workings of this system the young child has acquired without special training.

Cartoonists often capitalize on our knowledge of inflectional and derivational morphemes and their possible expression, for humorous purposes. Consider the accompanying cartoons.

It is worth noting that particular pronounceable items like /z/, /s/, /t/, "er," "un"[11] do not always express inflectional or derivational meanings. The /z/ in bug*s* signals plural, but the /z/ in bu*zz* or i*s* has no special significance, but is merely part of the pronunciation of a simple morpheme. The /s/ in hat*s* signals a morpheme, but the /s/ in bu*s* does not. The "er" in preach*er* and the "un" in *un*doing express morphemes, but the "er" in h*er* and the "un" in s*un* do not. There is no simple, one-to-one, always-and-only correspondence between morphemes and their expression, even as there is no such simple correspondence between sentence meaning and expression, as we saw in earlier examples of ambiguous sentences (in which one expression had several meanings associated with it), and sets of related sentences (in which various expression possibilities could relate to one meaning structure).

Compounds and Idioms

Besides including base morphemes and their expression like "tree" and "stand," inflectional morphemes like past and plural, and derivational morphemes changing an item from one word class to another, your lexicon includes compounds and idioms. These are lexical items clearly composed of subparts, each with its own meaning in isolation, but which, when the subparts are combined, often convey new and special meanings. Football is more than the meaning of "foot" plus the meaning of "ball." It identifies a type of object and a type of game. A restroom is not simply the meaning of "rest" plus the meaning of "room." The combination names a type of room which may (but also may not) be primarily for resting.

The relatedness of the morphemes in compounds is generally obvious to us though it can be quite varied. Note these examples from Fromkin and Rodman:

> ... a *bedchamber* is a room where there is a bed, *bedclothes* are linens and blankets for a bed, *bedside* does not refer to the physical side of a bed but the place next to it, and *bedtime* is the time one goes to bed. ... A *houseboat* is a boat which is a house, but a *housecat* is not a cat which is a house. A *boathouse* is a house for boats, but a *cathouse* is not a house for cats, though by coincidence some cats live in cathouses. A *jumping bean* is a bean that jumps, a *falling star* is a "star" that falls, and a *magnifying glass* is a glass that magnifies. But a

---

[11]I am representing these in their spelled form so as to avoid using unfamiliar phonetic symbols for vowel sounds that you will readily recognize from their spellings. But remember that we are still concerned with *sounds*, not with written forms.

> *looking glass* isn't a glass that looks, nor is an *eating apple* an apple that eats, nor does *laughing gas* laugh. (Fromkin and Rodman 1974, p. 120)[12]

But notice that, with some compounds, the combination results in a new and unpredictable meaning whole. Again some examples from Fromkin and Rodman:

> A *jack-in-a-box* is a tropical tree, and a *turncoat* is a traitor. A *highbrow* doesn't necessarily have a high brow, nor does a *bigwig* have a big wig, nor does an *egghead* have an egg-shaped head. . . . if one had never heard the word *hunchback,* it might be possible to infer the meaning. But if you had never heard the word *flatfoot* it is doubtful you would know it was a word meaning "detective" or "policeman." (Fromkin and Rodman 1974, pp. 120–21)

With idioms, the relation between the individual morphemes and the new total combination meaning is even less obvious—sometimes nonexistent. Even though you are not an acrobat or an infant, you can "put your foot in your mouth." If someone "has two left feet," we do not order special shoes. When someone "kicks the bucket" we are more likely to head for the funeral home than for the mop closet. These complex items are apparently entered in our mental lexicon as wholes, not as the meaning of each part plus the usual relations among them.

Semantic Features

When we think of simple morphemes like "lamp" or "break" or "itch," we may feel as if the meaning of each is a kind of indissoluble whole. But in fact, these morphemes are actually bundles or clusters of meaning features or elements called *semantic features.* Linguists have yet to identify in anything like a comprehensive way what all of these semantic features which we incorporate into our morpheme bundles might be. If I asked you to tell me what "break" means, you would probably say something like, "It means to come apart or to become damaged." Fine. We say of many things which come apart or become dysfunctional, that they broke.

The lawn mower broke.
The plate broke.

---

[12]Do not be troubled by the fact that, in written symbols, some compounds are written with a space between the two parts (laughing gas) and some are not (houseboat). We are not concerned with the written symbolization for our language, but with the language itself.

But there are many other things in our world which come apart, but we do not say of them that they broke.

> The paper broke.
> Her dress broke.

Textural properties of the object involved seem to be important to the meaning of break. Only some objects are breakable. Perhaps our notion of break includes a semantic feature of brittleness of texture (though notice that thread, which is not brittle, also breaks).

Break also seems to entail a certain specificity and completeness. A complex mechanism or organism (a car or a person, say) can go from a state of being fully functional to being damaged, but we do not generally say "The car broke" or "Mary broke." We either use break and specify the particular part which is no longer functional ("The fan belt broke" or "Mary's arm broke") or else we indicate a more general kind of breakage with an expression like "break down": "The car broke down" or "Mary broke down." When we do use break with a complex organism, as in "Mary broke under pressure," it has the force of suggesting a completeness in the breakage.

It is interesting to consider the many kinds of breaking (destructing?) we identify in English. Though they are all similar in including the notion of coming apart, each includes some specific meaning feature(s) which separates it from the others. Consider these few:

> If an item breaks by changing from a solid to a liquid through the action of heat, it "melts" (butter, ice cream, jello).
> If an item breaks suddenly, through ignition from within itself, it "explodes" (bomb, firecracker).
> If an item breaks in such a way that it blends with the surrounding liquid medium, it "dissolves" (sugar in coffee).
> If an item breaks as the result of a ripping motion, often leaving a jagged edge, it "tears" (cloth, paper).

Notice how the features of the literal interpretation are present when we use the breakage terms metaphorically:

> I melt every time he looks at me.
> She exploded when she heard what he had done.
> He dissolved into tears.
> Janet tore their argument to shreds.

Such informal speculation can be fascinating but, of course, we cannot hope through such activity to solve the problem of identifying the semantic features which our language incorporates. Fortunately, it is not our purpose here to do so. But such informal exploration of your own language meanings can help to reveal two important points: (1) The semantic component which you control is far more complex than you might have supposed, and (2) morphemes are not simple wholes, but rather clusters of semantic features or elements. I hope that such self-exploration will increase your awareness of what you know about your own language meanings, and, more important perhaps, help you appreciate the complexity of the semantic knowledge that the children you teach come to develop through their language interaction with people in their community.

We can only wonder at children's mastery of the semantic component of their language. Eve Clark has made the interesting suggestion that an important aspect of children's semantic development (the process by which, over time, their categories and labels come to match those of the adults in their community) may be their adding semantic features to their developing categories. Thus, for example, a child may initially categorize for "dogness" according to the simple feature "four-legged." If so, this category will also include sheep, goats, and cats. But as the child adds further semantic features to specify this category (for example, "barking"), the originally overgeneralized category will be reduced to one more nearly matching the meaning cluster the adults in the community call "dog" (E. V. Clark 1973). (We will consider this notion more fully in the next section.)

Although we cannot at this time be precise in our identification of the set of semantic features which we draw on and which cluster into various morphemes for the speakers of a language, we can identify with certainty what some of these features must be. The feature of being animate or inanimate differentiates the meaning bundles we represent as "hippo," "ape," "spider," "Brenda," "mailman," "old maid," "chairperson" from other meaning clusters we represent as "refrigerator," "rock," "pencil," and "mud." The feature of being human or nonhuman differentiates "hippo," and "spider" and "ape" from "Brenda," "mailman," "old maid," and "chairperson." The feature of being male or female separates "Brenda" and "old maid" from "mailman," and also separates "rooster" from "hen" and "billy goat" from "nanny goat." The feature of being concrete or abstract differentiates "Brenda," "rooster," and "rock" from "idea," "freedom," and "love." And so on. But beyond a limited basic set that we are fairly sure of, the question of what constitutes the set of fundamental semantic features that a language draws on is pretty open at this time. What is sure, however, is that there is such a set, and that the morphemes of a language are not single indissoluble meaning units, but rather bundles of meaning features. Put very informally, the entries in your mental dictionary are "defined" as composites of specific characteristics.

Our knowledge of the meanings of our language and of possibilities for their combination is something we generally take for granted. However, when we encounter unusual morpheme combinations we are jarred into an awareness of the magnitude of our semantic knowledge, and of what some of the semantic features we are using might be. My favorite nonnative example comes from a Kenya secondary school student. He was complaining in a written composition about his class leaders' unfortunate habit of making announcements, during meals, about the dirty condition of the school latrines. He argued, very persuasively, that mealtimes were not the proper times for such announcements, which "lessened one's taste for eating considerably." He painted a dire picture of students in great numbers falling ill from lack of food if such announcements continued to be made at meal times. He concluded his argument with this statement: "And so, if this continues to happen, many people's normality will be impeded, owing to underfeeding." We recognize this instantly as a sentence that a native speaker of English could hardly have come up with, mainly because of the co-occurrence of "normality" and "impeded." Part of the meaning that normality has for us is that it is a state or condition someone or something is in. And part of the meaning that impeded has for us is interference with active movement toward some goal. A state of being is not something which moves toward a goal, and therefore it is not something which can be impeded. We understand the student's meaning, because we share with him some of the meaning aspects (semantic features) of normality and impeded (the notion of interference in impeded, and the notion of a healthy or right kind of condition in normality). The semantic features we control constrain combination possibilities: Normality cannot be impeded; "plates break," they do not "tear"; papers and dresses do not "break" but do "tear"; roosters and proud people can "crow," but bravery and cars cannot. Part of your semantic knowledge is the constraints semantic features place on co-occurrence possibilities for morphemes.

Study this set of words listed in Roget's *Thesaurus* (1964, p. 533) under "Verbs. *walk.*"

amble	stroll	parade	hobble	trudge
canter	stride	prance	shuffle	wade
pitter-patter	strut	stalk	stagger	tiptoe
saunter	swagger	limp	reel	

All these words include the same basic set of semantic features that defines the general term "walk." Stated informally these would include at least the following set: action, locomotor movement, animate (that is, action of an animate being), alternating feet continuously. But the word "walk" is more general in meaning than the words in the above set. Each of the more specific walk words above contributes some additional semantic feature to "walk." "Stagger" adds unsteadiness, "stroll" adds slowness and leisureliness, "wade" adds through water, "prance" adds high stepping, "tiptoe" adds on toes with heels not touching the ground. Can you describe the specialness of each specific walk word, the semantic features(s) it includes that sets it apart from the more general "walk"? The more specific a morpheme is, the more the semantic features that characterize it and set it apart from other morphemes in the language.

Conclusion

We have barely begun to explore your semantic knowledge. But we know that it includes a knowledge of (1) how your community of language speakers views reality—categorizes it and relates the categories, and labels those categories and relationships; (2) the various kinds of meanings your language encodes; some heavy in referential content (like "cat," "see," "ugly"), others adding further refinement to basic meanings (inflectional morphemes like "plural" or "past"), others changing syntactic properties of a morpheme so that it can relate differently to other morphemes (derivational morphemes), others combining morphemes which, taken together, provide new meanings (such as compounds and idioms); (3) the possibilities for morpheme combinations, both within complex morphemes (what simple morphemes can combine to form complex ones and what the ordering principles are for these combinations), and also as co-occurrence possibilities within sentences; (4) the semantic features and how your language clusters them into morphemes (though this is often quite unavailable to consciousness); (5) which morphemes of your language are more and less general (include fewer or more semantic features). And this is only the barest beginning.

The growth and development of our semantic knowledge never ends. As our experience continues, our meanings increase. New experiences bring new meanings and expand and refine old ones. As teachers interacting with children in new and stimulating experiences, we are doing more about children's semantic growth than about their growth in the other two linguistic structure components (syntax, phonology). Interestingly, the prevailing view among many teachers is that their greatest contribution to children's language development in elementary school is in syntax (giving children grammar exercises designed either to teach them to identify parts of speech or to provide them with more adult-like sentence structures) *or* in phonology (giving children a knowledge of the sounds of their language through phonetic approaches to the teaching of reading, or trying to substitute more mature for less mature pronunciations). But nothing could be further from the truth. It is in the semantic domain that children's growth is most vigorous during the elementary school years. It is in new and rich shared experiences, which are part of the child's school life, that new meanings are born and expressed and familiar ones live and grow. This is the base of the child's continuing semantic growth. And because the semantic domain, so embedded in continuing experience, is an area where we too are learners, it is here that we may be doing our most important "teaching," for it is here that we, as real *learners* ourselves, model what continuing learning is.

SYNTACTIC COMPONENT

There is more to the deep or meaning level of language structure than semantic features bundled into morpheme units, and possibilities for the combination of morphemes within words and for their co-occurence in sentences. Syntax deals with the relational meanings in language; the basic unit of the syntactic component is the sentence. We have traditionally thought of a sentence as a complete thought (whatever that means), or as a string of words which, when written, begins with a capital and ends with a period. But what we are talking about here when we use the term *sentence* is an abstract construct, an ordered string of morphemes that comprise a proposition. This ordered morpheme string retains the meanings inherent in the individual morphemes comprising it ("boy," "run," "plural"), but it also contains relational meanings such as who performed the action, who had the action done to him or done for him, what was the location, how was the action performed. In English it is mainly through morpheme order and somewhat less through form ("quick-quickly," "mechanic-mechanical") that these relations are conveyed. The abstract construct sentence—a sequenced string of morphemes—relates to the semantic component of our knowledge in that it includes the meanings of the morphemic units; it also relates to the phonological component of our language knowledge (the component dealing with the sound system) in that we can associate a pronunciation with the morpheme string. Notice that we often actually utter only a portion of that string as, for example, when we answer "yes" to the question "Are you warm enough?" or "the" to the question "What's this word?" The underlying propositional meaning string is mentally present and what we actually pronounce is a reduced version of it: "Yes" (I am warm enough), or (This word is) "the." It is important not to confuse the abstract construct "sentence"—the organized morpheme sequence comprising a proposition—with its pronunciation. For our purposes "cat" and "plural" or "run" and "past" might be part of the sentence (S), but these would be actualized in the pronounced string as /kæts/ and /ræn/. Try to think of an S as the organized string of related parts, underlying the actual pronunciation.

Phrase Structure (*PS*) Rules and Recursion

We pointed out in the last chapter the incredible ability you (and all speakers of a language) have to produce and interpret sentences which are entirely new to your experience, sentences you have never encountered before. How can we account for this ability? Well, in a sense, novel sentences are not entirely new. The parts are selected and structured according to principles which are familiar even though the particular selection and sequence of elements is novel. Put another way, the particular sentence is new but its structural design or organizational framework is not.

It is possible to account for your ability to understand and create an infinite set of possible sentences in your language, by positing a finite set of principles which specify the possible organizations of sentence parts. Some of these principles deal with basic categories or classes of elements (noun, locative, intransitive verb) and possibilities for their combination. Various organizations convey various relations among the parts. In the sentence

> The girl kicked the ball into the street

we can identify the syntactic category or type of each morpheme:

The	girl	kicked	the	ball	into	the	street
determiner (or article)	noun	verb + tense (past)	determiner	noun	preposition	determiner	noun

We can also identify parts of the sentence string in terms of functional relations. One way to do this is to think of each functional segement of the S as the answer to a question.

The girl	kicked	the ball	into the street
(Who did it?)	(What did she do?)	(What did she kick?)	(Where did she kick it?)
subject (agent)	verb (action)	direct object	locative

Speakers of a language generally agree on what does and does not constitute a possible sentence in that language—an acceptable arrangement of morphemes. The question is, what is the standard that provides a basis for that judgment? It is possible to specify a set of selectional and organizational principles which, when applied to spoken sentences, will identify them as "acceptable" or "unacceptable." Linguists have worked and continue to work to specify a complete set of these principles. But it is crucial to note that positing such a set of principles is *not* the same as saying "This set of principles is, in fact, descriptive of the *actual* set of principles native speakers mentally use in determining which sentences of their langauge are grammatical, and in understanding and creating sentences." This may seem a picky distinction, but it is not. It amounts to saying that linguists do not know what organizational principles we, as speakers of a language, have in our heads. We can only say that (1) our language behavior is highly structured, very orderly, and nonrandom, and thus we can be sure that we have access to some set of principles for creating and understanding sentences and judging their grammaticality; and (2) it is possible to specify a set of organizational principles such that, if we apply them, we can account for all the strings of morphemes that speakers of a language recognize as grammatical sentences and none of the strings that speakers regard as ungrammatical.[13] We can say that the speaker of a language " . . . acts as if he knew . . ." and were using a set of principles like the set we propose (Slobin 1971, p. 53). We cannot say, however, that the set proposed in fact describes the actual mental set which underlies and accounts for our observed language behavior (for example, creating and understanding sentences, recognizing some sentences as grammatical and others as ungrammatical).

We saw earlier that, given an actual sentence, we can divide it into major parts. We recognize the function each major part serves in relation to the rest of the sentence. We also recognize that some phrases can be further divided. *Phrase structure* (*PS*) rules are posited to account for this knowledge we have. PS rules constitute a set of principles for identifying (labeling) and relating basic sentence (*S*) parts (called *constituents*). *S*s are described as being composed of phrases (constituents) which can be progressively subdivided into smaller constituents until we arrive at individual morphemes. (Remember, the claim is not that these rules are a picture of what is in your head, but rather that you behave linguistically *as if* these rules, or similar ones, are available to you.)

The sentence

The girl kicked the ball into the street

we can view as being composed of a constituent, traditionally called "subject," whose major element is a noun (or pronoun), and a second constituent, traditionally called "predicate," whose major element is a verb. Because the noun element and verb element are crucial, some linguists have called these two major sentence constituents the *Noun Phrase* (*NP*) and *Verb Phrase* (*VP*) of the *S*. Thus the first principle or rule proposed is that an *S* is composed of a Noun Phrase and a Verb Phrase. Linguists abbreviate this rule as

$S \rightarrow NP + VP$

which literally reads: "A sentence can be rewritten as a Noun Phrase plus a

---

[13]In actual fact, this set of principles has not been completely specified, and there is great debate as to the nature and form that such a set of principles will take.

Verb Phrase." It is then possible to specify ways in which each of these major constituents can be "rewritten"—further divided into their identified and labeled parts. Our original S is an instance of the NP being rewritten as the determiner "the" plus the noun "girl." Thus for this S:

$NP \rightarrow Det + N$

$Det \rightarrow the$

$N \rightarrow girl$

But you know, of course, that there could have been various types of NPs in the original S. For example:

$$\begin{Bmatrix} Joan \\ She \end{Bmatrix} kicked\ the\ ball\ into\ the\ street.$$

Thus linguists provide more general rules, such as:

$$NP \rightarrow \begin{Bmatrix} pronoun \\ (det) + noun \\ \ldots\ ^{14} \end{Bmatrix}$$

This would read that "an NP can be written as a pronoun or as a noun, possibly preceded by a determiner." Of course, the VP of an S would be similarly spelled out in terms of the possibilities for its composition.

The purpose here is not to elaborate in full the structural principles (PS rules) and their formalization that linguists have proposed, but rather to help you see how it is possible to provide a structural description for many thousands of possible Ss that the speaker calls "grammatical," in terms of a set of rules or general statements, which identify major constituents of S and the possibilities for their composition as subparts.

Another way to characterize this posited set of structural principles, accounting for some types of sentence units and their organization, is to sketch the sentence parts and relations in a tree-like diagram called a phrase structure tree.[15]

[14]This is not a complete set of possibilities.
[15]Note that this is only one of several such diagrammatic formalizations that has been suggested. Also, the particular model presented on p. 64 (Transformational Grammar) is only one of several approaches linguists have suggested. Other promising descriptions include Case Grammar (see Fillmore 1968 for original formulation) and Generative Semantics (see Parisi and Antinucci 1976 for an introduction to this approach).

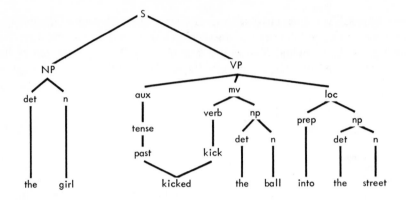

Here is a simplified tree diagram of our original sentence. Do not panic at the look of the *VP* part of the sentence. It is merely a graphic representation of some information that we could have spelled out in rules as we did earlier for the Noun Phrase: for example, *VP* → aux + mv + loc (Verb Phrase is to be rewritten as auxiliary plus main verb plus locative), with each of these subsequently spelled out into its constituents. The *VP* sketched here indicates that, in addition to the verb ("kick")—the main element of the *VP*—the *VP* also includes the "aux" information that the action is to be indicated as past tense ("kicked" rather than "kick") and that the location resulting from the action is specified as well. The sketch also indicates that the main verb itself consists of the verb proper ("kick") plus a following determiner plus noun, in this case "the ball." Notice that identifying this noun phrase in the tree diagram by small letters (*np*), makes it clear that its hierarchical status is not that of the main *N*oun *P*hrase of *S,* though it is composed of similar elements (det + noun). Similarly in the locational phrase, there is a noun phrase and again it consists of det + noun, but it, too, is not the major *NP* of the *S,* but rather a subpart of a major constituent.

Our sketch here has dealt with only one possible English sentence. The phrase structure rules and the corresponding tree diagram have provided a structural description in the form of a hierarchical set of labeled categories and relationships. But you can see that this sketch accounts for many thousands of possible sentences which are structurally similar but which include different specific morphemes.

Phrase structure rules can account for a tremendous number of sentences of a language. But we know that the set of possible sentences of a language is not just very large, but infinite; there is literally no limit to the set of possible sentences of a language. Any possible sentence can easily be made into another and longer sentence. If "That man is old" is a possible sentence of English, then so is "That man is very old," and so is "That man is very, very, very old." (I shall never forget my high school drama coach who, when distressed with some aspiring actor's poor performance at a rehearsal, would say, "That performance was absolutely the most wishy-washy, willy-nilly, shilly-shally, run-of-the-mill, bottom-of-the-barrel . . . etc. . . . that I have ever seen.") If "That man is his father" is a possible sentence of English, then so is "I know that that man is his father" and so is "You know that I know that that man is his father." (How many times have you heard children engage in this "I know that you know that I know . . . " game? Does that tell you anything about their language knowledge?) If "That boy is his son" is a sentence, then so is "That boy, who is a very good friend of mine, is his son" and so is "That boy is the son of the man I like very much but wish would stop smoking those foul-smelling cigars." The examples here are trivial, but the point is not. It is always possible to include a sentence within a sentence, and thus language must be, by definition, infinite. Linguists have tried to capture this fact of language in rules like:

$$np\text{------}> (det) + noun + (S)$$

This indicates that a noun phrase can include a sentence within it. Thus

> The girl *who was wearing blue socks* kicked the ball into the street.
> The girl kicked the ball *that had a leak in it* into the street.
> The girl kicked the ball into the street *that the men had just repaired.*

are all possibilities. Of course every *S* has its own *NP,* and if any *np* can always possibly include an *S,* which will also have its own *NP,* which can include an *S,* which will include an *NP* . . . well, you see, the possibilities are infinite.

Including an *S* within an *S* is called *recursion* and of course all languages have this recursive property. However, we do not generally communicate using sentences that are very recursive—sentence within sentence within sentence (although we do play games with such sentences as in "This is the house that Jack built"). Communication requires that, out of the structurally possible set of sentences, we use those which will be processed readily in actual life situations. But it is important to understand, as a basic fact about language, that there is in principle no limit to the set of sentences accounted for by a finite set of structural rules, even though many of the theoretically possible sentences are ones we would be unlikely to use in conversation.

What is important for us here is not a detailed version of phrase structure rules or their formalization as proposed by linguists, but rather the fact that part of our knowledge of language structure relates to our knowing that sentences include related subparts at various hierarchical levels, that these subparts are members of a finite set of types or classes in the language (like noun, verb, adjective, determiner), that only some arrangements of parts are acceptable to native speakers (and which ones), and that these arrangements themselves (as well as the morphemic units which ultimately comprise them) carry meaning.

Transformational (*T*) Rules

There is more to a native speaker's syntactic knowledge than an awareness of sentence subparts of various types in various relations, and an awareness that sentences can be included within sentences. Linguists propose another important type of rule or organizational principle in an attempt to account for the native speaker's sense of some sentences being variations of each other—various morpheme selections and arrangements conveying the same basic message or proposition (deep structure). Remember John and his little sister who kicked him in the shins? There we saw that by rearranging some sentence elements—by deleting some, by substituting some new items for the originals, by adding elements—we came up with a set of different versions of the original sentence. The rules linguists propose to account for this aspect of our knowledge are called *transformational (T) rules.* Doubtless you can see why: They account for the *transforming* of an *S* into various *S*'s which contain the same meaning.

If you study the interesting set of sentences below, you will recognize sentence 1, "Mary glipped a snoozle," as the most basic version (the *S* resulting from *PS* rules), and sentences 2 through 10 as transformations of that basic structure.

1. Mary glipped a snoozle.
2. It's a snoozle that Mary glipped.
3. What Mary glipped was a snoozle.
4. It was Mary who glipped a snoozle.
5. The one who glipped a snoozle was Mary.
6. A snoozle was glipped by Mary.
7. It's a snoozle that was glipped by Mary.
8. What was glipped by Mary was a snoozle.
9. It was Mary who a snoozle was glipped by.
10. The one who a snoozle was glipped by was Mary. (Fromkin and Rodman 1974, p. 164)

As you look at sentences 2 through 10 and compare them with each other and with the original, you can see cases of items being added, rearranged, substituted, deleted, or reduced. You can see that with phrase structure rules alone, we can account for only very basic, unadorned sentences like sentence 1. But we know that we can "say the same thing" in an endless variety of ways. *T* rules account for that.

In each of these sentences it is understood that the grammatical relationships among *Mary, glip,* and *a snoozle* are unvarying. That is, Mary is the one doing the "glipping" in all cases, just as it is "a snoozle" that gets "glipped" in all cases. To account for all these various syntactic forms, and at the same time reveal that the grammatical relationships are the same in each case—hence that the sentences are all nearly synonymous—is obviously too much of a job for the phrase-structure rules alone.

If we let the phrase-structure rules account for the basic structure of sentence [1] . . . and let transformations derive the other nine . . . sentences, we can explain the fact that in spite of the variance of syntactic forms all the sentences mean basically the same thing. (Fromkin and Rodman 1974, p. 164)

As you might guess, *T* rules, like *PS* rules, have been formalized by linguists so that they can readily be applied to identified types of structures. But what is important for us here is not a detailed study of all the proposed *T* rules and their formalization, but the recognition that there is some set of principles (however adequately or inadequately the linguists' description may have captured them), which speakers of a language know and which accounts for their recognition of stylistic variation. Further, the set of structural principles is basically the same from speaker to speaker. It is precisely the sharing of the same set of rules that makes us speakers of the same language. It is this underlying set of principles that children come to know. And linguists, with their formalized *PS* and *T* rules, are saying, "Speakers of a language perform *as if* they know and use (unconsciously) rules or guiding principles such as these."

PHONOLOGICAL COMPONENT

The human being is capable of making a wide range of sounds with his vocal apparatus. He can cough, whistle, sing, sneeze, and wheeze. He can also talk. Considering the diverse set of sounds all human beings can make so easily by means of an air stream passing up through the vocal tract and out through the mouth and/or nose, it is interesting that only a subset are the sounds of talk in any language. If we listen to a person speaking a language with which we are totally unfamiliar, a language for which we have no sound-meaning correspondences at all, we are still likely to recognize which of the sounds he produces are language sounds and which are not.

All the sounds used in human languages, however diverse they may appear, can be described in terms of a limited set of sound features relating to, for example, whether or not the vocal cords vibrate; whether the air stream passes through the mouth, or nose, or both; the position of the tongue in the mouth; the shape of the mouth; the position of the lips; whether the air stream passes through the mouth continuously (as in /s/) or whether its passage is stopped (as in /b/). We can indentify a set of significant sound features that all languages draw on. Clustering these features into various bundles, each language emerges with an inventory of basic consonant and vowel sounds that the native speakers recognize as being significant in conveying meanings in their language.[16] What is particularly interesting however, is that these basic sounds (significant sound feature bundles) are not clearly demarked in the actual stream of speech. The sounds in "She fell into the river but he grabbed her ankle and pulled her out just in time" form a continuous stream when spoken in natural conversation. But however continuous this sound stream is in time, the English speaker can break it into a set of significant sound units. You would say that the first word, "she," is a combination of a consonant sound /š/ and a vowel (V), the next word is the sound /f/ plus a V plus /l/, "into" is a V + /n/ + /t/ + V, "the" is the sound / ð / + V, "grabbed" is a /g/ + /r/ + V + /b/ + /d/, "ankle" is a V + /ŋ/ + /k/ + V + /l/, and so on.

The intention here is not to present a special set of written symbols for representing the basic sounds of English that the native speaker knows. For our purposes, V is a stand-in for a variety of specific vowel sounds. But it is important to emphasize that our concern here is with language *sounds,* not with the written symbols our alphabet uses (not always consistently) to represent them. Many languages have no written system at all to represent them; they are no less languages for that. English does happen to have a written system, and anyone who has ever been concerned with teaching a child to read it is aware that the written symbolization does not represent the sound system of our language through any simple set of one-to-one, sound-symbol correspondences. A given sound may be represented by different written symbols (the vowel sound of r*ai*n, r*ei*gn, c*a*me, or the /š/ sound of *s*ugar, *Ch*icago, sta*ti*on, *sh*ape). The reverse is also true; a single written symbol may represent various pronunciations (the different vowel sounds in f*i*n and f*i*ne, and the "th" in *Th*omas, *th*igh, and *th*y). What the speaker recognizes as a single basic sound may be represented by a combination of written symbols, as in the *Th*omas, *th*igh, *th*y cases, or in the /f/ written as "gh" in enou*gh* and as "ph" in ele-*ph*ant, or in the /ŋ/ written as "ng" in ki*ng.* The important point is to differentiate between the language and a written system devised to represent it. Our concern here is with what we know about the sound system of our language, a concern that would be no different however our language were written down, and even if it were not written at all.

We prize literacy so highly in our culture that the written word has a way of becoming "the real thing" rather than a symbolization of the real thing. We get to *believing* that grabbed has two /b/s, that the last vowel sound of ankle follows, rather than precedes the /l/, that king has four sounds, the last

---

[16]What I am calling "basic sounds" here, some call phonemes, others (for example, Fromkin and Rodman 1974) call phonetic segments.

two being /n/ and /g/. This is a sound-symbol confusion. (Contrasting Ki*m*, ki*n*, and ki*ng* helps to make the singleness of the /ŋ/ evident.) We explain casual pronunciations of "walking" and "having" as "dropping the g," and in fact often see these pronunciations represented in literature as "walkin' " and "havin'." Was there ever a /g/ in these words? What we mean is that in casual speech we often substitute final /n/ for /ŋ/. Sometimes people pronounce the past tense of "walk" without verbally expressing the addition of the past tense morpheme. We say they "dropped the ed." Is there any /-Vd/ in "walk*ed*"? We tend to confuse the sound component of our language with the written system devised to represent it. There are many languages that have no written systems to represent them, but obviously there are no alphabet systems that do not have languages that they represent. Written systems are one form of symbolization of language, but they are not, themselves, the language. When people of a language community devise a written system for their language, the language structure is not thereby affected in any way.

It is the sound system of your language then, not the related spelling system, that you recognize as being comprised of an inventory of significant or basic sounds—the sound bundles you pay attention to to differentiate meaning. For example, /bæt/, /pæt/, and /mæt/ are all pronunciations of English morphemes. The initial sound of each differentiates it from the other two. Notice that the initial sounds share some features, but are different in others; /b/, /p/, and /m/ are all made with the lips closed. But /m/ is nasal (made with air passing through the nose) while /p/ and /b/ are oral sounds (made with air passing through the mouth); /p/ is voiceless, while /m/ and /b/ are voiced (vocal cords vibrate during their production); /bæt/, /bæd/, and /bæn/ are all pronunciations of English morphemes also. The final sounds, /t/, /d/, and /n/ differentiate them and in fact form an analogous set to the /p/, /b/, /m/ trio. Can you describe the features of similarity and difference in the set /t/, /d/, and /n/ in terms of tongue position, nasality, and voicing?

The final sounds which differentiate "but," "bus," and "buzz" (/bət/, /bəs/, /bəz/) demonstrate another sound feature that is significant in characterizing basic sounds of any language. The tip of your tongue is in a similar position for all three of the final sounds. The voicing of /z/ sets it apart from the voiceless /t/ and /s/. But notice that the /s/ and /z/ are very different from /t/ in the way the air stream passes through the mouth. The air stream is completely blocked in the production of /t/ (thus /t/, like /b/, /p/, /d/, /k/, and /g/, is sometimes called a *stop* consonant), while for /s/ and /z/, the air stream passes continuously through the mouth, (and not surprisingly, these sounds are sometimes called *continuants.*) We can account for all the basic significant sounds in your sound inventory as clusters of a limited set of sound features, no two basic sounds (sound feature clusters) being identical in their total sets of features, but each one sharing some sound features with other basic sounds. We have considered only a few consonant sounds here, but vowel sounds as well share some features (such as voicing and continuousness) and differ in others (such as shape of mouth, position of the lips, position of parts of the tongue).

It is easy to see that you know the basic significant consonant and vowel sounds of your language. It is less easy to see that you have knowledge (though possibly not at a conscious level), of specific sound features. But the fact is, for some purposes, you treat various basic sounds in similar ways because of some shared sound feature. You pluralize chur*ch* (/č/), jud*ge* (/ǰ/), bu*s* (/s/), gara*ge* (/ž/), a*sh* (/š/), phra*se* (/z/) in the same way—by adding the syllable /əz/—because of a sound feature shared by all, and only by the set /s/, /z/, /š/, /ž/, /č/, /ǰ/. These are the "hissing" or "shushing" sounds of English, the class of sounds called *sibilants*. You may not have thought about this sound feature before, but given a nonsense word ending in any one of these six basic sounds (and only these six), you would have provided a plural form by adding /əz/; that is, you are treating diverse basic sounds in the same way —classifying them—on the basis of a shared specific sound feature. In pluralizing nouns ending with nonsibilant sounds, you classify them for the property of voicing, selecting voiceless /s/ for those ending with voiceless sounds (ha*t* + /s/, mo*p* + /s/), and selecting voiced /z/ for those ending with voiced sounds (bo*y* + /z/, gir*l* + /z/).[17] Likewise, you regularly add the /əd/ past tense only to verbs ending in /t/ (strut) and /d/ (fade)—the two English sounds which are nonnasal and stops and made with the tongue at the gum ridge. For other verbs, you select voiced /d/ for those ending in voiced sounds (tr*y* + /d/, hu*m* + /d/), and voiceless /t/ for those ending in voiceless sounds (ho*p* + /t/, dan*ce* + /t/). Again you are responding to particular sound features.

You also know which combinations of basic sounds are possible—which combinations the sound system of your language "allows." Asked to select an English name for a newly discovered object, from this possible set of names:

slenk   blenk   tlenk   glenk

there is one which you certainly would not choose. Which one is it? You would probably say that "tlenk" is impossible because of the combination "tl." You are right. You may say that the combination "tl" is too difficult to pronounce. But clearly this is not the case, as the sound combination /tl/ occurs in many languages of the world. However, English does not happen to be one of them. English combines /l/ with other stop consonants; notice the /bl/ of black, the /pl/ of plaque, the /gl/ of glass, and the /kl/ of class. But /tl/ and /dl/ do not cluster in English syllables. This is not a constraint imposed by human

---

[17]I am including here only regular forms, and excluding irregular plurals such as "children," "sheep," "data."

possibilities of pronunciation; it is simply a constraint from within a particular language. It is a simple fact of the language, and it is a fact that you know, though, as with so much of your language knowledge, you may be unaware that you know it.

If you try to pronounce the Swahili word for drum, *ngoma* (/ŋ*V*m*V*/), you may become aware of another important aspect of your phonological knowledge. In English, the sound /ŋ/, as in ri*ng* or thi*n*k, can occur at the end or in the middle of words, but not at the beginning. Though all sounds in *ngoma* also occur in English, you would know immediately that this could not be an English word. What is important here is not that you would know that it is not, in fact, an English word (after all, there are lots of English words you do not know), but rather that you would know that it *could not be* an English word. You know the constraints on the positions in which basic sounds can occur, and one of these is that, in English, the sound /ŋ/ does not occur at the beginning of words.

Another fascinating aspect of your phonological knowledge is how the pronunciation of certain sounds changes, depending on what sound(s) precede or follow them. If you pronounce the following three pairs

*p*ill	s*p*ill
*t*ill	s*t*ill
*k*ill	s*k*ill

you may be aware of a difference in your pronunciation of /p/, /t/, and /k/ when these sounds occur initially and when they are preceded by /s/. If you do not notice a difference, hold your hand in front of your mouth as you say each pair. You will probably be aware that the /p/, /t/, and /k/ in the first column are accompanied by a puff of air (aspiration) when you say them, while in the pronunciation of these "same" sounds preceded by /s/, the puff of air is absent. Here is a harder pair:

"cat" /kæt/	"cad" /kæd/

Can you hear any difference in the vowel sound as you pronounce the two words? The vowel sound of "cad" is longer in duration than the vowel sound of "cat." Notice that when we say a vowel sound is "long," we are not using this term as the reading teacher does to mean an alphabet symbol that "says its own name" or that Webster writes with a "-" above it. We are talking about the duration of the sound in time.

So far we have talked about only a small part of your knowledge of particular sounds and how they combine.[18] You also know much about the "tune" of the sentences of your language, the ups and downs, the stresses, the

---

[18]For further discussion of these four important aspects of the native speaker's phonological knowledge, see Langacker (1973), chapter 4.

pauses, and the various meanings conveyed by these sentence features. One way to attune your ears to the intonation possibilities (ups and downs of the voice) of your language is to consider the simple one-word sentences "Oh" and "No." Various intonation patterns differentiate between the "oh" of uncertainty (. . . well . . . I don't know really); the "oh" that means "How beautiful!"; the "oh" of understanding (. . . so *that's* what it means); the "oh" of disappointment; the "oh" of knowing a sly secret. The situation is similar with "no": different intonation patterns convey different meanings including at least the "no" of shock (You didn't!), of warning (mother to young child who is moving slowly, deliberately toward the forbidden object), of hesitation and uncertainty (. . . but . . .), of finality, and the straightforward negative reply to a question. You might want to try some of these "ohs" and "nos" out on friends or fellow students to see whether they can tell the meaning that your intonation conveys. But be warned! This can become very frustrating when you discover that these various meanings that you convey so easily and naturally in everyday conversation are more difficult to convey out of context when you concentrate on them so consciously. You will probably also be surprised to see how much you use nonverbal clues (facial expressions, the shrug of your shoulders) in addition to intonation patterns to convey your meanings.

Read these words aloud.

saw
who
yesterday
know
do
I
you

Now read this arrangement of the same words aloud:

Do you know who I saw yesterday?

The list and the question probably sounded very different. Perhaps you read the list with a rising intonation on each word, followed by a pause, and then a falling intonation on the last word (rise-pause, rise-pause, . . . fall). But when you read the sentence, you probably lost the pauses that were part of your list reading, and gave the sentence an overall rise, indicating that you were asking a certain type of question. The rhythm and intonation of the question were different from the rhythm and intonation of the list. Can you describe the rhythmic and intonational differences in the two possible readings of the ambiguous sentence

Did you ever see a horse fly?

(Sometimes it helps to substitute "la la la" for the words.)

You know which intonation patterns and rhythms are appropriate in conveying meanings in your language. You also know how to use and understand the feature of stress (emphasis). If you intended a neutral, strictly informational meaning, you would probably stress the words "told" and "tomorrow" slightly in the sentence

He told me they'd be arriving tomorrow.

But if you wanted to convey a special meaning, you would apply extra stress on various words, depending on your meaning:

He told me they'd be arriving tomorrow (Not *she* or you, but *he*)

He *told* me they'd be arriving tomorrow (He didn't *ask* me, he *told* me, or despite the fact that it didn't happen, he *told* me it would)

He told *me* they'd be arriving tomorrow (*Me,* instead of you or someone else)

He told me *they'd* be arriving tomorrow (Not *he* or *she*—one, but *they*—a group)

He told me they'd be *arriving* tomorrow (Not leaving, but *arriving*)

He told me they'd be arriving *tomorrow* (Not next week, but *tomorrow*)

This extra stress, which adds a special meaning to the neutral informational message, is called *contrastive* stress, for it focuses on one element as it contrasts with some expected meaning. As a speaker of English, you use and respond to this phonological feature of English with facility. Knowledge of stress, intonation, and rhythm are all important aspects of your phonological knowledge, every bit as important as your knowledge of the particular sounds of your language and the possibilities for their combination and pronunciation.

You know a lot about what matters in the phonological subsystem of your language—which particular sounds, out of all the possible sounds a human can make, are significant; what arrangements of sounds are possible; how sounds alter in combination; what stress, intonation and rhythm patterns are appropriate. But you also know what aspects of verbal sounds do not matter in the business of conveying meanings. The speed with which we say something, for example, does not alter the basic content of our message, nor does the pitch, or quality, or volume, or breathiness of our voice. It surely is the case that these voice features are sometimes associated with emotional or social meanings. For example, we may speak more rapidly when excited, with higher pitch when upset, or more quietly when telling a friend a secret. These are important meanings: I'm excited; I'm upset; I don't want to be heard. But we need to look beyond the rules of language structure to account for them.

Voice quality, speed, volume, and pitch do not alter the meanings of the propositions you make, the commands you give, the questions you ask.[19]

It seems strange that the very stream of speech sounds that is so full of meaning for the speaker of a given language, is just so much noise to the outsider. "Sounds are given meaning by the language in which they occur" (Fromkin and Rodman 1974, p. 3). I process the sound stream of Chinese, Yoruba, or Amharic as noise, while the speaker of Chinese, Yoruba, or Amharic processes the same sound stream as meaning conveying—in fact, is probably unaware of the *sound* at all, so closely related is that sound to meaning and so completely is his attention focused on that meaning.

The linguist's choice of the phrase "sound stream" is apt, for the sounds of spoken language do indeed flow continuously. Speakers sometimes pause for breath or for emphasis or to get their thoughts in order, but overall there is a continuous flow of sounds in speech. It is easier to hear this continuousness of the speech stream if you listen to people speaking a language you do not know, than if you listen to people speaking your own language. When you listen to your own language, the meaning "gets in the way." You tend to feel "breaks" in the speech stream that are not present in the sound signal itself, but are very much present in your mental organization of the sound signal you hear. To know a language is to know how the (physically) unbroken speech stream is (mentally) broken—the organizational structure of sounds, meanings, relations that the language system imposes. It is precisely because the sounds and meanings of your language are so inextricably entwined for you, that it is difficult to focus simply on the sound stream; for you it is not a sound stream, but a meaning stream as well.

Do you begin to wonder how it is possible that an infant, exposed to the continuousness of the sounds of language, ever manages to figure out the organization of that stream and its relation to meanings? But over time, virtually *every* child does build a mental organization for the language, that matches that of the adult in the language community. From an initial exposure to what, for the infant, must be noise, to the development of a full-fledged, highly complex, abstract language system matching the adult's seems an incredible journey, but it is one that every child makes for at least one language.

---

[19]You will recognize the difficulty here in limiting ourselves to "language structure." This is an important difficulty, as it underscores the fact that language is for communication; language structure does not actually exist in a pure form—in some sort of vacuum, apart from its use by real people in real situations to talk to each other about real experiences —to be sarcastic, to parody, to persuade, to show respect. But language structure is an important part of the whole, and by understanding this aspect more fully, we may ultimately come to better understand the whole, even though it is admittedly artificial, to some extent, to try to examine it out of the context of real communication.

This must surely stand as one of the greatest accomplishments of every human life.

LINGUISTIC UNIVERSALS

We have considered three major components of language structure: semantic, syntactic, phonological. All three are crucial to one's knowledge of a language. We are often struck by the tremendous diversity in these components from language to language; the meanings, syntactic organization, and sounds from one language to the next seem so very different. But are they? After all, human languages must be products of human intelligence. It goes without saying that humans could not have devised communication systems which they lack the ability to process. If humans, though diverse in many ways, are biologically similar in physical and cognitive characteristics, would we not expect that diverse languages—like the diverse humans who speak them—would also, at some deep level, possess important commonalities?

In fact, the underlying commonalities among languages are just as impressive as the surface differences among them. The important concept of *linguistic universals* captures this notion of linguistic commonalities which somehow relate to the commonalities of the humans who speak diverse languages. Some linguists are focusing their attention on semantic universals. Many feel that it is possible to specify a set of fundamental semantic features that all languages draw on. Though we do not know what all of these basic semantic features might be, we find that the properties of animateness, humanness, texture, shape, and function figure prominently in the meaning bundles that comprise the morphemes of many languages. How these features cluster into morphemes, and how prominent certain ones are, differs from language to language, but the fact of their occurrence in the semantic components of widely diverse languages is overwhelming.

The situation is similar in syntax. As we look at language after language, we find each one expressing similar relationships among sentence parts—attribution, location, agent-action. We find that word forms and/or word orders figure significantly in signaling these relationships. We find it possible to account for syntactic relatedness (stylistic variation) of the sentences of any language in terms of processes such as addition, deletion, substitution, rearrangement of sentence parts. And we find the same sentence types—statements, yes/no questions, information questions, negatives, commands—occurring across a range of historically unrelated languages.

In phonology, it is perhaps easiest to see how our human physiology would serve to limit the sound possibilities of language—given, of course, that languages use verbal sounds as their expressive medium. That all natural human languages *do,* is itself a universal! It is conceivable that other overt expressive systems could have evolved to convey meanings, but with the exception of a few specialized expressive systems (sign language for the deaf, for example), the human vocal apparatus is used as the major medium for expressing meanings.[20] Given that the human vocal organs are structured and function in certain ways for all normal humans, the range of possible sound features that languages could employ is obviously limited. We find it possible (and fruitful) to specify a set of distinctive sound features on which all languages draw, and which, variously selected, combined and used from language to language, account for the diversity in the phonological systems of human languages.

For each component, then, we are struck by the universal commonalities that underlie the surface diversity of languages. For all the diversity of the particular sounds, the particular organizational arrangements of sentence parts, and the particular meanings encoded by the various lexicons, languages are all actualizing in particular ways a fundamental set of universal meaning features, organizational possibilities, and sound features that the human mind and body are capable of. Just as all humans look noticeably different in specifics of appearance but share a basic set of universal physical characteristics that identify them as humans, so human languages differ in specific characteristics, but share a set of universal properties in the types of elements they include and the processes they employ. How could it be otherwise? Language, to be learned by *all* humans, must lie within the range of physical and cognitive possibilities and constraints common to *all* humans.

---

[20]Note also the tremendous nonverbal repertoire we all employ—an important system of gesture, body movement, and facial expression.

Chapter 4

Language Structure, Teachers, and Children

As teachers, we often see our role as one of diagnosing problems in our students and then providing experiences designed to eradicate those problems and substitute more desirable behaviors for them. The very term "diagnose," borrowed from medicine, suggests that we view the child in some important ways as an unhealthy, poorly functioning organism. After all, we seek our doctors' diagnoses when we are ill, not when we are in good health.

But in the area of language, at least, we might more appropriately view the child as an extraordinarily healthy organism, who will continue to flourish in the rich environment we can provide. We are not trying to rid the child of language "problems," but rather to enhance her remarkable continuing language development. Typically the child's language is alive and well, at whatever developmental stage we first encounter her—preschool, primary, or intermediate level—and our job is to provide an environment in which it will thrive.

The preschooler, given the opportunity and the desire, tells us about objects and events, asks a variety of questions, requests or demands what she wants. It takes a well-developed linguistic system (as well as a sophisticated knowledge of how to use it appropriately in various situations) to do this, and a well-developed linguistic system is exactly what preschoolers have. This is not to say that four-year-olds always formulate their sentences as adults do. Clearly, they do not. Their language includes pronunciations, word combinations, and vocabulary items which are different from the adult's. But these are more accurately seen as the healthy and necessary developmental differences of language growth in progress than as a set of "problems." Adults get around by walking, and eight-month-old babies get around by crawling. But notice that we do not view the eight-month-old's crawling as a "walking problem"; rather, we delight in the substantial accomplishment of mastering crawling, though we realize that the child will not crawl forever. Why then do we view the young child's far more impressive language accomplishment as being full of "problems," simply because it does not yet match our own? As adults, we often engage in complex abstract reasoning. Yet we do not view the four-year-old's understanding of her world through her manipulation of concrete objects and through her dramatic play as evidence of her having "problems" in abstract reasoning. Why then do we view her "comed" and "goed" as "language problems" and fail to see that they clearly demonstrate giant steps toward her working out the rules which underlie the diverse language she hears around her?

With primary level children, we tend to become caught up in the development of literacy—in teaching reading and writing skills. But it is important that we not confuse teaching a child to read and write her language with teaching a child her language. When we teach a child to read and write, we only teach her another symbolization system for the well-developed language system she already has. At primary level, we still hear children utter sentences which are not exactly like the adult's. But although a child's language includes sentences which contain deviant syntax, unusual pronunciations, or labels which express concepts somewhat different from our own, still, in the main, the child controls her language system, and we are only teaching her to process graphic symbols which represent it.

Just as many primary grade teachers confuse teaching the reading and writing of a language with teaching language structure, so many intermediate level teachers confuse teaching a child to *talk about* language structure with teaching her language structure. At the intermediate level, we may give children labels for their language structure, in an attempt to bring their knowledge of that structure to a level of conscious awareness; but this is vastly different from teaching the child her language structure. We are simply providing her with ways to talk about what she already knows unconsciously. At the intermediate level the child has virtually complete mastery of her language system, though she, like us, continues to develop vocabulary throughout the remainder of her life. We may give her labels such as noun, verb, adverb, adjective, subject, predicate, but we are not giving her the language structure which those labels identify. She controls that language structure already, and she has gained mastery of this complex linguistic system on her own through interacting with her environment.

As teachers, then, we must learn (1) to view the child's acquisition of language structure as a healthy ongoing process over time, (2) to sort out what we are and are not teaching. We may deliberately design instructional sequences to teach children to read, write, and talk about their language, but we do not design such sequences to teach them their language structure in the first place.

We know that language grows best in meaningful situations, that is, situations which are meaningful and interesting *to the child*. Therefore, we enhance the child's acquisition of all phases of language, including linguistic structure, when we provide and encourage experiences that are rich in meaning for her. The first question to ask perhaps, is, what does the child love most? What kinds of activities involve her totally? All these activities can, and must, include language, and they therefore provide the child with rich language data from which she can and will discern underlying organizational principles which relate expression and meaning. Involving a child in a veritable language bath all day every day in the rich and meaningful activities that fill our classrooms is the best possible way that we can enhance the child's growth of language structure.

As we become increasingly aware of the complexity and beauty of the structure of any language, we can only stand amazed that young children acquire it so effectively and with such apparent effortlessness. But a word of caution is in order. A child is often able to use language very facilely, and because she controls syntactic structure so well, even at the primary level, we sometimes fail to realize that the terms she uses with such apparent facility may identify concepts which are only partially developed.

How often at the primary and even at the intermediate levels we hear teacher-child interactions like the following:

T: Who remembers what we call these things that hang down from the ceiling? Do you remember . . . (pause) . . . what we just saw . . . (pause) . . . on the slides? . . . (pause) . . . Okay, I'm going to say it, and say it after me. Stalactites. They have to hang on tight. Stalactites. Everybody.

Children: Stalactites.

T: Okay, now we can see something else in this picture. It starts in the bottom. Who remembers the name for these? They go up from the floor . . .

Cs: Stalagmites.

T: Good. Stalagmites. Let's all say it.

Cs: Stalagmites.

T: Then, we see something that goes from the bottom of the cave all the way to the top, or from the top all the way to the bottom. Who remembers the name for this?

C: I know. I know.

T: What is it:

C: Stalagmites.

T: Well, a stalagmite starts at the bottom . . . what could be coming off the bottom?

C: Stalagmites.

T: Stalagmites. And what could be coming down from the top?

Cs: Stalactites.

T: Good, stalactites. And what could be maybe starting at the bottom and going up to the top and starting at the top and going all the way to the bottom? What could be called that? . . . (pause) . . . do you remember? Columns. Let's say that.

Cs: Columns.

T: Columns.[1]

How often we pull the children to supply the appropriate label, assuming that, if they have the label, they also control the concept which the label identifies. Yet children, being so facile with language structure, can talk of stalactites and stalagmites simply by manipulating the labels for these concepts which are only imperfectly understood. Some interesting current research deals with children's concepts of more and less, and with concepts of true and false. The evidence suggests that though children use and respond to these labels, they may in fact be functioning with different concepts than we assume. We need to be aware of when the child's verbalizations convey different meanings from our own, when they convey limited meanings, and when they convey no meaning at all.

One final word about language structure, teachers, and children. Teachers of intermediate level children often ask, "Isn't it important for a child to be consciously aware of linguistic structure—to know the names of parts of sentences, to be able to identify and label subjects and predicates, nouns and verbs?" We can best begin answering this question by asking another: How much of your language structure are you consciously aware of? I hope you are more aware now than you were before you began to read this section of the complexities of language structure. But even if you are, you will not find yourself using language in a more vivid, scintillating, and precise way as a result of this increased awareness. It is effective *use* of language in communication that is the major goal. As it is with you, so it is with children: Conscious awareness of linguistic structure can be fascinating in its own right, but it does not make you a more effective language *user*. A child might be fascinated with the study of language structure just as she might be fascinated by a study of microscopic creatures that live in a local pond. But *if* we choose to bring a child's awareness of her linguistic structure to a conscious level, we must be absolutely clear about what it is that we are doing. We are *not* teaching her

[1] I am indebted to Mimi Miran for this interaction.

language structure; this she already controls. What we are doing is no more and no less than equipping her with ways of talking about that structure. Further, we must never allow such activity to replace the endless rich communicative experiences which we provide for children. The conscious awareness of linguistic structure, being able to talk about the parts of language and their possible arrangements and combinations, must never substitute for the ability to use the language effectively in a range of communicative situations. As we will see in subsequent chapters, as teachers we stand to make our greatest contribution to children's language growth in the area of fostering effective and diverse use of language for communication, and not in the area of furthering their unconscious knowledge of language structure. Children take care of that aspect through their own interaction with the environment. We will turn our attention to the child's sequence and processes in the acquisition of language structure in Section Two.

SUGGESTED EXERCISES AND PROJECTS

Explorations in Children's Native-Speaker Abilities

Each of items 1 through 5 below deals with one ability that we said the native speaker of a language has. It is interesting to see to what extent and in what ways children's judgments of grammaticality and levels of grammaticality, recognition of sentence relatedness and ambiguity, and understanding and production of creative sentences are similar to and different from these abilities in adults. If done as small-scale studies, involving no more than six children, each of items 1 through 4 works well either as a long-term written project for an individual, or as a short-term combined written project for two or three people:

1. all members together design the instrument to use with children
2. each member runs it on several children
3. all members discuss, combining and relating their individual results
4. each member has the main responsibility for writing up part of the draft of the paper
5. all members react to and suggest revisions for entire paper
6. individuals carry out the revisions in final paper.

Some students who have done these projects have included the following sections in their final papers: statement of purpose, brief description of subjects used, brief description of procedure followed, discussion of results (summarizing chart and written discussion), discussion of limitations of study (how you would change/extend the study if you were to do it again) and new questions raised, tape transcript or data sheets used to record children's responses.

Remember that you often discover more about a child's language knowledge from his unexpected responses than from those that you predicted in advance. In giving the following set to children ranging in age from six to twelve,

> Mary broke.
> Mary cried.
> Mary around.
> Mary mooed.

a group of college students had predicted that the older children, like themselves, would rank the sentences in this order for levels of grammaticality:

> Mary cried (human noun + verb denoting human action)
> Mary mooed (human noun + verb denoting an action performed by animate creature, though not usually by humans)
> Mary broke (human noun + verb relating to inanimate object)
> Mary around (human noun + adverb—violation of possible word class combination)

The four sentences were read to one eleven-year-old. She was then asked, "Which sounds the best to you and which sounds the worst?" and they were read to her again. Without hesitation she replied, "Well, that depends on what Mary is. If Mary's a person, 'Mary cried' is best. If Mary's a cow, 'Mary mooed' is best. If Mary's a doll, then 'Mary broke' is best. And I don't like 'Mary around' at all." This was a most unexpected response, but one that told the students a great deal about the child's knowledge of her language (as well as about her ability to articulate that knowledge).

Item 5 works well as a written analysis done by one or two people, of 30 minutes' worth of children's interaction. Working as a pair on this study offers the chance for discussion and brainstorming about the children's language before writing up your study. It also divides up the difficult and time-consuming task of transcribing the tape.

1. Judgments of grammaticality.
   a. Select some children from six to twelve years of age (first through sixth grades), trying for representatives across the entire range. As far as possible get children who are similar in background (socioeconomic status, ethnic group, language dominance), and who differ just in age. Of course it will be most interesting if you can include children you teach now or have taught.

b. Prepare an instrument that includes about forty sentences, half of which you consider grammatical and a corresponding half which you consider ungrammatical. Remember that you should have a grammatical and an ungrammatical instance of each syntactic type of item you choose. Some examples are: regular past tense (grammatical: "The children climbed up the jungle gym"; ungrammatical: "He look at TV last night"); irregular past tense, animate/inanimate ("The lamp who/that fell down, broke"); number agreement ("The boys is/are going to the movies"); combining ("She is cold although/because the fire is hot" or "Before/after we eat dinner we go to bed"); reflexive ("I did it all by myself/himself"); regular plural, irregular plural, possessive, male/-female ("John likes to tie her/his own shoes"); complex comparatives ("That comb is big enough/small enough to fit in my pocket," or "That comb is too big/too small to fit in my pocket"); adjective order ("She lives in a big white house," "He has a brown new little puppy").

c. Randomize the order of your items, and then type them up in a final version so that each child in your study will respond to the same sentences in the same order.

d. Have each selected child respond to each sentence after you read it. (Of course you will have only one child present at a time.) You might give instructions something like "I'm going to read you a bunch of sentences, one at a time, and I want you to tell me, for each one, whether it sounds OK or not OK to you. I'll read any sentence for you as many times as you want me to." For every sentence which the child says is "Not OK," ask the further question, "What's not OK about it?" or "What sounds funny about it?" or "How would you change it to make it sound OK?" (This is important, as the child may be basing his or her judgment of OK-ness on something completely different than grammaticalness—for example, your unusual pronunciation of a particular word, or whether he or she likes the content of the sentence.)

e. Record each child's response to every item as you go along, either by hand or on tape.

f. Analyze your results. One way to do this is to make a summarizing chart and then provide a discussion. Some interesting questions to keep in mind are: Is there any evidence of a trend, from younger to older children, toward greater similarity to your own adult judgments? For which items is there greater/lesser agreement among the children? Between the children's judgments and your own? How can you account (*tentatively, speculatively*) for this similarity and difference of agreement?

g. It is crucial to remember that (1) your study is not an evaluative one in any way, so it makes no sense to say "So-and-so got X right and Y wrong." You are simply exploring the judgments of a few children, and how they are similar to and different from each other's and yours. (2) Since it is an exploratory and very small study, you must not make sweeping generalizations about, for example, "the seven-year-old's grammaticality judgments." Your statements will be very cautious and limited to your small sample ("Within this particular group of six children, there was some evidence of a trend . . . ").

2. Judgments of grammaticality levels.
   a. As in 1a above.
   b. Prepare an instrument that includes about twelve sets of three sentences which, for you, clearly range in grammaticality level. Generally we tend to regard as least grammatical those sentences which include extreme violations of expected word class (as in "John played symmetrical" where we expect a noun, rather than an adjective, to follow "played").
   c. As in 1c above.
   d. Have each selected child respond to each set of three sentences after you read the set. (Of course you will have only one child present at a time.) You might give instructions something like "I'm going to read you some groups of sentences, three to a group. For each group I want you to tell me which one sounds the best to you, and which one sounds the worst to you. I'll read a group as many times as you want me to so you won't have to worry about whether or not you can remember the sentences. You can hear them over and over, and you'll just tell me how they go in order from best to worst for how they sound to you." (Note: Some children, particularly the younger ones, may find your least grammatical sentence so "far out" that they do not respond to it at all and are, in fact, just judging between the two which they can process in some way. If this seems to be happening with a child you might ask specifically about the sentence which for you is least grammatical, for example "Tell me how you like this sentence just all by itself" (read it again). "Does that sound pretty good or not so good?")
   e. As in 1e above.
   f. As in 1f above.
   g. As in 1g above.

3. Recognition of sentence relatedness.
   a. As in 1a above, except use age range of seven to twelve. (My experience has been that many children younger than seven have difficulty dealing with nonsense sentences. Their energies often go into trying to make the sentence sensible.)
   b. Prepare an instrument that has three parts: (1) about five or six nonsense sentences with questions for the child to answer (for example, "The prat ruggled glingily down the slazoo. What ruggled? Where did the prat ruggle? How did the prat ruggle? What did the prat do?"); (2) about three pairs of sentences that do mean the same thing, and about three pairs of sentences that do not ("That's a big bunch of boys/That's a bunch of big boys," or "The dog chased the cat/The cat was chased by the dog."); (3) about five single sentences for the child to "say a different way" (production task).

    c. Randomize the order of your items within each of the three sections, and then type them up in a final version so that each child in your study will respond to the same items in the same order.

    d. Have each child respond to each item after you present it. (Only one child is present at a time, of course.) You might give instructions something like the following: (1) "I'm going to read you a pretty crazy sentence and then ask you some questions about it. You'll probably want me to read it for you several times, because it may be a little hard to remember at first. Just ask me; I'll read you any sentence as many times as you want me to." (It is *very important* that this not become a memory task, so you must say the sentence over as many times as you feel the child needs—perhaps after every question you ask. If the child seems shy about asking for several repetitions, just go ahead and provide them!). (2) "Now I'm going to read you some pairs of sentences, and I want you to tell me if they mean the same thing or different things to you. Of course I'll read them as many times as you want me to." If a child says the two mean different things, you might ask "How are they different?" (3) "Now here's a sentence." (Read it.) "Can you say that one a different way, but so it still means the same thing?"

    e. As in 1e above.

    f. As in 1f above. Some particularly relevant questions might be: When a child changes the model sentence for the production task, is the meaning changed? How? Is the meaning preserved but the form changed? How? Are both changed? How? For what kinds of sentences? Are there noticeable age differences relating to the kinds of changes the children make?

    g. As in 1g above.

4. Recognition of ambiguity.

    a. As in 1a above.

    b. Prepare an instrument that includes ten semantic ambiguities (in which the multiple interpretation depends on the meaning of a particular word or expression, as in "That movie was far out"). Also prepare ten syntactic ambiguities (in which the multiple interpretation depends on the various possible relationships among the parts of the sentence—"That's a beautiful woman's handbag"). Children's joke books and riddle books offer good sources for ambiguities.

    c. As in 1c above.

    d. Have each child—with only one present at a time—respond to each item after you read it. You might give instructions like, "I'm going to read you some things, and I want you to tell me what each one means." (read an item.) "What do you think that means?" (Response.) "Can it mean anything else? Would you like me to read it again so you can think about it some more?"

    e. As in 1e above.

    f. Analyze your results. One way to do this is to make a summarizing chart and then provide a discussion. Some interesting questions to keep in mind are: Is there any evidence of a trend, from the younger to the older children, toward the provision of more interpretations for the items? Are there any differences between the older and the younger children as to the actual interpretations they give, and/or which interpretation they seem to prefer? What interpretations did the children provide that you did not expect? For which items were (almost) none and (almost) all of the children able to provide more than one meaning? How is this to be accounted for?

g. As in 1g above.

5. Creation of novel sentences.

We have said that creativity is basic to language; communication proceeds mainly through the creation and use of specific sentences which are novel to both the speaker and the hearer. We recognize that creativity is basic to adult communication. But is it also basic to communication among children? Do they, too, interact mainly through the creation and use of novel sentences? To explore this question, tape record about thirty minutes' worth of children's interaction in as natural a situation as possible, *with no adult* in the immediate environment. (Needless to say, this will be most interesting if you study the children you actually teach.) You may have to tape the children several times to get them accustomed to the tape recorder, and also to get a total of thirty minutes' worth of audible conversation. (It does not all have to come from a single taping session.)[2]

As you will discover, taping is not easy. Two important things to remember are (1) to tape a situation or activity that children do in a localized area, so that your microphone will pick up most of their conversation (for example, housekeeping corner or table where three or four children usually sit to work; avoid the playground), and (2) to keep your taping equipment as unobtrusive as possible.

When you have thirty minutes' worth of audible taped interaction, transcribe it as exactly as you can, with all the "uhs," all the giggles, all the pauses, and all the inevitable inaudible spots where you simply indicate that you cannot hear what was said. Then study your transcript, trying to answer questions like the following in your written paper: Do children communicate mainly through the use of novel sentences, or through memorized ready-made

---

[2]One university student had considerable success with this project by suspending the tape recorder microphone from a light fixture above the center of a small, play dough activity table in the nursery school where she was working. Because the children were localized in the small area around this table, the microphone picked up most of their conversation. Also, the situation proved to be a very natural one, as the children became quite involved in working with play dough, conversing informally as they worked. The student wisely set up this taping arrangement and left it there for several weeks—sometimes with the tape recorder on, sometimes with it off—before she started taping the conversations she was going to study. By that time, the suspended microphone had become just another piece of classroom furniture to the children, and they were quite unaware of it.

ones? What are some examples of each type from your data? What proportion of the children's utterances is novel sentences? What proportion is memorized imitations? In what sense are the "novel" sentences new creations; that is, do the children create new vocabulary or new syntactic structures? What kinds? Or do they create within a predictable set of already established syntactic and semantic principles? What is the evidence here? For what purposes do the children use nonnovel (ready-made) language?

An interesting extension of this study is to compare the language creativity of your children's interaction with that of an adult interaction (taped and transcribed the same way that you did your children's conversation).

6. An exercise in differentiating meanings.

Pick a synonym cluster from Roget's *Thesaurus,* and try to differentiate the meanings of the particular words within your selected cluster. Can you identify the semantic feature or features which distinguish each entry from the others? What semantic features do all the words in the synonym cluster share (what makes them synonyms)? (This works particularly well as a small group discussion exercise.)

One interesting variation on this exercise is to try it with your intermediate level students. Can they tell the "special meaning" of each item?

A second variation to use with children is to ask your primary or intermediate level children to act out selected items from a synonym cluster, for example, various "walk" words.

If you and several of your fellow students or colleagues try one of these variations with children, you may want to get together afterwards to compare notes on your experience. What kind of linguistic knowledge did the children's behavior imply?

7. A discussion exercise on interestingly, intentionally deviant language.

Each member of a group (about five or so) brings several favorite examples of language used in interestingly not-quite-grammatical ways. Good places to look for such items include advertising, adult or children's literature, adult or children's conversation, and adult or children's writing. Together consider what the creator of that language item has done that makes it interesting in a special and unexpected way. What language rule(s) has he or she broken or bent? Why?

It is particularly interesting here to use children's favorite items from children's literature (what understanding must they have of language structure if they appreciate the author's deliberately deviant use of language?), or from their own oral or written language. However, note that the exercise deals with the intentional use of deviant language to provide special effects. Do not include items spoken by young children, which are simply the result of an early stage of language acquisition—deviant utterances which are not deliberately so.

8. *"Your own thing."* Design your own learning experience relating to the ideas in this section, discuss it with your instructor or an acquaintance knowledgeable in this area, and execute it.

SUGGESTED FURTHER READINGS

Two sources dealing with the structure of language, which are solid in their content, readable in their presentation, and appropriate for readers who are not professional linguists, are:

FROMKIN, V., and R. RODMAN, *An Introduction to Language.* New York: Holt, Rinehart and Winston, Inc., 1974. Especially chapters 3, 4, 5, 6.

LANGACKER, R., *Language and Its Structure.* New York: Harcourt Brace Jovanovich, Inc., 1973.

Section Two

LANGUAGE ACQUISITION

Chapter 5

Perspectives on Language Acquisition

INTRODUCTION

For centuries parents, scholars, and teachers have been fascinated and amazed by the phenomenon of language acquisition in children. How are we to account for the fact that *virtually every child, without special training, exposed to surface level language data in interaction, builds for himself—in a short period of time and at a prelogical stage in his cognitive development—a deep-level, abstract, and highly complex system of linguistic structure.* And that is only the beginning. In addition to acquiring the structure of the language of his community, the child acquires the complex underlying rule system governing its use: how and when to say what to whom. Let's think a minute about our italicized sentence above.

Virtually every child . . .

Except for those physical and cognitive skills which are clearly biological in their base, it is very difficult to think of abilities that all humans develop.

It is "given" in our biological inheritance as members of the species "human," that (almost) all of us eventually develop the ability to walk on two legs, to grasp objects with thumb and fingers juxtaposed, to make associations between events. But only some of us will learn to play an instrument, to multiply, to turn cartwheels, to whistle, to write. You probably know some young people or adults who cannot drive, swim, or play chess, but how many do you know who cannot understand and use language? Even when we look at the disabled members of the population (those with intellectual, physical, or emotional handicaps), we still find that most of them understand and use some form of language for communication. It appears that acquiring a language is a basic part of our human-ness: More and less intelligent children acquire language, more and less economically fortunate children acquire language, more and less physically able children acquire language, more and less emotionally healthy children acquire language. Whether a child grows up in a "traditional" society or in a "technological" one; whether in a large extended family or in a small nuclear one; whether on a Pacific island, in an urban ghetto or in a tribal farm compound; whether in a villa, a straw hut, an apartment, or a tent; whether with or without formal schooling; whether in a wet, dry, hot, or cold climate —the child will acquire the language of his community. Humans vary in which languages and dialects they acquire, in how rapidly they acquire them, in how many languages and dialects they acquire, in how talkative they are, in what they use language for, and in how effectively they express themselves verbally. But virtually all of them acquire at least one linguistic system for relating meanings and overt expressive symbols (usually verbal sounds).

Further, there is striking similarity in how all children learn their language. Naturally the specifics of the learning differ depending on characteristics of the language being learned, as well as on some other environmental factors. But it is possible to sketch a predictable general sequence of stages that children follow in acquiring language, as well as to describe certain cognitive processes that children seem to use as they try to figure out how the verbal sounds they hear relate to the meanings they understand. Researchers are currently able to speak with greater confidence about the "how" of sequence than about the "how" of process in language acquisition, and it is easy enough to see why. Describing a developmental sequence of stages a child passes through is more closely tied to the child's observable performance than is describing his mental processes in language learning. The more we move toward process description, the more we must infer from the child's behavior —speculate and conjecture about what might be going on in his head. But even though our statements about process are very cautious and couched in phrases like "the child *appears* to be operating according to a principle like X" or "the child behaves *as if* he is using a rule such as A," still the similarities across children are impressive.

The idea of being able to sketch a general developmental sequence of stages for some area of children's growth is probably not new to you. Piaget has been a leader in suggesting a sequence of stages children move through in their cognitive growth. We are all aware of a sequence of stages in children's physical development as well—we recognize that children hold their heads up before they sit up unaided, and that they stand alone before they walk alone. The suggested physical and cognitive development sequences are the result of careful observations of many children in a variety of both structured and naturalistic settings. And so it is in language acquisition. Though formal study of children's language as a separate discipline is more recent than formal study of children's physical and cognitive development, still the basis of the suggested developmental sequence is the same: It is a set of generalizations based on observations of what many children of various ages and backgrounds *do* and *say* as they learn language.

On reflection, the possibility of sketching a general sequence of stages of language acquisition for "all" children should be no more surprising than the possibility of sketching general developmental sequences for physical or cognitive growth for "all" children. Language acquisition involves a language and an acquirer. As was discussed earlier, human languages, however diverse they are in their surface details, are all remarkably similar in their basic elements and organizational schemes. As there are deep-level similarities across diverse human languages, so there are deep-level similarities across the diverse humans who acquire them. Similar physical and cognitive structures are part of the makeup of all of us, whatever kind of environment we happen to be born into and raised in. Clearly language acquisition is deeply rooted in the physical and cognitive structures and possibilities all humans share. Thus it should not be too surprising that we note a similar general developmental sequence and similar general learning processes at work across virtually all children acquiring language.

. . . without special training . . .

In many areas of children's learning, a goal is set and activities are provided to assure its attainment. We typically (1) divide the learning into "chunks" (such as subskills and basic concepts); (2) sequence the subskills or concepts in a simple-to-complex set of steps; (3) present them to the children and provide practice activities so that they will attain mastery of the concepts, skills, or processes; (4) test periodically to check for mastery and to guide subsequent learning activity. If we wanted a child to be able to add and subtract numbers up to six and to understand addition and subtraction as inverse processes, some of the sublearnings included might be the notion of each number up to six, the notion of set, the notion of set combination, the notion of subsets. We would sequence the sublearnings in some reasonable order, and would give the child many opportunities to work with objects in different amounts and to combine, uncombine, and recombine them. We would give him tasks to perform that would inform us of his progress toward mastery of the learnings, and we would use this feedback to guide our subsequent instruction.[1]

It is possible, though strange, to conceive of ways we could provide this kind of direct instruction for young children learning language. It would be possible to divide the language to be learned into basic parts—"parts of speech," types of sentences, types of sounds, semantic clusters, labels from categories of things in the child's environment. We could sequence these in some logical simple-to-complex series and provide opportunities for the children to practice each. We could periodically test for mastery as we went along. It would be possible in theory (but probably not in practice) to do this. But we *do not* do this, and it would probably be disastrous if we did! John Holt speculates about the absurdity and the disastrous outcome of such a procedure.

Bill Hull once said to me, "If we taught children to speak, they'd never learn." I thought at first he was joking. By now I realize that it was a very important truth. Suppose we decided that we had to "teach" children to speak. How would we go about it? First, some committee of experts would analyze speech and break it down into a number of separate "speech skills." We would probably say that, since speech is made up of sounds, a child must be taught to make all the sounds of his language before he can be taught to speak the language itself. Doubtless we would list these sounds, easiest and commonest ones first, harder and rarer ones next. Then we would begin to teach infants these sounds, working our way down the list. Perhaps, in order not to "confuse" the child . . . we would not let the child hear much ordinary speech, but would only expose him to the sounds we were trying to teach.

Along with our sound list, we would have a syllable list and a word list.

When the child had learned to make all the sounds on the sound list, we would begin to teach him to combine the sounds into syllables. When he could say all the syllables on the syllable list, we would begin to teach him the words on our word list. At the same time, we would teach him the rules of grammar, by means of which he could combine these newly-learned words into sentences. Everything would be planned with nothing left to chance; there would be plenty of drill, review, and tests, to make sure that he had not forgotten anything.

Suppose we tried to do this; what would happen? What would happen, quite simply, is that most children, before they got very far, would become baffled, discouraged, humiliated, and fearful, and would quit trying to do what we asked them. (Holt 1967, p. 56)

We know that the most important people in the young child's language environment, his family members and care givers, do not provide him with a rigorous language learning "curriculum." Rather, they engage with him and

---

[1]This is not to deny, of course, that much of the learning that occurs in our culture and in other cultures does not follow this pattern. People often learn by observation, modeling, trial and error, etc.

with each other (in his presence) in a natural kind of communication interaction which often involves linguistic structure far more complex than the child controls. The child is typically immersed in a kind of verbal bath day after day, interacted with through diverse language used in real and meaningful contexts. Much of the language of his environment is not directed to him. But much of it is—people explain to him, scold him, describe things to him, tell him anecdotes, wonder and speculate aloud with and for him, play with him, warn him, coax him, threaten him, answer him. Always there is language, verbal strings living in contexts which provide clues to the meanings they convey.

... exposed to surface level language data in interaction builds a deep-level system of linguistic structure.

An infant is exposed to a wide range of sounds—birds singing, objects falling, airplanes roaring, water running, people sneezing, people whistling, people talking. One wonders how the infant sorts out the sounds that convey language meanings from the sounds that do not! But consider the diversity within just the verbal strings. The child is exposed to a language "sample" including language addressed to him and language addressed to others, sentences which constitute well-formed (grammatical) strings and sentences which do not, sentences which involve linguistic structure he has mastered and sentences which are beyond his developing system, strings spoken by a wide range of individuals in a wide range of contexts. But one thing is common to them all: Each verbal string is an expression of some meaning. How does the child, *every child,* sort out which strings are well formed (grammatical) and which are not? How does he figure out how the noise strings are broken into meaning hunks? How does he figure out the principles according to which the strings of elements are organized? Above all, how does he figure out how those verbal strings relate to particular meanings?

The child's language environment includes a set of specific sentences, but it is not this set of specific sentences that he acquires. Rather, he deduces from these particular sentences an underlying set of organizational principles and sound-meaning relationships. He seems to understand that specific sentences are particular examples of basic principles, and it is those principles he works on. Children, even as young as two, do not talk to us by simply using the specific sentences that they have heard, but rather by constructing sentences according to their own early version of organizational principles *underlying* the specific sentences they have heard. The child's early linguistic system is different from the adult's and thus results in sentences like: Why you play with that? I not like it. He gived it to me.

The child will continue to revise his system over time and his resulting sentences will become more adult-like. But what is noteworthy about these early sentences is that they are not simple repetitions of the specific sentences he has heard, but are rule-governed constructions of his own created according to the underlying principles he has deduced. Every child is exposed to surface level language data in interaction, but builds a deep level system of linguistic structure. The system is one he . . .

builds for himself . . .

Many adults believe that children learn language because adults teach it to them. I vividly recall an informal conversation I had several years ago with an acquaintance who is a sociology professor and the father of three children. It went something like this:

> *Me:* It's interesting, isn't it, that we don't really "teach" a child his language. He learns it for himself.
>
> *Dr. X.:* (annoyed) What do you mean he learns it for himself? I *taught* my children their language, and that's how they learned it.
>
> *Me:* Oh? And how did you do that?
>
> *Dr. X.:* What do you mean "how did I do it?" I pointed to a book and said, "Book. Book. Book. Say it. Book." And the child said it. Then I pointed to a table and said, "Table. Say it. Table. Table." And he said it. That's how my kids learned English.
>
> *Me:* Oh.

This parent far underestimates the complex system that a language is. Like many adults, he is mistaking a limited set of verbal labels for *language,* the endless creativity of sentences according to a finite set of structural principles. He also far underestimates his children's abilities for language learning. But though there is a sense in which he overestimates his contribution to his children's language acquisition, there is also an important sense in which he *under*estimates his contribution. He has doubtless been far more important to his children's learning of language than he has ever dreamed, though not at all in the way that he supposes. He has been an important source of rich and varied language input for his children to "work on"; he has interacted with them verbally and nonverbally in various contexts and situations; he has provided opportunities for them to explore and "mess about" with their world and thus build the meanings basic to language; he has responded to and encouraged their communicative attempts. He may, as he claims, have taught his children some labels. Most parents do. But how minor that contribution is in comparison to his role as a rich language provider and constant interactant in communication with his children.

The "little linguist" analogy is one which has gained popularity over the past few years. It is helpful precisely because it focuses on the child as the active party in learning a language. According to this analogy, the young child is like a field linguist trying to figure out a language which is new to him. He hears unfamiliar verbal strings in particular contexts. The child, like the linguist, attends to the unfamiliar verbal expressions and the contexts in which they occur, and builds "hypotheses" (hunches?) about the sound-meaning relationships present. He "tests" his hypotheses or hunches by further observation, or by producing new sentences, trying them out, and seeing "how they fly." He is constantly getting feedback relating to his hypotheses, and also further exposure and interaction, both of which lead him to revise his hypotheses. This "little linguist" analogy does not mean that the child is aware of what he is doing (as the linguist is), but rather it offers an interactive model of the child and his environment which eventually results in the development of a complex abstract system of linguistic structure which moves steadily toward a closer match with the adult's. It is the child himself who processes the sounds of speech in his community, so as to derive underlying structure. We expose the child to language and interact with him through language, but he acquires linguistic structure through his own mental activity.

... in a short period of time ...

We are not surprised to find that entering kindergarteners are able to ask us a variety of questions, to tell us about things they've done and seen and things they like and don't like, to request things they want, and to direct others to do things. In short, though there is a range in rates of development across children, five-year-olds typically can use complex and varied language structures to serve a variety of purposes in their lives. Their language growth is still in process, but they generally have substantial control of language structure and use. Attaining this high level of control in such a short time is remarkable, given the complex system that a language is, and the fact that the child begins life as an infant immersed in a sea of undifferentiated sensations. Is there any other area of our lives where we accomplish something so complex so quickly? The kindergartener's language abilities don't surprise us; maybe they should.

... at a prelogical stage in his cognitive development ...

A great deal of a child's acquisition of linguistic structure occurs during the first five years of life. This is the period when he is most active in discerning a set of underlying structural principles from the speech that surrounds him. It is puzzling that one so young is able to engage successfully in activity which seems to demand so much high-level, abstract thinking. As we watch young children learn, we are struck by their heavy reliance on the movement of their own bodies in space and their physical manipulation of concrete objects. Piaget has stressed that, during the first two years of life, the child's own physical activity is his major way of knowing about the world. The infant understands the way the world is in terms of the way he is able physically to act upon it

—to squeeze it, shake it, bite it, etc. Yet the processing of language sounds so as to derive underlying structure would seem to require the mental manipulation of abstract symbols, rather than the physical manipulation of concrete objects.

Piaget has pointed out the four-year-old's inability to "conserve," that is, to recognize that objects and substances remain the same in amount, regardless of changes in their formal appearance. Shown two rows of six objects arranged in a one-to-one array

```
X   X   X   X   X   X
O   O   O   O   O   O
```

the four-year-old will tell us both rows have the same amount. But when the adult extends one row

```
X   X   X   X   X   X
O   O   O   O   O   O
```

the child will not recognize that both rows still contain the same number of objects; he will say the longer row has more. Confronted with two identical glasses, both containing the same amount of liquid, the child will tell us they both have the same amount. But when he sees the adult pour the liquid from one of the glasses into a tall thin glass, he will tell us that the tall glass contains more liquid than the first, because the liquid reaches a higher level in the glass. Given two identical balls of clay, the child will say they have the same amount. But when one is then stretched into a hot dog shape, the child will tell us that it has more than the first ball. In all these examples, the child is unable to take two dimensions into account and relate them logically. He focuses or "centers" on the dimension of extension—length or height, and ignores the dimension of density. Yet at the very age when he is unable to conserve, the child is integrating and synthesizing the abstract parts of a very complex linguistic system. It seems incongruous that his cognitive functioning is characterized by such physical activity, concreteness, and singleness of focus in most areas, yet his language acquisition activity seems to involve high-level (though unconscious) abstracting, relating, synthesizing, and integrating. How can the young child function in language acquisition at this complex cognitive level, when he is at such an early stage in his overall cognitive growth?

Let's end this introduction where we began it—with our initial italicized sentence. That sentence probably seemed innocuous enough at first, but you may now be aware that it raises fascinating and powerful questions about the incredible phenomenon of language acquisition:

Virtually every child, without special training, exposed to surface level language data in interaction, builds for himself—in a short period of time and at a prelogical stage in his cognitive development—a deep-level, abstract, and highly complex system of linguistic structure.

PERSPECTIVES ON LANGUAGE ACQUISITION

The Behaviorist View

Through the first half of this century, there was a prevalent view that language learning, like other kinds of learning, occurs as the result of the environment shaping an individual born with a given IQ (an innate general learning potential). This "behaviorist" position held that an individual is reinforced (positively or negatively) for responses to various stimuli. By administering positive reinforcement (praising, smiling) when a desired behavior occurs and administering negative reinforcement (scolding, correcting) when an undesired behavior occurs, one presumably strengthens the desired behavior and makes it more likely that that behavior will recur. Let's take a classic hypothetical example involving infants and language. Suppose a baby is lying on his back, happily babbling in his crib. Mother appears and begins to play with him. In the course of his babblings, the baby hits on the syllables "ma-ma" (an occurrence which, given the fairly predictable sequence of phonological development in infants, is quite likely). He gets a very positive response from his mother, as any mother knows only too well. He is hugged, cuddled and nuzzled, perhaps, all to the accompaniment of the mother's delighted squeals and chatterings. Surely any baby worth his salt will in time come to produce the sounds ma-ma in the presence of his mother, and cause a repeat of the pleasurable "aftermath." This view of language learning maintains that, as a child grows older, reinforcement becomes progressively more contingent on how nearly the child's language matches the adult's. That is, whereas ma-ma is positively reinforced as an appropriate response in an infant, it is likely that a mother will positively reinforce only utterances which are considerably more complex and adult-like when the child is three or four. Thus as positive reinforcement is employed only for progressively more adult-like utterances, the child moves steadily toward a more complex adult language system.

This description of the behaviorist view of language acquisition is somewhat simplistic and general. It does not do justice to the range of specific positions held within this school. Some behaviorists emphasize one aspect, some another, and certainly they elaborate the details of this general position differently, one from another. However, there is an area of common ground that justifies our speaking, at a general level, of "the behaviorist position." This common ground includes the belief that (1) children are born with a general learning potential which is part of their genetic inheritance (but without any specific learning abilities, such as a special innate capacity for acquiring language); (2) learning (including the learning of language) occurs entirely through the action of the environment shaping the individual's behavior; (3) behavior (including language) is shaped through the reinforcement of particular responses emitted in the presence of particular stimuli; (4) in the shaping of very complex behavior such as language, there is a progressive selection or narrowing of responses which are positively reinforced; although more simple and general responses receive positive reinforcement initially, such reinforcement is later given for responses which are more complex and which more nearly match the ultimate behavioral goal.[2]

At first glance this view is very persuasive. It squares with some of our own informal observations and intuitions about what children are and how they grow. Those of us who work with children doubtless feel that children do differ in their general learning abilities; that regardless of their environments, some are simply born with greater learning potential than others. Further, this view tells us that the environment plays a crucial part in one's learning, and that, too, is something we all feel is true. And no one would deny that important people in the child's world—parents, teachers, friends—do positively reinforce some behaviors (with smiles, hugs, praise, increased allowance, special privileges), and negatively reinforce other behaviors, and that they reward and punish different behaviors in seven-year-olds and in two-year-olds. And, finally, children do learn language, and this view tells us that they will.

Is the Behaviorist View Adequate?

Over the past several decades, scholars have gained richer insights into the complexity and creativity of human language, the language acquirer, and the processes of language acquisition. These insights have raised crucial questions that the behaviorist view has difficulty answering.

First, it is hard for the behaviorist view to account for the uniformity of language acquisition throughout the human species—virtually all children acquire a language, and they do so in much the same way. (This is what people mean when they say that language acquisition is "species uniform.") If language acquisition were simply the result of an innate general learning capacity plus a shaping environment, we would expect differences in language acquisition to reflect the wide range of IQ differences and environmental differences of young children. In fact, we would expect some children not to acquire language at all. Yet we see that even many mentally retarded children acquire

---

[2]For additional reading relating to this view see Skinner (1957), N. Chomsky (1959), and Staats (1971).

language, though they do not learn some other things. And though there are many specific differences from child to child in the learning of language, those differences are not nearly so vast as a behaviorist theory would predict. If language acquisition were simply a matter of environment shaping the child's language, the resulting shapes and the sequence and processes leading to those resulting shapes would be far more diverse than they in fact are.

Second, there is the other side of this "species uniform" coin, the "species specific" argument. The behaviorist position would predict that intelligent beings other than humans could acquire language too. If language acquisition is a function of innate IQ plus environmental shaping, we should be able to take intelligent chimps, put them in a language shaping environment and end up with chimps that communicate through human-like languages.

Researchers opposed to the behaviorist position have insisted over the years that language acquisition is restricted to the human species, that it is "species specific." They have argued that, though animals do commmunicate, none of them does so by means of a system involving a finite set of principles which accounts for a literally infinite set of possible sentences. Animal communication does not include the possibility of endless creative construction, the creativity which is at the very heart of human language and sets it apart from all other communication systems. So the argument ran . . . until recently.

Recent research with chimps, however, has caused some modification of this original strong objection to the behaviorist position. Raised in various special settings designed for language learning (some laboratory settings and some more natural settings), some chimps have done astonishing things. The major question of the chimp research has been, "Can chimps learn to arrange and rearrange a finite set of symbols according to a limited set of organizational principles, to communicate *creatively*—that is, to express messages in specific ways that they have not been previously exposed to?" Chimp researchers answer "Yes"; some opponents of the behaviorist position answer "No." The chimps involved in these experiments use language symbols other than verbal ones, for the obvious reason that physical differences between chimps and humans prevent chimps from using their vocal apparatus in human ways. But human speech is not necessary for human language, as the sign language of the deaf clearly indicates. Some chimps have been taught to use the hand signals of the deaf (American Sign Language), others manipulate small plastic tokens on a magnetic board, and still others type geometric designs to convey messages. But in each case the goal has been to see whether chimps can manipulate these symbols so as to create novel expressions, just as humans do.

The results of the chimp research to date have been impressive. Chimps have been able to respond appropriately to complex commands such as "Sarah" (chimp's name) "insert apricot red dish, grape (and) banana green dish" (Fleming 1974, p. 35), and to respond differently to "Roger tickle Lucy" (chimp's name) and "Lucy tickle Roger" (p. 46), demonstrating a grasp of

underlying organizational relations. Some chimps have demonstrated remarkable inventiveness. One, seeing a duck for the first time, signed "water bird"
(p. 38); another, who had used the sign "food" for radish, finally tasted a radish
and thereafter signed it either "cry hurt food," or "hurt food," or "cry food"
(pp. 44, 46). Like human children learning language, chimps have generalized
labels learned in particular contexts to new contexts. For example, after learning "more" in the context of tickling, one chimp started using the "more" sign
when she wanted more of a variety of actions and objects (p. 32). Many of these
chimps deliberately string "words" (signs or manipulable tokens) together into
combinations they have not been taught so as to express new meanings. Like
the stringing together of words we see in young children, the chimps' combinations are clearly patterned and nonrandom, and express meanings and relations quite like those early expressed by young children.

In short, child language researchers who find the behaviorist position
untenable as an explanation of language acquisition have had to modify their
species specific argument in light of these amazing chimp accomplishments.
These originally skeptical researchers are somewhat less adamant now about
the creation of novel messages through a finite set of symbols and rules being
a possibility that exists only for humans. Nevertheless, they point out that after
years of concentrated efforts to teach chimps a human-like language, the
chimps have progressed only to the level characteristic of most two- or three-
year-old children. But they admit we do not yet know how far chimps can go.

In summary then, in pointing out limitations in the behaviorist position
on language acquisition, the species uniform argument holds more strongly
than the species specific one, which holds only with some modification of the
initial strong position.

Third, the behaviorists' heavy reliance on stimulus-response-reinforcement learning poses serious problems. Children eventually come to use full
adult forms of language, forms produced in accordance with an underlying
system of structural principles like the system of the adult. Yet in the natural
communicative interaction that forms the basis for the child's language learning, he is very rarely verbally reinforced positively or negatively for the forms
he uses. The work of Brown and his colleagues demonstrates that parents
verbally reinforce their children according to the truth value of what they say,
rather than for the forms they use. One study took language samples of three
children who were observed extensively in their homes, and

> . . . contrast(ed) the syntactic correctness of the population of utterances fol-
> lowed by a sign of approval—*That's right, Very good,* or just *Yes*—with the
> population of utterances followed by a sign of disapproval—*That's wrong* or *No.*
> The results are simply stated: there is not a shred of evidence that approval and
> disapproval are contingent on syntactic correctness. (Brown, Cazden, and Bel-
> lugi-Klima 1971, p. 409)

The parents of the three children did give verbal signs of approval and disapproval for what the children said, but the approval and disapproval were contingent on the truth value of the child's utterance, not on the form. Two examples of utterances given verbal approval by the mother are "He a girl" (spoken in reference to the mother) and "Her curl my hair" (spoken while the mother was curling the child's hair). Two examples of utterances given verbal disapproval are "There's the animal farmhouse" (spoken of a lighthouse) and "Walt Disney comes on, on Tuesday" (the program came on on a different day). Brown, Cazden, and Bellugi-Klima conclude:

> It seems, then, to be truth value rather than syntactic well-formedness that chiefly governs explicit verbal reinforcement by parents—which renders mildly paradoxical the fact that the usual product of such a training schedule is an adult whose speech is highly grammatical but not notably truthful. (1971, p. 410)

The behaviorist position claims that correct (adult-like) structures come to prevail and immature forms drop out due to the reinforcement they receive. But this claim does not square with systematic observations of parents actually reinforcing their children's utterances. Children's language forms become steadily more adult-like, despite the fact that they are not specifically reinforced for form.

Occasionally a child is corrected for using a form, however. The following two well-known examples demonstrate the difficulty a child has recognizing what, specifically he is being corrected *for*.

> *Child:* Nobody don't like me.
> *Mother:* No, say "nobody likes me."
> *Child:* Nobody don't like me.
>
> (eight repetitions of this dialogue)
>
> *Mother:* No, now listen carefully; say *"nobody likes me."*
> *Child:* Oh! Nobody don't likes me. (McNeill 1966, p. 69)

> "Want other one spoon, Daddy."—"You mean, you want THE OTHER SPOON."—"Yes, I want other one spoon, please, Daddy."—"Can you say 'the other spoon?' "—"Other . . . one . . . spoon."—"Say . . . 'other.' "—"Other."— "Spoon."—"Spoon."—"Other . . . spoon."—"Other . . . spoon. Now give me other one spoon?" (Braine 1971, pp. 160–61)

According to the behaviorist view, reinforcement is contingent on specific behavior. It is hard to see how negative reinforcement could be playing an important role in the child's learning of form, for when it is given (and remember, it very rarely is), it is very general; it is given in response to a form that has many elements, any one or several of which could be wrong. How could the child make use of this global negative reinforcement to increase the likelihood of his using more mature forms? This kind of reinforcement lacks the specificity that most behaviorists would claim is important.

Also, as a child learns a language, we see many earlier adult forms drop out, only to be replaced by less adult forms, which are in turn eventually replaced by the original adult forms. For example, early in his development a child uses adult irregular verb and noun forms (came, went, ran, men, feet), but then replaces them with overregularizations (comed, goed, runned, mans, foots), and eventually goes back to the appropriate irregular forms (Ervin 1964). Surely the child was not negatively reinforced for his earlier adult-like irregular forms and positively reinforced for the non-adult regular forms. Yet his earlier adult forms are replaced by non-adult ones. A view of language learning which sees developmental changes in form as the result of reinforcement is hard put to explain this very predictable sequence in children learning English.

Fourth, as mentioned previously, the child is exposed to many particular sentences, yet what he learns is not those specific sentences, but the organizational principles underlying them. What young children say is in the main not sentences which are repetitions of those they have heard, but rather sentences they have created according to their own early version of the adult's underlying rules. It is difficult to see in what sense the young child is being—or *could* be—reinforced here. He utters specific sentences that he has created. If positively reinforced, how could he know that that reinforcement is contingent not upon the specific sentences themselves, but on the principles underlying them? If the child is unable, when corrected, to recognize what in his sentence the correction applies to, how can we expect him to take the enormous abstract leap of linking reinforcement to his building of a deep-level system of linguistic structure?

Fifth, how could the child learn a system so complex in such a relatively short period of time if he begins at level zero, with nothing given but a general learning capacity? There are other far less complex learnings that he masters less well despite rigorous stimulus-response-reinforcement training schedules. It seems incredible that given only general intelligence as a starting point, language acquisition could occur in such a short time.

The final problem also concerns the behaviorist notion of general intelligence capacity as the only given at birth: It is the young age at which children engage in language acquisition. How can they work so successfully on such a complex abstract symbol system before they can deal cognitively with many other areas of complex abstract symbolization and logic? If they have only a general, overall intelligence capacity, why do they perform in the area of language acquisition so far beyond their level of functioning in many other areas? Why doesn't general intelligence cover all areas equally? Or, granting individual differences in children due to environmental variations (an assumption compatible with the behaviorist position), why doesn't it happen that in some children language acquisition abilities outstrip cognitive functioning in other areas, while in other children, other abilities advance more rapidly? But this does not seem to happen. In virtually all children, it is language acquisition abilities that pull out in front of other cognitive functioning.

In summary, many child language scholars have found the behaviorist account of language acquisition untenable, as it is unable to account for (1) the species uniformity of language acquisition, (2) the species specificity of language acquisition, (3) the independence of language development from reinforcement for form, (4) children's inferring of deep-level structure from an exposure to surface structure, (5) the relatively short period of time, and (6) the earliness—the prelogical period of children's lives, during which they acquire so much of a complex linguistic system.

The Innatist View (Strong Version)

Partly in response to these apparent inadequacies in the behaviorist view, another view of language acquisition gained ground, variously called the "innatist," "rationalist," or "nativist" position. It differs from the behaviorist position in two major ways: (1) It redefines and gives increased importance to innate factors in language acquisition, and (2) it reinterprets the role of environmental factors in language acquisition.

Pendulums swing in the field of language acquisition no less than in other disciplines. Thus the earliest shapers of and spokesmen for the innatist view (particularly Noam Chomsky and David McNeill) articulated an extremely strong version of this position, perhaps partly as a reaction to the strongly prevalent behaviorist view of the time. Chomsky and McNeill maintained that every child is born with universals of linguistic structure "wired in." That is, the child does not have to learn those features common to the structure of all human languages, for he is born with the skeletal framework of linguistic structure innately specified; the semantic, syntactic, and phonological possibilities of human language are already present. According to this view, the child presumably does not have to learn, for example, that the verbal strings he hears relate to meanings; that those strings affirm, negate, question, command; and what the basic syntactic elements of language are. These features are common to all languages and thus relate in some way to shared physical and mental characteristics of all humans. Being a human, the child already has a start on "knowing" what kind of system a language is in its basic design. He has a start on cracking the particular linguistic code of his speech community because he already "knows" what kind of system that code must be. His job then, is to figure out how the particular language system of his community actualizes linguistic universals. He does not have to learn *that* one can ask information questions in his language, but rather *how* one asks information questions in his language: Does one use question words? What are they? Does one rearrange sentence elements? How? He does not have to learn that one expresses meanings through verbal expression, but rather what the particular set of distinctive sounds are (out of all the possible ones) that his linguistic community uses. Which sound feature bundles are used? How do they combine? How do they modify each other in combination? In short, he knows what kind of system human language can be, and his job is to discover which particular subset of the semantic, syntactic, and phonological possibilities his language community happens to use.

This strong version of the innatist position has received support from biologically based research relating to language development. Lenneberg (1964) drew attention to some important ways in which language acquisition is more akin to genetically determined skills (such as walking on two legs) than to culturally transmitted ones (such as writing). When the child is born, he is unable to walk and unable to write. However, he has an innate biological predisposition for learning to walk on two legs, but no such biological predisposition for writing. Learning to write is mainly a matter of training. Lenneberg pointed out that using language, like walking on two legs, is a behavior which shows (1) limited variation within the species (wide individual variation in the specifics of its execution, but striking similarity in its basic design throughout the species); (2) no beginning point for the behavior within the evolutionary history of the species (we can't find a point in the history of our species when man began to walk on two legs or began to use language as we know it); (3) "evidence for inherited predisposition" (Lenneberg 1964, p. 584) —humans are "biologically constituted" for a certain type of locomotion and for symbolic communication through language; (4) apparent existence of organic correlates (language acquisition, like walking, follows a predictable course of maturational development, more than a course predicted primarily by type or amount of training). In contrast, writing, a culturally transmitted skill, shows wide variation within the species (vastly different systems from culture to culture, some cultures having none at all), a beginning point within the history of the species, "no evidence for inherited predisposition," (inability to write is simply a "deficiency in training which can be quickly corrected by appropriate practice"), and no apparent organic correlates.

Lenneberg pointed out some correlations between stages in language development and stages in physical maturation (for example, motor coordination, structural and biochemical changes in the brain). In studying language recovery in adults and children who had incurred brain injury, Lenneberg found the prognosis to be "directly related to the age at which insult to the brain is incurred" (Lenneberg 1967, p. 142). If the injury to the language area of the brain occurs in the early years, the brain is still "plastic" enough that another area can take over the function of language acquisition. However, this does not seem to be the case after puberty, the time of life at which the brain has stabilized. Lenneberg has posited a "critical period" for language acquisition, ending at puberty, by which time the brain has matured (structurally, biochemically, neurophysiologically), and after which time "automatic acquisition from mere exposure to a given language seems to disappear . . . and foreign languages have to be taught and learned through a conscious and labored effort" (Lenneberg 1967, p. 176).[3]

Thus, Lenneberg's work linking language acquisition to biological maturation supported the earliest and strongest version of the innatist position, which made two major claims about the innate component of language acquisition: (1) that the child's genetic inheritance was greater than had been supposed—the child was not simply a "blank slate" at birth; and (2) that genetic inheritance for mental abilities was not simply a general ability to learn but, rather, that it included a specific predisposition for language acquisition.

Notice, however, that Lenneberg at no time claimed that language acquisition was an entirely inherited phenomenon.

> The appearance of language may be thought to be due to an innately mapped-in *program* for behavior, the exact realization of the program being dependent upon the peculiarities of the (speech) environment. As long as the child is surrounded at all by a speaking environment, speech will develop in an automatic way, with a rigid developmental history, a highly specific mode for generalization behavior, and a relative dependence upon the maturational history of the child. (Lenneberg 1964, p. 600)

According to Lenneberg, exposure to language in the environment is a necessary and sufficient condition for language acquisition in children. But in drawing attention to the characteristics of language acquisition which are biologically based, rooted in our species membership, Lenneberg's work did support the view that children are born with an innate predisposition for language acquisition, a special capacity apart from general IQ.

The innatists reinterpreted the role of "nurture," environmental influence, as well as the role of "nature," innate input, in language acquisition. The early claim was that the environment was important in language acquisition in two major ways: (1) exposure to language in the child's environment "triggered" his innate language acquisition "device," setting his language acquisition course in motion; and (2) language exposure provided linguistic data for the child's innate mechanisms to work on so as to discover the particular details of his language which set it apart from other human languages. Thus the environmental contribution was viewed primarily as providing language exposure for the child.

[3]For more recent research relating to Lenneberg's ideas, see Krashen (1973) whose study suggests that brain lateralization occurs much earlier than Lenneberg proposed, possibly by around age five.

The Innatist View (Modified Version)

This strong position underwent substantial modification during the 1970s in both the nature and the nurture claims. It is the modified version of this position that will provide a framework for us throughout the remainder of this section. While still allowing that the innate contribution to language acquisition is substantial, many innatists now propose a different description of its character. They view the innate component not as a body of (unconscious) "knowledge" about the structure of human language, but rather as a substantial innate cognitive potential for processing human language so as to derive its structure; they see the child's innate endowment not as content—something known—but rather as processing abilities for finding out. Slobin, an important proponent of this modified version of the innatist position, responded to a presentation by McNeill, an advocate of the stronger, "content version" of the innatist position, as follows:

> ... it seems to me that McNeill takes a "content approach" ... while I would favor a "process approach." It seems to me that the child is born not with a set of linguistic categories but with some sort of process mechanism—a set of procedures and inference rules, if you will—that he uses to process linguistic data. These mechanisms are such that, applying them to the input data, the child ends up with something which is a member of the class of human languages. The linguistic universals, then, are the *result* of an innate cognitive competence rather than the content of such a competence. The universals may thus be a derivative consequence of, say, the application of certain inference rules rather than constitute the actual initial information in terms of which the child processes linguistic input. (Slobin 1966, pp. 87–88)

There is currently a significant Piagetian-influenced move toward viewing the child's innate processing abilities for language as just one manifestation of deep-rooted and more general cognitive abilities. Doubtless this is an area in which vigorous research will continue for some time. But whether the result of this research supports the view of the child as having special specific innate processing abilities for human language, or as having more general innate cognitive abilities for symbol processing—abilities which he uses in language acquisition as well as in other areas—in either case, the modified innatist position on language acquisition seems to be affirmed: (1) There is a substantial innate contribution to language acquisition, and (2) the innate component includes cognitive abilities that are well adapted for processing human language so as to derive underlying organization.

The innatist position has also undergone some modification in the role it ascribes to the environment. We currently hear less about the environment "triggering" the child's innate "language acquisition device" which then moves steadily along a language acquisition course, and we hear more about the child learning language through his interaction with his world. "Interaction" is indeed the crucial word—*action*—verbal and nonverbal *doing* between the child and others. This word conveys, as it is meant to, that the child's development is a two-way street: He is not simply shaped and molded by the environment, but he also shapes and molds it, changing it and to some extent controlling it for his use in further learning. The following three brief examples show the child actively influencing and controlling his environment toward his own language growth.

First, children influence the way their mothers talk to them. Recently there has been much study of the language mothers (and others) use when talking to young children. It is now quite clear that mothers talk to their infants differently than they talk to adults or older children. Mother adapts her language so as to accomplish meaningful communication with her child. She uses shorter, simpler sentences than in adult conversation, she relies heavily on concrete contextual support, she incorporates a high proportion of basic meanings and relationships early understood by young children. She repeats a lot, and she exaggerates her intonation. She is cueing on signs from the child —signs of comprehension and noncomprehension and signs of continuing participation or nonparticipation in the interaction. She does everything she can to keep the child in the interaction. It is not simply a matter of mother using adult language to the child and the child passively taking it in until it becomes his own. Rather, the behavior of each is simultaneously shaping and being shaped by the behavior of the other as they interact. Many of the cues that mother and child are using as they interact are nonverbal. What does mother *do* as she talks with baby that gives clues to her meanings? What does baby do in response—what body movements and facial expressions guide mother's next move in the interaction?

Second, the young child seems to actively control the linguistic environment so as to get the data he requires. We said earlier that this "little linguist" is actively working on the language he is exposed to so as to figure out how the sounds he hears relate to meanings, and what their underlying organization is. Some researchers have pointed out that the child's early question "What dis (dat)?" ("What's this/that?") elicits the data he needs to discover the semantic categories and labels in his language community. His later (endless) "why" questions serve to provide many examples of causal relations. It has been observed that the child's use of the What's this/that question coincides with a sudden marked increase in his vocabulary. This question enables the child to elicit examplars and nonexamplars of categories, to find out which things are and are not dogs, babies, shoes, books. Is the child using these powerful linguistic tools in order to find out what he wants to know about the language that surrounds him? Guided by his innate propensities for language learning, through his *interaction* with people and things in his environment, the child seems to be actively seeking and using experience that helps him in his language learning task.

Third, the child's active use of things (as well as people) is important in his building the fundamental understandings that we see (hear?) him first express when he "bursts into speech" (Nelson 1973). As he moves his body about in space and encounters and acts upon objects (shaking them, grabbing them, biting them, squeezing them, dropping them, throwing them, etc.) he builds understandings which are basic and necessary to his language growth: notions of self and other, of the separateness of objects, of things located in separate spaces, of "causers" and "happenings caused," of recurrence of actions and things. The environmental "stuff" on which the child acts and with which he interacts to build himself the meanings expressed in a language, includes far more than narrow linguistic "data." There is no passivity here—rather, *action* which is *inter*—between child and others and between child and environmental objects. You can see that this interactive view differs in emphasis from the earlier innatist position that saw the environment "triggering" innate mechanisms that caused language acquisition to magically unfold. You can see, too, that this interactive view differs drastically from the behaviorist notion of the child simply being shaped by the environment.

IN CONCLUSION

It is important to note that the innatist view of language acquisition, in its strong early form and as subsequently modified, was not dreamt up out of the blue to thwart behaviorists. It grew out of insightful observations of many real children in diverse settings learning and using language. It is not simply convenient to say that language acquisition is species uniform and species specific; rather, it has been noted by many observers of children that they all learn language and do so in a variety of natural settings by following an impressively similar general course, and that members of other species do not naturally acquire a communication system that allows for endless creativity within a finite set of organizational principles. It is not simply convenient to say that reinforcement for form is not crucial to acquiring a complex linguistic system. Rather, extensive research has provided ample evidence that children are not typically reinforced for form, and that on those rare occasions when they are, they are unable to make use of the reinforcement. It is not simply convenient to say that children devise a deep-level linguistic system on the basis of the surface level data that people around them use in interacting with them. Rather, researchers say this because they have observed that children, across a wide range of diverse settings, communicate typically by creatively constructing novel sentences which are describable in terms of a preliminary set of underlying systematic principles, rather than by parroting familiar sentences.

Further, it is sometimes claimed that, while the behaviorists rely on empirical evidence, basing their conclusions entirely on actually observed behavior, the innatists are "mentalistic," relying heavily on unfounded conjectures about what is going on in children's minds. But in fact both views of language acquisition are rooted in actually observed behavior. The difference between them is a difference in how to interpret the behavior which is observed. Is this observed behavior the result of innate general IQ plus reinforcement for responses to stimuli, or is it the result of special innate processing abilities plus constant interaction with the environment?

When the dust from the behaviorist/innatist debate settles, it seems we are left with the following inescapable assumptions which will provide the framework for our study of the sequence and processes of language acquisition:

1. What is being acquired[4] is a system of linguistic structure which is a finite set of underlying principles allowing for the creation of an infinite set of novel sentences.

2. The one who is acquiring this system of linguistic structure is a human born with innate potential for processing the overt symbols of language so as to derive underlying structure—meaning and organization.

3. The language acquirer is in an environment which provides exposure to and interaction through language, both of which are necessary for language acquisition. The child's task is to figure out how the verbal strings of sounds he hears in real situations relate to the meanings in those situations.

4. The child is the active party in his own learning. He uses the environment for language acquisition. He interacts with people and things in his environment, building hypotheses about language, gathering further data, testing hypotheses, and refining them as he goes. He is an active pattern seeker and user.

5. Simple imitation, practice, and reinforcement for linguistic form, although they do occur, cannot account for acquisition of linguistic structure.

[4]Again, we are focusing only on the acquisition of linguistic structure for a start. Children acquire far more than this when they learn a language, especially the many various ways to use this structure in different situations.

Chapter 6

Language Acquisition: Developmental Sequence

INTRODUCTION

As with some other important areas of children's development (physical, cognitive), it is possible to describe a predictable general sequence of language acquisition stages virtually all children go through in a given order, though at varying rates. In this chapter we'll first consider an overall sketch of the sequence of preschool language development, and then study a more detailed discussion of that general sequence. Roger Brown's five stages provide a general framework for this discussion (R. Brown 1973). The first two stages are discussed in detail, and then important aspects of language acquisition that span several stages are presented: the child's development of negatives, of interrogatives, of sentence combining, and of a linguistic sound system. Finally we'll consider four aspects of later (school-age) language development: (1) refinement of language structure, (2) elaboration of language use, (3) development of metalanguage—ways of talking about language form, (4) increased independence of language from immediate context.

PRESCHOOL DEVELOPMENT: A SKETCH

Over time, the language forms that children use become more like those used by the adults in the community. Below are seven excerpts from mother-child interactions, selected to demonstrate a typical progression in language acquisition. These short episodes involve different child-mother pairs. (Episode 4 involves an adult other than the mother.) However, all include children from similar background (middle-class Anglo), and all episodes were gathered in as natural a setting as possible (in the home, with mother and child engaging in an activity that was a regular part of their daily routine). Study the seven episodes to see what differences you notice from one to the next. What changes do you see as the child progresses? Jot down your observations of each episode, if you choose, before going on to read the discussion. (Episodes 4 and 5 should be considered together, as they represent the same stage of development, but demonstrate different language features of that stage.)

As you study the episodes, try to keep two things in mind. First, what is being demonstrated is a general developmental sequence characteristic of early language growth in children. Though the general course of development is similar across children, the rate at which children develop is highly variable.[1] I have not included the ages of children in the episodes, so that you will not be tempted to make age-related statements about "the language of three-year-olds" or "the four-year-old stage," but rather will be able to focus on a developmental progression which children go through at different rates, though in the same basic sequence.

Second, remember that we are attempting to describe the child's developing linguistic structure, and this means describing something which she has, not something which she lacks. It is tempting to look at an episode involving a child's early language and say, "She doesn't have articles," or "He makes mistakes in verb tenses," or "She has trouble with plurals." To say this would be to say that the young child's language system is different from the adult's and we knew that already. When we get to the end of listing features of adult language that the child "does not have" or "has trouble with" (that is, uses differently than we do) we have said nothing about what the child *does* have, what her language system *is*—the very thing we are supposedly attempting to describe. We know that the child's early language is a system of some sort. Her early sentences are designed, nonrandom, patterned; they are constructed in

---

[1]Even in a single child, one can observe what appear to be faster and slower periods of development, though the "spurt" or "slack" is doubtless more apparent than real, for the internal development that we cannot observe may be proceeding very steadily and what we call "spurt" or "slack" may simply be the appearance of the overt behavior reflecting that steady development.

accordance with the child's rule system. Our question is, what is the nature of that system? What is language from the child's point of view? How does it change over time?

As you study these episodes, try to avoid describing the children's language as a set of deficiencies ("The child lacks. . . ." "He makes mistakes with . . ." "She has trouble/difficulty with . . ."). Here are some sentence frameworks that might help you focus your expression and your thinking on the nature of the language system the child does have:

This child expresses _____ (possession, plural, information questions) through the pattern _____.

This child combines units of type _____ with units of type _____ in the order _____.

In this episode the child is using elements like _____, _____, and _____ that were not present in earlier episodes.

EPISODE 1²

C: Nununuhnuh

M: You wanta get down? Huh?

C: Dahdah mummun nunah nahnahmah

M: Where you goin? Where you goin? Where you goin? No, no, no, no.

C: Mamama

M: Come here.

C: Dahdah

M: Daddy's lunch. Daddy's lunch. Daddy's lunch.

C: Nanana dedah dede

M: Get back.

C: Nuhna nahnuhnuh

M: No. (Child is fooling with tape recorder.) Huh? Where you goin, huh? Where you goin, huh? Where you goin, huh? Where you goin, huh? See this baby? See this baby?

C: Dede

M: You're gonna fall off. No, see the baby? Here,H———, H———, H——— (child's name). Here let me have that. Let me have it.

C: (Fusses.)

M: Did you get all that out? You can't have that, darlin'.

C: (fusses.)

M: No, come on. Find something else to play with. Come on. Here. Here you go.

²I am indebted to Chris Leach for this episode.

EPISODE 2[3]

M and C are playing in yard in child's sandbox.

M: Do you want to swim in your swimming pool today? Do you want to get in the pool? Or not? (Pause.) Do you know where your teaspoon is? The big one.

C: (Looks around but does not try to find spoon.)

M: Here it is. Whee. (Dumps some sand out.)

C: (inaudible)

M: Want to use this? Can you fill up the spoon first?

C: (Fills a container, patting it with a shovel.)

M: Are you ready to turn it over? Want to turn it over?

C: (Starts turning it over during M's questions.) Yeah.

M: OK, pat it some more.

C: (Pats some more.) Me.

M: OK. Turn it over. Oh. Quick. Quick. Turn it over quicker or it's all going to fall out.

C: (Turns it over quickly.)

M: That's a girl. Oh, it all came apart. Oh, too bad. Too bad. Let's do this one. (Picks up another container.) Here you want to help fill that up?

C: (inaudible)

M: You want to use that one?

C: (Looks at tape recorder.) Carole.

M: Carole's. That's not a radio.

C: (Returns to filling container.)

M: Shall we turn it? (Pause.) Do you want to turn it now?

C: Here.

M: Right over here? Poop.

C: Pow.

M: Are you going to go bang and pow mine down? Oh, don't do that. Don't do that!

C: (Steps on the sand castles.) Off. Off. Off.

EPISODE 3

M and C are playing with toys in C's room.

M: I'm going to build a tower. (Begins building with blocks.)

C: (Pushes tower over.)

M: What did you just do?

C: Me . . . tower fall down.

M: Tower fell down. Yeah. Will you build a tower?

C: (inaudible)

[3]I am indebted to Carole Urzúa for episodes 2, 3, and 5.

M: You build one.

C: (Builds tower.) One tower.

M: One tower. You want to build two towers?

C: (Gets up to look into cylinder that contained blocks and is now empty.) Allgone.

M: All gone? There's plenty around here, I think. Enough for you to do something else.

C: (Puts cylinder over her own head.) Allgone.

M: Where's D———? (Picks up cylinder from front of C's head.) There she is!!

C: (Puts cylinder back on her head again.)

M: Where's D———? Oh. She disappeared for good. (Lifts cylinder.) Oh, there she is!

C: (Indicates her toy doll named Judy.) Judy.

M: Judy? You want to play it with Judy?

C: Hat on. (Puts cylinder on doll.)

M: Hat's on. Judy's hat's on.

C: Horsie do it.

M: Horsie do it? OK. You go over there and see if you can do it with the horsie.

C: (Puts cylinder over top of big horse on springs.) Hi. Hi, horsie. (Looks back at M and smiles.)

M: Did you get the horsie?

C: (Sees duck.) Duck?

M: Kiss the duck. (Extends duck to C.)

C: (Comes over and hugs M.)

M: You know what I see over there? I see your big bus is over there and it's turned over. Do you know that?

C: Mommy. (Puts cylinder over M's head.)

M: Mommy? OK.

C: Where Mommy?

M: Where's Mommy? (Lifts cylinder.) Boo.

C: (Squeals delightedly.) Wear hat.

M: Wear a hat? Are you going to wear a hat? That hat's too big for you to wear.

C: (Puts cylinder on top of her own head. Squeals.)

M: You squealer.

. . .

C: Sit down.

M: Sit down?

C: (Puts cylinder over her own head.) Where? Where?

M: Where's D———? She's gone. She's all gone.

C: Allgone Mommy. (Takes off cylinder.)

M: Mommy all gone. Hey, where's the cow? (M puts cow under the cylinder.)

C: See cow.

M: The cow's all gone.

C: Cow allgone. (Looks around.)

M: Where is it? Where is the cow? Do you know where the cow is? (Lifts cylinder.) Huh. D———, look at this.

C: See cow. (Laughs.)

EPISODE 4[4]

M and C are playing in C's room. C has stuffed rabbit.

M: Is this yours?

C: Mommy gave me that.

M: Does it have a name?

C: Uh uh.

M: What color is he?

C: It's a bunny.

M: Are you going to undress your black baby? What does she have on?

C: Some pants.

. . .

C: (At scribble book.) I draw the puppy.

M: What, L———?

C: I draw the puppy's nose.

. . .

M: Oh, you know what?

C: You know what? I can draw two puppies.

M: OK. You do that for me. Is that one puppy right there?

C: Uh uh.

. . .

M: Tell me something about the goblins.

C: Goblins scare me.

M: When did the goblins come and scare you?

C: Goblins scare me.

M: What do they look like?

C: (No response.)

. . .

[4]I am indebted to Suzy Heitzeberg for this episode. (Consider episodes 4 and 5 together.)

M: What does Santa Claus look like?

C: Um, my mouth.

M: What does he have that's real big and white?

C: A chin.

EPISODE 5

C: Mommy, can I have a Butter Crunch? (From an ad.)

M: No, honey.

C: Can I have a Hershey bar?

M: No, honey.

C: What I can have?

M: How 'bout some raisins?

C: OK.

. . .

C: I say no.

M: No what?

C: Not like.

M: You don't like cabbage?

C: No.

M: Well, just leave it there, OK? Just leave it there.

C: Eat the fish.

M: You can eat some fish.

C: Put the cabbage here.

M: (Puts cabbage where child indicated.) Yeah, let's put the cabbage . . . let's put the cabbage like you do when you don't care for something. You just sorta leave it there. You taste it and you be polite and you taste it and then you just put it there and then you just eat everything else. Would you like some more fish?

C: I like more fish.

M: All right. Child, you're gonna have table manners yet!

EPISODE 6[5]

M: You want to put your new stockings on?

C: Yes.

M: Here they are. I (inaudible).

C: And these. I'll show you. I'll show you, Mommy.

M: OK.

[5]I am indebted to Shirley Hollibaugh for this episode.

C: How 'bout these? (Finding a different pair of stockings.)

M: All right. Those are OK.

. . .

M: What'd you make for breakfast this morning?

C: I made some cookies, some cookies.

M: No! That's not what you made for breakfast! What'd you make for breakfast?

C: Donno.

M: 'Member? In the bowl, I mean in the pan. Oatmeal? Say it.

C: Oatmilk.

M: It's not oat milk, it's oat*meal!*

C: (Strongly) I know to say it!

M: Well, say it right.

C: Oatmeal!

M: Oatmeal! That's right. Did it taste good?

C: Yep. There was taste good (inaudible).

M: Was it warm?

C: Yep.

M: What'd you tell me about the knife?

C: I, that's ... my, my ... playing knife ... and cuts you up.

M: Might cut me?

C: Yep.

M: You shouldn't play with knives, should you?

C: I can play with mines.

M: What happens when you play with Mommy's?

C: Donno.

M: They hurt you, right?

C: Yep.

M: Might be dangerous, huh?

C: Yeah. I say it was dangerous.

EPISODE 7[6]

M: What did you do at school today?

C: Working—just was working. Teacher has a magnet game. Some things are magnet and some things are not. The ones that are sticky stick and the ones that are not sticky don't stick.

M: Did you play on the jungle gym today?

C: No, I'm a watcher.

[6]I am indebted to Jamie Ber for this episode.

M: What's a watcher?

C: I watch everybody fall off and if they do, I go and get the teacher.

M: Did you have a nice ride on the school bus?

C: Yes. Do you know what Mr. B——— (the bus driver) says?

M: No, what?

C: "Shut up, R———" (child's name) and he turns the radio up real loud.

. . .

M: What do you want to be when you grow up?

C: I am a fireman!

M: What do firemen do?

C: They put out fires, rescue people if they fall from a real tall building and go in spook houses and if someone is missed, like a fireman, the ambulance and the rescue people, they find him.

. . .

M: What's your favorite kind of sandwich?

C: A mustard sandwich. Take some bread and fold it up and put some mustard in the middle of it. Don't you know?!?

. . .

M: What do you want for breakfast tomorrow?

C: After this night?

M: Yes.

C: Cheerios in a bowl with milk on top.

. . .

M: It's time to go to bed, R———.

C: If you say "It's time to go to bed, R———" one more time, you are going to upset me.

M: I'm sorry, but it is time.

C: You're upsetting me!

You might question whether C-1's language is language at all (throughout this discussion I will refer to the child in each episode with C- and the number of the episode). Isn't this just a baby making noise? No, it is something more than random noise making. The baby repeats a limited set of syllables in this sample, most of them consonant + vowel combinations. This repetition shows some articulatory control that was not present earlier for this child. Earlier verbal noise making is more diverse and does not show the patterning evident here, either in consonant + vowel syllable structure or in deliberate syllable repetition. C-1's language demonstrates some nonrandomness, which is a characteristic of language.

In this first episode one wonders whether C-1's "Mamama" and "Dah-dah" are words. How can we tell when "Dahdah" is a repetition of two syllables and when it is a word, a deliberate sound string intended to convey a particular meaning? The mother in this episode responds to "Dahdah" as a meaningful utterance since the child speaks it in the presence of the father's lunch and, the mother assumes, with some reference to that. Generally when we begin to observe the child uttering particular sound sequences in particular situations, we assume that the child has established some sound-meaning connection. It is this assumed connection that distinguishes words from verbal noises. The crucial question is, "Is there a particular sound-meaning connection for this child?" We would have to observe the child's use of these sound strings in diverse contexts to be sure. However, it would seem, even from this very limited episode, that the child is at least at the brink of "wordness."

Often a sound-meaning connection is different for the child than for the adult. It is not unusual to hear a mother say of her child, "———is the word she uses for———." Here the sound sequence may be quite unlike that which the adult would use to express that meaning. On the other hand, a child's early word may sound very much like an adult's, yet denote a different area of meaning as is the case, for example, with the child who calls all animals "doggie."

Notice the turn taking in this first conversation. We often take it for granted that two participants in a conversation take turns when they interact. If for some reason both speak at the same time, they tend to apologize and one gives the floor to the other ("Sorry. Go ahead."), thus acknowledging that both know that the appropriate way to dialogue is to take turns at speaking. But turn taking in an interaction is behavior which is learned. The baby's earliest cooing and gurgling occur simultaneously with the mother's verbalizations. In episode 1 there is some evidence of early development of what one sociolinguist has called "communicative competence" (Hymes 1972), the ability to interact verbally in accordance with principles of social appropriateness of language use. Taking turns in conversation is one such principle that speakers of a language learn and use early.

In episode 2 there is no question as to whether or not the child is communicating with words, deliberate sound sequences which *mean*. The child's "me" following her mother's "OK, pat it some more" might mean "me —I'm the one who's patting it." Her "Carole" as she looks at the tape recorder possibly means "That's Carole's" and her "here" possibly is said to indicate "I want to turn it over right here." This child is getting considerable mileage out of a few one-word utterances. Notice the absence of sound-making "fillers" (though if we looked at a larger segment of this child's language in a wide range of situations we might find some "playing with sounds"). We also see in this episode a rooting of the child's language in her action, a characteristic typical of early language. It helps us to understand what the child is saying if we can also see what she is doing; "pow" as she moves to pow the sandcastles, "off, off, off" as she step, step, steps on them.

We know that a child's language growth doesn't have to do only with what she says, but at least as importantly it has to do with what she comprehends in the speech of others. But the question "What language does the child comprehend?" is the most difficult of all, and the earlier the stage of language development the harder it is to answer. C-2 does not overtly respond to the mother's opening series of questions, though it would seem the mother is using these forms precisely in order to get some sort of verbal or nonverbal (action) response from her child. After her mother asks, "You want to use that one?" (referring to a container), C-2 looks at the experimenter's tape recorder and says, "Carole." But does C-2 behave in this way because she did not understand what her mother was saying, or because she did not understand a crucial *part* of what her mother was saying, or because she was not even listening, or because she preferred to do something else? There is usually no way to tell for certain.

On the other hand, Mother says, "Turn it over. Oh. Quick. Quick." and C-2 does turn it over quickly. Mother says, "OK, pat it some more" and C-2 does. But is this because she understands her mother's verbal suggestions, or simply because it is in the nature of the game itself to pat the sand and to turn it over quickly? Or did she understand some nonverbal signal, a gesture or facial expression, and not comprehend or perhaps not even attend to the verbal signal itself? To attempt an answer, one must observe a child extensively so as to note overall patterns in the child's verbal and nonverbal behavior in different situations. Even then the question of comprehension remains tantalizing. Our overriding tendency is to assume that the child's responses, being similar to those *we* would make in that situation, indicate that she understands what *we* would understand in that particular situation. Maybe . . . but then again, maybe not.

Overall, movement from episode 1 to episode 2 involves movement toward "wordness." In episode 1, repeated sound sequences and tentative hints of words were playing an important part in the interaction. In episode 2, words —items we can identify with confidence as sound-meaning relations—have emerged to play an important part in interaction.

Particularly noteworthy in episode 3 is the child's word combining. Some researchers consider this early combining the beginning of syntax for the child. And what powerful use C-3 makes of this expressive device. In a total of twelve word combinations for the child in this short episode, we find her using language for different purposes. She reports and comments on her actions: "tower fall down" (presumably meaning something like "I made the tower fall down"), "one tower" ("I'm building one tower") "sit down" ("I'm going to sit down"), "see cow" (spoken once when she does see the cow and once when she doesn't). She initiates and maintains games: "hat on," "horsie do it," "where Mommy," "allgone Mommy," "wear hat." She greets: "hi, horsie." Structurally we find constructions involving verbs expressing actions, nouns as agents (doers) of actions and also as objects, locational expressions ("on," "where," "down"), modifiers in "one" and "allgone" (expressing the nonexistence of an entity). This child seems to use to the full whatever expressive devices she has, in this case two or three words in combination. The young child wrings tremendous expressive potential out of simple two-word combinations, expressing through them a variety of meanings and relationships.

In episode 3, as in episode 2, the child's saying and doing are of a piece, her words live in her physical actions. It is through her saying and doing together (and with the willing participation of a very sensitive, cooperative mother!) that C-3 initiates and controls throughout this episode.

You'll notice that "allgone" is written as one word for the child, but as two ("all gone") for the mother. This is not a misprint but rather an attempt to convey how the item functions differently for the child and for the adult. The mother's lexicon includes two separate items, "all" and "gone," each of which enters into various combinations with other lexical items. But study of the large body of language data collected on this particular child reveals that "allgone" works for her at this stage as a single, inseparable unit denoting absence. Remember, our question is, "What is the child's language system?" and in the system of this child at the time of this episode, "allgone" functions as the expression of a single morpheme.

Episodes 4 and 5 demonstrate what Roger Brown has called "an intricate sort of ivy" that begins "to grow up between and upon the major construction blocks, the nouns and verbs" that are the predominant elements in early speech (Brown 1973, p. 249). You can notice an increased length in the utterances of C-4 and C-5 over those of C-3. It is partly this "ivy" that accounts for the increase in length. C-4 and C-5 include in their utterances a variety of grammatical morphemes, those bits and pieces that are not heavy carriers of semantic content, but which refine meanings and contribute to smoothness and fluency. Now there are articles ("a," "the," "some"), "be" forms ("It's a bunny."), plural morphemes ("mittens," "bears"), possessive morphemes ("puppy's"), prepositions ("on," "with," "through"), and auxiliaries like "can."

C-4 and C-5 are using a variety of sentence types—affirmatives, negatives, interrogatives, imperatives. Notice the variety in negatives: "Uh uh," "I can't," "I didn't," "No," "Not like." The interrogatives occur in the fixed routine sequence in episode 5. Notice that C-5 says the two yes/no questions as they occur in the ad: "*Can I have X?*" But when she asks the information question "What *I can* have?" she doesn't invert the subject-verb order as it occurs in the ad. Clearly she is not simply imitating the ad, but in this instance is structuring the expression according to her own developing system of rules. This unreversed subject-verb order in information questions is a familiar phenomenon in children's development of interrogative forms.

In episode 6 there is evidence of combining several underlying propositions into a single utterance. In the child's "I, that's . . . my, my . . . playing knife . . . and cuts you up," there are four underlying propositions, something like "That's a knife," "The knife is mine," "The knife is for playing," and "It cuts you up." Underlying C-6's "I know to say it" are the two propositions "I know something" and "I say it," and underlying her "I say it was dangerous" are "I say something" and "It was dangerous." Notice too that C-6's language in this episode is less dependent on her immediate action and setting than was the case with children in previous episodes. She and her mother discuss events that happened previously and objects which are out of sight, as well as those in the immediate situation.[7]

Both the expression of several underlying propositions in a single utterance, and the lessened dependence of the child's language on the immediate context, are particularly apparent in episode 7. In this informal, before-bed conversation, C-7 and his mother talk about his actions, but their talk is not a part of action he is engaged in at that moment. Surely the most structurally complex utterance in this episode is C-7's reply to his mother's question "What do firemen do?" "They put out fires, rescue people if they fall from a real tall building and go in spook houses and if someone is missed, like a fireman, the ambulance and the rescue people, they find him." This reply includes at least the following underlying propositions. (Analyses here will differ slightly, depending on how some adjectives and adverbs are treated.)

> Firemen put out fires
> Firemen rescue people
> People fall from a building
> The building is (real) tall
> Firemen go in houses
> The houses are spooky (type)
> Someone misses someone
> Someone misses a fireman
> The ambulance finds the fireman
> The people find the fireman
> They are rescuers (type)

The seven episodes included here span a four-year age range: C-1 is under one year, and C-7 is under five. Over this span one sees a steady increase in

---

[7]For further discussion of the young child's early movement away from dependence on the immediate context, see Sachs (1977).

the length and complexity in the forms of children's verbal expression. The work of many researchers, especially Brown and his colleagues, suggests that increases in length and complexity are related.

PRESCHOOL DEVELOPMENT: A CLOSER LOOK

Mean Length of Utterance (MLU)

Brown and his colleagues closely observed the early language development of three children over a period of several years. It became apparent to them that the length of a young child's utterances was a better indicator of language development than was chronological age. If we describe the language system of several children of the same age, we find marked differences. But if we describe the language system of several children whose utterances (spoken sentences) average the same length, we find impressive similarities. Brown and his colleagues used the child's average number of morphemes per utterance as their length measure. They calculated a mean length of utterance (MLU) for a child by counting the number of morphemes in 100 of the child's consecutive utterances (that is, in 100 sequences that would be sentences for the child), adding the total number of morphemes from the 100 utterances, and then dividing by 100. They posited five stages in early language acquisition, each stage defined by MLU. For each stage they also suggested an upper bound (UB), that is, what would typically constitute the longest utterance (in morphemes) in the child's sample. One can view Brown's stages as MLU spans as well as central MLU points.

STAGE	MLU (POINT)	MLU (SPAN)	UB
1	1.75	1.5–2.0	5
2	2.25	2.0–2.5	7
3	2.75	2.5–3.0	9
4	3.50	3.0–3.5	11
5	4.00	3.5–4.0	13

Based on Brown (1973), p. 56.

Up to Stage 5, an MLU of 4.0, increasing length reflects increasing complexity. Typically, a young child might say

Daddy go

and later

Daddy going

and still later

Daddy is going.

As the child's language develops, it moves from a system which at most combines two or three uninflected, heavy content items (especially nouns and verbs), to a system which incorporates expression of inflections like past tense and plural, grammatical morphemes like articles and prepositions, and embedded and conjoined constructions, all of which contribute to both length and complexity of expression. Because of this length-complexity relationship, MLU is a good indicator of early language growth.

After an MLU of 4.0, however, utterance length is no longer a very helpful measure of language growth. You can probably already guess why. Just think of all the shortened forms we regularly use in conversation. If someone asks you, "Are you going to be able to make it to the party by 8:00?" you may simply answer "Yup." But that one "yup" that you actually speak relates to a much more complex underlying structure that you have access to and are drawing on—something like "I am going to be able to make it to the party by 8:00." And so it is with children. After an MLU of 4.0, the length measure does not reflect the complexity of what children know, the system that enables them to produce deleted forms.

Stage 1

Brown's stages provide a useful framework for viewing early syntactic growth, so long as we remember that development is continuous. We impose segmentation on this continuous process to make it manageable for study; the segments or stages are not demarked in the growth itself. *We* put them there. Keeping that uppermost in our minds, we can profitably look at Brown's characterization of these early stages of language acquisition.

Stage 1 is sometimes called "the two-word stage." A striking feature of the utterances of a child with an MLU of around 1.75 is that many of her utterances are two morphemes long, and some of them are even longer. C-3 is an example of a child in Stage 1.[8] Some researchers have dubbed the language of this period "telegraphic," as the morphemes the child expresses tend to be heavy carriers of content—nouns, verbs, some adjectives and adverbs—just as would be the case in a telegram where we pay by the word and

[8]Of course a far more substantial sample of the child's language than is present in episode 3 is necessary to establish a child's MLU. This episode has been extracted from a large body of data for C-3, and her MLU for that larger body of data places her in Stage 1.

thus select the heaviest content carriers we can find. There is a noticeable absence of grammatical morphemes like articles (a, the, some); auxiliaries (can, will); "be" forms as main verbs (It *is* red); and "be" forms which precede verbs in adult constructions (*is* going). C-3 expresses the meaning "The cow is all gone" by saying "Cow allgone." She conveys her meaning very satisfactorily, as she would not have done had her two uttered morphemes been "the is."

Through the use of heavy content items in short combinations, the child in Stage 1 expresses what Brown and his colleagues have characterized as a set of about ten "major meanings and relations." These meanings and relations account for a high proportion of the Stage 1 child's utterances though, of course, not for all of them. What is particularly impressive is that these major meanings and relations are evident in the expressions of Stage 1 children acquiring a variety of languages. Let's look at these major meanings and relations.

Below you will find several examples of important Stage 1 meanings and relations. Accompanying each example is a description of the situation in which the child's utterance was spoken. Try to figure out the meaning or relationship demonstrated in each group of examples before you read the discussion following the examples. For example, you'll study examples a, b, and c of Cluster 1 to try to determine the type of meaning expressed in all three examples. A line has been left beside the number 1 so that you can write out what you think the meaning or relation is that is being demonstrated in the examples. You'll proceed in the same way throughout the ten clusters. Clusters 1 through 3 exemplify three major meanings. You might want to study those three sets and respond before going on to Clusters 4 through 10, which exemplify seven relations that can be expressed as two-term relationships. What kind of items is the child relating in each one? Study all seven before you respond.[9]

CLUSTERS 1–3: MAJOR MEANINGS

1. _____

    a. Adult says, "What's this?" Child answers, *"This doll."*

    b. Adult and child are looking at a picture book. Child points to a picture of a house and says to adult, *"See house."*

    c. Adult asks child, "Where's the baby?" Child touches doll nearby and answers, *"Here baby."*

2. _____

    a. Child begins turning a toy wheel in order to make noise, and says *"More noise."*

---

[9]All examples are real instances of children's language taken either from language acquisition literature or from personal observation.

    b. Mother has some raisins. Child extends open hand toward mother and says, " *'Nother raisin.*"

    c. Child and mother have been walking outside. Mother starts toward the house. Child pulls on mother's hand, so she'll keep walking and not go inside. Child says, *"More bye-bye."*

3. _____

    a. Child stops turning a toy wheel that had been making noise when he turned it, and says *"No more noise."*

    b. Child looks at empty breakfast plate and says, *"Allgone egg."*

    c. Mother and child are inside with the front door open. Mother closes the door and child says, *"Allgone outside."*

CLUSTERS 4–10: RELATIONS

4. _____ + _____

    a. Mother is writing a letter. She asks child, "What's Mommy doing?" Child answers, *"Mommy write."*

    b. Child is looking out the window watching his father walk toward his car. Child says, *"Daddy go."*

    c. Mother is dressing child (Kathryn) and encouraging her to stand up so mother can pull her overalls on. Child says, *"Kathryn stand up."*

5. _____ + _____

    a. Child is preparing to throw a ball. Child says, *"Throw ball."*

    b. Child is "feeding" a toy cat a raisin and says *"Eat raisin."*

    c. Child is preparing to pull a Teddy bear in a toy wagon. Child says, *"Pull Teddy."*

6. _____ + _____

    a. Mother is busy making bread. Child looks at her and says, *"Mommy bread."*

    b. Adult says to a child (Kathryn), "Throw me the ball." Child answers, as she prepares to throw the ball, *"Kathryn ball."*

    c. Mother is putting child's book away on the shelf. Child says, *"Mommy book."*

7. _____ + _____

    a. Adult asks child, "Where did Janet go?" Child answers, *"Go movie."*

    b. Adult asks child, "Where did you put your socks?" Child answers, pointing, *"Put there."*

8. _____ + _____

    a. Doll is "eating" at the table. Child says, *"Baby table."*

    b. Adult asks child "Where's Mommy?" Child answers, *"Mommy kitchen."*

    c. Child is trying to put a shoe on her mother's foot. Child says, *"Shoe foot."*

9. _____ + _____
    a. Child points to her father's place at the table and says, *"Daddy chair."*
    b. Mother is taking a new dress out of its box. Child says, *"Mommy dress."*
    c. Child touches her mother's nose and says, *"Mommy nose."*

10. _____ + _____
    a. Child reaches for a microphone, draws back suddenly and says, *"Microphone hot."*
    b. Adult says to child, "Bring me a book to read to you." Child brings a book about animals and says, *"Animal book."*
    c. Adult says to child, "Oh that's a big ball." Child says, *"Big ball."*

Brown's term for the meaning expressed in the examples in Cluster 1 is "nomination," which is just a twenty-five-cent word for labeling, naming, or identifying. The child is connecting verbal labels with certain objects. Adults often encourage this by engaging children in "the naming game." We'll ask a child to "Show me your eye" or we'll ask, "Where's your nose?" Clearly we don't mean these in a literal sense: How do we "show" someone something which is already in full view? And how would we react if the child responded to our "Where's your nose?" by actually telling us the location of her nose: "It's in the middle of my face." This isn't what we mean. In the naming game, a paraphrase for "Show me your———" or "Where's your———?" might be "Demonstrate to me that you know which part of your body is called———." And the child knows the game and typically responds to our cue by touching the appropriate item and giving the label—"This X" or "Here X."

Notice that the child's "See house" in example 1b is nomination, but C-3's "See cow" in the earlier episode (p. 117) is not. We must look to the context of the utterance for clues to the child's intended meaning. In 1b, the adult and child are engaged in a naming game with a picture book. The child identifies one picture as an item called "house." But C-3 says her "see cow" in very different situations. Her mother hides the toy cow under a cylinder and says, "Hey, where's the cow?" and then reveals it. The child's responses, "see cow," once when the cow is concealed and again when it is revealed, are clearly statements about the cow, and not attempts to label the object. Here we have two utterances which, taken at face value, are very similar but which in context are used to express quite different meanings for the young child.

Brown has called the meaning demonstrated in the examples in Cluster 2 "recurrence." You might have identified this meaning as "Child wants more of something." The child asks for more activities as in "more bye-bye" (which we might paraphrase as "I want to go outside some more"), and also more things as in " 'nother raisin."

The third major meaning of this early period exemplified in Cluster 3, Brown calls "nonexistence." Here the child indicates through verbal expression that she recognizes the absence of something. You can find further examples of this in episode 3.

Clusters 4 through 10 can be expressed as two-term relations of the form ——— + ———. Clusters 4, 5, and 6 relate various components of a basic

agent + action + object

pattern. The examples in Cluster 4 express an agent + action relation, those in Cluster 5 express an action + object relation, and those in Cluster 6 relate agent + object. It is significant that the first expressed element in categories 4 and 6 is an *agent,* a *doer,* of some action. The semantically oriented term "agent" is preferable to either the syntactic term "subject" or the term "noun" here because there are many grammatical subjects and many nouns which are not agents—doers of actions—and these do not occur significantly in Stage 1 relations. The word "plate" in "The plate broke" or "The plate is broken" is a grammatical subject and a noun, but it is not an agent; it does not do the breaking, but rather it becomes broken through the action of someone. Observations of the speech of Stage 1 children suggest that it is the semantic concept of doer and what the doer does (Cluster 4: agent + action), or doer and what the doer does something to (Cluster 6: agent + object) that are the relations the child notices and expresses in Stage 1 speech.

Notice that, in surface structure, many of these Stage 1 utterances seem remarkably similar. In fact there is a well known example in language acquisition literature in which a Stage 1 child was observed to use the sentence "Mommy sock" on two different occasions, once when the child, Kathryn, picked up her mother's sock, and again when her mother was putting the child's sock on her (Bloom 1970, p. 5). In the first instance, the context would suggest that the child's sentence expressed possession, meaning something like "This is Mommy's sock," and that in the second instance, the child was expressing an agent + object relation something like "Mommy is putting the sock on Kathryn." Here is a case rather like the adult's "Hunting lions can be dangerous": A single surface structure can relate to two different deep structures. And in both the child's case and the adult's, it is the context that helps to disambiguate the surface structure.

Slobin has pulled some further interesting examples from Bloom's work (Slobin 1971, pp. 46–47). The following five of Kathryn's Stage 1 sentences could simply be viewed as all cases of the child putting two nouns together:

1. cup glass
2. party hat
3. Kathryn sock
4. sweater chair
5. Kathryn ball

But in real contexts, the child was using them to express very different semantic-syntactic relations:

1. conjunction ("I see a cup and a glass.")
2. attribution ("This is a party hat.")
3. possession ("This is Kathryn's sock.")
4. location ("The sweater is on the chair.")
5. agent-object ("Kathryn will throw the ball.")

Some linguists have called Stage 1 utterances like those in Cluster 6 "verbless sentences." Verbless, but not actionless, surely. Though the action is not named in these sentences, its meaning must be present just as the notion "you" is present in adult imperatives ("Close the window") where it is not expressed. Apparently at this stage the child's rule system generates agent + object expressions as grammatical sentences. Yet these verbless sentences remain puzzling. We feel that the verb encoding the action in a sentence is somehow the core of the sentence. We are aware, too, that action is central to the young child's life: Her growing understanding is dependent on her doing. Why does a child develop a language system that does not require expression of this central fact of her life? Like most why questions about language, it is interesting, but not very productive to ask it. We can only say that the Stage 1 child's language does include utterances of the agent + object type, and that these are OK (grammatical) expressions for the child. Within real contexts, any two-term expression from the agent + action + object string is possible, the items generally occur in that order, and convey to adults the agent + action + object relations appropriate to the situation.

Clusters 7 and 8 include location. Actions, as in Cluster 7, and entities, as in Cluster 8, can be located. (This is reminiscent of Cluster 2 in which both actions and things could recur.)

The examples in Cluster 9 demonstrate the young child's expression of the possessive relationship, naming first the possessor and then the object possessed. Cluster 10 demonstrates what is often called an "attributive" relationship. (You might have labeled this "description" or "adjective-noun" or "modification.") The order of the two elements is not as fixed as in the other relational clusters; either attribute + entity, or entity + attribute will do. (In the adult system both orders are acceptable also, as in "The *ball* is *big*" or "That's a *big ball.*")

Of course all the child's utterances in Stage 1 are not two-morpheme combinations. Some are one word, and some are more than two. Stage 1 is perhaps better regarded as a span than as a particular point in the child's development. During this span the child's MLU increases. Thus, toward the end of this period, more longer-than-two-morpheme combinations occur.

One cannot help but be impressed by the evidence of pattern in this early period in the child's language development. The child's language is clearly rule governed and creative. The child seems not to be imitating other's comments, but rather expressing her own meanings creatively, within the set of structural possibilities her system allows. That is exactly what we do as adults, of course, only we create within a different system of structural possibilities for relating sounds and meanings.

Stage 2

Brown defines Stage 2 as centering on an MLU of 2.25 and including the span of 2.0 to 2.5. What accounts for the increase in the MLU? What expressive devices are children now using that make their sentences longer? We can identify three that are important here: (1) the emergence of grammatical morphemes included in the child's speech, (2) the stringing together of two-term relations, and (3) the expansion of a term in a relation.

We mentioned in our brief discussion of episodes 4 and 5, the grammatical morphemes that begin to be in evidence as the child's MLU exceeds 2.0 —Brown's "ivy" that creeps in and around the heavy content items that are the building materials of Stage 1 speech. Brown and his colleagues have studied the emergence and development of fourteen grammatical morphemes including present progressive ("-ing"); the prepositions "in" and "on"; plural; regular and irregular past tense; regular and irregular third person singular forms (he or she goes, skips, rises, says, does); possessives; articles; auxiliary *be* (*is* going); and *be* as a main verb (Brown 1973).

It is important to recognize that though many of these grammatical morphemes first appear in Stage 2, they do not suddenly occur in all contexts where the adult would use them. It may be many months between the child's first use of the preposition "in" to express containment ("put in," "in box"), and use of this preposition for all containment situations where the adult grammar would require "in." Sometimes it is as if a rule which is obligatory for the adult is optional for the child. The "as if" here is a deliberate hedge in that we cannot know just what rules the child operates with. We do know, however, that alternate forms (constructions expressing containment with and without the use of "in") do occur and seem to live quite happily side by side in children's language for a period of time (the period of time differing from morpheme to morpheme and from child to child). More or less gradually the child's use of the particular grammatical morpheme comes to resemble the adults' use, reflecting a progressive modification of the child's underlying rule system toward that of the adult. In Brown's words:

> In Stage II we find the first appearances of noun and verb inflections and of such little words as articles, spatial prepositions, copula and auxiliary *be* forms. None of these "grammatical morphemes" is acquired suddenly and completely. Each of them is for a considerable period of time sometimes present and sometimes absent in obligatory [for the adult] contexts. The proportion of times a form is present gradually rises with time. (Brown 1973, p. 398)

A second factor accounting for the increased length of the utterances in Stage 2 is the stringing together ("concatenation") of constructions which would earlier have stood as complete utterances for the child. Taking an example from our earlier episodes, we find in episode 5, "Put the cabbage here," an action + object + location construction. At an earlier point, two terms of this construction would have been typical: action + object (put cabbage), or entity + location (cabbage here), or action + location (put here). Here is another example from episode 4: "I draw the puppy," a three-term construction (agent + action + object) composed of two-term relations familiar from Stage 1: "I draw" (agent + action), "draw puppy" (action + object), or even "I puppy" (agent + object).

It is hard not to ask *why*. If the child can express a set of two-term relations at a given point in her development, why can't she express those very same relations in a string? Why only one by one? Is this the result of some sort of memory constraint or of some processing limitation? Again, we don't know for sure. However, the movement toward increased combinatory capacity is a developmental phenomenon that occurs quite predictably in children's acquisition of language.

The following two examples from episodes 4 and 5 demonstrate a third major factor accounting for the increase in MLU in Stage 2.

I draw the puppy's nose.
I like more fish.

Here we again have concatenation in that the child has strung together

agent +	*action* +	*object*
I	draw	the puppy's nose
	like	more fish

But in addition to concatenation, we find that within one term of this relationship, the object, the child has produced an expanded construction. Note that the expansions clearly grow from Stage 1; the expressions "more fish" and "puppy nose" would be no surprise in Stage 1. What is new is their incorporation within a major term. There is a hierarchical structure evident here in that a major component has subcomponents.

The continuity of the child's growth through Stage 1 and into Stage 2 is impressive. We see clearly in the speech of the Stage 2 child that she has incorporated, refined, elaborated and expanded the meanings and expressive devices available to her in Stage 1. The child does not leap from one stage to the next, but rather grows steadily in language, at every point building on what has preceded. Thus familiar meanings find more explicit expression (possessive inflection, use of "a," "the"), new expressions suggest that earlier meanings have become more refined (verb + ing), earlier structures are combined (agent + action + object) and elaborated (object that is a phrase), but the seed from which these developments have grown is clear.

Development of Negatives

Already at Stage 2, it begins to be difficult to stay with a stage-by-stage description of the child's developing language. We have said that grammatical morphemes begin to appear in Stage 2. However, the child's adult-like mastery of them typically develops steadily over several years after their first appearance. When we move beyond Stage 2, this continuousness in the development of complex aspects of language is even more striking. Brown identifies the use of "sentence modalities" as a particularly salient characteristic of a child's language in Stage 3 when the MLU is around 2.75. "Sentence modalities" can be roughly paraphrased as "sentence types," such as declarative (affirmative statements), negatives, interrogatives (questions), and imperatives (commands). Because the development of these structures is very much in evidence in Stage 3, Brown has labeled this stage "Modalities of the Simple Sentence." However, because this development actually begins long before Stage 3 and continues long after, researchers have found it fruitful to study the development of negative and interrogative structures as ongoing processes cutting across all stages.

What do we mean when we use negatives, when we say "no"? Clearly we mean different things:

Yes, we have no bananas.
No, I don't want that.
That is not true.

At the very least, our meanings for negatives include nonexistence, rejection, and denial, as in the sentences above. The semantics of negation include these meanings for at least some children in the "one-word stage," that is, the stage prior to Brown's Stage 1 (Bloom 1970). The following examples are from children in the one-word stage:

NONEXISTENCE

No more cleaner (said when the cleaner was gone).
No more juice (said when the juice was gone).
No pocket (said on finding her mother's skirt lacked a pocket).

REJECTION

No (said while pushing object away).
No dirty soap (said while pushing worn sliver of soap away in bathtub). (Bloom 1970, pp. 172-73)

DENIAL

No dirty (said with reference to a clean sock the mother had just said was dirty). (Bloom 1970, p. 149)

What about the syntactic devices that develop to express the child's meanings of no? Klima and Bellugi-Klima (1971) have sketched a developmental sequence for negation. They identify a first period during which the main device for expressing negation is to affix a "no" to the beginning of a sentence as in

No money.   No singing song.
No sit there.   No play that.

This device is used for various meanings of "no" as in the following examples of rejection and denial:

Adult: Get in your high chair with your bib, and I'll give you your cheese.
Child: No bibby.
Adult: Oh, you don't want your bibby?

Adult: Well, is the sun shining?
Child: No the sun shining.
Adult: Oh, the sun's not shining? (Klima and Bellugi-Klima 1971, p. 418)

Later the child begins to insert the negative element within the sentence, and the set of negative words expands to include "don't" and "can't" as single, inseparable units in addition to the earlier "no" and "not."

That no fish school.	I can't see you.
There no squirrels.	You can't dance.
He no bite you	I don't want it.
I no want envelope.	I don't know his name.
That not 'O,' that blue.	

(Klima and Bellugi-Klima 1971, p. 418)

Still later, elements like "can't" and "don't" separate for the child: that is, she uses "do" and "can" alone in interrogative structures, and therefore we assume that she has now analyzed "can't" and "don't" as the morpheme combinations "can" + "not," "do" + "not."

Later still, we observe "negation spread" as in these examples from a child with an MLU of 4.7:

I'm not scared of nothing.
Little puppies can't bite no one, right?
Don't never leave your chair.
He can't have nothing.
I never have none. (Bellugi 1971, p. 105)

And, finally, the special set of indeterminates that adults use in negative sentences ("anything," "anyone," "any") find their way into the child's system.

This syntactic development occurs over a period of several years and, as you might expect, the changes are gradual. In time, certain forms come to prevail over others, but various negative forms will exist side by side in the child's emerging system at any particular time.

Development of Interrogatives

Questions are generally requests for information.[10] There are three main interrogative structure types in English for asking questions. Here are a few examples of each type:

[10]We frequently use interrogative structures for purposes other than to gain information. For example, "Can you reach my pencil?" or "Could you hand me that?" are not requests for information; "yes" or "no" would be inappropriate responses. They are requests for action. When teachers ask questions like "What is the capital of Montana?" they are not seeking the information the question implies, but rather, whether or not the student knows what the capital of Montana is. "Tag questions" like "It's hot, isn't it?" or "You like that, don't you?" do not really seek information, but mainly serve to engage one in conversation. The form/function distinction will be elaborated in Section Four.

YES/NO

Have you seen him recently?
Can you come tomorrow?
Are you coming down with the flu?
Did you get your A in statistics?

INFORMATION

What are you taking?
What are you doing
When are you going?
Why are you going?
Where are you going?
How are you getting there?
Whose is it?
Who won?
What fell?

POLAR

Did you talk to Mark or Jim?
Did Mary or Jim answer?
Did you talk to Mary yesterday or the day before?
Did you talk to Mark about that, or did you decide to just skip it?

As the name implies, yes/no questions are used by adults to elicit from the listener either agreement or disagreement with the proposition in the question. Such questions generally involve a reversal of the subject and the first part of the verbal element from standard sentence word order. This reversal is sometimes called the "flip-flop transformation": *"You have* seen him recently" becomes *"Have you* seen him recently?" *"You can* come . . ." becomes *"Can you* come. . . ." Questions including some form of "do" can be described in reversal terms also, even though the related simple declarative sentence "You got your A in Statistics" does not include the "do" element in its surface structure. It is as if the "do" element is inserted and then reversed (*"You did* get your A. . . ." *"Did you* get your A . . .?"). Sometimes we ask yes/no questions without this syntactic reversal, conveying by intonation alone that we have asked a yes/no question: "You've seen him recently?" "You can come tomorrow?"

Information questions generally seek fill-in-the-blank information:

You are taking (*something*).
You are doing (*something*).

You are going (*some time*).
You are going (*for some reason*).
You are going (*some place*).
You are getting there (*some way*).
It is (*someone's*).
(*Someone*) won.
(*Something*) fell.

The first seven sentences can be viewed as undergoing three changes to become the related information questions: (1) The appropriate question word is selected to fill in the blank (what, where, whose); (2) that word is moved to the beginning of the sentence; and (3) the subject and first verbal element are reversed, just as they were for yes/no questions, resulting in sentences like "What *are you* doing?" (rather than "What you are doing?"). There are, of course, many more kinds of information questions than are given in the above examples (how much/many, what kind, how big, which, which one) but the structural principles for them are all basically similar. A few questions, like the last two in the list, require only the substitution of the appropriate question word for the blank:

| (Someone) won. | Who won? |
| (Something) fell. | What fell? |

Polar questions are choice questions. The speaker provides several choices and assumes the listener will select the accurate one. It's a question we use when we think the answer is one of several possibilities, and we're just not certain which one. Notice that the choice, ——— or ———, can involve any basic portion of the sentence—subject, verb, object, location, time, entire clause.

Children must learn which utterances are questions, what questions mean, and how to express them. And, as with negation, their development of interrogatives changes over a period of several years.

Young children seem to be in a good environment for learning about questions, since a high proportion of the mother's speech to her young child is in the form of questions. In fact, it is not surprising to find in the literature reports of observations of mother-child pairs in which 50 percent of the mother's utterances to her child are questions (Savić 1975).

Ervin-Tripp has suggested that children recognize questions early, and respond to them differently than to other sentence types: "The age for studying the initial discrimination of questions must be from the very onset of speech, at least well before 1:9, when we find such discrimination already well established in our youngest subject" (Ervin-Tripp 1970, p. 81). Indeed, by 1:9, children typically ask a variety of questions themselves. It is interesting that young children will respond to a question by providing information—that is, they will respond to a question as if it *is* a question, even though they will sometimes provide the wrong type of information, the kind of information required by a different question type. The child below seems to be answering the adult's attribute questions as if they are questions about the direct object.

M: What color is he? (referring to child's stuffed rabbit)
C: It's a bunny.
M: What kind of house did the little pig build?
C: A house.

And these two examples come from Ervin-Tripp.

Adult: Who's watching Daddy?
Child: Shaving.
Adult: Who's eating?
Child: Meat.

Here the child apparently interprets the first question as a question about the father's action and the second as a question about what is being eaten. Clearly children comprehend certain types of questions earlier than others. Though they may know that an utterance is a question and seeks information, they may not recognize what kind of information the particular question seeks. Then they may respond by giving information that would be required by a type of question already in their repertoire.

Not surprisingly, the child generally comprehends a given question type before she produces it. However, comprehension and production sequences seem to be similar; those questions understood earlier are those produced earlier, and those understood later are produced later, with the production lagging some months behind the comprehension.

The work of different researchers who have studied children's acquisition of the semantics of questioning is not exactly comparable, as different researchers have studied slightly different sets of questions and they have studied them in somewhat different ways (Brown 1968; Ingram 1970; Ervin-Tripp 1970; Savić 1975). However, there is general agreement about some important question types. "What" (direct object), "where," and "yes/no" questions are among the earliest comprehended and produced, with "why," "how," and especially "when" questions coming much later, and "who," "whose," and "what-do" questions generally falling somewhere in between.[11]

---

[11]"What" direct object questions are questions about the direct object portion of the sentence. "What did he eat?" Answer: "A steak." Not all questions with "what" ask about the direct object (*"What* broke?" or *"What* kind of ice cream do you want?" or *"What* one do you like best?"). "What-do" questions ask about the entire verb phase (predicate) of a sentence, as in "What did he do?" Answer: "Ate a steak."

When you think back to the child's Stage 1 meanings and relations, this general acquisition sequence for the semantics of questions is not surprising. "What" and "where" questions focus on naming and on location. Remember that expressing nomination and expressing location of actions and entities are an important part of Stage 1 language. The intermediate questions, "who," "whose," and "what-do," relate to the child's early meanings also. "Who" asks about agents (or objects), "whose" about possession, and "what-do" about action. These meanings, too, are basic to the child's early expression. But the meanings required by "why" (causal relations), "how" (means or instrumentation of action), and "when" (time concepts) occur later in children's understanding and in their verbal expression.

Klima and Bellugi-Klima (1971) have studied children's acquisition of the syntactic structures of questioning. They find children to go through a predictable sequence that spans several years. They have examined the syntax of questioning in children at three periods, roughly corresponding to Brown's Stages 1, 3, and 5. Here are some examples of yes/no and information questions of children in the three periods they studied (Klima and Bellugi-Klima 1971, pp. 421-23).

	yes/no questions	*information questions*
Period 1	Mommy eggnog?	What(s) that?
(around Stage 1)	I ride train?	What cowboy doing?
	Sit chair?	Where kitty?
	Ball go?	Where horse go?

In this period the child expresses yes/no questions by speaking a sentence with rising intonation. Without that intonation contour, each of the above would be a simple statement for the child. (Note the familiar Stage 1 meanings and relations in these questions.) Information questions at this point include only "what" and "where" types and are of the form "what X," "what X doing," "where X" and "where X go."

	yes/no questions	*information questions*
Period 2	See my doggie?	Where baby Sarah rattle?
(around Stage 3)	Mom pinch finger?	What me think?
	You can't fix it?	What the dollie have?
	This can't write	Why you waking me up?
	a flower?	Why not . . . me can't dance?

While the sentence + rising intonation is still the main device for asking yes/no questions, modals like "can't" and "don't" are in evidence along with the heavy content words. Information questions have expanded to include additional types ("why" "why not"), and the question word often precedes a full-blown sentence (NP + VP) and not simply an NP with or without "do(ing)" or "go(ing)."

	yes/no questions	*information questions*
Period 3	Does the kitty stand up?	Where I should put it
(around	Is Mommy talking to	when I make it up?
Stage 5)	Robin's grandmother?	What I did yesterday?
	Did I saw that in my book?	What he can ride in?
	Oh, did I caught it?	Why kitty can't stand up?
	Will you help me?	Which way they should go?
	Can't it be a bigger truck?	How he can be a doctor?

This is a particularly interesting period. In yes/no questions the child's use of auxiliary elements has expanded considerably (note "does," "did," "will" in the examples). Especially noteworthy is the child's reversal of subject and first verbal element—the "flip-flop." But notice that this reversal is not present in the child's information questions. This is puzzling. Why would this flip-flop occur regularly in the one question type (yes/no), and just as regularly not occur in the other (information)? Obviously the information questions are more difficult in that they require (for adults) other adjustments in addition to the reversal. They also require the selection of an interrogative word and its placement at the beginning of the sentence. But if the different situation for the two question types were merely a matter of how many adjustments must be made, then we would expect that, with information questions, sometimes the child would make one adjustment, and sometimes another; sometimes she would say "What you are doing?" (placement of question word at beginning, but no reversal), and other times "Are you doing what?" (reversal, but no placement of question word at the beginning). But this is not what happens. Children have not been observed to use questions of the latter type ("Are you doing what?"), but quite predictably ask questions of the former type ("What you are doing?"). We don't know *why* it happens this way; we only know *that* it happens this way.

Below are excerpts from an extended conversation (play session) between two four-year-old girlfriends. No adult was present when this play session was tape recorded in the one girl's bedroom. They express negatives and ask questions in a wide variety of ways. How many can you identify and describe? (C-1 and C-2 here are not the children of episodes 1 and 2.)

C-1: What's that gonna be?

C-2: That's the thing that keeps the door closed.

C-1: And what this gun' be?

C-2: That's the (inaudible).

C-1: (They begin to play house.) Now, Mommy! I don't want to.

C-2: Well, you have to.

C-1: I don't want to go to sleep. Okay?

C-2: You have to.

C-1: What?

C-2: You have to.

C-1: Well, I'm gonna play this game all night.

C-2: You better not 'cuz I'll spank you.

C-2: (Sneezes)

C-1: Bless you, Mommy! (Both laugh.)

C-1: Now, Mommy.

C-2: What?

C-1: I'm doing all this all night, so spank me.

C-2: (Spanks her.)

C-1: What you going to do now?

C-2: Put you to sleep. Now, go to bed.

C-1: (Makes loud noise.) Mommy?

C-2: What?

C-1: I'm not going to . . . go to sleep. I'm going to pop you in the tummy.

C-2: I'll *punch* you in the tummy. (Both laugh.)

C-1: Now. I'm not going to put my pants on under my 'jamas, okay? Mommy. (Calling) It's morning time. I didn't go to sleep. What's gonna happen now?

C-2: You're gonna have to go to sleep.

C-1: In the daytime?

C-2: Yeah. Take a nap.

C-1: I'm not going to.

C-1: Look out the window. Oh! Hey Mommy! A ghost outside! Okay, Mommy? Okay, Mommy? (Meaning, "Do you agree to pretend there's a ghost outside?")

C-2: Okay.

C-1: There's a ghost outside. Look out the winda. See a ghost?

C-2: Yes . . .

C-1: What we should do?

C-2: We should move. To another house.

C-1: Okay. We're moved. We moved to another house.

C-2: Okay. Now we put all our stuff in. Oh, yeah.

C-1: Mother?

C-2: The ghost . . .

C-1: I think I hear a giant!

C-2: Giant? There's no giant at night.

C-1: Why?

C-2: There's no giants at morning.

C-1: Uh-huh. (Yes.)

C-2: No, there isn't.

C-1: You see one?

C-2: No, I don't.

C-1: Well, I do.

C-2: I don't see one.

C-1: I do.

C-2: I don't.

C-1: I do.

C-2: I do not.

C-1: I do.

C-2: Now, be quiet.

C-1: I'm watching the news.

C-2: No, you aren't.

C-1: Uh-huh! Uh-huh!

C-2: You aren't.

C-1: Uh-huh! Now you be quiet.

C-2: You be quiet.

C-1: You be quiet.

C-2: You be quiet.

C-1: *You be quiet!* (Screams it.)

C-2: You be quiet!

C-1: I think I'm gonna die.

C-2: No, you're not.

C-1: Yes, I am.

C-2: No, you won't.

C-1: I need a nurse.

C-2: No.

C-1: Yeah!

C-2: No.

C-2: Well, better be quiet.

C-1: Why?

C-2: 'Cuz there's a monster coming!

C-1: Okay. (Whispering.) I see a monster! What we should do?

C-2: He's coming in the door—now he's in the house—wait—hide—hide.[12]

[12]I am indebted to Genevieve Kerr for this example from her data.

Development of Sentence Combining

Another important aspect of children's language developement that spans a period of several years is the combining of several propositions into a single sentence.[13] As adults we accomplish this combining in a variety of ways. Consider a few ways we can combine propositions:[14]

a. This is the house and Jack built it. (Two clauses or propositions of equal status combined.)

b. This is the house that Jack built.
   This (thing) that Jack built, is the house. (One proposition is given prominence and the other elaborates a noun in that proposition.)

c. When Jack built the house, rats were all about.
   Rats were all about when Jack built the house.

   Before Jack built the house, he was troubled by rats.
   Jack was troubled by rats before he built the house.

   After Jack built the house, the rats ate the malt.
   The rats ate the malt after Jack built the house.

   (Two propositions of unequal status are combined in a time relationship.)

d. Jack killed the rats because they ate the malt.
   Because the rats ate the malt, Jack killed them.

   If the rats get in the house, they will eat the malt.
   The rats will eat the malt if they get in the house.

   (Two propositions of unequal status are combined in a cause-result relationship.)

e. Jack's building the house surprised me. (From *"Something* surprised me.")
   Jack likes to build houses. (From "Jack likes *something.*")
   You know that Jack built the house. (From "You know *something.*")

   (One proposition "fills in the blank" in another.)

Acquiring the capacity to combine propositions in these various ways would seem to be a very complicated business. But the first few conversational turns of C-7, in our earlier example, show that this four-year-old is using many of these proposition-combining devices, often in combination with each other.

M: What did you do at school today?

[13]I have relied heavily in this section on Clark and Clark's (1977) very clear and informative discussion of work in this area. You may want to read their discussion after you have read chapter 7 of this text.

[14]Remember, a good way to find the propositions within a sentence is to find the verbs. Each one will generally be the nucleus of a proposition.

C: 1. Working—just was working. 2. Teacher has a magnet game. 3. Some things are magnet and some things are not. 4. The ones that are sticky stick and the ones that are not sticky don't stick.

M: Did you play on the jungle gym today?

C: 5. No, I'm a watcher.

M: What's a watcher?

C: 6. I watch everybody fall off and if they do, I go and get the teacher.

M: Did you have a nice ride on the school bus?

C: 7. Yes. 8. Do you know what Mr. B——(the bus driver) says?

M: No, what?

C: 9. "Shut up, R——" and he turns the radio up real loud.

In sentences 3, 4, 6 (twice), and 9, the child combines propositions with "and," giving them equal status (as in examples a above). In sentence 4, one propositions elaborates a noun in the other (as in examples b above): "ones that are sticky," "ones that are not sticky." In sentence 6, he combines propositions in a cause-result relation (" . . . if they do, I go . . .") as in examples d above. And in sentences 6 and 8, he combines propositions by making one "fill in the blank" in the other as in examples e: "I watch *something* → I watch *everybody fall off*"; "You know *something* → You know *what Mr. B—— says.*"

Lively research is underway relating to these complex developments in children's language acquisition. Some research suggests an earlier preference for combining propositions in an equal way (as in examples a), rather than in ways that give one prominence over the other. Slobin and Welsh (1973) gave a two-year-old called "Echo" sentences to repeat after a model. Some of them included unequal clauses. "Repeating" these after the model, Echo restructured them either by repeating only the main clause, as in:

Model: Mozart (name of child's bear) who cried came to my party.
Repetition: Mozart came to my party. (p. 487)

or else by joining them as two equal clauses:

Model: Mozart who cried came to my party.
Repetition: Mozart cried and he came to my party. (p. 493)

Model: The owl who eats candy runs fast.
Repetition: Owl eat a candy and he run fast (p. 494).

Model: The man who I saw yesterday got wet.
Repetition: I saw the man and he got wet (p. 494).

In their spontaneous, nonelicited speech, young children first combine propositions as equal clauses, typically using "and" or "and then." Later they begin to combine propositions of unequal status using adverbials like "before," "after," "because." Initially they express the main clause first, but later they combine the clauses in either order.

In addition, children's acquisition of complex structures shows an earlier preference for keeping clauses intact and not interrupting them by inserting other clauses. Sentences of the type

> This is the house *that Jack built.* (uninterrupted main clause)

would typically precede sentences of the type

> This (thing) *that Jack built,* is the house. (interrupted main clause)

We would assume that C-7 was using structures like

> I have the ones *that are sticky.* (uninterrupted main clause)

before structures like

> The ones *that are sticky* stick. (interrupted main clause)

C-7's "I watch everybody fall off" and "Do you know what Mr. B———— says?" are further examples of uninterrupted clauses in combination.

Eve Clark has noted another developmental trend in the acquisition of sentence combining. When two events are mentioned in a sentence, young children assume that the one which is mentioned first occurred earlier in time than the event mentioned second. Given sentences to act out with toy objects like

> The boy patted the dog before he kicked the rock.
> After the boy patted the dog, he kicked the rock.
>
> Before the boy kicked the rock, he patted the dog.
> The boy kicked the rock after he patted the dog. (Clark and Clark 1977, p. 359)

younger children will make the boy pat the dog and then kick the rock for the first pair, but will make the boy kick the rock and then pat the dog for the second pair. A reasonable assumption is that children's earlier productions of complex sentences relating events in time will reflect this comprehension pattern; that is, that their earlier sentences with time adverbials will mention events in the order of their occurrence. The comprehension-precedes-production assumption is not foolproof by any means, but it usually works.[15] Clark and Clark (1977) found the children's earliest adverbials to be "when," "if," and " 'cos" (because), and later to include "before," "till" (until,) and "after" (p. 358).

---

[15]For an interesting discussion of production preceding comprehension see Berko Gleason and Weintraub's (1976) paper on the "trick or treat" routine.

Limber has studied the development of combining devices like those in examples e above (called complements) in which a clause fills the "something" blank. Studying children from two to three years old, he identified an early set of verbs children were using including a "want" group ("want," "need," "like") and a "watch" group ("watch," "lookit," "see"), as in

I don't want you read this book. (I don't want *something.*)
Watch me draw circles. (Watch *something.*)
I see you sit down. (I see *something.*)
Lookit a boy play ball. (Lookit *something.*) (Limber 1973, p. 177)

At an earlier stage these verbs typically occur in the child's speech followed by simple nouns—"want that," "see Mommy." Limber suggests that the step from verb + noun ("want + juice" or "watch + me") to verb + clause ("want + you fix it" or "watch + me do it") is a small one, often occurring within a month after the child's first use of the particular verb in any construction (p. 175). As Limber's subjects approached three, their repertoire of verbs taking complements ("something"-blank fillers) expanded to include a variety, for example, "think," "said," "remember," "wonder," "wish," "pretend" (p. 176).

In summary, a child's development of sentence-combining devices shows movement along several dimensions: (1) from a stringing together of equal clauses, toward a joining of clauses of unequal status; (2) from the order main clause first, toward variable order of unequal clauses; (3) from uninterrupted main clauses, toward use of interrupted ones (insertion of subordinate clauses within main clauses); (4) from order of mention coinciding with order of occurrence, toward variable order of clauses; and (5) from use of small semantic-syntactic sets (of adverbials; of complement verbs), toward more expanded sets.

Development of Sound System

We have said very little so far about children's acquisition of the sound system of their language. We know that children move from making sounds to making sense. But currently there is considerable debate as to whether earlier sound making is continuous or discontinuous with the "true speech" that begins at around a year when children begin using identifiable words, sound strings that make sense.

There is some agreement that two distinct sound-making periods can be identified during the first year, a vocalization or prebabbling period, and a babbling period. During the first, which lasts roughly for the first six months, children vocalize in a random way. Their vocalizations include a wide range of sounds and do not demonstrate a pattern or control.

This is what the child produces. But there is evidence that the child is making some important perceptual sound distinctions during this period also. For example, she discriminates between the sound of the human voice and other sounds, between angry and friendly verbal expression, between male and female voices, between various intonation and rhythm features, and between certain speech segments (Clark and Clark 1977, p. 377).

During the second six months, the babbling period, the vocalizations are different. The sound productions exhibit greater pattern and articulatory control as children verbalize strings of repeated consonant + vowel syllables. Their cries are more differentiated for surprise, hunger, and discomfort. They babble with more melody—the suprasegmental features of their language (intonation, stress, rhythm) are more in evidence. Some of the sounds that were present in their vocalizations in the prebabbling period are now gone.

As the child moves into "wordness" or true speech, there is a corresponding decrease in her babbling. Her first words may differ markedly from adult pronunciations, though they are likely to be simplifications of the adult pronunciations involving the omission of final consonants (/b/ + vowel for "ball"), the reduction of consonant clusters (/tik/ for "stick"), the omission of unstressed syllables, or the reduplication of syllables (Clark and Clark 1977, p. 397). At first, the child may have variable pronunciations for the same word. A similar general sequence in the acquisition of particular sound elements is evident in many children, with each element generally being produced at the beginning of words before it is produced in the middle or at the end of words, with /l/ and /r/ usually being among the last sound elements acquired, and with consonant clusters (e.g., /pr/, /kl/, /str/) being acquired after single consonants.

The child must learn to perceive the significant sound features of her language and she must also learn to produce them in her own speech. Examples like the following are common:

> Recently a three year old child told me her name was Litha. I answered "Litha?" "No, *Litha*." "Oh, Lisa." "Yes, Litha." (Slobin 1971, p. 65, quoting G. A. Miller)

148

One of us . . . spoke to a child who called his inflated plastic fish a *fis*. In imitation of the child's pronunciation, the observer said: "This is your *fis*?" "No," said the child, "my *fis*." He continued to reject the adult's imitation until he was told, "That is your fish." "Yes," he said, "my *fis*." (Berko and Brown 1960, p. 531)

Such examples suggest that children perceive distinctions which they do not produce in their speech. Clark and Clark posit this as evidence that young children store "adult-based representations" of words in their minds, rather than representations based on their own pronunciations. They find further evidence for children's adult-based representations in the fact that (1) they identify meanings based on their perception of the sounds of the words they hear, (2) they change their pronunciation over time toward the adult pronunciation, and (3) when they begin to produce a given sound segment (such as /s/), it spreads to other words in their repertoire where it does belong, but not to words where it doesn't belong, according to the adult pronunciations.

In the development of the sound component of language, the actual practice of particular sounds and sound combinations seems to be as important as mental representations of sounds in guiding children toward adult-like pronunciations. Overt practice assumes greater importance in this area of acquisition than in the area of semantics or syntax. Articulatory skill becomes more controlled and refined with use. The development of this component is heavily physical and as in the development of other physical abilities (standing on your head, swimming), practice helps to bring the skill under control.

There is much research to be done in the area of the child's acquisition of the sound system of language. At this time it is impossible to give a certain answer to the question of whether or not early vocalizing is continuous with later true speech. It appears that there is continuousness in the development of suprasegmentals (intonation, rhythm, stress), in steadily increasing articulatory control, and in mental representations of words; however, there appears to be discontinuity in the development of a particular set of sounds from early vocalizing to the use of these sounds in the child's first words.

LATER DEVELOPMENT

We can identify four areas of continuing language growth through the elementary school years: (1) language structure—the ongoing expansion and refinement of semantics and syntax (and to a lesser degree, phonology); (2) language use—the increasing ability to use language more effectively to serve a variety of functions in diverse communication situations; (3) metalanguage—the growing ability to talk about language in a conscious way, as a particular kind of code; (4) language as an independent symbol system—the increasing independence of language from contextual support.

Language Structure

The child's semantic growth continues because her experience continues and expands. New experiences require growth in her semantic system in two ways. First, as she encounters new people, objects, properties, activities, information, relationships, her language must expand to include ways of talking about them. But sometimes the new element in an experience is the act of considering a familiar experience at a conscious level. Experiences of anger, of numerousness, of weight, have been part of the child's life for a long time as she has felt frustration and she has manipulated objects in various quantities and of various weights. But considering anger as an entity—a particular type of feeling with identifiable behavioral signs, considering number as a property of collections of objects, considering weight as a characteristic of objects—these are new experiences in that they are new ways of looking at aspects of the world. "Angry," "seven," "two more," "heavier" become part of the child's semantic system as these concepts become hers. Sometimes the new experience will involve considering specific entities as members of higher order classes: for example, viewing oaks, maples, and birches as "deciduous"; porpoises, dogs, and cows as "mammals"; grandmother and grandfather as "senior citizens." Other times the new experience will involve further differentiation within a domain so that things that were "little" or "teeny" may be seen as—and called —"three centimeters" or "a half inch," and what was "big" might now be "wide" or "long" or "tall" or "fat," and "dogs" might now be "dalmations," "poodles," "golden retrievers," and "mutts." But the basic principle holds: As the child's experience expands, her semantic system expands also.

The child's expanding experience alters her semantic system in a second way. As she encounters categories which are in conflict with the system she has worked out, she is forced to revise her semantic system. Overextensions continue to disappear as she modifies her system in light of new experiences. "Horse" serves well until she encounters mules and donkeys; "camel" is fine until she encounters a dromedary.

Children's syntactic growth continues during the elementary school years also. When they enter school, children typically have an impressive command of the structure of at least one language, are able to express themselves in ways that others understand, and generally are able to understand what others say to them. However, until around age ten (perhaps longer), children are still working out the exceptions to the general rules they have acquired for how language works. These exceptions include both particular forms ("brought" does eventually triumph over "brang" and "eaten" conquers "aten"), and larger constructions—phrase structures. Carol Chomsky studied school children's acquisition of structures which are exceptions to general patterns in English. For example, typically in an affirmative English sentence the nearest np (noun or pronoun) preceding a particular verb is the performer of that action:

> *I* want to go (I want, I go)
> *I* want *Mary* to go (I want, Mary goes)
> *I* persuaded *Mary* to go (I persuaded, Mary goes)
> *I* begged *Mary* to go (I begged, Mary goes)
> *I* forced *Mary* to go (I forced, Mary goes)
> *John* asked to go (John asked, John goes)
> *John* told *Bill* to go (John told, Bill goes)
> *John* told *Bill* what to do (John told, Bill does)

But there are some exceptions to this usual pattern. In the following examples, the nearest np preceding a verb is *not* the performer of that action:

> *I* promised Mary to go (I promised; I go, *not* Mary)
> *I* asked John what to do (I asked; I do, *not* John)

Chomsky reasoned that exceptional syntactic patterns like these would be acquired later by children. She tested forty five- to ten-year-olds to find out. Her results support several important conclusions: (1) acquisition of exceptional syntactic constructions typically continues until around age nine or ten, and probably beyond that for many children; (2) acquisition of these exceptional cases follows a predictable sequence; (3) acquisition of these structures proceeds at a variable rate across children; exceptional syntactic structures which some children master by age five or six, other children don't control until age nine or ten. It appears that for later syntactic development as for earlier, the rate of acquisition varies considerably, but the sequence of development is remarkably similar across children.[16]

Language Use

I have imposed the distinction between development of language structure and development of language use or function so that we can study language growth in manageable chunks. However, the distinction has no basis in the reality of language acquisition. Children do not learn the structure of language and then

[16]For a full description of this fascinating research into acquistion of exceptional syntactic patterns, see C. Chomsky (1969). The present discussion is based on her own description and analysis of her work. For important objections which have been raised regarding Chomsky's methodology and analysis, see Maratsos (1974), E. V. Clark (1971, especially pp. 746–47; and 1973, especially pp. 96-98); and Macnamara (1971).

learn how to use language to serve their communication purposes. Rather, they learn language always within the context of real communication, by using particular language structures to serve particular purposes, and by listening to and interacting with others who do the same.

> Children have to build up structure and function at the same time. As they learn more about structure, they acquire more devices with which to convey different functions. And as they learn more about function, they extend the uses to which different structures can be put. (Clark and Clark 1977, p. 373)

Like the objects they manipulate, language *is* what language *does* for young children. And for older, school-age children, language is also very much a matter of doing: persuading, informing, entertaining, seeking information. This functional aspect of language is so important that it is developed more fully in its own section (Section Four). But a few words are in order here.

The school-age child's social world is bigger and more diverse than that of the preschool child. The six- to twelve-year-old interacts with a variety of people for a variety of purposes. She interacts with an expanded group of peers, with people older and younger than herself, with familiar people, with strangers, with people of higher and lower status than hers, with individuals, with groups. The channels of her interaction expand to include written channels, which often involve greater formality, precision, explicitness of expression, and more extensive use of certain language structures (such as passives) than oral channels. She interacts with others in a wider range of settings—in classrooms, on playgrounds, in libraries, in other children's homes and neighborhoods. In this bigger social world, her language must serve some new functions and must more effectively serve some familiar ones. The child's wider world of interactants, of interaction situations, and of interaction purposes pushes her language to become more "widely adapted" (Brown 1973, p. 245), and thus a more effective and powerful communication tool. We communicate with someone some place for some purpose. As the someones, the some places, and the some purposes become more diverse, the child's communication range increases to accommodate this diversity.

Metalanguage

During the elementary school years, children's ability to focus on language structure in a conscious way increases also. This is not to be confused with either the acquisition of language structure or with the development of language function. Being able to talk about language (metalanguage) is different from mastering that sound-meaning system of structure which allows for the interpretation and the creation of novel sentences (linguistic structure), and it is different from being able to use language effectively in social interaction.

Asked to identify grammatical and ungrammatical sentences as "sounds okay to me" or "sounds not okay to me," five- and six-year-olds are often unable to focus on the form of the sentence apart from the meaning. For example:

Adult: "The children climbed up the jungle gym." Does that one sound okay or not okay to you?

Child: Not okay.

Adult: Can you tell me why? What sounds not okay to you?

Child: There's no jungle gym.

Adult: "All the dogs raided the garbage cans." How 'bout that one? Does it sound okay to you or does it sound not okay?

Child: No, not okay.

Adult: Why? What sounds not okay about it?

Child: Well, because dogs shouldn't raid garbage cans.

Adult: Here's another one. "What will John do with his car?"

Child: Beats me! It sounds okay.

They are unable to focus on these forms *as forms,* rather than as communications. Contrast the above children's responses with these responses of an eleven-year-old.

Adult: "John went to the store, but Mary went to the store."

Child: No, it should be "John and Mary went to the store." That would sound better.

Adult: "We went to see him." How does that one sound? Okay or not okay?

Child: Well, okay, but it sounds kind of cut off.

Adult: "He hurt himself." What about that one?

Child: That sounds cut off too. Make it a little longer. "He hurt himself when he was playing football."

This child is focusing on the language as a formal code.

School language programs have traditionally placed considerable emphasis on children's learning to talk about language and to do so using certain terminology. (I have never understood why *talking about* language structure —identifying parts of speech, subjects, predicates, infinitive phrases—has been emphasized so much in elementary language arts programs, and why *use* of language for real and effective communication has been emphasized so little.) This practice of encouraging children to talk about language in certain ways may be rooted in the prevailing and (I believe) misguided notion that talking about language in specified ways influences one's ability to use language more effectively. But, in fact, the ability to talk about a linguistic code, and the ability to use language effectively in communication, are quite separate. There is no reason to suppose that someone who is able to recognize and label adjectives will speak and write more descriptively; there is no reason to suppose that someone who is able to identify parts of sentences (subject, predicate, complement, infinitive phrase, adverbial clause) will speak and write more fluently. Lewis Carroll used language remarkably, yet his ability to label parts of speech may have been no better than yours and mine. And many linguists, who should be able to identify linguistic units better than most, communicate abysmally in speech and writing.

Language as an Independent Symbol System

Children's language becomes less tied to the immediate context as they grow older. Bloom suggests that this is the major development from around six to twelve years.

> Clearly, the most important development in language in the school years is the child's increasing ability to use the linguistic code, both to speak and understand messages, independently of eliciting states or conditions or of the circumstances in which speech occurs. Linguistic interaction among adults is relatively free from the context in which it occurs; adults do not talk about what is immediately apparent to their listener ... This transition from maximum dependence on contextual support to speech which is independent of the states of affairs in which it occurs is the major accomplishment in language development in the school years. (Bloom 1975, pp. 283-84)

This development is intimately tied (as are most aspects of language growth) to the child's cognitive maturation, which involves further development of the ability to manipulate symbols of various kinds, including language. Since we regard manipulation of linguistic symbols apart from context as a high-level use of language, we tend to foster this line of growth in schools. We generally encourage children to move from more concrete uses of language (to describe objects which are in view or to tell what they are doing as they do it) toward more abstract uses (considering hypothetical situations: "Suppose you were a member of the First Continental Congress or the one in charge of the water control board of our city . . .").

Up to this point we have been mainly concerned with how the form of children's utterances changes over time. We have found that children move through a predictable general sequence in terms of how many of what type of units they organize into creative constructions. But how can we account for this predictable movement? Chapter 7 deals with some important factors that influence this predictable developmental sequence.

Chapter 7

Language Acquisition: Active Processing in an Interactive Environment

INTRODUCTION

We have said that a child acquires language through interaction with his environment. A child plus an interactive environment. *What is the nature of the child?* What abilities does he have that are well suited to figuring out how verbal noises that surround him relate to meanings, and how does he use these abilities in the language learning task? *What is the nature of the environment?* How does it contribute to the child's learning of a language? What does the environment provide and how does a child use it?

We do not have complete answers to these questions. However, the vigorous language acquisition research of the recent past has contributed many important insights so that we are beginning to understand what some significant pieces of the language acquisition puzzle are and how they fit together. What I am calling "recent" research is in an important sense not recent at all. Many powerful contributions have been the result of building on past knowledge—rediscovering, incorporating, reinterpreting, synthesizing earlier child language studies with more contemporary observations of children learning language. Not only has recent research reached back, building on important insights from earlier studies; recent research has also reached *out,* building on knowledge and research methods from related but traditionally separate disciplines; for example, cognitive psychology, anthropology, sociolinguistics. Both the reaching back and the reaching out of recent research have resulted in some rich insights relating to the two major questions of this chapter: What does the active *child* do in learning a language? What is the nature of the *environment* in which he does it?

THE CHILD

Prelinguistic Interaction

The child develops patterns of interaction long before he uses linguistic symbols of expression. Much of the study of these early interaction patterns has focused on mother-child interaction. What is particularly striking is the picture that emerges of an actively differentiating, initiating and responding infant from birth.

Focusing on something with another person is basic to communication. During his first few months, the child develops skills that are important to this sharing of focus with someone else. It is well documented that within his first month, the child distinguishes people and things, responding differently to the two. The young infant responds distinctively to eye contact, a crucial ingredient in interaction and mutual focus. He responds to adult smiles and vocalizations by increasing his own smiling and vocalizing, and he is able to imitate adults' facial expressions and gestures within his first month. By four months, the infant will follow another's line of regard, enabling him to attend jointly with another (Bruner 1975, p. 8). In short, the infant is not a passive being, but is well equipped to participate actively in interaction.

Some researchers, most notably Bruner, see the child's prelinguistic communication as continuous with his later use of conventional linguistic symbols in communication.[1] The continuousness that Bruner is interested in is not the movement from babbling to speech, but rather the growth into social interaction. In the early interactions of mothers and their prelinguistic children, Bruner finds some important precursors of language. One thing the child must learn is that speakers communicate intentions. Through their words, they request things of others, seek information, make assertions. Mothers of prelinguistic infants typically impute communicative intentions to their infants' vocal and nonvocal behavior.

[1]Though note Dore's (1975) disagreement. In his view, children's earlier indicating— by cries and gestures—is discontinuous with their later use of referring expressions (p. 37).

Some real incidents reported by Snow suggest the cartoonist is right, for example, the following "conversation" between a mother and her twelve-month-old child:

> *C:* abaabaa
> *M:* Baba. Yes, that's you, what you are. (Snow 1977, p. 17)

The interaction between C-1 and her mother (p. 114) offers further examples. In this type of interaction, " ... the child sometimes conform[s] with the interpretation, sometimes not, but learn[s], en route, what interpretations his efforts evoke and how these may be modified" (Bruner 1974-75, p. 267).

Also in the context of mother-child interaction in the first year, the child develops procedures for engaging another in joint attention, and for following another's initiation in focusing attention.

> ... there is present from a surprisingly early age a mutual system by which joint selective attention between the infant and his caretaker is assured—under the control of the caretaker and/or of the child, eventually managed by joint pickup of relevant directional cues that each provides the other. (Bruner 1974-75, p. 269)

These developments may be prerequisite to the child's later use of linguistic devices for the purpose of referring: "look dat" or "a mouse" or "see doggie" or "that house." The mother's and child's early joint attention occurs through mutual gazing, either one following the other's line of regard.

Mother and child also frequently engage in joint action sequences, such as peekaboo, pushing an object back and forth, or handing one another objects in turn. These routines may make both a cognitive and a social contribution to the child's movement "from communication to language." These action sequences involve agents of actions, actions themselves, objects of actions, instruments of actions, locations—the very elements that the child's earliest language encodes. In these play sequences, various members can be substituted in each category. For example, various people can be the agents of the peeka-boo action (child, mother), and various instruments can be used as the hiding device (the hands in front of the face, the child's dress pulled up over the face, a curtain, a chair). In give and take games, the object given and taken can vary, the action itself can vary (handing the object, pushing it, rolling it), and the agent and the recipient can alternate so the child is in one turn the agent and in the next turn the recipient. Thus the joint action sequence is segmented in the very way that language is. Bruner reasons that the close correspondence between the segments of action sequences and the segments of the language sequences that encode them aids the child in the cognitive aspects of his language learning task.

But the social aspects of these sequences are important to the child's development into language also. These sequences are executed mutually, with each participant contributing in a different and appropriate role. Sometimes the joint action involves the accomplishment of a task—mother steadying a box for the child to put shapes in, or the child handing the mother shapes one by one for her to put in the box. Communication is such a mutually accomplished task, requiring each participant to contribute in an appropriate role.

By the end of his first year then, the child is able to give communicative signals that his mother will respond to in predictable ways, to initiate and to respond to mother's initiations of focus on an object, to initiate and take appropriate turns in joint action sequences, and to "comment" (perhaps in prelinguistic or in nonstandard linguistic ways) on objects of joint focus or action. The joint action sequences of his first year have aided his conceptualization of segments that are encoded in his earliest language (agents, actions, objects, locations) as these segments have been clearly marked and used in his action routines with mother. These action sequences have also fostered the interaction cycle of give and take, initiate and respond. Thus when the child begins using words to express himself, a well-developed interaction cycle is already present. Basic ingredients of purposeful communication have been developed through joint attention and joint action: reciprocity, signaling, responding, adapting, alternating, focusing, initiating. It is a small next step for the child to put standard words into this well-developed communication cycle.

The Cognitive Base of One-Word Speech

First Morphemes.   When he does begin to use words, what are those words likely to be? What is it in the child's environment that captures his attention so much that he notices the linguistic label his community uses for it (or devises one of his own)? Katherine Nelson (1973) studied the early vocabularies (the first ten words and the first fifty words) of eighteen children over a one-year period, from the time the children were around one year old to the time they were around two. There were some surprises in her findings. Eleven of these children had "shoe" as one of their first fifty words, five of the children had "hat," and four had "sock," but not a single one had "diaper." Yet surely diapers were present in these young children's immediate environments far more than hats, shoes, and socks; the chances are that these children wore diapers constantly, but not so hats, shoes, or socks. Seven of these children had "clock" (meaning both clock and watch) in their first fifty words, but only one had "crib," though we would assume the children had more experience of cribs than of clocks and watches. Of these eighteen children, six —exactly one-third—had "key" in the first fifty words, but not a single one had "table," yet tables are surely more frequent in young children's experience than keys are. How are we to account for the fact that shoes, socks, hats, clocks, and keys were much noticed and early named by these children, while many more frequently encountered items—diapers, cribs, tables—were not?

The work of the cognitive psychologist Piaget provides an answer. He describes a predictable sequence of stages in the cognitive growth of all children. The first of these, lasting roughly from birth to two years he calls the sensorimotor period. During this period a child builds an understanding of his world by acting upon things physically. The things of his environment *are* whatever he is able to *do* to them—some things are suckable, others biteable, others squeezeable. It is through the child's physical action upon the environment that his view of reality changes: He moves from perceiving reality as a continuousness of undifferentiated sights, smells, sounds, tastes, and tactile sensations impinging on his sense organs at birth, to perceiving reality as separate entities, actions, people in space.

Against this Piagetian background, the presence and absence of certain items in children's early vocabularies seems less surprising. What does the one-to two-year-old notice particularly? What he acts on physically. A child *acts on* hats, shoes, and socks, but a diaper is something that is *done to* him, in a sense; he "gets diapered." Clocks and watches make interesting noises (tick, clang, dong, cookoo), and keys can be grasped, jangled, shaken, and bitten, but what can a child do to a table or crib? Tables and cribs are just *there.* (I wonder what a child's notion of "table" or "crib" is anyway, since he is so small that he must be perceptually aware of only a portion of a table at any given time. If he is standing up, then "table" must be the table leg. If he is sitting in his highchair, then "table" must be a smooth surface—very different indeed from the leg. If he is standing beside his mother who is preparing food on the table, is the "table" what he sees as he looks up, the underneath portion perhaps? How does a child put these various visual perceptions of "table" together? To some extent, this is the problem the child must solve with any vocabulary item. What any lexical item represents is different at different times and in different situations. But perhaps a child can experience, physically and sensorily, a graspable key or hat or shoe as a totality, a single entity, in a way that he cannot experience table or crib, and this may make his understanding and naming of these items easier.)

The phrase "acts on" is Piaget's: The child in the sensorimotor period "acts on" his environment. Notice that this interpretation of the child's interaction with his world sees the child as active in his own learning and experiencing. The child does not sit passively while things in the environment happen to him, but rather he reaches out, grabs, kicks, bites, squeezes, sucks, shakes. The child is born to learn, it seems, and to learn in different ways at different times, depending on his changing cognitive structure. His way of learning during the sensorimotor period is by acting on his world physically. Out of his sensorimotor experience he formulates the concepts and understandings he names with his first words.

Nelson also noted in her study that thirteen of the eighteen children had the word "car" in their first fifty words. The properties of motion and change are important here. Young children notice objects that do things. What the child notices is the basis of his understanding, and what he understands is what he will express through language. Nelson concludes:

> Frequency of personal experience, exposure to words, strength of need or desire cannot apparently explain the selection of these words. They are personal, selective, and for the most part action related. It is apparent that children learn the names of the things they can act on, whether they are toys, shoes, scissors, money, keys, blankets, or bottles as well as things that act themselves such as dogs and cars. They do not learn the names of things in the house or outside that are simply "there," ... This general conclusion is of course in accord with cognitive theories (e.g., Piaget's) emphasizing the importance of the child's action to his definition of the world, but it implicates equally the importance of actions external to the child. Thus, the words the child learns reflect the child's mode of structuring the world. Their properties are those of high salience to the child exhibited either through his own interactions or through their apparent changes. (Katherine Nelson 1973, pp. 31–32)

Like Nelson, Brown (1973) is interested in accounting for the types of items children's early language does and does not include, and the order in which children acquire items of different types. It would be a reasonable hypothesis that a child would first learn those items which he hears most frequently. These would be grammatical morphemes like articles, "be" forms and endings on verbs and nouns. This hypothesis would be based on the assumption that the learner is a somewhat passive being whom the environment shapes and on whom it imprints language items. Since "the" and "be" are imprinted many times, they would become part of his language system early.

But, in fact, in all the language acquisition literature across the centuries, "the" and "be" forms (and comparable forms from languages other than English) have never been reported as children's first words. These are the very words that are conspicuously absent from one-word speech and from Stage 1 (two-word) speech. It turns out that there is no significant relationship between frequency—how often a child hears an item—and how early or late he acquires it. Clearly, a child must hear an item in order to figure it out and incorporate it into his developing system. But beyond some minimal level of exposure, frequency is unimportant. It is not how many times a child hears an item that is important but, rather, it is what he selects, notices, attends to, and uses— acts on—in his way that is important for his language growth.

Remember that one-word and two-word (Stage 1) speech are comprised mainly of heavy content words. When the child does begin to acquire grammatical morphemes, around Stage 2, he does so in a fairly predictable order. Brown and his colleagues have studied in depth the acquisition order in three children, from one-word speech, through Stage 1 and Stage 2, and Brown (1973) suggests some language features that apparently contribute to the salience of some morphemes for the young child. One such feature is "phonetic substance": Is the morpheme a full syllable, like "on" or "here" or is it part of a syllable like the /z/ of "Mommy's" or "doggies"? Is the morpheme one which is typically unstressed, e.g., articles as in "*the* big box," "*a* new one," "*some* soap"? Brown's work indicates that greater phonetic substance (full syllable, stressable) contributes to perceptual salience for the child.

The positions in which a morpheme can occur will also influence order of acquisition. Items occurring in final position gain a child's attention. We would expect morphemes which frequently occur in final position (for example, mine in "No, no, that's mine") to be acquired before those which generally occur initially in sentence segments ("the" or "a").

Children also seem geared to notice those items which play significant semantic or syntactic roles. A child will tend to acquire a morpheme which plays a major semantic role (pronouns which can be agents) before he acquires a morpheme which only modulates meaning (plural, or third person singular morphemes as in "goes"). And he will tend to acquire earlier those morphemes which play significant syntactic roles (subjects, verbs, objects, modifiers), than those which play lesser roles (auxiliary elements).

Morphemes vary considerably in the amount of new versus redundant information they carry. Pronouns carry more information than do third person singular verb endings, which are in fact highly redundant. In the sentence "He goes every week," the /z/ of "goes" indicates that the subject is third person singular, but that information is already present in the word "he." The third person singular morpheme is highly redundant, and children typically acquire such redundant forms later than more informative ones.

Morphemes also vary significantly in the changeableness of their form. Many grammatical morphemes change form depending on their context. The regular past tense morpheme will be /t/, /d/, or /əd/, depending on the final sound of the verb with which it combines. However, the progressive morpheme, -ing /ɪŋ/, is always added to the verb in just that form. Those morphemes which are more stable in form and are not conditioned by context, are earlier additions to the child's system.

Thus it appears that children notice and earlier incorporate forms which tend to have greater phonetic substance, which can occur in final position in utterances, which are semantically significant, which are syntactically significant, which are informative rather than redundant, and which are stable in form, whatever the context of their occurrence. These features, taken together, account very well for the acquisition order from one-word speech through Stage 1 (heavy content items) and Stage 2 speech (beginning of acquisition of grammatical morphemes). Children are guided not by the frequency of forms in their environment, but rather by their own strategies of noticing, by what has salience for their own active processing.

Early Acquisition Strategies.   In studying her group of one- to two-year-olds, Katherine Nelson (1973) focused on another aspect of children's early language learning that shows the child acting upon his environment for his own learning. She felt that she could, with some confidence, identify six different strategies the children in her study were using to learn their language, six different ways they were in a sense "acting on" the language data around them. Four of the strategies correlated with greater linguistic maturity at age two (according to her syntactic and vocabulary measures), and two of the strategies correlated with less linguistic maturity at age two, suggesting that different strategies are useful at different stages of development.

It is important to remember what a correlation is. It simply tells us that certain factors occurred together significantly more or less frequently than chance would predict. In Nelson's study the one factor was linguistic maturity at age two, and the other factor was the presence of a particular language learning strategy. Four of the strategies she identified were much in evidence in the children who, at age two, got higher scores in her linguistic maturity measures, and two of these strategies were very much in evidence in the children who, at age two, got lower scores in her tests of linguistic maturity. What correlations do not tell us anything about is cause-result relations. It is altogether possible that two factors occur together for quite other reasons than the study examines. Further, even if there were a cause-result relationship or one factor was influencing the other, a correlation would suggest nothing about the direction of influence—which factor was to some degree responsible for the presence of the other. The very most that correlations can do is suggest the *possibility* of the presence of *some sort* of relationship to be explored further. With these cautions in mind, let's look at the strategies Nelson observed.

Some of the children in her study preferred a "productive strategy," and some preferred a "comprehension strategy." That is, some of the children were producing language a lot, saying things, and getting feedback from others' responses to their productions. Some of the children produced less and seemed to be observing more, attending selectively, watching to see how meanings and verbal expressions related. Both comprehension and production strategies correlated with high linguistic maturity at age two.[2]

The excerpt below, from the conversation of a nineteen-month-old girl and her mother, demonstrates a production strategy at work:

> *C:* I sit down.
> *M:* Oh, you're sitting down?
> *C:* I sit down with cup. I sitting. I sit down.
> *M:* Uh-huh. You're sitting down there.
> *C:* Sit down there.
>
> *C:* Sit down?
> *M:* Yeah, you can sit down.
> *C:* (She sits down.) I sit down.
> *M:* Okay. You can sit down. Okay.
> *C:* Sit down on boat.
> *M:* Sit down on the boat.[3]

Another strategy that correlated positively with linguistic maturity at age two was a "questioning strategy." It is only a correlation, remember, but intuitively it is satisfying. If a child is working on figuring out the labels that go with objects in his environment (and this is clearly an important aspect of his language learning from age one to age two), then asking "What dis?" or "What dat?" would seem to be an efficient way of eliciting precisely the kind of data he needs to build and modify his hypotheses about what things are called.

Perhaps the most tentative of Nelson's observed strategies is what she calls "functional definition" of language, that she feels guided the child's attention. On the basis of proportion of words of different types in the children's early vocabularies, she felt she could distinguish two subgroups: (1) a "referential" group of children whose first fifty words included a high propor-

---

[2]These two strategies may remind you of different learning styles or preferences you have seen in children of other ages in other learning situations. Some children seem to "learn by doing," but many children we teach appear to prefer an observation strategy; they watch and put the pieces together in their heads. Teachers usually assume that the more overtly expressive child is brighter and the observer less so. Comments like "She's very quiet. *But* she's bright enough" are typical. "But" is the crucial word here—quiet *but* bright. We rarely hear teachers say, "Oh she's so quiet and bright." I know of no research that supports our tendency to assume that overtly expressive children are more intelligent than children geared toward observation. Without meaning to push Nelson's research too far, I would suggest that it supports the effectiveness of an active observation strategy in one important area of learning, that of learning a language. There is no reason to suppose that an active observation strategy is not an efficient strategy for other kinds of learning as well.

[3]I am indebted to Carole Urzúa for this example from her data.

tion of common nouns (object labels) and who seemed to view the primary function of language as naming objects; and (2) an "expressive" group of children whose first fifty words included proportionately more words used in social expressions ("stop it," "thank you") and fewer object names, and who, Nelson felt, saw language as serving a primarily social-affective function. At age two, the ten referential children in her study scored higher overall in the vocabulary measure, and the eight expressive children scored higher overall in the syntactic measure. It is important to remember that all the children's early vocabularies included items of various kinds. All that is involved here is the relative proportion—a sort of preference—for naming as opposed to expressive vocabulary items.

One factor that seemed to relate significantly to the course of linguistic growth of these children was whether or not the child's functional definition of language matched the mother's. Referential mothers of referential children, and expressive mothers of expressive children, provided language data consistent with their children's hypotheses, data that their children could use. If the child was working on the assumption that language was for naming things, it helped if his mother was providing lots of object labels; it was helpful to the child who was working on the assumption that language was for dealing with people if his mother was providing lots of social expressions. But where the mother's and child's views of language mismatched, the child seemed less able to use the data the mother provided. Nelson found instances of children of mismatched child-mother pairs remaining stationary in their language growth for a period, then apparently revising their functional definition of language by bringing it into line with mother's, and then proceeding, now able to use the language data mother was providing.

The referential/expressive distinction is admittedly somewhat tentative, but it does raise some interesting questions. Where would the child's early notion of the primary purpose of langauge come from? Wouldn't it be likely to come from the child's interaction with the mother? If so, how could mother's and child's functional definitions of language mismatch? Answers to these questions do not fall within the scope of Nelson's study, and to my knowledge subsequent studies have not dealt with them.

The two strategies Nelson identified which correlated with less linguistic maturity at age two were "imitation" and "repetition." Those children whose language production included a higher proportion of spontaneous imitation of adult utterances, and those whose productions included a higher proportion of repetitions of their own utterances (saying the same thing more and creating novel and diverse utterances less), attained lower vocabulary and syntactic measures at age two. As these are only correlations, it would be impossible to say either that imitative and repetitive strategies result in slower language learning, *or* that slower language learners use imitative and repetitive strategies. Nelson suggests that different strategies may be more or less useful at different points in children's growth.

Besides raising some interesting new questions, Nelson's work on strategies underscores two points made already: (1) by the time children are a year old, important aspects of a communication framework have been established, and (2) children go about the business of figuring out a language in their own active way, selectively attending to and acting upon the language data which surround them.

The Cognitive Base of Combinatory Speech

Moving from one-word to combinatory speech, we find Brown asking the question: What would the Stage 1 child have to understand about his world in order to express the meanings and relations of Stage 1 speech? What are the cognitive bases of Stage 1 speech?[4] Again Piaget's work provides a frame of reference that makes possible a rich, coherent, and persuasive interpretation.

Think back to Brown's three "major meanings" expressed in children's Stage 1 speech: nomination, recurrence, nonexistence. What must the child understand in order to express nomination: "this doll," "see house," "here baby." He must at least recognize that there are separate entities in space. At first it may seem strange to think that anyone ever has to learn this; the separateness of things seems so obvious to us. But remember, we are talking about a young child who, we assume, started out as a receiver of undifferentiated sensory stimulation. Only through his interaction with things in the environment does the child come to differentiate among things. This sense of separate-thing-ness is basic to his expression of nomination.

In order to name, the Stage 1 child must also realize that despite certain variations in an object, it remains the same thing. Whether Mommy is standing or sitting, talking or quietly reflecting, whether she is in the kitchen, in the bedroom, or in the car, she is still *Mommy,* one and the same entity. When the child applies the same name to various objects (for example, calling his toy plastic key, his father's car key in a key case, and his mother's key on a key chain, all "key"), he must have recognized some shared characterstic(s) as basic to them all, thus making them members of a category "key." He must have these basic understandings of a word before he is able to associate verbal labels with particular items. Nomination is no small accomplishment.

Where would the prerequisite understanding for naming come from if not from the child's experiences of physically acting on the people and objects in his environment? The notions of separateness of objects, and the significant

---

[4]The following discussion relies heavily on Brown (1973), especially pp. 198–200.

sameness of people and objects in different states and conditions are notions built through the child's sensorimotor experience.

What about recurrence—"more bye-bye," " 'nother raisin," "more noise"? In order to express this meaning, the child must understand that the situation which did exist but presently does not, can exist again. This is another notion that the child has built through his own repeated actions with things in his environment. The infant kicks the mobile in his crib. It moves, making interesting patterns and sounds. He kicks it again. The interesting patterns and sounds are repeated.

Brown reminds us of two apparent precursors of the language of nomination and recurrence. Piaget identifies two early "schemas" (action patterns) typically occurring around four to eight months. In the "recognition schema," the infant, in the presence of a particular object, moves his body in the way he typically acts on the object. For example, he sees the bottle, focuses on it, and begins sucking movements, or he sees his rattle and moves his arm in a shaking motion. It is as if the child provides a physical "label," through body movement, for an object which he recognizes as separate and distinct. The "recurrence schema" Piaget calls "making interesting sights last." Here the infant engages in some particular physical movement with the apparent intention of causing a pleasurable event to recur, as in the mobile example above.

When the child expresses nonexistence—"no more noise," "allgone egg," "allgone outside"—he demonstrates an ability to "anticipate based on signs." Looking at an empty plate and saying "allgone egg" makes sense precisely because there was good reason to suppose there would be an egg on the plate. Children make—express—sense in terms of the way the world is. The child has come to associate specific events with specific signs—eggs with plates, noise with wheels turning, outside with front doors, juice with cups— through his sensorimotor activity, his eating, drinking, turning wheels, opening and closing and going in and out through doors.

In expressing possession, the child acknowledges some sort of relationship or closeness between particular people and particular objects. As with his anticipation based on signs, the child is relating two different things that, in his experience, have regularly been associated in some way. While I find no basis for attributing to the child an understanding of the highly abstract notion of ownership, it does appear that the child has discerned a pattern: That particular chair has to do with Daddy ("Daddy chair"), that particular dress has to do with Mommy ("Mommy dress"), that particular nose has to do with the dog ("doggie nose").

A major cognitive understanding underlying the child's expressions of attributes of objects ("microphone hot," "animal book," "big ball"), is that objects have inherent properties: The object is not the property, but has the property. This seems a highly abstract notion. It is hard to think where it comes from, if not from the child's physical encounters with objects of various sizes, textures, temperatures, and types. The variety of experience is important here. It would be impossible for a child to recognize, and verbally signal, that a ball is "big" if he hadn't had experience of balls (and other objects) of different sizes. The child is able to identify a particular book as an "animal book" rather than some other sort of book, precisely because he has experience of books which are and which are not animal books but books of some other type.

Many of the Stage 1 child's sentences involve two terms (in order) of the agent-action-object relation. It would seem that a child who says "Kathryn stand up" (agent-action), "throw ball" (action-object), and "Kathryn ball" (agent-object meaning "Kathryn is throwing the ball") differentiates (1) between actions and entities, and (2) between entities which are agents and those which are "done to" or acted on. Again it is hard to really believe that one ever has to learn something so obvious as the fact that objects are separate from the actions involving them. But remember that, for the small child, things in the environment *are* what he *does* to them. This differentiation of actor and action is one that comes about through the child's increasingly varied physical interactions with an increasing range of objects and people. As he finds that he is able to grasp, bite, or kick a wide range of objects, grasping and biting and kicking must come to exist for him apart from the objects grasped and bitten and kicked, as well as apart from himself as the grasper and biter and kicker.

The notion of agent or causer which the child expresses in agent + action or agent + object sentences has a precursor in the child's physical expression. We often see very small children deliberately take their mother's hand and physically encourage her to do something for them—for example, to wind a toy that they themselves are unable to manage. This is clear indication of the child's recognition that people (mothers) are causers, can make events occur. The child's later verbal symbols "Mommy push" or "Kathryn throw" express this understanding in a new way.

And finally, the child's locational expressions attest to an understanding of events and things being in distinct locations in environmental space. The child's first two years involve much in the way of picking things up and putting them down—locating, dislocating, relocating objects in various places. Particularly interesting are the child's early "where" questions—"Where baby?" or "Where Mommy go?" At an earlier time, when a person or object was out of sight, it had simply ceased to exist for the baby. Dangle a watch in front of a small infant and then hide it behind you and the child will cry, for it is gone, nonexistent. But dangle the same watch in front of the same child a few months later and when you hide it behind you, he will crawl around behind you to find it. Now out of sight no longer means out of existence. It hasn't ceased to exist; it has simply been displaced, moved to a new location. This understanding of displacement that the baby demonstrates when he crawls around behind you looking for the watch, is expressed in verbal symbols when he asks, "Where clock?" or "Where clock go?" He knows the watch has not ceased to exist; it is simply in some other location out of sight, and the question is *where.*

In summary, language acquisition is clearly cognitive in its foundation. The Stage 1 child's language is deeply rooted in and dependent on his cognitive growth, the mental construction of reality that he has built through his sensorimotor experience.

> ... the [child's] first sentences express the construction of reality which is the terminal achievement of sensorimotor intelligence. (Brown 1973, p. 200)
> [Stage I relations can be viewed] as the linguistic expression of sensorimotor intelligence. (Dale 1976, pp. 24–25)

In chapter 6 we saw continuousness in the child's movement from one syntactic stage to another. Now we see continuousness in the child's movement from early physical expressions to verbal expressions of nomination, recurrence, agent-action, and location. It is as if the child has replaced one set of expressive symbols, physical ones, with another set of symbols, verbal ones. There is continuity in what is being expressed, and in the use of symbols to express. Yet the child's movement into verbal symbols represents a major advance in that his new symbol system is one which is potentially unlimited. So long as the child is dependent on the movement of his own body in relation to objects in his immediate environment, his expression must be limited to here and now. But as he grows in his understanding and in his ability to use verbal symbols to express his meanings, he moves into an expression system that will ultimately not constrain him in time or place. Perhaps it is our awareness of the greater power of linguistic symbols over prelinguistic, physical ones, that is the basis for our making a sharp distinction between "linguistic" and "prelinguistic" stages in children's growth ("Is Joey talking yet?" "Suzie's first word was————."), despite the fact that both represent continuous developmental expressions of similar kinds of meanings, and despite the fact that an important part of the child's expression will always be nonverbal, as it is for the adult.

I have dealt with the Stage 1 situation in depth, not because I expect everyone reading this book to be interested in two-year-olds, but rather because this rooting of language growth in cognitive growth has profound implications for any adult who works with children through elementary level. Language acquisition researchers have studied this cognitive base for language most at the very early level of development and thus we understand it best and can describe it more precisely at that level. But we know that one's real experience of the world—*whatever his age*—is the only possible basis for his developing language. We produce and interpret language in terms of our understanding of the meanings it conveys. That understanding is the sum of our experiencing in the world. As our understanding grows, so does the possibility of our producing and interpreting language more powerfully. One's continuing understanding of the world through his experiencing of it is the only basis for language growth.

The Cognitive Base
of Continuing Semantic Development

The same word often has different meaning for a child and an adult as in the following examples:

Grandmother is caring for her three-year-old grandson and finds crayon marks on the wall.

Grandmother: Oh, C———. Look at this! How did this get here?

C: I did it, Grammy.

Grandmother: You did that?

C: Yes, but it was a accident. I couldn't find a piece of paper.

Mother and her three-year-old daughter.

M: People are always telling you to "share," aren't they? What does "share" mean?

C: It means I get to play with somebody else's toys.

Yet we know that, over time, the child's meanings of "accident," "share," and other words become more like the adult's. How does this happen?

Looking at the semantic growth of children in the late sensorimotor period and beyond, we see again that children figure language out—make sound-meaning associations—in terms of their developing cognitive processes and understandings. One important source of information about the world, is the perceptual properties of objects: How does an object taste or smell? How does it feel when you touch it? How does it look? What is its size and shape? How does it sound? Eve Clark puts forward an interesting and persuasive perception-based hypothesis regarding the young child's semantic development (E. V. Clark 1973). She asks: How does a child associate a meaning with a pronounced sound string that he hears in particular contexts? Clark's hypothesis, called the Semantic Features Hypothesis, asserts that the child seizes on some particularly salient (to him) perceptual feature of the object in question (say, "doggie"), assumes that feature to be its "definition" (four-leggedness), and uses the term for objects possessing this defining feature (calling horses, sheep, cows, and dogs "doggie"). Upon receiving feedback about his use of the term ("No, honey, that's not a doggie. That's a kitty. Nice, soft kitty."), and learning more about other similar objects, he adds further semantic features to his original defining one that will differentiate among various objects possessing that original feature (features that will differentiate dogs from other four-legged animals).

We are assuming, as discussed earlier, that morphemes can be described as bundles of semantic features. Clark's hypothesis suggests that young children begin by "defining" a word in terms of a particular feature, and subsequently add further features to their "definitions." Thus, over time, children's use of words comes to match adults' use of the same words. Put another way, children's definitions eventually comprise the same bundles of semantic features that the adults' do. Note, however, that this match (near-match) happens over time; as children are developing their language, their words often do not mean what we think they mean.

Support for the Semantic Features Hypothesis comes from several sources. In diary studies, there are examples from many languages of children using a term to refer to items other than those the adult would use the term for. This is known as "overextension." The following examples show children using various perceptual characteristics of objects as the first defining semantic feature. (The examples are from English unless otherwise indicated.) Because the child's early use of the new term is based on a perceptual feature also available to adults, the child's category often overlaps with the adult's and thus

OVEREXTENSION RELATING TO	CHILD'S WORD	FIRST USED TO REFER TO	SUBSEQUENTLY USED TO REFER TO (I.E., OVEREXTENDED TO)
Shape	mooi	moon	cakes, round marks on windows and in books, tooling on leather book covers, postmarks (round), letter O
	kotibaiz	bars of crib	toy abacus, toast rack with parallel bars, picture of building with columns on facade
	tick-tock	watch	clocks, watches, gas meter, firehose wound on spool, bathroom scales with round dial
Size	fly	fly	specks of dirt, dust, all small insects, his own toes, crumbs of bread, small toad
	bébé (French)	baby	other babies, all small statues, figures in small pictures and prints
Movement	bird	sparrows	cows, dogs, cats, any animal moving
Sound	fafer (French)	sound of train (chemin de fer)	steaming coffee pot, anything that hissed or made a noise
Taste	cola (French)	chocolate	sugar, tarts, grapes, figs, peaches
Texture	va (Russian)	white plush dog	muffler, cat, father's fur coat

Based on E. V. Clark (1973, pp. 79–83; 1974, p. 112).

the adult often understands what object the child is referring to in a given situation.

The Semantic Features Hypothesis would predict this early overextension. Mother points to the full moon and says, "Oh, look at the moon. See the pretty moon." The child does see the moon, but what is it that makes a moon a "moon"? If the child assumes it is its roundness (that is, that its "definition" is [+ round]), then other round things will also be "moon"; the term "moon" will be overextended.

The Semantic Features Hypothesis also predicts that further features will be added to the child's definition as environmental feedback indicates that it is necessary to further differentiate between various objects which possess the original defining feature. Remember, the child is having new experiences and encountering new objects all the time, and these must be distinguished. Thus he must restructure his earlier overextended category.

> The present hypothesis claims that the child will gradually add more specific features to the word as new words are introduced to take over subparts of the semantic domain. The addition of other features to the word combined with the introduction of new words will require the further differentiation of quasi-synonyms, and a considerable restructuring of the semantic domains of overextensions. (Clark 1973, p. 84)

Clark offers the following example of overextension and restructuring, a tentative sequence in one semantic domain, based on composite evidence from several diary studies:

	WORD	SEMANTIC DOMAIN	POSSIBLE CRITERIAL FEATURE(S)
Stage I[a]	bow-wow	dog(s)	shape
Stage II	bow-wow	dogs, cows, horses, sheep, cats	shape
Stage III	(a) bow-wow	dogs, cats, horses, sheep	
	(b) moo	cows	sound (horns?)
Stage IV	(a) bow-wow	dogs, cats, sheep	
	(b) moo	cows	sound
	(c) gee-gee	horses	size (tail/mane?)
Stage V	(a) bow-wow/doggie	cats, dogs	size
	(b) moo	cows	
	(c) gee-gee/horsie	horses	
	(d) baa	sheep	sound
Stage VI	(a) doggie	dogs	
	(b) moo	cows	
	(c) gee-gee/horsie	horses	
	(d) baa lamb	sheep	
	(e) kitty	cats	shape, sound

[a] These stages are not related to Brown's stages.
  Clark (1973), p. 85.

So far we have dealt only with the child's acquisition of those words that have an ostensible referent, things we can point to. But we find overextension and restructuring in other areas of the child's semantic acquisition also. Researchers studying semantic acquisition of relational terms (Donaldson and Wales 1970; H. Clark 1970; Donaldson and Balfour 1968; E. V. Clark 1973; 1974) in children around three to five years old report that children go through a predictable stage of interpreting both polar points of a dimension as if they mean the greater one (for example, "less" and "more" are both interpreted as meaning "more"; "big" and "small" are both interpreted as meaning "big"; "tall" and "short" are both interpreted as meaning "tall," and so on with "long" and "short," "high" and "low," "fat" and "thin," "wide" and "narrow.") Notice that in adult usage, for each pair, one member is used as the name for the dimension, and in each case it is the member having the greatest extent. If we want to know the size of something, we ask "How *big* is it?" not "How small is it?" Or if we want to know the width of something, we ask "How *wide* is it?" not "How narrow is it?" Indeed, "width" (not "narrowth") is the name of the dimension. These are the "unmarked" terms, the terms that name the dimension in a neutral way, without suggesting that something is long or short, wide or narrow. And in telling the extent of something, we might say it is "three feet *long*" or "ten feet *high,*" but only in special cases (called contrastive or marked cases) would we say something was "three feet *short*" or "ten feet *low*" (for example, we might say this if we had established that something was too short or too low for a given purpose and then we might try to ascertain how much too short or how much too low it was for the specified goal).

The Semantic Features Hypothesis can account for the child's gradual movement from labeling both polar points on a dimension as the greater one, to labeling both extreme points differently. According to this hypothesis, children first learn the "unmarked" member of the pair, the term that also names the dimension. Thus "wide" and "tall" and "high" are perhaps entered into the child's lexicon as [+ extent] (having extent) and only later differentiated from their opposites by the addition of the features [+ polar], with the negative poles ("narrow," "short," "low") then defined as [− polar].

A similar situation obtains with "more" and "less." For a time, children interpret both as meaning more. Clark suggests that children first are defining "more" and "less" with the semantic feature of "having amount" ([+ amount]). Thus both "more" and "less" would form a category defined by having amount.

... where extent is the best exemplar of amount, the child's entry for *more* has added to it the feature [+ Polar]; but since the child knows that *less* also "means" [+ Amount], he will assume it too contains the feature [+ Polar]. Finally, in the last stage of the acquisition of these meanings, the child learns that *less* refers to the other end of the scale, and thus contrasts in meaning with *more: less* is [– Polar]. (Clark 1973, p. 91)

Kindergarten and first grade teachers are well aware that their children are more successful in math with questions about "more than" than they are with questions about "less than" or "fewer" ("Which set has more/fewer? Show me the set that has more/fewer than this set. Can you find the set that has two more/fewer members than this set?") Many children of this age are still developing the meanings of these terms.

Notice that the child's early focus on the greater extent or amount is consistent with children's performances on Piagetian conservation tasks. Three- to five-year-olds focus on water that rises higher in a narrower glass, objects that extend further in a strung out row, clay which is extended in a hot dog shape. Children seem to be perceptually oriented toward noticing greater extension. It is not surprising that their learning of some aspect of their language, semantics in this case, will use and reflect their cognitive orientation —their ways of noticing things in their world.

In a study Clark did with four-year-olds, on opposites, she found children overextending in another way. Her subjects interpreted "big" as the opposite of "small, short, thin, low, young, and shallow . . ." and "small" or "little" as the opposite of "big, high, tall, long, wide, thick, and old" (Clark 1973, p. 92).

. . . these data provide considerable evidence that the pair *big-small* is overextended to cover the domain of the other more specialized dimensional terms such as tall-short, high-low, wide-narrow, long-short. . . . (p. 94)

Perhaps "big" is first extended to cover all the dimensions of greater extent since it is the most general; i.e., it requires the fewest semantic features to define it. The features [+ Dimension] and [+ Polar] will do for "big" as well as for "long," "tall," etc. It is only with the inclusion of further features (such as [+ Vertical], [– Vertical]) that "tall" and "long" become differentiated out from "big."

Children's developing understanding of the terms "same"/"different" and "before"/"after" have also been studied. Whether asked to give the experimenter an object from an array of familiar objects that was the same or one that was different from a particular object, young children would select an object that was the same. In other words, they interpreted both same and different as meaning same (Clark 1973, p. 91). With the terms before and after, young children have been observed to move through a predictable sequence of stages: (1) not understanding either term but assuming that the first event mentioned was the first to occur, (2) later interpreting before to mean both before and after, and (3) interpreting the two as opposites.[5] One cannot help but wonder whether teachers of kindergarten and first grade children might do well not to assume that their children have adult meanings for those terms so basic to our trade: Show me the set that has *less (fewer)*. How many *less (fewer)* does this set have than this set? Can you find one that is *different* from this? How is it *different*? What did the second Billy Goat do *before (after)* he met the Troll?

What is particularly important for us here is that we see, once again, the young child actively involved in figuring out language for himself, and doing so by systematically using the cognitive strategies available to him, strategies that serve him well in figuring out other aspects of his world as well. We see him using sensory information to the full, and making hypotheses about word meanings based on his organization of sensory input. We see him applying his hypotheses as he uses his new words in various contexts, and ultimately revising his definitions and subsequent use of words by making his definitions more precise, adding further semantic features to his originals in order to differentiate more accurately among objects. He is the active party in his own learning; he is the hypothesis maker, tester, reviser; he works always within a given cognitive structure and always within an interactive environment.

Children as Active Processors

The Role of Reinforcement, Practice, and Imitation.   Ervin-Tripp and Miller early noted a phenomenon, "overgeneralization," in the child's acquisition of inflections (past tense, plural) which is perhaps analogous to the semantic "overextension" noted by Clark (Ervin 1964). Their observations deal with the child's acquisition of irregular past tense forms and irregular plural forms. They collected frequent texts from seven children from the time they were two until they were four. During this time the children all regularized the plural of "man" ("man," "mans") and "foot" ("foot," "foots" or occasionally "feet," "feets"). That is, they overgeneralized the regular formation of plural to these irregular forms. But the developmental course of irregular past tense verb forms was especially interesting. The children first used the adult forms ("came," "went") and later abandoned these for the regularized, overgeneralized forms ("comed," "goed"). Finally the children moved to the adult forms for these irregulars ("came," "went"). But the interesting question is, how can we account for this very predictable pattern (observed in many children since

[5]For discussion of children's interpretations of "ask" and "tell" and of "brother" and "sister," see Clark (1973), pp. 96–98 and 98–101.

Ervin-Tripp and Miller's original study) of the child originally using the adult irregular verb tense forms which he hears all around him, and then dropping these forms—which he continues to hear—for the regularized forms which the adults around him do not use. Apparently in his earliest use of irregular forms, the child has not analyzed the verbs into action + tense. They are for him simple unitary names for actions.[6] But as the child is exposed to and perceives a regular pattern for expression of past, he overgeneralizes the observed pattern to forms where the adult does not use it.[7] The importance of this fact of language acquisition cannot be overstressed, for several reasons. First, it flies in the face of the notion that children learn adult syntactic forms because they are positively reinforced for using them, and they stop using nonadult forms because they are negatively reinforced for their use. Children are not negatively reinforced for saying "came" and "went" and positively reinforced for saying "comed" and "goed." And yet this is the direction in which they quite predictably move at one stage in their development. Second, this fact causes us to question the importance of practice of particular forms. The behaviorist view assumes that more practiced forms become more firmly entrenched speech habits. But here we see a pattern of development repeated in child after child, in which the earlier "practiced" forms drop out to be replaced by forms totally novel to the child's experience. Third, this finding raises questions about the central role often attributed to imitation in children's acquisition of a language. The question of the role of imitation in language acquisition is a very complex one. We know young children do sometimes imitate what adults say—slang expressions, exaggerated intonation patterns, particular words, social formulas. And we know that children certainly do end up speaking the language of their own community rather than some other. This must be imitation in some general sense. But imitation in the sense of repeating exactly what the adults around him say seems unimportant as a process which advances the child's syntax to a more adult level.[8] In the case of overgeneralization, the child is creating new forms according to his own developing rule system, not imitating the forms he hears around him. His creations are often utterances that adults do not produce. Rather than reinforcement, practice, or imitation, the process which is very much in evidence in the child's overgeneralization is that of

[6]Notice the irregular verbs are those that occur most frequently in the child's environment.
[7]In their data, Ervin and Miller found the children using overgeneralized past tense forms before they produced more than a few (if any) regular past tense forms (like "walked," "waved," "departed"). It appears that children are highly sensitive to patterns. Though most of the verb forms they hear are the frequent irregulars, they quickly discern and use a regular pattern after limited encounter with it (Ervin 1964).
[8]For an examination of the charges against imitation playing a significant role in language acquisition, and a suggestion of some ways in which imitation may make a significant contribution, see Ruth Clark (1977).

seeking, finding, and using patterns. The little linguist, the hypothesis maker, is at work.

It may be difficult for adults to see the child's move from "went" to "goed" as a developmental advance. But clearly it is. The child's early unanalyzed action word "went" becomes a complex morpheme of action + past, expressed as "go" + /d/. And it is powerful evidence of the child evolving a creative underlying rule system rather than committing to memory a list of specific forms.

Studies of sentence repetition in children cast further doubt on direct imitation as an effective strategy for advancing a child's language complexity. Sentence repetition studies have been of two types: (1) observations of children repeating utterances they hear in naturalistic settings (spontaneous imitation), and (2) observations of children repeating carefully designed sentences presented by a model in a structured situation (elicited imitation). In the naturalistic situation it has been observed that children don't imitate sentences that are beyond the complexity of the sentences they create and use on their own (Ervin 1964; Brown and Bellugi 1964). When a child spontaneously repeats a sentence, it will typically be of a type he would produce on his own. In the elicited imitation situation, children reformulate (rather than repeat) the input sentence according to their own language system, if it is beyond the bounds of their rule system. Thus their imitation may omit elements or reorganize elements, though it will generally retain the input order of elements. Children apparently imitate primarily those structures which are accounted for by the underlying rule system they already possess. If young children do not imitate sentences involving structures more complex than those they have already acquired, it goes without saying that their rule system is not advanced by simple imitation. In general, in spontaneous and in elicited repetition situations they imitate what they already control the rules for; they tend not to imitate structures involving rules beyond those within their control, but rather reformulate such sentences to conform to their current rule system.[9]

Slobin and Welsh raise a further argument against the importance of imitation in language acquisition—this one having to do with what it is the child is imitating and what it is the child is acquiring.

> Imitation probably is not an important device in language acquisition, because the aspects of language which the child must acquire are not available to be imitated: He is exposed only to surface structures of sentences, but what he must acquire are deep structures and the transformational rules which relate deep and surface structures. (Slobin and Welsh 1973, pp. 485–86)

[9]Elinor Keenan (1977) has, with justification, taken strong exception to the equating of repetition and imitation in this line of research. She maintains that in natural situations, children's repetitions may serve many communicative purposes other than imitation.

Since children predominantly imitate only those structures which their underlying rule systems account for, Slobin and Welsh assume that elicited imitation might be a technique which would provide insight into the rule system the child controls. Working with the two-year-old they call "Echo" (mentioned earlier), Slobin and Welsh found that if she understood a model sentence, she would often "repeat" the model sentence according to her own syntax. She would process the meaning, and then give it back according to her own rule system:

Model: The pencil is green.

Repetition: pencil green (p. 487)

Model: The little boy is eating some pink ice cream.

Repetition: little boy eating some pink ice cream. (p. 487)

Model: This one is the giant, but this one is little.

Repetition: dis one little, annat one big (p. 490)

Model: The man who I saw yesterday got wet.

Repetition: I saw the man and he got wet.

Model: The man who I saw yesterday runs fast.

Repetition: I saw the man and he run fast (p. 494)

This elicited repetition technique offers possibilities for finding out what kind of rule system a child has at a given point. Interestingly, it appears that through elicited imitation, we may learn more about the child's language than the child learns about ours.[10] The child as active language processor and hypothesis builder is a more powerful explanation of language acquisition than the child as imitator.

Operating Principles.   Slobin's work on operating principles supports the notion of children as active noticers and users of patterns in language acquisition. Slobin and his students have vigorously collected their own data and have intensively studied data collected by others on first language acquisition in more than forty different languages including Greek, Hindi, Hungarian, Turkish, Japanese, Finnish, Czech, Russian, Navaho, Samoan, Italian, Serbo-Croatian, Swedish (Slobin 1973, pp. 177–79). Slobin looks for commonalities in the way children learn language across widely diverse languages. His assumption is that the commonalities will be a function of children's language

---

[10]Remember too the difficulty children have in imitating corrections of their utterances. "Nobody don't likes me" and "other one spoon" were very resistant to change in a situation very like elicited imitation in which the parent provided a model for the child to repeat. (In listening to adults interact with young children in natural situations, one often has the impression that adults imitate children more than children imitate adults.)

acquisition strategies—their mental processing—rather than a function of the particular language being acquired. If children acquiring languages which are so very different are proceeding in very similar ways in the language learning task, Slobin assumes that in these learning similarities we may be tapping those "process mechanism(s) . . . set(s) of procedures and inference rules . . . that children use . . . to process linguistic data" (Slobin 1966, pp. 87–88). He cites a number of commonalities observed and, based on these, posits some operating principles, "a sort of general heuristic . . . which the child brings to bear on the task of organizing and storing language" (Slobin 1973, p. 191).

For example, prefixes tend to be acquired later than suffixes. Children learning a language which expresses a particular meaning (such as location) as a suffix, control this linguistic feature earlier than do children learning a language in which this same meaning is expressed as a prefix. This is one bit of evidence supporting Slobin's suggested operating principle (or child's self-instruction) "Pay attention to the ends of words" (1973, p. 191).[11] Another operating principle, "Pay attention to the order of words and morphemes" (p. 197), is suggested by the fact that children, whatever language they are learning, typically preserve the order of the input language. They may leave out items the adult would include, but those items children do include in their speech at any given point tend to be in the order the adult language would require.

Several of Slobin's suggested operating principles are stated in avoidance terms—"Avoid rearrangements" and "Avoid exceptions." We have already seen examples of avoiding rearrangements in those early information questions English-speaking children ask: "Where *you are* going?" "Why *he is* doing that?" And the avoidance of exceptions principle would account for the over-generalizations applied to irregular verbs and plurals, noted earlier—the "comed," "goed," "foots," and "mans" cases which are so typical. Another interesting operating principle Slobin suggests is "Underlying semantic relations should be marked overtly and clearly" (p. 202). That is, the child seems to proceed on the assumption that if there is a particular meaning, it will find a particular expression in the surface structure. The English-speaking child's early forms like "putted" and "sheeps" suggest the use of such a principle. In the adult language, we have a surface form "put" which doesn't indicate past, and a surface form "sheep" which does not indicate plural. But the young child seems to assume that if the meaning of past is intended, then it should be clearly indicated in the surface structure, thus "putted"; and if the meaning of plural is intended, then it should be clearly indicated in the surface structure, thus "sheeps."

[11]This discussion is simplified from Slobin's (1973) article, "Cognitive Prerequisites to the Development of Grammar." For more extensive development of the procedure, supporting data, and complete set of proposed operating principles, see the article itself.

Slobin suggests more operating principles and offers more support than I have indicated here. But this should suffice to indicate that children (universally, it appears) go about the task of language acquisition using similar mental processing schemes. They are especially geared to noticing certain aspects of the input language data (order of parts, general patterns), and to utilizing the information they perceive in predictable ways in building their language system.

Notice again the close interaction of language and cognition. Are these operating principles cognitive strategies or linguistic strategies? Of course they are both: cognitive strategies employed in the acquisition of a language system. One thing that makes Slobin's work persuasive is that it draws on a broad and rich data base, namely, observations of children acquiring more than forty different languages, many of them totally unrelated. Is this "mentalistic study" (an accusation sometimes made about language research)? Yes, in the sense that it makes tentative statements about mental processes that may be operating in language acquisition. But it does so based on the solid intensive and extensive observation of real children's actual behavior, what children *do* and *say* as they learn language.

The Interaction of Linguistic and Cognitive Complexity. Slobin suggests that order of acquisition will reflect the influence of both cognitive and linguistic complexity. Children express the "semantic intentions" or meanings of which they are capable, those which they understand. As some understandings are cognitively simpler, we would expect them to be expressed earlier in children's speech. In English, for example, the syntactic form of the following questions is the same and thus linguistically they are all equally complex:

Where did you go?
Why did you go?
When did you go?

But, as we know, children typically ask (some form of) where questions before they ask when or why questions. This order is cognitively influenced. The sensorimotor child lives in a concrete, spatially oriented world, an environment of things in places. His earliest understandings include location. Why questions involve causal relations between events. This is an understanding which is cognitively more difficult than an understanding of location and, not surprisingly, these questions typically come later than where questions. Later still come when questions, requiring some grasp of abstract and elusive time concepts. Understanding of time concepts develops later than understanding of location and simple causality, and so of course their expression (as when questions) comes later also.

But in some instances it is linguistic complexity rather than cognitive complexity that accounts for acquisition order. Studying young bilingual children's acquisition of their two languages, Slobin finds cases in which children express a given meaning, such as location, in one language but not in the other. Clearly they understand the concept involved, or could not express it in either language. Looking at the languages in question, Slobin finds the syntactic devices for expressing that notion to be simpler in the one language than in the other. Thus children master expression of location earlier in the language in which such expression is syntactically simpler, and later in the language in which expression of location is syntactically more complex.

We have already discussed the continuity across Brown's syntactic stages, and also from prelinguistic to linguistic expression. But Slobin adds to this notion of the continuousness of language development: *"New forms first express old functions, and new functions are first expressed by old forms"* (1973, p. 184). It is a sentence that takes some thinking about, but it is an important idea well worth the effort. By "functions" Slobin means something like "understandings," and by "old forms," he means forms which are already within the child's repertoire. This sentence might be paraphrased as "The child will first use a new structure to express an already familiar meaning; and he will express new meanings first by using already familiar structures." Either a new form or a new meaning, but not both. The child moves steadily, incorporating something new within a framework that is familiar. A child might first express the notion of juice being in the cup by saying "juice cup." Later, the same child might express this as "juice *in* cup." This expression is a "new form" expressing an "old function" (understood meaning). A humorous example of the reverse—a new meaning first being expressed by the forms already within the child's control, comes from Slobin's three-year-old daughter: " 'Anything is not to break—just glasses and plates' " (1973, p. 186). She had come to a new and rather complex idea, something like "Nothing is breakable except glasses and plates." Lacking this complex expression for her new idea, she did the best she could with what she had. She used the language forms already within her control to express this new notion.

Functional Need ("Communication Pressure") Hypothesis.

It is often asserted that children learn a language because they need to be understood in their communication with others in order to have their needs and desires met. It is claimed that this need is what propels a child to the mastery of a language.

It is certainly true that a well-developed language system provides an effective base for communicating one's needs and desires. Brown points out the need for a child's language to become "more widely adapted" as he moves into situations involving more interaction with those outside of his home (for example, when he goes off to nursery school) (Brown, 1973 p. 245). However, in view of the following, it appears that this functional need argument as an explanation of the child's acquisition of a language has been overstressed: (1)

a child's early communication of cries and coos or one- and two-word sentences is very effective for getting his wants and needs met. Why, then, would he bother to develop a more complex system? Dale gives this example:

> My son Jonathan at age twenty-six months requested the repetition of some favored activity by saying *'gain,* with a characteristic rising intonation; at age thirty-one months he said *Do that again, Dad.* The latter sentence is far more complex linguistically but no more effective. (Dale 1976, p. 141)

(2) All children develop a language system which is far more complex than the meeting of needs and desires would require. All children develop complex syntactic transformations and diverse vocabulary, when simple sentences and limited vocabulary would suffice for the fulfillment of needs. Why develop a vocabulary that includes "big," "huge," "enormous," "gigantic," "horrendous," "fat," "tall," when "big" would do? Why develop a syntactic system that generates "I want that ice cream that is yellowish white with the little crunchy bits in it," when you can get the same ice cream by saying much more simply, "I want ice cream. It is light yellow. It has bits in it. The bits are crunchy"?

(3) Children differ in their needs and desires and in how ready and able the adults in their environment are to meet them. Yet *all* children develop this very complex language system. These facts mitigate against this functional need hypothesis as accounting for the fact that children acquire language, and it certainly gives no clues at all as to how they do it.

So where does all this leave us? Back where we started, perhaps, with a human being born to do this thing called acquiring a language. He is a being in possession of powerful species-related, cognitive abilities for processing linguistic symbols (input data) so as to derive underlying structure. We see a child in a natural environment actively using these powerful abilities which are his in a highly creative way.

THE ENVIRONMENT

Four General Principles

Many people who regularly interact with children (parents, teachers, caregivers) want to know what is the very best kind of environment we can provide for children's language to grow in. We look to language acquisition research to suggest some possible answers. And indeed, recent research in this area is exciting and suggestive. But there are as yet no firm answers and certainly no simple ones. It would be naive to hope for any at this point, given (1) the fact that systematic study of environmental aspects and attempts to relate them to aspects of children's developing language are still fairly young; (2) the fact that virtually all children acquire a language, whatever their environment, so long as that environment includes language (on what basis do we say that such-and-such is an important factor in a child's language learning environment when we know that children whose environments do not include that factor do, in fact, acquire a language?); and (3) the overwhelming complexity of language, of children, of learning, of the environment, and the even greater complexity of relations among them. Perhaps one of the major contributions of studies of environments in which children acquire language has been to raise better questions which in turn give rise to more focused study.

Researchers have observed children's home environments and have described some important aspects of the situations and types of interactions they have found there. A picture is emerging from this research of an environment which shapes to, responds to, and interacts with (rather than directs) the language acquiring child. Nelson's work with one- to two-year-olds contributes to this picture.

Nelson (1973) investigated the following aspects of her eighteen subjects' home environments, and established significant correlations for each aspect with at least one of her various measures of language growth.

ASPECTS OF THE PHYSICAL ENVIRONMENT

———1. amount of time the child spent daily watching TV

———2. number of outings per week

———3. amount of time spent with other children

———4. number of adults the child saw during the week

ASPECTS OF VERBAL ENVIRONMENT WITH MOTHER

———5. acceptance by mother of child's language as meaningful

———6. rejection by mother of child's language as difficult or impossible to understand

———7. more directive pattern of interaction—high use of directives by mother

———8. less directive pattern of interaction—higher use of questions by mother

Which of these features would you expect to correlate with greater language growth (+) and which with lesser language growth (−)? Space has been left beside each item for you to make your + and − guesses before going on to a discussion of Nelson's correlations. Why would you expect these + and − correlations?

Briefly and simply stated, Nelson got significant positive correlations between one or more language maturity measures and the following environmental factors that she looked at: (1) number of outings per week (the children in her sample who had more outings per week scored significantly higher on some linguistic maturity measure); (2) number of adults in the child's environment (the more, the better); (3) mother's acceptance of her child's communications as meaningful, whatever their form; and (4) less directive maternal pattern of interaction. The remaining items—amount of TV watching time (the more, the worse), amount of time spent with other children (the more, the worse), mother's rejection of inadequate forms of expression as not conveying meaning, and the more directive interaction style (including a high use of commands by the mother)—significantly correlated with lower scores for these young children on some of Nelson's language measures.

Two cautions are in order here. First, what we have are only correlations, and correlations do not suggest causal relations. At best they suggest areas for further study. Second, Nelson herself is the first to caution that many specifics can not be generalized across time. She points out that it is likely that different strategies for acquiring language and, by extension, different environmental factors for the child to use in his learning, will be appropriate to different stages of his growth. Such caution statements are frequent in her work. For example, talking of the child's preferred learning strategies, she says:

> . . . it might be proposed that repetition . . . is an accommodative strategy . . . appropriate at a point where language acquisition has begun but is not advanced. (p. 54)

And discussing the high rate of mother questions in interaction with her baby, she says that:

> . . . a high rate of mother questions was positively related to comprehension at twenty months but not earlier. Thus, a single variable may have different effects at different stages. (p. 71)

Thus, it would be absurd to use this research as a basis for a decision to keep all preschool children away from other children and away from TV for (1) these specifics may not be generalizable across various stages in the child's language growth, and (2) the basis is only correlation, not cause.

The real importance of Nelson's correlations is in the support they lend to several general principles relating to children's environments, principles which find further support in other research as well.

1. *Environmental features which match the child's ways of learning about his world are helpful.* This principle would render the negative TV correlation unsurprising. The children in Nelson's study were between one and two and a half and deeply into the sensorimotor period. If the sensorimotor child's way of learning is by exploring and altering things in his world by manipulating

them—acting on them physically—would we expect TV to offer the stuff of his learning? Remember, the child's language is rooted in the understanding he is building through his active experiencing. It may be that types of experiencing other than TV watching are more appropriate, more "what he's into" in his ways of learning at this early time.

Another of Nelson's correlations that may relate to principle 1 is the directiveness of the mother. Compare the mothers' directiveness in episodes 2 and 3 in chapter 6. It is easy enough to see which mother takes a more directive role, including a high use of commands, and which mother follows the child's lead and asks questions more than she gives commands. Given that the child's approach to learning is an active one, we would expect that the child in the less directive environment would have the room he needs for actively observing, exploring, hypothesizing in his own way. In Nelson's words:

> . . . the effect of this characteristic [maternal directiveness] is to restrict the child's concept formation by substituting the mother's concept selection for his own. (1973, p. 84)

> . . . mothers who are highly directive interfere with the process of vocabulary building, a process that is facilitated by the child's orientation to objects and their names. (p. 86)

> The . . . directive factor analyzed in mother talk was the factor most consistently—and negatively—correlated with positive characteristics of child talk and maturity of child language. This factor was interpreted as one which imposed the mother's views and expectations and prevented the child from effectively formulating and naming his own concepts. (p. 94)

An environment which encourages the child to "do his thing," namely to actively explore and observe and manipulate so as to formulate his own concepts and name them, this environment would seem to match the child's early ways of learning.

2. *Environmental features which are responsive to the child and which shape to him in interaction are helpful.* Again one wonders about Nelson's TV finding. TV programs do not respond to what children do and say; people do. It has been suggested that hearing children of deaf parents might learn language by watching TV. But Ervin-Tripp (1971) finds that this does not happen. Why not? TV can provide a tremendous amount of exposure to language. So what is lacking here? Precisely the back and forth initiation and response, the reciprocity that is the core of the communication cycle.

Nelson suggests that the correlation between spending more time with other children, and a slower rate of language acquisition lends "support to the idea that other children are poor language models" (p. 62). This may be the case. However, it may also be the case that agemates are less able to respond to and shape to the young child, less able to understand and accept his communication as meaningful, less able to interact with him meaningfully than are adults and older children. It may be the interaction abilities rather than the "poor language model" that are important here.

This environmental feature of amount of time spent with other children appears to be one that, while not correlating with strong language acquisition in Nelson's very young subjects, might be expected to correlate with strong language growth at a later stage. It remains for future research to deal with this question. But it seems likely that, as the child at age three or four moves out into the world more, perhaps heading for nursery school, the new demands placed on him to interact with a wider range of people, including many more children, will encourage him to expand his language into a more widely adapted instrument for communication. Mother, after all, understands just about everything, including his grunts, whines, and wails. But other children do not. Increased contact with other children *after* he has built himself a basic beginning language system may contribute to his widening that system for more extensive communication.

The more/less directive dimension makes sense in terms of this responsiveness principle (as well as in terms of the first principle, learning style match).

> ... the most salient relationships between mother and child speech are those involving the mother's active role in directing the child's behavior, which has a negative impact, and of responding to his verbal behavior, which has a positive impact. (p. 93)

Again, C3's mother provides a vivid example of a parent responding to her child's verbal behavior.

3. *Environmental features which focus on meaning rather than on form are helpful.* The accepting/rejecting dimension of Nelson's correlations may relate to this principle. The terms "accepting" and "rejecting" are so emotionally loaded that it is important to clarify them as used by Nelson. She is not talking here about acceptance or rejection of the child per se, but rather about acceptance or nonacceptance of his language as meaning conveying. Two of Nelson's short examples help to make the accepting/rejecting contrast clear. Here is an example of an acceptance pattern:

> *Mother:* Jane. Here's a bottle. Where's the bottle? Here's a bottle.
> *Jane:* Wah wah.
> *Mother:* Bottle.
> *Jane:* Bah bah.
> *Mother:* Bah bah.
> *Jane:* Bah bah.

Mother: Oh, bah bah. Here's a ball.

Jane: Baw.

Mother: Ball. Yes.

Jane: Uh. Uh boo?

Mother: Ball.

. . .

Mother: Is that a car?

Jane: Bah.

Mother: Yes, car. Here's another car.

Jane: Gah.

Mother: Car, yes.

Jane: Bah. Daddy.

Mother: Daddy. Daddy's car is all gone (pp. 104-5).

And here is an example of a rejecting pattern:

Paul: Go.

Mother: What? Feel.

Paul: Fe.

Mother: What's that? A dog. What does the dog say? One page at a time. Oh, that one over there. What's that one there?

Paul: Boah.

Mother: What? You know that.

Paul: Bah.

Mother: What?

Paul: Ah wah.

Mother: What?

Paul: Caw.

Mother: Car?

Paul: Caw, awh.

Mother: Little kitty, you know that. (pp. 105–6)

Paul's mother seems to be saying "If you want me to understand you then you're going to have to talk more like I do." But the message that Jane's mother seems to be giving is "We're communicating through these noises we make back and forth and we've got a good thing going. Let's keep it up." (It would be hard to be more accepting of the child's language than to abandon your own adult language and use the child's instead, as Jane's mother does with her "bah bah.") This kind of adult response appears to be an encouragement to language.

The most striking example I know of this acceptance of the young child's language as meaningful came in the form of an informal conversation I had recently with an English professor from the University of Texas. Powerful, effective, expressive language is his trade. He is an English professor; he is also a father. Our conversation centered on the remarkable early language accomplishments of his now twenty-year-old daughter, accomplishments he recalled with fondness and pride.

"Why, she was talking in complete sentences by the time she was ten months old!" he told me.

Now this English professor probably views "complete sentences" as utterances that include articles (like "the," "a"), various forms of "be," auxiliaries (like "can" and "do"), inflections like past tense and plural endings, as well as heavier content items like nouns, verbs, adjectives, and adverbs. Descriptions of early and rapid language learners exist in language acquisition literature. However, we have yet to find a ten-month-old who was talking in utterances including articles, auxiliaries, various forms of "be." It is unlikely that his daughter is the first. But the professor's remark is important not because of what it tells us about his daughter, but because of what it tells us about him. He did what many parents apparently do. He heard through his daughter's expression to the meaning he felt she intended. Within the context of their interaction, both he and his daughter focused on meaning. The supportive interaction cycle, plus the immediate situation, plus the child's nonverbal gestures and expressive signs, plus the child's verbalizations equaled a totality of meaning which he remembers as "talking in complete sentences."

This father is typical of the many parents who assume their children *mean* when they verbalize, and who respond to their children's verbalizations as if they convey meaning. Suzie says "abah" and mother or father tells the researcher, "That's Suzie's word for juice," or baby howls and mother explains, "That's the way he cries when he is hungry." We cannot know for sure how this meaning focus of parents' interaction with their young children contributes to their language development. But we assume that it does contribute and that it reinforces what children already seem to know at a tender age: that language interaction is primarily a matter of sharing meanings, not a matter of exchanging forms. It is interesting that many adults who focus on meaning in their interactions with one- and two-year-olds, focus primarily on form in their interactions with the same children five or six years later, though the children still understand language to be a meaning-based business.

> *Child:* Me and Johnny went . . .
> *Adult* What? You mean "Johnny and I went . . . " Where did you go?
> *Child:* Oh, nuthin'.

4. *Environmental features which provide for variety and diversity in nonverbal and verbal areas (exposure and interaction) are helpful.* The positive

correlations in Nelson's study between number of outings and number of adults in the child's environment may relate to this principle. If the child's language is rooted in his own experiencing, then we would expect that the wider the range of experiences he has, the richer will be the meanings that will find verbal expression. A greater number of outings would seem to contribute to this richer experiential—and language—base. Further, if a wider range of adults interacts with the child, we would assume that the child is being exposed to and interacted with via a wider range of expression possibilities. If he is involved in building hypotheses about sound-meaning relations based on the language "data base" of his exposure and interaction, then we would expect that exposure and interaction involving a wider "data base" will result in the building of more powerful hypotheses that will take that diversity into account. It is interesting to note that the children of working mothers in Nelson's study, those children who spent substantial time with other adult caregivers, made greater gains than the children of nonworking mothers (p. 60). It is a reasonable assumption that more limited exposure and interaction will result in the building of narrower hypotheses, while more diverse exposure and interaction will result in the building of more encompassing hypotheses.

These four suggested principles are of course tentative, but they do receive support from some other research. The principle of diversity in the verbal environment is supported by an interesting early study done by Cazden (discussed in Cazden 1972). Her subjects were twelve black children, ranging in age from twenty-eight to thirty-eight months. The children all attended a day care center eight to ten hours a day where the child-adult ratio was thirty to one. Cazden reasoned that if one evaluated these children's language and then gave them a heavy dose of a particular type of intervention, one could assume that the differences in the children's language before and after the intervention were attributable, at least in part, to the intervention strategy used. She divided the children into three groups, four children in a group: two experimental groups (an "expansion group" and an "extension group") and a control group. The children in the groups were comparable in age, talkativeness, and MLU. In a playroom for forty minutes a day for twelve weeks (a heavy dose), an adult interacted with each individual child in the two experimental groups in a specified way. In interacting with each of the four children who comprised the "expansion group," the adult would provide the adult form for everything the child said in his developmental form. For example, if the child said "Dog bark," the adult would say "Yes, the dog is barking." In interacting with the four children in the "extension group," the adult would deliberately *not* "repeat" (in the adult form) what the child had said, but rather would meet the child's idea with a relevant, but different, idea. For example, if the child said "Dog bark," the adult might answer "Yes, but he won't bite" or "I guess he's mad at the kitty" (Cazden 1972, p. 125). The four children in the control group received no special treatment, but were familiar with the adult experimenters and the playroom, and played there from time to time. The language of all twelve children was evaluated before and after the twelve-week session, so it was assumed that if greater gains were made during that time by the children in one of the experimental groups over the children in the control group, then the particular intervention strategy could be said to have contributed to accelerating the children's language growth.

The researcher's expectation at the outset of the study was that the children in the expansion group would show the greatest gains. The assumption was that the adult's provision of the adult form at the very moment when the child's attention was focused on the meaning that form encoded, would maximize the likelihood of the child's connecting that meaning with that form. It was further assumed that pairing adult form and child's meaning in this way 100 percent of the time would be maximally efficient.

The children in the expansion group did make greater gains than the children in the control group. But interestingly, the children in the extension group made slightly greater gains than the expansion group children. Why?

Several partial explanations have been offered. McNeill suggests that the inflated rate of expansion with the expansion group probably resulted in some misinterpretations on the part of the adult (McNeill 1970, pp. 109–10). In normal adult-child conversation, adults expand the child's utterances roughly 30 percent of the time (Brown, Cazden, and Bellugi-Klima 1971, p. 404). If one expands *every* child utterance, it may be that the form provided by the adult encodes a meaning other than the child intended. Such mistakes in interpretation could not be expected to aid his acquisition of adult sound-meaning relations.

But Cazden herself has suggested that "depressed attention" in the expansion group might have been a factor contributing to the less-than-expected effectiveness of this expansion procedure. Remember, the child's focus is on meaning, not on form. In fact, examples like the "nobody don't like me" and " 'nother one spoon" conversations suggest that the young child often does not hear the differences between his own expression of a meaning and the adult's expression of the same meaning. If the child says, for example, "Dog bark" and the adult says, "Yes, the dog is barking," perhaps the child thinks to himself "Yeah, that's what I just said." Imagine how sustained your attention would be if you were in a situation in which your conversational partner "repeated" (at least in your perception) everything you said. That is, after all, a favorite technique children use when their deliberate intention is to tease one another. This inflated use of expansion seems to violate principle three in that it focuses on form rather than on meaning.

One reason given for the slight superiority of the extension approach over the expansion technique relates to principle four, the diversity principle. In the extension approach, the child was hearing a wider and more diverse range of adult language forms, and it would seem that his language hypotheses would need to be wider to take this diversity into account. Also in this approach the adult was responding to the child in a meaning-filled way. It is in the context of meaningful communication, in the give-and-take of real interaction, that language acquisition is at its best.[12]

Brown, Cazden, and Bellugi-Klima's (1971) study of parents' verbal reinforcement of their children's utterances lends indirect support to principle 3. This principle claims that meaning focus in interaction is helpful. Their study (discussed earlier) established that parents do focus on the meaning rather than on the form of their children's utterances. Extensive observations of natural interaction between adult and child in the home demonstrate that verbal reinforcement is contingent on the truth value, the meaning, of the child's utterances, rather than on the form. Cazden identifies it as a major paradox of language acquisition that though neither parent's nor child's attention is on linguistic form, the child learns form well.

"Baby Talk" (or "Motherese")

There is a substantial and rapidly growing body of research on mother's (and other adults' and even older children's) language to young children. This research strongly supports principle 2 which suggests that a responsiveness and shaping to the child is helpful for his language growth. This research is particularly impressive in that it includes data from a wide variety of languages and cultural groups, e.g., Danish, American Indian languages, Syrian Arabic (Ferguson 1975, pp. 2–3). We find one indisputable fact whatever the language and culture in question: Adults talk differently to young children than they talk to other adults. The form of language adults use when talking to young children is called "baby talk" (sometimes "Motherese"). Notice this is not what the layman means by this term. Traditionally baby talk has referred to language forms we attributed to young children. But this is not what we mean by the term here. Baby talk is defined as a language version which "consists only of language material identifiable as primarily appropriate for speech to young children" (Ferguson 1975, p. 7). In the languages studied, researchers have found baby talk to include phonological, syntactic, and semantic features —modifications of the adult language in each of these areas, that adults deem appropriate for interacting with babies and young children.

Noam Chomsky's insistence in the 1960s on the gross imperfection of the language sample that the language-acquiring child was exposed to, gave impetus to this line of baby talk research. Chomsky (1965) maintained that one

---

[12]For a comparable study with Anglo subjects from thirty-two to forty months old, which found a "recast" sentence intervention procedure (similar to expansion) to correlate with greater linguistic gains than did a "new-sentence procedure" (similar to extension), see Nelson, Carskaddon, and Bonvillian (1973).

of the strongest supports for the view that language was to a considerable degree "innately specified," was that the language the child is exposed to—the corpus of data that he must work from to figure out sound-meaning relations and underlying linguistic structure—is such a mish-mash of false starts, backtracking, hemming and hawing, that a child could not possibly discern underlying rules from such a corpus. Chomsky claimed that the actual performance of speakers is so far removed from the idealized competence (intuitive knowledge of underlying rules) that the child achieves, that it is inconceivable that the child could acquire linguistic competence from performance data. The child must, he concluded, be born with the universals of linguistic structure already present as part of his genetic inheritance (Chomsky 1965).

It is undeniable that, when adults engage in informal conversation, all the performance imperfections that Chomsky has noted are evident. However, it has become increasingly clear that adults talk to young children differently than they talk to other adults. Study the two interactions below.[13] The first involves a mother telling an adult interviewer about her three-year-old daughter. The second involves *the same mother* talking with her three-year-old daughter with no one else present. List all the baby talk features that you can find in the second conversation. One guiding question might be "What aspects of the mother's speech to her child would seem funny or inappropriate in conversation with me?" Those features which are appropriate in her interaction with the child but which would seem inappropriate in her interaction with you or another adult, are baby talk features. What differences do you notice between her speech to the adult interviewer and her speech to her child?

CONVERSATION 1

Mother: She was potty trained at one-and-a-half.

Interviewer: Gee! That's good!

M: Potty trained early, walk slow. But you know, I've always heard it's better if they're a slow walker because it takes so much coordination to crawl, and I don't know if this is true or not, but I've always been told that the longer a child . . . (pause) . . . crawls, the more coordinated they'll be. I don't know if that's true or not, but I know when . . . (pause) . . . there are children who are uncoordinated, sometimes for practice they'll make them crawl. She was a *good* crawler and she wasn't, you know, when she first started crawling she wasn't one of those that crawled on her stomach, you know. She just started crawling. She wasn't a scooter, whatever, you know. Some kids scoot and some roll, you know. (Getting out baby book.) Jill started crawling . . . (looking through book, pause) . . . I have this in here somewhere. Oh! Ah . . . (pause) . . . I think she was almost thirteen months old when she started. Okay . . . (pause) . . . sat up at six months. I remember, she, it took her a long time to sit up, too, or sit up, but she stood

<hr>

[13]I am grateful to Shirley Hollibaugh for allowing me to use these conversations from her data. (The child's name has been changed here.)

up at eighteen, er . . . (pause) . . . eight months, but she didn't start walking until um . . . (pause) . . . you know, walking across the room . . . um . . . let's see . . . (pause) . . . I always meant to write all this (laughing) and just never did!

CONVERSATION 2

M: (Preparing child for bath; child has a rash.) C'mon. Take your c. . ., take your clothes off and (inaudible) your (inaudible) on. Mommie's puttin' some baking soda in it. Okay?

C: Okay. Don't take these away to me. (Refers to bathtub toys.)

M: Don't take them away to you?

C: No.

M: Why? (Drawn out with falling and then rising pitch.)

C: Cause I wants too many more. Right?

M: Hurry up. Take your 'jammies off.

C: I's . . . (pause) . . . take 'em off.

M: (Softly) Want me to help you?

C: Yeah.

M: (Almost a whisper) Come 'ere. You still itch?

C: Yep.

M: Wonder what's *makin'* (unusually high pitch) those bumps? They're all oooooover you!

C: Yeah.

M: What's makin' 'em, I wonder.

C: Donno.

M: Oh! My goodness! (Rising pitch, drawn out syllables.) Look! All over you! (Laughing.) Isn't it funny?

C: (Weakly) Yeah.

M: Huh?

C: Yeah.

M: Ya' wanna get in the water now and see if that helps?

C: Yeah.

M: Wadda ya wanna do today?

C: Donno.

M: Wanna go see Na-ma? (Child's grandmother.) Wadda ya wanna do?

C: Donno

M: Go (inaudible) to Na-ma's and play?

C: (inaudible) and put my, my, b . . . put my, that on. (M dressing child)

M: What on?

C: My . . . new shoes.

M: Jill, those shoes don't *go* with your *pants*. Corduroy pants? You don't wear Sunday shoes with corduroy pants.

C: Do!

M: Why?

C: We do!

M: Who says?

C: M . . . m . . . Becky.

M: (Drawn out, sing-song, low to high pitch) Becky says? (Laughing) When did Becky tell you that?

C: Cause she did.

M: Uh uh. (Meaning no.)

C: Uh huh! (Meaning yes.)

It is hard to imagine that a young child could figure language out if, in fact, the language used with him were like that in conversation 1 above. In fact, it is hard to believe we adults really talk to each other like this at all. But we do. Our competence and performance are quite discrepant—which was precisely Chomsky's point.

Some phonological features of baby talk that have often been observed and which you might have found in the mother-child conversation above, are exaggerated intonation contours (ups and downs of the voice), lengthening (stretching a word or syllable out in time), use of higher than normal pitch, whispering, exaggerated stress or emphasis, and substitution of sounds which are easier for children to pronounce for those which are more difficult (for example reduction of consonant clusters). Some syntactic features that have been noted include the omission of inflections, auxiliaries, and "be"—"dolly walk" rather than the adult "The dolly is walking," or "Baby do it?" rather than "Can the baby do it?" or "You a good girl?" rather than "Are you a good girl?"

The length of sentences adults address to young children tends to be significantly shorter than the length of sentences they use with other adults. Also, the sentences they address to young children tend to be syntactically simpler than those typically used in adult-adult dialogue, including less embedding. It's interesting too, that the adult's sentences to young children are notably more well formed than the sentences they use in conversations with adults; the child-addressed sentences contain substantially fewer performance inperfections, disfluencies of all kinds. (The differences in length, simplicity, and well-formedness of sentences are particularly evident in the sample conversations above.)

One interesting feature of baby talk is the avoidance of first and second person pronouns ("I" and "you"). Expressions like "Joanie all done now?" (rather than "Are you all done now?"), and "Mommy doesn't like that" (rather than "I don't like that") are common across language groups. It is plausible that the adult feels intuitively that the constant third person references ("Mommy," child's name) are simpler than the first and second person pronoun references ("I," "you") which change depending on who is speaking and who is being addressed. We often find special word forms in baby talk— "bye-byes," "tummy" and in the sample conversation above, "jammies" and "Na-ma"—that would be inappropriate in normal adult conversation.[14]

A high amount of repetition, paraphrase, and question forms have been noted in maternal speech to young children. Mothers frequently repeat either exactly or with some slight alteration both what they say and what the child says. The frequent use of questions may be an unconscious attempt by the adult to maximize the likelihood of a child responding verbally and thus really conversing, for question forms more than any other sentence types pressure the listener to give a verbal response.

The content of adults' talk to young children tends to focus heavily on the here and now, on objects, people, and activities present in the environment as they interact.[15] Snow has observed another interesting aspect of the content of mothers' speech to their children. She analyzed the speech of nine Dutch mothers to their two- to three-year-old children, in terms of Brown's Stage 1 meanings and relations (Snow, 1974). She wondered whether mothers were sensitive to the meanings young children understand and express, and whether they would incorporate these meanings in their speech to their children. Would a high proportion of their talk with their children be about locations of entities and actions, nonexistence of things and people, agents and the actions they engaged in? If so, this would support the notion that mothers adapt their language in ways that will make it more likely the child will understand the mother's meaning. Obviously, the child is more likely to understand what his mother means when she talks with him if she expresses the same kinds of meanings that he expresses when he talks.

Snow analyzed only the mothers' sentences that were more than one word long. Of those, she found that 76 percent were adult expressions of Brown's major meanings and relations of Stage 1 including the mother's frequent nomination questions "What's this?" and "what's that?" This very high percentage suggests that mother is cueing on the child's understanding. Of course the mothers in the sample could not tell us "I talk with Susan a lot about what things are called and where they are located and whose they are and who does what because I know she understands these things. After all, these are the things I hear her talk about all the time." But though these mothers could not tell us this, it appears they have unconsciously picked up

---

[14]Further support for the existence of these baby talk features is that their use in adult-adult dialogue changes the nature of the dialogue, giving it a joking quality, a mocking tone, an endearing tone.

[15]For further discussion of adults' language to young children, see Blount and Padgug (1976); Ferguson (1964); Cross (1975); Snow (1972; 1977b).

on the kinds of things their children understand, and they are using these as the content of their talk, "knowing" that their children will understand them.

The character of baby talk is influenced by the language level of the child with whom the adult is interacting. As a child grows older and becomes more advanced linguistically, his mother's language to him includes fewer baby talk features than it did when he was younger. The mother in the conversations above doubtless included more baby talk features and used them more frequently in conversing with her child when her child was younger than three, than she did in this sample. We talk to three-year-olds differently than we talk to one-year-olds. This is powerful evidence of our shaping to the child. In interaction, the context in which language acquisition occurs, we and the child adapt and shape to each other.

Further evidence of this shaping comes from a study by Snow in which she had mothers talk to their two-year-olds in two different situations, the "present condition" in which the child was in the room with the mother, and the "absent condition" in which the child was not in the room and the mother talked into a tape recorder (Snow 1972). (The tape recorder was also on during the "present condition.") The mothers talked very differently in the two conditions. In general, the mothers used more baby talk features in their speech when the child was present—simplified sentence structure and few third person pronouns. It seems that mothers' langauge is influenced by cues they receive from their children—facial expressions, body movements, vocalizations. Mother is shaping her language to her child in response to signals of his attention and involvement.

Ferguson has helpfully categorized the baby talk features he has studied into (1) features that serve to simplify, such as deletion of inflections and avoidance of first and second person pronouns; (2) features that serve to clarify, such as repetition and exaggerated intonation; and (3) features that serve to express affection or signal that the conversation is meant for the child, such as increased use of diminutive forms, use of high pitch, whispering (Ferguson, 1975).

It appears then, that the language-acquiring child does not have to learn language from such a messy corpus as Chomsky proposed. Universally adults provide children with a language sample that makes the significant phonological, syntactic, and semantic segments and relations more obvious than they would be in normal adult conversation. As Snow says, "No one has to learn to talk from a confused, error-ridden garble of opaque structure" (1977b, p. 38).

A study by Cross suggests a connection between mothers' ways of responding to the child, and the child's acquisition of language structure (Cross 1975). Instead of trying to get a representative sort of cross section for her study of mother-child interaction, Cross chose to study sixteen mother-child pairs including only very linguistically accelerated eighteen- to thirty-month-olds. What she wanted to know was what do the mothers of very rapid language learners do when they talk with their children that might account for their children's rapid development. Interestingly, Cross relates that when she asked the mothers in her study this question before she began her observation, all the mothers insisted that they did not alter their speech for their child in any way.[16] A typical comment was "Oh, I just talk to her as if she were an adult." Of course this turned out not to be the case. Cross identified many features of the mothers' speech that marked it as speech to young children. But the particularly interesting feature of her study was the high proportion of mothers' utterances that were directly contingent upon what the child had said. She was impressed by:

> ... the relatively few occasions when these mothers attempted to control the focus or direction of the conversations, and by the correspondingly high proportion of interaction sequences in which they allowed the child to initiate (and terminate) the topic.
> ... Fifty-five percent of the mothers' utterances incorporated exactly, or referred to, the child's previously expressed topic. (Cross 1975, p. 133)

Here is a picture of mothers tuning into and building on and from what their children are telling them. It is a picture of mothers following children's initiations in conversation.

In a recent study of two mother-child dyads from the time the children were three months until they were twenty months, Snow focuses on evidence that mothers' verbal interaction with their babies is particularly influenced by their desire to engage their children in conversation—reciprocal interaction (Snow 1977). Mother is responding to baby, but, Snow suggests, her adapting of her verbal behavior is more a response to her baby's abilities as a "conversational partner" than to her baby's ability to comprehend speech. "I would suggest that the interactions between these mothers and babies can best be described as conversational in nature, and that the changes in the maternal speech result from the development of the baby's ability to take her turns in the conversation" (Snow 1977, p. 11). The biggest change in mother's language, Snow observed, came at around the time baby was five to seven months and had become better able to "take turns" in conversation, rather than at around twelve months when the child was beginning to use speech and thus give clear signs of comprehension. Accounting for mothers' language modification in terms of a "conversation model" makes sense out of the fact (1) that mothers talk to tiny noncomprehending infants at all, (2) that they talk in face-to-face position, (3) that they talk to them least while feeding, the time when the child could not give a verbal response, (4) that they use an unusually

[16]Comments on her paper, presented at Child Language Forum, Stanford University, 1975.

high proportion of question forms, the very forms that "require" a response from the conversational partner. Snow found that the mothers responded to many of their baby's behaviors—burps, smiles, yawns, sneezes—as if they were communication units:

> *C:* (Smiles)
>
> *M:* Oh, what a nice little smile! Yes, isn't that nice? There. There's a nice little smile.
>
> *C:* (Burps)
>
> *M:* What a nice wind as well! Yes, that's better, isn't it? (p. 12)

Mother would often take both roles in the conversation if the baby did not participate:

> *M:* Oh, you are a funny little one, aren't you, hmm? Aren't you a funny little one? Yes. (Snow 1977, p. 13)

They tended to phrase their questions so that any response on the baby's part could be interpreted as a reply. When the babies were over a year and were using one-word speech, Snow noted numerous instances in which the mother would respond to her daughter's one word as initiating a new topic of conversation:

> *C:* (Makes blowing noise)
>
> *M:* That's a bit rude.
>
> *C:* Mouth.
>
> *M:* Mouth, that's right.
>
> *C:* Face.
>
> *M:* Face, yes, mouth is in your face. What else have you got in your face?
>
> *C:* Face (closing eyes).
>
> *M:* You're making a face aren't you? (p. 18)

Snow suggests finally that perhaps mothers' desire to converse with their children accounts significantly for the character of their speech to young children.

> Mothers' desire to communicate reciprocally with their children . . . may well be a crucial factor in limiting the topics discussed and thus the semantic and syntactic complexity in mothers' speech. (p. 20)

Whatever the basis for adults' modifying their speech to young children, whether to the end of maximizing the likelihood of the child's comprehension, or whether to the end of engaging him in interaction, or both, it is clear that this simplification, clarification, and expressiveness in our speech to the child does occur and that it does render more transparent the structure of language which he is working to internalize. We assume this aids his language growth. If we were to deliberately set out to design a method of aiding the child, the resulting "curriculum" would look much like baby talk: It would simplify, clarify, and express in ways that would gain and hold the child's attention.

It might seem paradoxical to propose that adult modification of language to children, a narrowing of the children's language data, will aid their language development; and on the other hand, to maintain that wider, more diverse exposure to language will aid their language development. Wider language or narrower language, but not both. But I think the two are not contradictory. It is as if the child has a variety of language samples and each is shaped for him, thereby making it more accessible for his processing. Thus the child receives a diverse yet useable corpus.

SUMMARY

The picture that has emerged in this chapter is one of an active and powerful language acquirer interacting with people and things in a responsive environment. Several major themes have been stressed relating to the nature of the activity the child engages in as he acquires language:

The continuousness of the child's growth in language. We have studied a predictable sequence of general syntactic stages a child moves steadily through, and within this general framework of successive stages, we have focused on a predictable sequence of development of grammatical inflections, negatives, interrogatives, and sentence combining. Using a Piagetian frame of reference, we have seen that there is continuity from the child's prelinguistic primarily physical expression into his linguistic expressing of meaning. We have seen, too, that there is a continuous growth of the communication cycle that the child's verbal expression becomes a part of as it grows. We have seen continuity in the child's use of new forms to express familiar meanings, and in his expression of new meanings through the use of already familiar forms; the child moves out into new territory always bringing along and using something which is familiar. I have used the word "growth" repeatedly to capture this notion of the child's steady, continuous progression. I have assumed, along with Nelson, that "there is a basic continuity in language developmental processes and structures. The same types of structures and processes are utilized throughout development, and changes in them are gradual and continuous" (Nelson 1973, p. 2).

The rooting of the child's language growth in his cognitive growth. We have looked at the sensorimotor base of the child's earliest lexical items, and the meanings he conveys in his earliest word combinations. We have examined

a variety of preferred language learning strategies that children employ—
different ways that they cognitively process the language around them so as
to figure out its sound-meaning relations. We have explored the perceptual
base of the child's early strategies for attending to and figuring out what words
mean; we have seen the child focus on perceptually salient properties of objects
(shape, texture, extended dimension) as he builds his semantic system, adding
more properties to his "definitions" as he goes. We have noted some tentative
"operating principles," guiding heuristics suggested by the similarities in the
language learning behavior of children from various linguistic communities.
The child's own cognitive orientation guides him in what he attends to and
how he uses it to solve the language "problem."

The child as the active party in his own learning of language. We have
seen the child actively figuring out underlying relations in language. The child
is an active observer, comprehender, questioner, producer, explorer, hypothesis maker, tester, and reviser. In short, " . . . the child is viewed as an active
information processor, model builder, and problem solver" (Nelson 1973,
p. 3).

Several basic and presumably helpful general characteristics of environments for this active language learner to move about in have also been suggested:

**An environment which is compatible with the child's own ways of learn-
ing.** We have examined studies suggesting that the child have latitude to
explore his environment freely, and that he be able to act on a variety of
materials physically. We have pictured an environment in which the adult
provides stuff for the child to mess about with if he chooses, but does not direct
the child's activity with the objects provided. Thus the child "formulates and
names" his own concepts, rather than mouthing the ready-made concepts of
someone else.

An environment which is responsive to the child, which shapes to him.
Research has found an interaction pattern in which the mother follows the
child's lead to be helpful. Nowhere are responsiveness and shaping to the child
more evident than in the much studied modification of adult language to young
children. Whether as an aid to children's comprehension or whether as an
attempt to engage the child in conversation or both, adults provide a language
sample for the children they interact with, which makes the underlying organization of language maximally apparent.

**An environment which focuses on the meanings expressed in language,
rather than on the forms of their expression.** We have found that adults do
interact "meaning-full-ly" with their young children. They rarely correct their
children for forms, and when they do, the child is usually unable to modify

his utterance on the basis of the correction provided, so it seems unlikely that this could be helpful. Research suggests that acceptance of the child's utterances as meaning conveying, whatever their form, is a helpful pattern of interaction. And we have seen that many adults bend over backwards to attribute meaning to children's verbal productions.

An environment which provides linguistic and nonlinguistic diversity. Research indicates that the greater the diversity within the child's environment for him to explore and use, the richer will be the concepts he builds and the language hypotheses he formulates, as these concepts and hypotheses will need to take into account his diverse experiential base.

Shall we say, finally, that the child's acquisition of language is universal or unique? Say that it is both. It is universal in that every child shares with every other human the fact of acquiring a human language at all, as well as the general sequence and processes of its acquisition. Language acquisition is part of the child's human-ness—marks him unmistakeably as a member of the species human.

But language acquisition is also part of the child's uniqueness. Every child builds language out of his own personal and unique experiencing. His use of language is creative from the outset. It is built out of his meanings and his alone. It expresses what he has to say in the ways he chooses to say it. Thus every child constructs, at one and the same time, a system which is universal and unique.

Chapter 8

Language Acquisition, Teachers, and Children

This chapter title suggests the question teachers raise so often, not without a noticeable edge of frustration: "All this stuff about language acquisition is fine, but what does it have to do with me? In the first place, I don't teach four-year-olds, I teach eight-year-olds. And in the second place, I'm not a mother at home with one child; I'm a teacher in a classroom with twenty-five kids." True enough. Homes and classrooms are different; four-year-olds and eight-year-olds are different; mothers and teachers play different roles in children's lives. But some aspects of language and its acquisition are, I believe, so deeply rooted and so pervasive that they cut across the specifics of setting, age, and role, and thus have implications for us. In this chapter we'll consider these aspects—specifically, the seven major themes from the last two chapters, identified in the summary of chapter 7. Whether we're talking about homes or classrooms, four-year olds or eight-year olds, mothers or teachers as adult interactants:

The growth of language is a continuous process for children. Language is a human's major means of communication and therefore children's growth in language is growth in communicating. The continuousness of this growth is evident in several areas. One is form. We have seen that children's continuing interaction through language which is an integral part of the environment in which they are actively participating results in their replacement, in time, of less mature language forms with adult ones. When will a child replace "buyed" with "bought" or "brang" with "brought"? When she notices that and how her forms and the adults' are different. What causes her to notice? How much exposure to the adult forms does she need in order to hear the difference? We don't know, anymore than we know how much exposure a given child needs to a mass in different shapes before she realizes that it is the same amount whatever its shape. We cannot force the realization, and in language acquisition we are likely to lose ground if we try.

> *Child:* I brang my lunch today.
>
> *Teacher:* You did? Well I brought mine today too. And Johnny brought his and I think Jo brought hers, didn't you, Jo?

generally works better than

> *Child:* I brang my lunch today.
>
> *Teacher:* You *brang* it? Don't you mean that you *brought* it? Can you say that? "I *brought* my lunch today."
>
> *Child:* (Carefully) I . . . *brought* . . . my . . . lunch today. (Cheerfully) And Tammy brang hers too.

The child has her own internal clock for using the interactive environment to build an adult-like language. But we know that, just as her notions of conservation of mass will come through her messing about with and acting on clay and other substances, so her use of adult language forms will come through her messing about with language—her acting on language by using it in talking and listening in communication.

The content of children's language grows continuously also. Their expanding experience provides an ever expanding base for the content of their communication. Their experiences of today and the language that lives in them become part of the luggage they carry with them into tomorrow. It becomes crucial, then, that real interaction live in real experience, that the school day be full of the reciprocal give-and-take of real communication, listening and talking with people about shared experiences and shared concerns.

We also see continuousness in the child's language as it becomes more widely adapted to various social situations. This, too, is growth which is based on a widening of the child's experience. As she interacts with a wider circle of individuals (neighborhood children, schoolmates, teachers, other children's parents, unfamiliar adults) in a wider range of situations, her language repertoire expands. Her early growth will be toward understanding and making herself understood by "outside others" in "outside places" (for example, nursery school teachers), in order to accomplish basic communication; the first goal is to comprehend and be comprehended. But ever increasing social interaction shapes a child's language eventually into a variable and often subtle social tool which goes well beyond meeting the demands of basic communication. The child's language becomes more socially appropriate as well as more comprehensible. This increased adaptability of the child's language to diverse social settings contributes to her control of the environment generally. As she becomes better able to interact effectively and comfortably in various situations, this wider interactive base provides possibilities for new experiences, which further enhance her language adaptability, which opens further possibilities for new experiences . . . and the cycle goes on. Even in the preschool child we see evidence of the emergence of various styles within her language repertoire. We see her talking "more politely" to an outside adult, using simplified sentence structure and exaggerated intonation patterns when talking to a baby, adopting a formal and directive style when role playing a teacher. We see her using some established telephone conversation conventions ("Hello? Is Paul there?" "Well, what I'm calling about is. . . ." "See you next Tuesday. Bye."), speaking more quietly in library or church than on the playground, following certain clear exchange patterns in argument ("I can too" "Cannot." "Can too." "Cannot." "Can!" "Can't!"). This aspect of language growth continues as the child's social experience grows.

From the beginning of language development, a child uses her language for various purposes (Section Four develops this topic further.) Through the years there is continuous growth in language function for the child as she both adds new language functions to her range, and also develops additional means for accomplishing familiar functions. From the outset certain functions are present: Babies use language to let others know what they want, to get others to do things for them, to express feelings. But this range expands to include using language to entertain others, to relate events, to fantasize. Typically, children's school experiences involve new emphasis on use of language for intellectually oriented purposes—comparing or contrasting, providing evidence in support of opinion, explaining with precision, reasoning logically. Adding new means to their store for realizing a particular function can be illustrated by the function of requesting, getting someone to do (or stop doing) something. The two-year-old may say "more juice." The four-year-old may say "I want more juice," or may demand "Give me more juice," or may soften the request by saying "May/Can I have some more juice?" or "Could you get me some more juice?" An eight-year-old may use more subtle devices like "I'm still thirsty," or "That sure is delicious juice; orange is my very favorite," or "Is there any juice left?" Like other aspects of language growth, children's growth of language functions—both the adding of new functions and the continuing refinement within functions—happens within contexts of real and meaningful communication experience.

This is as true of expressing functions through written channels as through oral ones. Increased opportunities and desire for real communication provide the continuity for the child's spilling over from oral into written channels. There is (should be) continuousness from oral into written channels of expression. The child has reasons to interact with people beyond the immediate time and place. She wants to communicate with people beyond the area that her voice can fill and at other times than this moment and this once. Perhaps she has a title or an idea about a painting or a collage she has made that she wants others who look at it in her absence to know about. Or perhaps she needs to get information from a local government official about where exits on the new highway going through town will be and how the school neighborhood will be affected, so she needs to write a letter. She wants to "hear" the ideas of others expressed at other times and other places and thus reading is important to her. Written expression makes wider interaction possible. And the continuousness is evident again—from prelinguistic gesture into verbal expression into written expression, but never leaving any expressive form behind, just expanding further her expressive repertoire. *Form, content, function, and channels of expression* all show continuous development. Growth in all these areas has its best chance in the interactive classroom environment where children use their developing *forms* to express their ever expanding *content* for various *functions* (purposes) and in diverse *channels* in order to communicate more widely and more effectively with others.

I have used the term "language growth" repeatedly. Growth. The notion of growth is frustrating; it is so slow. We don't have time in these days of "back to basics," accountability, behavioral objectives, and ladders of skills for the slow steadiness that is growth. But language acquisition is just such a growth process. We do not, cannot, give children our ready-made concepts or our language to express them. Each child must build her understanding and expression out of personal experience. We serve her well if we provide worthwhile experiences, and the endless opportunity to express what she feels and what she understands as she engages in them. We serve her well, too, if we leave our pathology notions of child language behind us. Ours is not to hunt for deficiencies ("diagnose") to erradicate ("treat"), but rather to understand the growth in progress and exploit opportunities for enhancing it. We know that the child's language has grown steadily and continuously in form, in content, in social flexibility, in function up to the moment she arrives at the school door. What reason would we have for supposing that that continuous growth would stop or slow down now, at the very time she comes to an environment, our classroom, which offers more people to interact with every day than she has ever had at home, and a wide range of daily experiences to communicate in and about? The possibilities for contributing richly to the child's steady language growth are there, but only if we see our classrooms as communities for communicative interaction, rather than as locations where children mindlessly follow our dictates. We would do well to understand the child's continuous language growth process and, believing in it, align ourselves with it.

The growth of language is deeply rooted in the child's cognitive growth. We have dealt with children's language growth through their interaction with others, their oral and written communications. But moments of silence and aloneness can contribute to language growth also. Have you ever watched a child staring long and hard, and silently, at a spider spinning a web, at a speckled rock, at an upside down turtle trying to right itself? Have you ever watched a child concentrate intently, and wordlessly, on painting a picture or building with an erector set? Have you ever watched a child look up and stare off into space in a puzzled wondering way after reading a poem or story? Often we don't watch; we are too busy "teaching." But when we do, we know that much of a child's cognitive growth—wondering, watching, figuring out— happens silently. This, too, is the stuff of language. Where there are thoughts, ideas, feelings, the child will one day search for and create their expression whether in speech or writing, whether for herself or for sharing with others. These silent experiences are basic to language growth in another way too. They expand and deepen the child's understanding of the expressions of those she hears and reads.

We feel that we contribute to children's cognitive growth (and thus to their language) when we tell them things clearly and simply so that they can understand them. But we do so only if we touch base with their experiencing; that is where cognitive growth happens. Ten-year-olds, like Nelson's two-year-olds, must "formulate and name their own concepts." Often in our hurry to reach our behavioral goals that children be able to say and do certain things in certain situations, we bypass the very experience that would contribute to their formulating of concepts. We sometimes mistake their mouthing of our concepts for their having formulated and named their own.

The child's own understanding is the basis of her language expression and her response to the expression of others. Whether her understanding grows through her play, her quiet contemplation, her messing about with things, or her conversing with others, it is her deepening and broadening meanings that will need, and will find, richer language means of expression.

The growth of language involves the child as the active party in the learning process. Children learn. That's an innocuous sentence, isn't it? But a powerful one. Teachers teach; that is, they engage in activities and interactions with children intended to foster their learning. Whether or not in fact these activities and interactions do result in children's learning is another question. "Learn" is an active verb if ever there was one. We don't "learn children"; *children learn.* Our language encodes our realization of the active nature of the child in her learning by providing a structure of doer (child) + action (learns). Our language reflects our understanding that learning is something someone does, not something which is done to someone. We can lecture, discuss, question, demonstrate, explain, scold, assign, test, praise, punish. But do what we will, learning comes finally from one place alone: *within the child herself.* What the child notices (an active verb), she will attend to (another active verb); what she attends to, she will learn (an active verb); what she learns she will express herself and understand in the expression of others.

We and the things we do stand outside of children. Children's learning happens from within. Thus our task (and it is no easy one) is to connect the "without" and the "within"—to provide experiences that gain or use children's notice, that engage their attention and involvement. This is far more difficult than bombarding them with information that we feel is significant, for it means our noticing (active verb) where they are, what they are into and care about, what they find stimulating and respond to in an involved way. It particularly means watching children in informal settings where they are freest to be themselves, and are less likely to shape their behavior to please us and be what they feel we want them to be.

Donald Graves (1978), surveying the elementary classrooms where children's writing does and does not occur in the U.S., England, and Scotland, has found that children's writing is happening—is alive and well—in only a small percentage of classrooms. In those classrooms where children's writing is thriving, he has found, not surprisingly, that the teachers differ markedly in many ways. However, he has identified some striking and unmistakeable similarities among this diverse group of teachers. One of these is the teacher's awareness of the personal and individual interests of the children.

> These teachers knew their children's interests, learning foibles, and personal struggles. They often said, "Margaret is interested in collecting cocoons now," or "Andrew is into rocks." Their responses contained specific information about child interests. Yet there was a curious lack of skills check-off lists, behavioral objectives, detailed plans and the like. (Graves 1978, p. 639)

It is the child's particular interests that become the basis for her writing (and, by extension, for her other language use) in the hands of these skillful and perceptive teachers.

There are increasingly impressive indications that we have much to learn by watching children play. In playful situations the child's actions do not carry the consequences that they do in "real life." Thus play is safe; it allows the child to try out new behaviors and actions in a buffered, nonthreatening situation. In the safe setting of play, the child can, and apparently does, figure out, practice, consolidate, integrate new learnings. Thus play contributes significantly to furthering the child's understanding, and also shows us what the child is working on (playing on?), figuring out, practicing, integrating. Of course, her play shows us this only if we are watching.

What is the content of a child's play? Insects? Is she constantly asking you for a jar to house the creepy-crawlys she is always finding on the playground? Structures? Is she a builder of complex Lego or block structures? Or is rhythm the stuff of her play—dances, handclaps, jump rope rhymes, singing games? Whatever the interests of our children at play, we can make a place for them in our classrooms. Think of the endless possibilities for experiences which might be meaningful to our insect collector and her friends: collecting a wide variety of insects, preparing environments for them, observing and comparing their behavior in natural and "prepared" environments. Think of the language possibilities here as the collectors observe and compare their insects, plan and construct the environments for them, discuss and record their observations, write out instructions for other class members as to how each insect should be cared for, what it should eat and how often, how it should be handled. And of course they'll want to read or listen to you read *Charlotte's Web* and *Cricket in Times Square*. Will that get them into discussions of insect and animal characteristics that are and aren't preserved in the fictional tales?

And what of our budding builder and her builder friends? Will they want to build structures of various types, to observe and compare buildings in the community, to talk with an architect or engineer parent, to get hold of and study blueprints and possibly construct models from them, to gather leftover building materials from local construction sites, to study local building codes, to draw up blueprints for and construct a model of their dream school, to move into an exploration of structures in other geographical areas where climate and life styles are significantly different? What rich language possibilities there are here as the builders discuss and compare their observations; plan their constructions together; contact and talk with architect, engineer, construction workers; write for old blueprints or for copies of local building codes and possibly discuss the code with a knowledgeable local official; write off for, read, discuss information about structures in other places and in former (and in future?) times; follow written instructions for making their own constructions.

And think of the vital uses of language for the rhythm group as they perhaps collect dances, handclaps, jump rope rhymes and singing games from children in other grades, other schools, other neighborhoods; from parents, grandparents, and older members of the community; from written sources (Abrahams 1969; Opie and Opie 1959; 1969), as they engage in sharing favorites with others—teaching and learning rhymes and routines, and as they create new routines of their own.

Once you start really thinking about it, the possibilities are endless. But the point is this: Our careful observations of our children's play can alert us to what they are "into." This we can incorporate in the classroom experiences we make available. Children's language lives and grows when it is an integral part of their meaningful activity, when they are *using* language in activities which are purposeful and engaging to them.

The growth of language is aided by an environment which is geared toward the child's ways of learning. Differences in ways of learning are influenced by developmental level. We expect that learning through manipulation of objects, through making things, and through physical activity will be important to our first and second graders, whereas our fifth and sixth graders, although not leaving these concrete expriences behind, will be more comfortable than our younger students with manipulating language symbols apart from the physical experience. While our younger children are more geared to solving problems close to themselves and within their immediate environment (for example, how to distribute supplies equitably), our older children may get involved with problems which have relevance beyond the context of themselves and their immediate environment (Are green stamps a ripoff? Should the government penalize consumers for buying gas guzzler cars and provide financial incentives for buying more economical ones?). Also, while our younger children learn more through oral channels, much of our older children's learning comes through written channels.

But whatever the children's ages or developmental levels, there is wide individual variation in preferred strategies related to learning. As with Nelson's two-year-olds, so with our ten-year-olds, individual children attend to different things in their environment and utilize different learning strategies as they assimilate new understandings into their cognitive structure. Again, observing children at play or in free activities can help us. As we watch children in free settings, we see wide differences in how much structure and what kinds of structure different children prefer; in whether a child prefers to work, play, learn predominantly alone or with others, and in smaller or larger groups; in whether a child chooses to be active in cohesive, more permanent social groups, or whether she prefers a more transient, free-floating pattern of moving from group to group; in the amount and type of physical movement a given child employs; in whether her involvement is more that of observer or that of participant, and in whether and how this changes over time and with different groups of children; in whether a child is given to working on pragmatic solutions or creative solutions, to real problems or imaginary ones. If we are going to provide for each child's ways of learning (and we must if we are concerned about the child's growing language), then it is clear that we are going to have to provide for a range in the dimensions mentioned. We can do this by (1) including a variety of specific activities for developing particular concepts (some physical activities, others quiet; some individual activities, others small-group or large-group; some highly structured, others more loosely structured); and (2) including in the classroom environment many activities which are open-ended and which individual children can use in different ways.

Having animals in the classroom is one example of an open-ended, flexible activity that different children will use in their own preferred ways. The brief conversation below between an adult visitor and some kindergartners grouped around their gerbil's cage hints at some of the different ways in which these children were using this experience and also demonstrates how language was a rich integral part of their meaningful experience.

Adult: What's that brown thing in there with the gerbil?

Boy: It's a log. It's a plastic log.

Adult: It's not a real log, is it? (Pause) It looks like he likes to chew on that.

Girl: He's chewin' on it. I hope he hasn't swallowed it.

2nd Girl: I bet he has swallowed it!

Boy: He'll be dead by now, then.

2nd Boy: Yea, eatin' the toy or sumpin'. Spittin' it out!

Girl: We can make lots and lots of room for him.

2nd Girl: This is where he plays.

3rd Girl: Yea, and this is where he sleeps. And this is where he exercises.

Girl: Yea. (pause) Yea.

Boy: He jumps offa this—and down. Wheeeeee!

Girl: Look. This goes in here.

2nd Girl: (to gerbil) It's time to go to sleep now. C'mon.

Girl: Hey, wake him, he may not (inaudible).

Boy: Does something like to go in here? Or does this go in the exercise room?

2nd Girl: This goes in the exercise (she's cut off).

3rd Girl: This goes in the playroom. (Pause) That's right here.   And this is where he rest-es.

2nd Girl: This is where his sleeping room is.

Girl: This is where he goes to the bathroom.

3rd Girl: (to the gerbil) Now, do you want to play or exercise? (Pause) Do you wanna play or exercise? I think you wanna play right now. You can exercise later. You can have a apple. (To 2nd Girl) Do you think he should have a apple?

2nd Girl: Of course. (Pause) C'mon.

Boy: Here we go! (Pause) He's got the apple.[1]

Some of the children in this class had been physically very active with the gerbil, getting food for it, building items for its environment. Others delighted in sitting and watching it closely for long periods. Groups formed and re-

[1] I am indebted to Marian Coffee and Michael Henniger for this episode.

formed naturally around the cage—groups of various sizes and composition. There were pragmatic problems to be solved—what to feed the gerbil, where to get the food most economically and conveniently, what to use for a water dish that would fit into the cage but wouldn't tip over, how to care for him on weekends. But there were more creative problems to be dealt with, too—what kind of gadgets and devices could the children make and provide for their gerbil's play and exercise? The gerbil offered something meaningful for everyone. And of course, because the experience was meaningful in different ways for each child, it offered many opportunities for real communicative growth for those involved children. In professional jargon, you could call this an example of an "individualized oral language development activity." In plain talk, it's an example of children's language living and growing in meaning-full experience.

The growth of language is aided by an environment which is responsive to the child. In his article about reading called "Twelve Easy Ways to Make Learning to Read Difficult* (*and One Difficult Way to Make It Easy)," Frank Smith (1973) provides the following as the one difficult way: "Respond to what the child is trying to do" (p. 195). This is as relevant and important a guideline in all other areas as it is in reading. I know of no more difficult or more on-target challenge to teachers than this. It implies, first of all, that we see and understand what it is that the child is trying to do. This means perceptive observation on our part—that we actually watch and listen, and that we bring to bear on our watching and listening a solid knowledge base relating to how children learn. Second, it implies that, once we understand what the child is trying to do, we respond to that appropriately. Both are challenging, especially for beginning teachers.

Anyone who has ever been a teacher knows that beginning teaching can be a scary business—twenty-five of "them" and only one of me, and what will I give them to do all day every day? Will they like me? Will I be able to control them? For many beginning teachers, survival is a major goal. Some research suggests that earlier in their careers, teachers are focused mainly on their own performance, and that it is not until they are farther down the road in their teaching experience and have become secure in their role, that they are able to shift their main focus from what they are doing, to what their children are doing (Fuller 1969). At that point the main questions become "What does Janet seem to care about? How does she learn? How does she interact with others? What is she trying to do and how can I help her get on with it? How can I expand what she is doing?" The work of many researchers referred to in the preceding chapter (Cross, Blount, Ferguson, Cazden, Nelson) provides a clear picture of young children's language growth proceeding vigorously in environments which are responsive to the children's initiative. I believe that this continues to be the kind of environment that contributes to language growth throughout the elementary school years. It makes no sense to assume that, starting at age five or six, the child does a complete turnabout so that a directive environment in which she plays a submissive, passive role will be helpful. That the classroom is a more directive environment than the home is generally true. But this is a function of our trying to fit the child to the institution, rather than providing an institution that fits the child's own developmental tendencies.

If there is one way above all others for us to be responsive to children, it is to listen to them. This implies that children's talk be valued and encouraged in our classrooms. Yet some studies indicate that many classrooms are weighted toward structured large-group lessons which are teacher dominated. One such study, a study of children's and teachers' questioning in fourth- and sixth-grade social studies classes, found teachers asking an average of 47 questions per 20-minute period, while the entire group of children averaged a total of 6.9 questions per 20-minute period (Davis 1971). Another study of social studies in fourteen classes from second to sixth grade found that, of the total number of questions collected, only 1.67 percent were asked by children (Dodl 1966). Child-selected activities, child-suggested activities, child-created activities, child-controlled activities in which the teacher serves as a roving on-the-spot consultant, are more conducive to children's language participation and growth than are teacher-controlled "discussions."

Nothing encourages one to talk so much as the presence of an interested listener. Many parents often listen to their children; teachers should too. But this is difficult—twenty-five children and only one teacher, so many pressures (get the milk money and the attendance slip down to the office, get Thomas to the resource room by 9:15). But there are several important things we can do to free ourselves to be interested listeners for our children. First, we can make child-chosen, child-initiated, and child-group activities more central to our program. Then we can move about among our children, and our interacting with individuals or small clusters of children about what they are interestedly doing is *a part of* our scheduled activity, rather than an extra we get to when-if-ever the scheduled activity is done (the worksheets, the workbook pages, the written comprehension questions on the reading assignment). Kohl (1969) suggests starting with ten minutes a day during which the children can follow any of a number of optional activities you have provided which you think may be interesting to them, or any activity of their own devising. One option is ". . . sitting and doing nothing if they choose" (p. 71). (When children are sitting quietly and not moving about, are they really "doing nothing"?) He suggests that you

> make it clear that nothing done during that period will be graded, and nothing need be shown or explained to the teacher. That ten minutes is to be their time and is to be respected as such. Step out of the way and observe the things your

pupils choose to do. Step out of the way, but don't disappear. Make it clear that you won't tell people what to do or how to do it, but that you will be available to help in any way you can, *or just to talk* (italics added). For ten minutes cease to be a teacher and be an adult with young people, a resource available if needed, and possibly a friend, but not a director, a judge, or an executioner. (Kohl 1969, p. 71)

Strategically placed, for example, in the middle of the afternoon, the original ten minutes might in time extend a few minutes at either end, eventually becoming a significant block of time during which our children could, *if they chose,* talk with us and/or with each other about things which they care about.

Secondly, we can use our teacher aides, parent volunteers, or older student assistants who come into our rooms from upper classes, to be additional listeners for our children. Typically, we dispatch these aides to the hall with one or two children to work on multiplication tables or a phonics drill. However, their contribution to our children's language could be significant if they functioned, instead, as interested listeners and as nondirective, participative adults.

Third, the more we can be with our children in their informal free times, the more opportunities we will have to listen to them and share their delights. On the playground, at lunch, on the ride to a field trip—these are rich opportunities for listening.

It is interesting that we express a real concern for developing listening skills in our children, yet seem less concerned with developing listening skills in ourselves. Current books about language arts stress the importance of our children learning to listen. Goals like the following are familiar: "Listening to sense that a problem exists," "Listening for implications and consequences in a problem," "Listening to get facts straight in a problem," "Listening creatively to plan procedure" (Lundsteen 1976, pp. 443–44). But how much do we engage in these behaviors? Is it likely that we will effectively teach children to do what we don't do?

As teachers we sometimes tend to talk at children rather than with them. It is a simple fact that the way one speaks to another influences the way that other uses language in return. In what we generally call "teacher-led discussions," we frequently use our language in ways that influence children to use their language in more limited rather than more expanded ways. There are three particularly prominent features of teacher talk which encourage children to use their language in restricted ways, and all three are prevalent in teacher-dominated, rather than teacher-responsive, verbal situations. The three are parroting, fishing, and using limiting questions.

(Teacher has placed one large ball to represent the sun and is using a smaller one to represent the earth.)

T: Now here we have the earth revolving around . . . (pregnant pause). What does the earth revolve around?

C-1: The sun.

T: The sun. Right, Marie. But as it moves around the sun, it also keeps turning, like this (turns ball) on its own . . .

C-2: Center.

T: Well, it's kind of . . .

C-3: AXIS!

T: Its own *axis.* Right. And do you know what we call that? (pause) When it goes around on its own axis? We say the earth ro . . . (hopeful pause)

C-2: Revolves?

T: No, not revolves. We say it ro . . .

C-3: Rotates!

T: Rotates! That's right. It rotates on its own axis. And that makes day and night. Now if we live right here on this side of the earth where my finger is, are we having day or night when the earth is like this? (T indicates spot away from sun.)

Cs: Night.

T: We're having night. Yes. And when we're turned like this so that the side we're on is facing the sun . . . ?

Cs: Day.

T: *Day.* We're having *day.* Very good.

Can you hear the parroting here, the teacher's repetition of the children's answers? We need to be aware of our own parroting because it works against children's language growth. I often wonder what effect our parroting has on children's feelings of competence. Mightn't a child wonder "If my answer was right, how come it couldn't stand on its own? What was the matter with what I said that the teacher had to say it after me—the very same thing?" Further, our parroting has the effect of closing episodes. It's as if, with our repetition of the child's response, we say "There now, that one's done" rather than meeting the child's response with a remark, a comment, a question, a wondering that would propel the interaction forward. We get into a pattern of

T initiate —————— C respond —————— T repeat (closure)

repeated over and over, rather than a pattern of building in which teacher and child both initiate and respond, and the discussion often goes from child to child.

I think our parroting also encourages children not to listen to each other, not to use each other as learning resources. After all, why should a child listen to what another child says when he knows the teacher is going to say it again anyway. This is an unfortunate consequence of our parroting, for it is important for children's language growth that we maximize the opportunities for real interaction among them.

Can you find the examples of fishing in the teacher-led discussion above, the instances in which the teacher has a particular response in mind and the children's job is to find it? In fact, all of the teacher's questions are of this type, but it is perhaps best illustrated when the expected response is not forthcoming, and the very reasonable "incorrect" responses are ignored. The teacher pulls for a particular response, responds positively to that one, and ignores other responses, *intelligent responses, the very ones* that could be used to further children's learning. Going further with the differences between "center" and "axis" or "revolve" and "rotate," just might teach someone something new. But through fishing questions and acceptance of only expected responses, the teacher does more to test (finds out which labels the children, some of them, know) than to teach.

It is dangerous to lead children to believe that learning is a matter of psyching out teachers to find out what specific response gets a smile, and more dangerous still to foster the belief that learning is a matter of saying particular things in particular ways. Fortunately our older students often let us know when we are fishing. If in response to a question I have asked, a student prefaces the answer with "Well, I don't know if this is what you want but . . ." I know immediately that I have asked a fishing type question.

Closely related to fishing questions are limiting questions, those questions that do not invite children to think, wonder, justify, explore, explain, convince, but only to provide a simple label or fact. Most often limiting questions require one- or two-word responses. The teacher's questions in the above discussion are all of this type. We look in vain for the enticing questions: "Suppose. . . . What might happen then?" "How do you know that . . . ?" "How do you think people found out that . . . ? What might they have noticed?" "I wonder why . . . ?" "What do you think would happen if . . . ?" "How come when X happens, Y happens?" "Can you show us how/why . . . ?" "If X happened, what might happen to Y?" "How is X similar to/different from Y?" "Has X ever happened? *Could* it ever happen? Under what conditions?" Limiting questions restrict rather than expand possibilities for children's learning. And of course, they also necessarily restrict the children's language, their expression of what they understand.

Compare the language of the children in the above teacher-led discussion about the earth's movement with the language of the kindergartners in the following teacher-led discussion.

T: Everyone got a chance to weigh back in October which was a long time ago and then a few days ago everybody got through weighing again. Now some of you gained some pounds and some of you didn't gain any. (She refers to chart.) The black line was how much you weighed in October and the red line is how . . .

All the children: much you weigh now!

T: Now where they are right together, that's a person that didn't gain any.

C-1: I didn't gain any.

T: Can you tell me who . . .

C-2: Annie.

T: . . . There are some people on here, where there's only one square, rectangle between the red and black line. . . . How many pounds did they gain?

All the children: One!

C-2: I gained one.

T: Now let me see if you all can tell me how many pounds this person gained. . . .

All children: Two.

T: . . . and how many pounds did this person gain?

All children: None!

C-3: Teacher, I want to tell you something about that . . .

T: All right.

C-3: First I weighed 61, so probably your scale is wrong or my scale is wrong, because I weighed 61 and now I weigh 60 on my scale.

T: Well, what happened to you?

C-2: She lose weight!

T: How many . . . from 61 she used to weigh, now she weighs 60, how many do you think she lost?

All children: One.

T: One what?

C-2: One pound.

T: That's right. Well maybe you did, Eileen. Sometimes we lose weight during the year.

T: Now one person on this, one person on this chart gained a lot of weight, in fact they gained more than anybody else.

(Children all talking at once.)

T: Let Kevin come up and find not the person who *weighs* the most, but the person who *gained* the most.

C-5: Gained?

T: Gained means to get bigger . . .

C-5: Taller?

T: No, I don't mean to get taller, I mean bigger.

All Children: Mike . . . I know . . . I know . . .

C-6: 1 . . . 2 . . . 3 . . . 4 . . . 5 . . . 6 . . . 7.

T: 7 pounds. Is this person the heaviest person in the class?

All Children: No . . . Eileen . . . Larry . . .

C-1: I see someone who gained four!

C-2: Me too!

C-3: I see someone who gained one. That's me. I have a blue one on top.

T: All right, I'd like for everyone that didn't gain any weight to stand up . . . didn't gain any weight . . . Oh, I thought we said you lost weight!

C-5: Yeah, I lost weight, but I didn't gain any.

T: Oh, you're right then.

C-7: I bet we are all going to get to the top when we grow. . . . She only got one . . .

C-5: If I gained four pounds, I'd be all the way to the top.

T: If you gained one pound stand up . . . one pound.

(Children talking as they stand up or stay seated.)

T: OK, sit down. If you gained two pounds would you stand up?

C-1: Hey, I didn't gain two pounds, I gained two and a half.[2]

It is clear that the learning and the language of the children are more powerful in the second discussion than in the first. The teacher is more responsive: She questions in ways that invite the children to think and interact in new ways, and she is ready to follow their initiatives. They also are encouraged to talk with each other. In teacher-led whole group discussions, it is more difficult to be responsive to children than in activities involving fewer children and more child direction and initiative. This is one reason to use teacher-led discussions sparingly. But even here, responsiveness is possible, especially if we avoid parroting, fishing, and using limited questions.

If we are to be responsive as teachers then, it seems we might well focus our efforts on observing our children more and cueing on their interests and concerns and learning styles, on talking less and listening more (and better), on interacting with our children in free situations, on providing a maximum amount of child-child interaction, on making child-selected and child-designed activities a major part of our program, on making our talk less controlling and directive, and on providing activities which are open ended. We would expect children's language to thrive in such an environment.

The growth of language is aided by an environment which focuses on meaning rather than on form. Communication is the goal of language from prelinguistic symbols into oral channels into written ones. Children know this, mothers and fathers know this. But teachers sometimes forget that (1) the child's getting her message across is more important than the forms she uses to do so, and (2) the paradox—and truth—of language growth is that the child focuses on meaning but she learns form. Cazden suggests that

> . . . one important function of knowledge about language for teachers is to put the language forms used by children back where they belong, out of focal awareness. Normally, in out-of-school conversations, our focal attention as speakers and listeners is on the meaning, the intention, of what someone is trying to say. Language forms are themselves transparent; we hear through them to the meaning intended. But teachers, over the decades if not centuries, have somehow

[2]I am indebted to Marian Coffee and Lisa Leiden for this episode. The names of the children have been changed.

gotten into the habit of hearing with different ears once they go through the classroom doors. Language forms assume an opaque quality. We cannot hear through them; we hear only the errors to be corrected. One value of knowledge about language—its development and its culturally different forms—is not to make the language of our children more salient to our attention. Quite the opposite. That knowledge reassures, and lets language forms recede into the transparency that they deserve, enabling us to talk and listen in the classroom as outside, focusing full attention on the children's thoughts and feelings that those forms express. (Cazden 1976, p. 10)

"But how will the child learn to say 'brought' instead of 'brang' if I don't call it to her attention?" She will learn exceptional forms the way you and I and most human beings of the world did: through being exposed to and using language forms in meaningful interaction contexts, forms in the service of communication.

This means that:

1. *Verbalization must not replace language* in our classrooms. The classic example that I know of verbalization substituting for language is the following from Bereiter and Englemann's *Teaching Disadvantaged Children in the Preschool.* The authors cite this excerpt as a fine example of the teaching of "classifying things as weapons or nonweapons."

Teacher: (Presents picture of rifle.) This is a————.

Child B: Gun.

Teacher: Good. It is a gun. Let's all say it: This is a gun. This is a gun. Again. This is a gun. Let's say it one more time: This is an alligator.

Child D: It ain't neither. It a *gun.*

. . .

Teacher: Okay, I'll start again. This is a gun. Is that right? This is a weapon. This is a gun. This is a weapon.

Child D: No it ain't no weapon.

Teacher: (Presents pictures of knife, cannon, pistol.) This is a weapon. This is a weapon. This is a weapon. These are weapons. Say it with me. This is a weapon. This is a weapon. This is a weapon. These are weapons: Let's hear that last one again. Make it buzz. These are weapon*zzz.*

. . .

Teacher: Here's the rule: (claps rhythmically) If you use it to hurt somebody, then it's a weapon. Again. If you use it to hurt somebody, then it's a weapon. Say it with me. If you use it to hurt somebody, then it's a weapon. One more time. If you use it to hurt somebody, then it's a weapon. (Bereiter and Englemann 1966, pp. 105–8)

Whatever these children and this teacher are engaging in, one thing it most definitely is *not: language.* There is no language apart from meaning. Language is *communicating*—the back and forth, the give and take of ideas, not (as in this example) the mindless parroting of rigid, fixed forms. Where in this drill is the meaning that we know to be the very base of language? Where is the creativity, the novel expression, that is the core of language? Where is the communication here, interacting with someone about something for some reason? The teacher and children in this drill are practicing something which is diametrically opposed to language in its meaninglessness, in its rigidity, in its purposelessness. The children may get very good at doing drills of this type, giving fixed responses to fixed questions on cue. What they are *not* getting better at through this activity, is *languaging*. My concern is that such activity adversely affects children's language growth.

If we build out from the interests and concerns we observe in our children, it is unlikely that we will fall into the verbalization trap. Moffett's (1973b) second- and third-grade teachers started with a "burning issue," their children's concerns about the petty stealing of supplies—pencils, rulers, erasers. It would seem, on the face of it, an unpromising starting point for rich language, but in fact it was a very powerful starting point precisely because the children were extremely concerned about this issue. As the children tried to solve the problem of petty stealing, their activities included initial discussion in small groups and the recording of the main ideas from each group's discussion; discussion among the recorders from the initial groups; planning and making posters about stealing; planning a publication about stealing—brainstorming in small groups, recording ideas, presenting ideas to a panel, selecting the best ideas for what to include in the publication; going around to other classes to explain the campaign; preparing a questionnaire and conducting a survey on attitudes toward stealing; writing articles for the class publication, reading them to others, discussing the articles, offering feedback to authors of the articles, rewriting and proofreading the articles, and selecting the final group of articles to be circulated to other classes; going in pairs to other classes to get reactions to their suggestions for dealing with stealing; small group discussion of these reactions (main ideas recorded); final discussion about specific ways to implement the campaign throughout the school (Moffett 1973b, pp. 49–50, 139–42). Here the children were using language meaningfully across all channels: they were listening, speaking, reading, writing with purpose.

> As one of the teachers said, the project may not prevent stealing, but it works well for language development. For motivating pupils to speak and write, and to do so in real and meaningful ways, it seems indeed very successful. The teachers felt that the pupils came alive and became involved in language as they never had before. Four features of the process account for this, I believe, and would be desirable traits of other speaking and writing assignments for this age. (1) Though paramount to the teachers, speech was, in the pupils' eyes, incidental to the goal of social action; it was a means to a real-life end, solving the problem

of stealing. (2) The various speaking and writing tasks formed a long-range continuity that imparted practical sense to each task and accumulated momentum as one led into the next. (3) Pupils were allowed to socialize, make decisions with peers, and exercise some independence as groups. (4) The high motivation cut out distraction and impelled the children to interact within their groups (p. 50).

2. *Talking about language must not replace using language.* The following sequence from a third-grade language arts text would be a poor substitute for any experience of the "burning issues" children.

NOUN DETERMINERS

Study the following sentences. Each word in color is a noun. What word comes before each noun?

These examples follow with each capitalized word printed in blue.

The APPLE is good.	The APPLES are good.
A PEACH is good.	These PEACHES are good.
An ORANGE is good.	Those ORANGES are good.
That PEAR is good.	Two PEARS are good.
This CARROT is good.	Three CARROTS are good.
One MELON is good.	Four MELONS are good.

Each of the words before a noun is a *noun determiner.*
Read the sentences in each group again. All the nouns in the first group are singular nouns. All the nouns in the second group are plural nouns.

Which noun determiners go with singular nouns? Which go with plural nouns? Which noun determiner is in both groups?

Think about noun determiners. Do they come before or after nouns? What are some noun determiners? (Hand, Harsh, Ney, Shane 1975, p. 152)

Next the children are to practice.

FOR PRACTICE

Oral Read each of these sentences. Use a noun determiner in each sentence.

1. ____shoe is small.
2. ____bee stung me.
3. ____rabbits jumped out.
4. ____elephant is big.

5. ____grapes are ripe.
6. ____monkey fell.
7. ____boys are big.
8. ____pencil is sharp.
9. ____balloon broke.
10. ____girls ran fast. (p. 153)

What are these third graders able to do or what do they know after completing this exercise that they didn't know or weren't able to do before? Well, they may be able to define "noun determiner," or to identify certain words in sentences as examples of "noun determiners." Some children may even be able to list, on cue, which noun determiners are used with singular nouns, with plural nouns, or with both—at least, they may be able to do this until the chapter test is over, after which time this memorized item will fly because it was irrelevant to the child's real life in the first place (unlike the burning issue of petty theft). The real question is: Is the child a more effective user of language after completing such an exercise? Are *you*? Perhaps you hadn't thought about noun determiners before, which is highly likely, as there are certainly more interesting things for you to be thinking and talking about. Has your use of language improved after this (renewed) acquaintance with the label "noun determiner"? I daresay it hasn't, precisely because using your language in communication with others makes you a more effective communicator; labeling syntactic items simply makes you a better "syntactic item labeler" (at least for a few days). Talking about forms doesn't help you express meanings more effectively.

(Though our main concern here is with differentiating between talking about language and using language, the temptation to raise a peripheral question about this type of drill is irresistible. Why is it that we find such an abundance of incredibly dull, sterile, and artless "language" examples in, of all places, *language arts* textbooks? We would have to go a very long way to find a third grader who, in her own natural conversation, ever said anything so dull or unlanguage-like as "Four melons are good." Is this really what we want to surround our vital and involved language learner with?)

3. *Structuring a simple-to-complex sequence of forms is inappropriate.* The communication itself will determine the language forms the child uses and responds to: Who is sending the message (speaker or writer), who is the receiver (listener or reader), what is the purpose of the communication, what is the situation in which it is carried on? If the child is sending the message, she will "express the intentions of which she is capable" through the linguistic devices she controls, probably moving gradually (as Slobin suggests young children do) into new forms to express familiar meanings or familiar forms to express new meanings. Our child sender will probably do some selecting and shaping of her expression depending on who her listener (or reader) is. Some-

one familiar? A stranger? Someone older? A younger child? Someone of higher status, perhaps another teacher? A public librarian? A school board member? She will also select and shape depending on her purpose. Is she trying to inform, to entertain, to persuade, to gain information, to comfort? And she will shape, too, in response to the situation—the time, place, number of people involved, formality. If we focus on language use for effective communication, then organizing a curriculum for simple-to-complex sequencing of syntactic structure or vocabulary has no place. Shall we say "We'll begin by having the children use simple sentences and next month we'll add conjoined structures?" Or "This week we'll use the vocabulary in Thorndike's Basic 500 and next week we'll add 'appreciate,' 'sincere,' and 'fertility' "? No, we and our children use the language forms that will help us accomplish effective communication.

Children will become more effective interactants as they have more opportunities to interact. Structuring the language curriculum for children's continuing acquisition of language forms or for their more effective use of them in communication is no more necessary for ten-year-olds than for two-year-olds. That "curriculum" is based, in school as at home, on children's interests and concerns. Natural shaping does occur in real communication events at school no less than at home—simplifying, clarifying, paraphrasing, emphasizing—but it happens not through sequenced curriculum, but through feedback as to whether one has been understood and whether one has achieved the purpose of the communication.

4. *Contrived situations must not replace real ones.* It is easier to get charts of flowers or grasshoppers and have a class "discussion" about them than it is to have the children get a supply of real flowers or grasshoppers to examine. But the level of involvement and correspondingly the level of the children's language in the real situation will far exceed that in the picture chart situation and will make the flower or grasshopper search worth all the trouble. (And of course, there are lively language possibilities in the real business of figuring out how we can get enough flowers or grasshoppers for all of us, as well as in the actual gathering of them.) Listen to the language of children in clusters of four or five, as they "mess about" with different types of flowers and discover the "themes and variations"—basic parts and specific differences among them. New meanings find expression as they wonder, question, inform, argue, reason through language. It is not long before "stamen" and "pistil" become useful replacements for their "long thing with the fuzzy stuff at the end" or "tube thing with a ball at the bottom." This is in striking contrast to the language of the picture chart which typically goes something like this:

T: I have a chart here for you today boys and girls, about the parts of a flower. Did you ever think about what kinds of parts flowers have?

Cs: (general mumbling).

T: Well they all have pretty much the same kinds of parts.

C-1: They all have petals.

T: Right, Jamie. They all do have petals. Now here's something else they all have. See this long stick-like part? It's called a stamen. You've probably seen these before. If you look inside a flower you see the stick-like part that is fuzzy on the end. Have you ever seen that?

Cs: Yeah. I have. I have, teacher. Me too!

T: Well, that's the stamen and. . . .

The situation is stilted and the language in it is lifeless. The real situation, however, lives for the children, and their language lives in it.

5. *Staged performance must not be emphasized over interaction.* Performing in front of others, whether putting on a play for an assembly or for parents' night, acting out a story for a younger class, or doing show and tell, can be a great experience for children of any age. Performing seems to be high in motivational value. But in terms of children's language experience and growth, it is likely that the greatest value is in the attendant activities rather than in the performance itself, that is, in the planning, the creating, designing, decision making, and publicizing. Language often lives in these activities in a particularly vital way, possibly because communication is terribly important in these activities in which children are working together toward goals they care very much about. This is not to say that there is no conflict; but remember, argument is a valid language function and can be engaged in more or less effectively. But it does seem to be the case that language lives in shared experience. Preparing to perform for others is one particularly exciting shared experience for children. It's important to stress, however, that the importance for language growth is more in the interaction involved in reaching the goal, than in the performance itself.

Knowing that I am interested in children's language growth, teachers often tell me when I wander into their classrooms, "We do a lot of oral language development in my class. Every week I make sure that every single child has a chance to get up in front of the others and tell about something." This may be a valuable experience for children. But it would be a mistake to see this as one's (oral) language program. Performing before a group of twenty-five peers is something we are rarely called upon to do as adults or as children. Yet we know that we communicate with others every day, using our language for a variety of purposes. Thus involving our children in using their language for a variety of purposes in interaction with each other and with others constantly, constitutes a language program, as performing weekly before twenty-five peers will never do.

The growth of language is aided by an environment which provides rich diversity of verbal and nonverbal experience. On the face of it, the school would seem to be especially well designed to provide great diversity in verbal and nonverbal experience for children. If we exploit the resources available within the classroom, within the school, in the neighborhood, and in the larger community, our children are bound to have many rich experiences. Language lives and grows in these, as our children select, plan, engage in, and relive them later in their talk and in their writing. And because the school makes available a range of real situations, interactants (oral and written), and purposes for using language, we stand in a special position to expand the child's language beyond the instrument she brought from home.

Often throughout this chapter it seems we have focused as much on learning as we have on language. That is because language and learning are so inextricably intertwined. We have seen that children's language growth is rooted in their cognitive growth and that all their verbal and nonverbal experiencing are language related. We move now to consider this language-cognition relation. We know that cognitive growth contributes to language growth. Does language growth also contribute to cognitive growth?

SUGGESTED EXERCISES AND PROJECTS

1. *Meanings and relations.* You know that Stage 1 major meanings and relations include the following categories: (1) nomination, (2) recurrence, (3) nonexistence, (4) agent-action (5) action-object, (6) agent-object, (7) action-location, (8) entity-location, (9) possession, (10) attributive. Assign the following examples to categories by placing the appropriate category number on the line preceding the situation description and child's utterance. You may find some items can belong to either of two categories. For these, what additional situational information would help you decide which meaning or relation the child intended?

   ———(Child named Kathryn is at breakfast table. Points to her father's juice and then to her own.) "Daddy juice. Kathryn juice."

   ———(Mother is putting child's toys in toy box.) "More play."

   ———(Child sees mailman coming.) "Mail come."

   ———(Child is looking for pockets in dress.) "No pockets."

   ———(Child picks up a toy car.) "A car."

   ———(Mother puts child's shoe in closet and closes the door.) "Allgone shoe."

   ———(Adult: "That's a little tiny button isn't it?") "Tiny button."

   ———(Adult: "I have to go home now.") "Go home?"

   ———(Mother is washing child's sweater.) "Mommy sweater."

   ———(Adult: "Bring me a book and I'll read you a story.") "Book shelf."

   ———(Child slams door.) "Close door."

   ———(Child points to picture of a boat.) "Pretty boat."

   ———(Child is looking at a picture of a dog. Adult: "Where's the doggie's nose?") "Here nose."

   ———(Adult pointing to picture. "He's hiding the doll.") "Hide doll."

————(Child named Paul is eating lunch.) "Paul lunch."
————(Adult: "I found your shoe under the chair.") "Find chair?"
————(Child is building with blocks. Reaches for another block.) " 'Nother block."

2. *Analysis of child language sample.* In as natural a setting as possible, record, or have a mother record, a total of thirty to forty minutes worth of language from one child (age two to four). Transcribe and analyze your recorded data. Find the MLU for your sample (see Brown 1973, p. 54, for procedure for determining MLU). Discuss the semantic, syntactic, and phonological features of the child's language system (as evidenced in the child's performance), and the purposes for which you feel the child is using his language. It will help if you number the child's utterances sequentially in your transcript, so that you can readily cite supporting examples from your data for the points you make in your discussion.

3. *Study of child-child language.* Record twenty to thirty minutes worth of good (audible) conversation among several children between two and five years old, playing together in as informal a situation as possible and *without an adult* in the immediate vicinity. Transcribe your tape. Then (1) analyze it for any differences you notice between the children's use of language and your own, and (2) cite as much specific evidence as you can from your recorded data of the children's knowledge of language rules— of principles underlying their verbal behavior.

4. *Replication of Berko Gleason study.* Replicate Jean Berko Gleason's (1971) morphology study (the "wug study") with four or five children, ages four to seven. You'll conduct the test with each child individually, describe your results, and compare with Berko Gleason's.

5. *Replication of Chomsky study.* Replicate Carol Chomsky's (1969) "promise" and "easy to see" studies, *or* her "ask/tell" study with four to five children ages five to ten. Conduct the test(s) with each child individually and discuss your results.

6. *Sentence repetition test.* Construct and administer a sentence repetition test of approximately twenty-five items to each of five children ages two to five. Be sure your test includes sentences of a variety of types (affirmative statements, negative statements, commands, questions), of varying lengths, and of varying complexity. Record each child's responses and transcribe them exactly. Analyze your results. Are there differences from younger to older children? What are they? What kinds of changes do the children make in their repetition of the model? Do they substitute items?

Delete items? Rearrange items? Which ones? How can you account for these changes? Do you see any patterns here?

7. *Study of mother's speech to young child.* Tape record an informal conversation between yourself and the mother of a two- to three-year-old (about fifteen minutes worth). (You might tell the mother that you are taping because you don't like writing things down and would rather just talk with her informally, but you do want to have the information from the conversation, in case you want to refer to it later.) The focus of your conversation will be for the mother to tell you about her child. Get her to talk *as much as possible.* Then have her, at some time when you are not present, tape about fifteen minutes worth of her informal interaction with her child— for example, child's play time after nap, child's bath, lunch time. Transcribe both tapes. Analyze the mother's language to compare the language she used when she talked with you, an adult, and the language she used when she talked with her child. Note any semantic, syntactic, phonological features of difference in her language in the two situations (length of sentences, complexity of sentences, variety of vocabulary, variations of pronunciation, stress or emphasis, use of playful nonsense words, number of well-formed sentences).

8. *Adults' language to children of different ages.* In as natural a setting as possible, have a parent tape about thirty minutes of family interaction involving at least one parent and two children of different ages. For example, a mother and father and their one- to two-year-old and four- to seven-year-old at dinner would be ideal. Transcribe your tape. (There are bound to be points at which the sound is inaudible. Just transcribe as completely as you can, leaving blanks for the segments it is impossible to hear, and indicating by a question mark those segments of which you are uncertain.) Analyze your transcript noting especially any differences in the adults' language with each other, with the older child, and with the younger child. Also, how does the language of the older child change when interacting with the adults and when interacting with the younger sibling?

9. *Survey.* We hear adults express many commonly held misconceptions about how a child acquires a language. Design a questionnaire relating to how children acquire their language and have at least twelve adults respond to it. Discuss your results. What notions about language acquisition are most prevalent in your sample? Do the ideas of parents differ from those of nonparents? If so, how? Be sure to frame your questions so that they are open enough that respondents' answers will be informative (not simply "yes" or "no"), yet limited enough that people will not simply throw the questionnaire in the waste basket because it is too much trouble

to respond. An appropriate item might be: "Some adults feel that praising children for certain behaviors strengthens those behaviors, and that giving negative verbal reinforcement for certain behaviors discourages those behaviors. How important do you feel an adult's positive and negative verbal reinforcement (praising or correcting) is, in moving the child toward a more adult-like language system?" It would be inadvisable to phrase this as a yes/no question ("Do you think X is important?") as your responses would be minimally informative.

10. *Children's interests and language experience.* If you are currently working with a class or group of children, get some index cards and write one child's name on each card. Then, below the child's name, list three special interests of that particular child. It is likely, at this point, that you will need to observe your children more closely for awhile in order to come up with three interests for each one. (This in itself is helpful, as it will clue you in to which of your children are kind of "blending into the woodwork.") After you have at least three special interests listed for each child, think of some language experience that you can provide and help each child move into that relates to one of the three interests you have listed. Write your ideas down, one on the back of each child's card. Implement as many of these ideas as you can. Which of the ideas turn out to be on target? Which ones simply miss? Why? How does your original idea change when the child gets involved? How does it expand—for this child? For other children who join in? What might you do next?

11. *"Your own thing."* Design your own learning experience relating to the ideas in this section, discuss it with your instructor and/or an acquaintance knowledgeable in this area, and execute it.

SUGGESTED FURTHER READINGS

Some useful works relating to the sequence and/or process of language acquisition in children, include the following:

BAR-ADON, A. and W. LEOPOLD, *Child Language: A Book of Readings.* Englewood Cliffs, N.J.: Prentice-Hall, Inc., 1971.

BROWN, R., "An Unbuttoned Introduction," pp. 4–59, in R. Brown, *A First Language: The Early Stages.* Cambridge, Mass.: Harvard University Press, 1973.

CHUKOVSKY, K., *From Two to Five,* trans. and ed. Miriam Morton. Berkeley: University of California Press, 1963.

DALE, P. S., *Language Development: Structure and Function* (2nd ed.). New York: Holt, Rinehart and Winston, 1976.

HOPPER, R., and R. NAREMORE, *Children's Speech: A Practical Introduction to Communication Development.* New York: Harper & Row Publishers, Inc., 1973.

SLOBIN, D. I., *Psycholinguistics* (2nd ed.). Glenview, Ill.: Scott, Foresman and Company, 1979.

Films relating to language acquisition, that might be of interest, include:
Child Language: Learning Without Teaching. Sterling Educational Films, Inc.
Development of the Child-Language. Harper & Row Publishers, Inc.
Early Words. John Wiley & Sons, Inc.

A film that is compatible with the ideas presented in this section, and relates entirely (and vividly) to classroom practices is:
Oral Language Development: Views of Five Teachers. Agency for Instructional Television.

Another film of interest that relates to children's language development over time is:
Shared Nomenclature. Ohio State University. Film Lab Service, Inc., 4019 Prospect Avenue, Cleveland, Ohio 44103

Two books relating directly to teaching, which are helpful in that they are not prescriptive so much as suggestive—sparkers to get your own ideas going—are:
HOLT, J., *What Do I Do Monday?* New York: E. P. Dutton, 1970.
KOHL, H., *On Teaching.* New York: Shocken Books, Inc., 1976.

A language arts and reading textbook that many teachers have found helpful is:
MOFFETT, J., and B. J. WAGNER, *Student-Centered Language Arts and Reading, K-13: A Handbook* (2nd ed.). Boston: Houghton Mifflin Company. 1976.

Two helpful introductions to the ideas of Jean Piaget are:
FLAVELL, J. H., *Cognitive Development.* Englewood Cliffs, N.J.: Prentice-Hall, Inc., 1977.
GINSBURG, H. and S. OPPER, *Piaget's Theory of Intellectual Development* (2nd ed.). Englewood Cliffs, N.J.: Prentice-Hall, Inc., 1979.

Section Three

LANGUAGE AND COGNITION

LANGUAGE AND
COGNITION

Chapter 9

Language in Learning

INTRODUCTION

We saw in the last section that language acquisition is clearly dependent on cognition. Children figure out the language in their environment by using powerful processing abilities, hypothesizing, testing, confirming, disconfirming, revising underlying rules for sound-meaning relations. We saw that children's processing of language at different stages is inextricably bound up with their cognitive orientation, whether sensorimotor or perceptually based. We saw evidence of some tentative general operating priciples (Slobin), as well as some idiosyncratic preferred strategies (Nelson), in children's cracking of the linguistic code. Language acquisition is a highly cognitive process.

But the major question for us in this section is the other side of the language-cognition coin: *Can language contribute to cognitive growth?* Fortunately for us, psycholinguist Frank Smith provides "a conceptual framework for teachers" which deals with this question without getting bogged down in the illusive and mysterious realms of mentalism—vague wonderings about "mind," "thought," "idea" (Smith 1975). Smith's approach is the one we will use here. He assumes that every human builds, out of personal experience, a cognitive structure or *"a theory of the world in the head"* (p. 11). This theory, or personal notion of what the world is like, shapes both the way we look at past experience (recall, summarize, interpret it), and the way we look at new experience. Every human attempts (1) to *comprehend,* that is, to make sense out of the world by *"relating new experience to the already known,"* fitting new experience into our existing cognitive structure or "theory" (p. 10); and (2) to *learn,* that is, to alter our existing cognitive structure when experience does not make sense, when it does not square with our "theory." Our theory of what the world is like provides us with a set of expectations. When our ongoing experience fits our expectations, everything is fine; the new experience makes sense, we comprehend. But when the new experience is out of line with our expectations, we are forced to reexamine those expectations and modify them to make room for the new experience—it must fit, it must make sense. Using Smith's conceptual framework, we can rephrase our original question as: Can language help one to make sense out of the world? Can language help one *comprehend* and *learn?* In this chapter we'll consider the use of language to help children comprehend and learn, especially as language is used in (1) questioning, (2) focusing attention, (3) making understandings more precise, (4) making understandings more retrievable, (5) reinterpreting past experience, and (6) going beyond present personal experience. We'll also consider the important role that interaction plays in the child's comprehending and learning.

How are the two little girls in the following two episodes using language to help them make sense out of their world?

(A two-year-old girl is coloring on paper and talking with her mother about the crayons.)

C: That green?

M: Um-hm. It's a very light green.

C: Oh. Brand new?

M: Um-hm. I think that one is brand new.

C: Those too old?

M: Well, some of them are old and some of them are new. The little ones are old and the longer ones are new.

C: Baby one old?

M Um-hm.

C: Throw away?

M: Oh no. We're not going to throw them away yet. They are still good. We can still draw with them.

(Same little girl several days later, in the bathtub, playing with toys.)

C: Gammy make those? (Refers to bathtub toys.)

M No. Grammy didn't make those.

C: Grammy got those?

M: No. Mommy and Daddy got those.

C: Oh. Brand new?

M No, they're old.

C: Throw away?

M: Well, we may think about it. They're not really good blocks. Maybe Santa Claus'll bring you some better blocks. OK?

C: OK. (Child indicates another toy.) Gammy Gammy gave those me?

M: Yes, your Gammy gave those to you.

C: Oh. Brand new?

M: Uh-huh. They're brand new. Remember, they came in that package? Before Thanksgiving?

C: (Child indicates a different toy.) Mommy Daddy get those?

M: Yea.

C: Oh. Old?

M: Not too. Got them to go on the airplane to see Gammy. 'Member?

C: OK.

M: They're pretty new. Pretty new.

C: Pretty new?

M: Uh-huh.

C: (Child indicates a different toy.) Those new?

M: No, those are old.

C: OK. (Child indicates a different toy.) Those, that old?

M: Pretty old.

C: Pretty old?

M: Uh-huh.

C: Those old? Gammy give it me?

M: No, Gammy didn't give those to you. Mommy and Daddy got those.

C: Oh. Those brand new?

M: No, they're old.

C: Still brand . . . still . . . still brand new?

M: No, they're not still brand new. They're old.[1]

[1]I am grateful to Carole Urzúa for letting me include these episodes from her dissertation data.

(A four-year-old girl comes in from playing and eats lunch in the kitchen while her mother is preparing soup. As she enters the house, a neighbor child calls to her, asking if she wants to have a game of throwing leaves in the hair. Mother intervenes.)

M: I don't go for that, not in the hair.

C: Wanna do it on the tummy? (Laughs.) Where's the rice?

M: In the pan.

C Get the old sugee bowl, the old sugee bowl . . .

M: Get the old what?

C: The old sugee.

M: Oh.

C: That's sugar.

M: Oh, sugar.

C: (Laughs.) I said it funny. (Drums hand on bowl and says "bum didee ump" in time to drumming.) Know what? S——— has a brother and he's onny three. K———'s still three. How come you're giving me all that rice? Just give me a few?

M: Um-hm.

C: You ca' have some if you want to.

M: Thank you. I don't think I want any now.

C Numnumnumnumnumnum. Get the, get the sugar bugar mugar. Sugar, bigger, pigger. This is gonna taste yummy yumyumyumyumyum. Put some up here. (Eats some rice.) Yum yum yummy yum. Tastes good. Mom, know what? That's J———'s company. J——— has some company company and that child is one of his company.

M: Um-hm.

C: Just like we had company. Get that. That's hot. I mean is there sugar on that?

M: Is there sugar on what?

C: Those vegetables.

M: (Laughs.) No, that's not sugar.

C: What is it?

M: What do think it is, what else could it be?

C: Rice?

M: No, it's not rice. It rhymes with rice, though.

C: Ice.

M: Ice! Right!

C: How come ice is on it?

M: Because it's frozen.

C: Yumyum, yumyum, yumyum, etc. (Hums.)

C: How come you're—are you gonna have the vegetables? Are you?

M: I'm cutting them up to put in some soup.

C: What kind of soup?

M: It's gonna be vegetable and chicken and rice.

C: yum yum. It tastes good to me. I don't like them. I don't like the broccoli. I don't like all that. What is in there? Is there potatoes?

M: No.

C: What are those white things?

M: Cauliflower.

C: Do you like those?

M: Um-hm.

C: I don't like cauliflower. Augh!! Yukky!! Does it taste good to you?

M: Yeah, it tastes yum to me.

C: It tastes yukky to me.

C: How come M————'s (C's brother) not allowed to play, um, go across the street? C———— said that.

M: Well, M———— isn't. That's right. He's not allowed to go across the street.

C: Well, well he asked you one day. You said he could.

M: Well, yea, he can go across if, if he comes and asks me. But he has to ask me every time he goes across. So I always know where he is.

C: Is that the soup?

M: Yep.

C: Oh. And dates?

M: Dates?

C: Are dates in here?

M: Oh, no. Dates are in another yellow container. That's chicken.

C: Oh. Mamma, I'm getting full.

M: Okay.

C: I'm just gonna take one more bite. Is that corn?

M: Yep.

C: Frozen corn too? Everything's frozen. That, that, that, and that. Is that frozen?

M: No.

C: Just the container. Tomato soup?

M: No, tomato sauce.

C: Tomato sauce. Now I'm gonna go out and have the tea party. But no but I'll tell her, R———— that no putting rocks and stuff on me.[2]

Clearly each of these little girls is trying to make sense out of her world, trying to relate new experience to the theory of the world she has built from her past experience and to further elaborate her theory—of new and old (and pretty new and brand new), of where things come from, of vegetables (what kinds there are and what one does with them), of others' likes and dislikes, of

[2]I am indebted to Julie Niehaus for this episode from her data.

rules. Language is helping them make sense of their experience and figure out what kind of world they live in.

The claim of this chapter is that language is a powerful tool in comprehending and learning. This is not a claim that language is the only tool, nor that it is a necessary tool for making sense out of one's world, but only that it is a most important one. Language helps one to comprehend and learn in various ways, perhaps the most important being questioning.

QUESTIONING

Most children are active questioners. One four-year-old told his mother, "I'm a why-er, you are a because-er!" (Chukovsky 1968, p. 31). A child's questions serve many purposes—seeking permission (Can I go?), requesting (Will you tie my shoe?), initiating social interaction (Know what?). But as the four-year-old "why-er" suggests, one important function of the child's questions is to seek information. A child's questioning for information gives him considerable control over his own comprehending and learning (provided, of course, that he is in an environment in which he is able to exercise it freely). By questioning, a child is able to initiate and actively search for what he wants to know in order to continue building and revising a theory of the world. We see the child as the active party in his own learning once again. It is what *he* notices and wonders about that gives rise to his questions.

We hear people talk informally of children's "innate curiosity." We don't know whether curiosity is, in fact, innate, but we do know that the child's earliest verbal language includes questioning. Even when the child is limited to one-word utterances, questioning is present (Dore 1975) and can be identified by the rising intonation contour of the voice, as well as by aspects of the situation itself (for example, waiting expectantly for a reply and looking away after the reply is given). When children move into combinatory speech, two morphemes and beyond, both yes/no and information questions are much in evidence. It is likely, initially, that one- and two-word questions serve primarily as requests for a verbal response from a conversational partner. But early on children appear to employ questions to gain information as well as simply to engage in conversation. It is difficult to escape the conclusion that the two-year-old in the earlier episode is using questions primarily for cognitive purposes—to figure out some aspect of her world.

You remember that the syntax and the semantics of questioning develop over time and that the semantic development here corresponds closely to a cognitive development sequence—acquisition of what and where questions preceding why questions, with when questions coming still later. Children appear to develop sequentially the linguistic means for seeking the kind of information they are cognitively able to use; first means for categorizing and locating objects, then seeking causes, then locating events in time. Whatever the initial impetus for children's questioning and whatever the various social functions children continue to use questions for as they develop, it appears that one early and significant function of children's questioning is intellectual—the seeking of information about physical aspects (That green? Those too old? How come ice is on it? What are those white things?) and social aspects (Do you like those? Does it taste good to you? How come M——'s not allowed to go across the street?) of the world. In view of (1) the earliness of children's expression of questions and use of questions to gain information, and (2) the notable cognitive-linguistic correspondence in the semantic development of questioning, one wonders whether Britton is right when he says that a child begins "with the drive to explore the world he is born into," and that speech does early become its "principal instrument" (Britton 1972, p. 93).

FOCUSING ATTENTION

Young children's language often serves to help them attend to and execute tasks. Consider the following examples.

(A four-year-old is drawing a picture. Her grandmother is present. The sentences in italics are addressed to her grandmother, the others to herself.)

I'm going to draw a picture now.
Big park and another bit of it coming below. Two bits of it. Colour it in and make it all into one park. Draw St James's Park.
Look! Now I'm going to draw a person walking around.
A little round head. A little eye and another little eye. A little nose. A little mouth. And how big the body is and there's the feet. Hands.
I'm drawing a little girl in the park.
That's a little girl walking round. What nice coloured clothes she's got on. What lovely coloured clothes. Clothes. Coloured clothes. . . . (Britton 1972, p. 54)[3]

(Here is a child talking quietly to herself as she puts her doll to bed.) Putting her to bed. In the bed. Like that. Puts legs down. (Child looks around.) Now . . . well . . . a cover. Where's a cover? I'll have to find a cover . . . in the box (Child turns over the contents of a box) . . . here . . . *that'll* do for a cover . . . there . . . put it round . . . make you warm. . . . There . . . that's nice and warm baby. (Based on Tough 1977, pp. 48–49)

The child's talking here is clearly not directed to anyone else. It is not interactional in any way. The talk is a running commentary that seems to aid in keeping the child "aware of the actions he is performing" (Tough 1977, p. 47).

[3]Quoted with permission from Mrs. E. W. Moore, formerly of the University of London Institute of Education.

Also, when the child encounters an impediment to his action, this talk seems to direct his activity toward the recognition of the problem and the solving of it. The child's talk seems to keep him on course and help him resist distraction.

It would be easy to dismiss this monitoring use of language as the child simply talking to himself idly while playing. But if we remember how important the child's activity is to his building of a theory of the world, then we are likely to see this action-related use of language as an important aid to his comprehending and learning.

Obviously the talk of others can serve to focus one's attention also. Much of adults' talk with the child seems to be for the purpose of directing the child's attention to certain aspects of what he is doing or observing. In the following episode, can you identify instances in which the teacher is using language to focus the child's attention?

> (A five-year-old and his teacher are watching a spinning top.)
> T: Where are all the colours now do you think?
> C: Gone—they've gone away.
> T: Have they really gone away?
> C: No, but you can't see them.
> T: The colours are really still there, do you think?
> C: Mm. 'Cos you can't see them.
> T: The colours are still on the top, but we can't see them. I wonder why can't we see them?
> C: It's going too fast. You can't see them because it's going round fast.
> (The top loses speed.)
> T: Look—what can you see now?
> C: The colours again—red and blue and all colours.
> T: Why can you see them now?
> C: Because it's nearly stopped—it's going slow—you can see them.
> T: What did it look like when it was going round fast?
> C: It just looked like lines—sort of white and black wasn't it? (Tough 1974, p. 82)

When we turn from situations of direct action (drawing, playing with dolls) or observation (of a spinning top) to situations of "thought," again we find that language can aid in directing attention as children conjecture about a situation. What instances can you find in the following two episodes of language serving to focus attention on aspects of situations that children are conjecturing about? Here are a teacher and some six- and seven-year-olds.

> T: I am going to ask you a question. Here's something for you to think about. Do you think the bird was clever to choose that place [under the school roof] to build a nest?
> Cs: Yes. Yes. It was a good place, etc., etc. (several taking part).

T: Why is it?

C: Because the cats can't get at it. . . . Because it is too edgery to go along. . . . It's too narrow to go across, and because they've got small feet. . . . Well, they wouldn't be able to get on . . . and they would just fall off.

T: You don't think the cat could balance along there? And somebody said it's out of the rain, yes? What's another good reason why the bird would build a nest there?

C: Not a very good reason. . . . Because Mark . . . he was trying to get . . . he had a big . . . he had a big cage and he was climbing up to get the bird down. (Based on Rosen and Rosen 1973, p. 49)

And here is a teacher talking with her eight-year-old children about unkindness.

T: What makes you unkind?

C-1: Well . . . um . . . sometimes if children are older than others . . . and then they're nasty to them.

C-2: They tease them.

T: Yes they do, don't they? I wonder why that is?

C-2: They want to.

T: Do you think that when there are a lot of boys together that sometimes that makes a difference?

C-1: Yes. . . . If you get one . . . one bad person . . . an . . . um . . . then all the others um . . .

C-2: Turn bad.

C-3: Yes. . . . Like one bad apple in the barrel turns the rest bad.

T: Yes, that's true.

C-3: Not that to good . . . not that one good makes the rest good . . .

T: You don't think that happens if you've got one good one?

C-1: No, that never happens.

C-3: But if you leave one good one in with bad ones, I think the good one'll turn bad.

C-1: Yes.

C-4: And the . . . and the . . . an' the nasty children . . . an' . . . they'll make the . . . um . . . good children be nasty . . . or . . . or . . . they hurt and everything. They're always unkind with everybody.

C-2: I'm never unkind. (Laughs)

C-5 I don't believe it.

C-2: Don't you?

C-5: No. I don't.

C-3: Everybody's unkind sometime in their life. I wouldn't like someone who wasn't unkind *at all.* (Based on Rosen and Rosen 1973, p. 83)

Even as adults we often find that the very act of verbalizing helps us block out distractions and focus our attention on a demanding task. Have you ever found yourself reading a poem or difficult passage of an article out loud in order to grasp its meaning more fully? In the act of verbalizing we seem to marshall our forces of attention.

In summary then, children's own talking, as well as the talk of those they interact with, can help them focus attention on what they are doing (drawing a picture, or putting a doll to bed), observing (a spinning top), or thinking about (the location of a bird's nest, or reasons for unkindness).

MAKING UNDERSTANDINGS MORE PRECISE

One high school English teacher had a recurrent struggle with her accelerated group of students. As they wrestled with elusive poetic images, she would ask, "What do these lines *mean?*" One floundering student after another would respond, "I *know* what it means; I just can't *say* it." The teacher's answer was always the same: "If you can't say it, you don't know." I think her meaning might be more accurately paraphrased, "If you can't say it, then you don't know it in the precise and clearly delineated way that I want you to." It's possible that our theory of the world, our "knowing," involves much that we cannot articulate. But it is certain that those understandings that we can articulate, we do most surely know, comprehend. Further, it is likely that in the struggling act of representing (re-presenting) our understandings in spoken or written form, we render those understandings more precise, give our nebulous ideas a definite shape they did not have before. Is this why we so often ask our students to "Tell me what you mean by————," or "Tell me how you know that————?" Are we only evaluating their comprehension? Or are we also trying to help them comprehend more fully, more precisely through the demanding activity of articulating their ideas?

MAKING UNDERSTANDINGS MORE
RETRIEVABLE

Often as teachers, in class discussions like the above (about the bird's nest location and about unkindness), our tendency is to supply the expression for the difficult idea the child is struggling to put into words. We finish the sentence for him when he pauses, or we fluently paraphrase his emerging and half-expressed idea. But I believe that the struggle itself is important both for the child's thinking and for his languaging. If we can hold our tongues we do the child a service. There is no surer way for him to become the master of an idea than to render it expressible.

Language labels aid recall. Early studies indicate that those properties of objects which have readily available labels in a particular language are more accurately and easily recalled later by speakers of that language, than those properties of objects which lack such clear, simple, obvious labels. Brown and Lenneberg (1954) studied subjects' recall and recognition of colors. They showed each subject four colors simultaneously, then removed them, and then had the subject select the original four colors from a chart of 120 colors. No color names were used. As expected, those colors that were clear examples of simple, obvious categories (that is, those that had unambiguous labels) were most easily and accurately identified on the chart. For example, a true yellow was more reliably recognized in the array than a yellow-orange example. Using the same procedure with monolingual Zuni Indians, whose language does not have separate labels for yellow and orange but regards them as a single color category, the experimenters found that the subjects frequently confused yellow and orange (that is, selected orange from the 120-color array when the original color had been yellow, and vice versa), whereas monolingual English speaking subjects never confused these two, which are distinctly labeled in English. Interestingly, though no color names were used throughout the experiments, subjects reported that, after seeing the original four colors, they "stored" them as names and then proceeded to identify them on the 120-color chart. Those most easily named were those most accurately recognized later. We frequently have similar experiences to this, for example, when we try to hold in memory the color of a particular pair of pants so as to find a matching top when we go shopping. We seem to hold the color in mind more as a label (such as canary yellow or sky blue) than as an image. In such situations we are more likely to match accurately the true examples of reds, oranges, yellows, greens, blues, and purples, than the more marginal ones (in terms of labeled color categories) in, say, the between-blue-and-green range.

Two other researchers conducted an experiment based on Brown and Lenneberg's color experiment, but using pictured facial expressions as the items to be recalled (Frijda and Van de Geer 1961). Subjects were shown photos, one at a time, of a particular actress' face in different expressions. They then had to select the same photo from a group of sixty. The results were similar to those in the Brown and Lenneberg experiment. Those facial expressions that were most "codable," that had the most agreed-upon descriptive labels, were most accurately recalled and selected from the larger array.

Other studies suggest that language influences not only the ease with which we recall something, but the nature of the recollection as well. Besides remembering part of the perceptual information from an experience, a person remembers a label for that experience. The associations we have for the label itself become part of the recollection. In one study, subjects were presented with line drawings and each drawing was given one of two labels for each subject (Carmichael, Hogan, and Walter 1932). One line drawing was $\vdash$. Those subjects for whom this drawing had been labeled "seven," when asked to draw it later, tended to distort the figure as 7. Those for whom it had been labeled "four" tended to reproduce it later as ꜔ . The subjects recalled their associations with the label "seven" or "four," as well as the perceptual image of the line drawing itself. The line drawing ⧖ was reproduced as ⧎ by those subjects for whom it had been labeled "curtains in a window," but was reproduced as ◇ by those subjects for whom it had been labeled "diamond in a rectangle." Thus the event recalled is a different event from the one actually experienced, partly because of the associations the "recaller" has for the language label that is part of the recollection. When we "re-collect" an experience, part of what we "collect" are the associations that are part of the label we use to name the experience. What this research says to teachers is that in encoding his experience in language, in talking about it, the child will make an experience more readily retrievable. Also, the way the child labels and talks about the experience will influence the way he remembers it later. The associations he has with the labels themselves will become part of the remembered experience. The kind of sense the child makes out of personal remembered experience will be affected by the language which was part of its storage.

REINTERPRETING PAST EXPERIENCE

Britton tells us "Language is one way of representing experience . . . we habitually use talk to go back over events and interpret them, make sense of them in a way that we were unable to while they were taking place" (Britton 1973, p. 19). Here is language serving to aid us in making better sense of our past experience. The word "represent" is important here. Language can provide a means by which we "re-present" past experience—present it again, isolate it, consider it, reinterpret it in light of our ever changing and growing "theory of the world in the head." And of course our theory not only shapes our interpretation of past experience (contributes to comprehension), but that theory is also shaped and modified by subsequent experience (contributes to learning) in that our theory must be able to account for all our experiences, not just some of them. The symbols language provides for re-presenting our experience are a powerful means of making that experience an "object" we can "act on," shaping it to fit our theory, and also an "object" which further shapes our theory. Britton speaks of our symbolizing reality by means of language "in order to handle it" (Britton 1972, p. 20) as some sort of object. Thus language provides one important means for our comprehending and learning, for our making sense out of our past experience.

GOING BEYOND PRESENT PERSONAL
EXPERIENCE

The notion of language aiding us in going beyond the present situation is a favorite of Bruner's. He believes that, in time, children develop language as a cognitive instrument such that they can use language symbols to represent, manipulate, and transform "the regularities of experience" apart from the direct experience itself. We can see children grow in their ability to use language to "go beyond" in at least three areas: (1) going beyond the actually present here-and-now experience, (2) going beyond the personal experience, and (3) going beyond the real or possible experience.

Going Beyond the Present Experience

Though much of young children's talk is closely tied to their action of the moment, there is evidence that two- to three-year-olds are beginning to go beyond the here-and-now experience in their thinking and talking. They may talk about events which have recently happened or soon will. The following two-year-old is talking with her mother, who has picked her up from the sitter, about events that happened recently.

> *M:* What did you do today with Kimberly? Can you tell me?
> *C:* I played toys with Kimberly.
> *M:* You played toys with Kimberly?
> *C:* I put the toys away.
> *M:* You put the toys away?
> *C:* I put the tinker toys away.
> *M:* Oh, the tinker toys.
> *C:* Was messy.
> *M:* It was messy?
> *C:* Yep.
> *M:* Oh.
> *C:* In Kimberley's room. (Sachs 1977, pp. 59–60)

And this three-year-old is talking with her mother about going to her grandmother's ("Na-ma's") later in the day.

> *C:* ... go to, to Na-ma's and play.
> *M:* Wadda ya gonna play at Na-ma's?
> *C:* So we (inaudible) to, to babies.
> *M:* You gonna play with the babies?
> *C:* Yep. To Na-ma's.
> *M:* What else?
> *C:* So play, play with the toys.
> *M:* With the toys? What else?
> *C:* Puppy.

M: Would you like to play with Skippy? (Skippy is the puppy's name.)

C: Yep.[4]

Going Beyond the Personal Experience

Joan Tough's study of three-year-olds suggests that some children this young are beginning to be able to go beyond their own experience, projecting themselves into the experience of others. Here are some examples of three-year-olds using language in an empathetic way.

> Jane refers to a child who was crying before she came into the observation room:
>
> *Jane:* She doesn't like Terry teasing . . . that's horrible . . . and she's crying 'cos she didn't like it.
>
> Tim talks about the figures in the snowstorm novelty:
>
> *Tim:* The cowboy wouldn't like going up and down on the see-saw . . . it would make him feel sick.
>
> Michelle is telling the observer about an accident at home when her mother fell over their dog:
>
> *Michelle:* Lassie didn't mean to . . . not to hurt my mum . . . she didn't. (Tough 1977, p. 58)

And here are two three-year-old boys discussing the kind of garage they will make out of an available shoe box. The discussion involves one child going beyond his own experience to incorporate the other child's.

> *C-1:* Well, you know, garages have to have doors.
>
> *C-2:* Sometimes they don't.
>
> *C-1:* Garages have to have doors that will open and shut.
>
> *C-2:* My grandad has one and he puts his car in and that hasn't doors.
>
> *C-1:* But a garage has doors—and you lock the door so nobody can take it—the car you see.
>
> *C-2:* My grandad has a car thing and it hasn't doors on. It just keeps the rain off you.
>
> *C-1:* Oh—well—shall we make a garage or a car thing like your grandad's?
>
> *C-2:* Well, I don't know how to put doors on.
>
> *C-1:* I would think of glue or pins or something like that.
>
> *C-2:* No—put it this way up see—and cut it.
>
> *C-1:* Yes, that might be all right.
>
> *C-2:* Right—Mark—right—I'll get the scissors. (Tough 1974, p. 21)

---

[4]I am indebted to Shirley Hollibaugh for this excerpt from her data.

Going Beyond the Real Situation

We sometimes see young children go beyond a real situation to an imagined one. Some of the imagined ones are situations that could occur (for example, dramatic play of domestic activities), and some are situations that, for adults at least, could not occur (such as dramatic play involving monsters and ghosts). Consider again the play session between the two four-year-old girls (pp. 141–43); this session involves both types of imagined situations.

Sapir sees the possibility of going beyond the present personal experience as being heavily dependent on language.

> If a man who has never seen more than a single elephant in the course of his life nevertheless speaks without the slightest hesitation of ten elephants or a million elephants or a herd of elephants or of elephants walking two by two or three by three or of generations of elephants, it is obvious that language has the power to analyse experience into theoretically dissociable elements and to create that world of the potential intergrading with the actual which enables human beings to transcend the immediately given in their individual experiences.... (Sapir 1956, p. 7)

He may be right. However, I see no way at this time to determine clearly whether language makes it possible for us to go beyond the actual, present, and personal, or whether language merely expresses our having done so. At the very least however, we can assert with confidence that language supports our going beyond. Thus language makes a significant contribution toward our comprehending and learning, toward our building a theory of the world which includes what *is* and what *is not,* and also what *could be* and what *could not be.*

It is a predictable aspect of children's language growth that they will gradually move from their language, relying heavily on personal, present, direct experience, toward a greater independence of language from immediate situation. Perhaps this is what Bruner means by language becoming a "cognitive instrument" for children. Over time, children become better able to represent hypothetical situations and manipulate language symbols apart from an actual situation. Remember that some see this progressive independence of language from context as the child's greatest language achievement over the elementary school years (L. Bloom 1975, quoted on p. 154). If Bruner is right, the child becomes able to transform reality to create and consider different hypothetical possibilities through his languaging.

THE IMPORTANCE OF INTERACTION IN COMPREHENDING AND LEARNING

One implication throughout this discussion has been that interaction, the use of language in communication, contributes to comprehension and learning.

Our theory of our world grows and changes as we encounter others' experiences, interpretations, and ideas. This encounter most often happens through language interaction, whatever the expressive channel: talking and listening, reading and writing. New questions and wonderings often arise in interaction. The comments, observations, and wonderings of someone else can get me wondering about something I hadn't considered before. The very presence of a knowledgeable conversational partner may encourage me to express my wonderings and get feedback from my partner that starts me on some new wonderings. The provision of new information may give rise to new questions.

But it is not only in the area of stimulating us to ask new questions that interaction can play an important role in comprehending and learning. We have seen already that our attention is often directed in an interactive situation, whether the focus of attention be a spinning top, or a consideration of safe locations for birds' nests or of children's unkindness. Further, we are often motivated in an interaction situation to put words to our impressions, thus making them more precise. We will struggle to give an idea an expressible shape so that it can be communicated to someone else. Interaction (communication) is a powerful motivator. Interaction can also play an important role in one's recalling and reinterpreting past experiences. Children are eager to tell us about what they are doing or making, or to tell friends about recent experiences they have had. These interactions may serve a cognitive purpose as well as a social one, in that they influence the way the occurring experience will later be recollected, and they provide a setting and motivation for reliving and reinterpreting the past experience.

And, of course, it is in interactive situations that we often encounter others' experiences and understandings that encourage us to extend and modify our own theory of the world. In interaction, we have access to "the beyond" —beyond the present, beyond the personal, beyond the possible. The example of the two three-year-olds making a garage from a shoe box is not a trivial one. C-1 insists that garages must have doors. His experience tells him that garages have doors that open and shut and can be locked. C-2 confronts him (insistently) with a counter example, his grandad's "one" that he puts his car in and that keeps the rain off the car, but that most definitely does not have doors. And C-1, as a result of this encounter, modifies his theory to include both garages (with doors that open, shut, and lock), and also "car things" that don't have doors. The "car thing" is beyond his personal and direct experience, but he makes a place for it in his theory. Through interaction, he has gone beyond the limits of his own personal experience. Through interaction, he has learned.

Piaget has been a leader in focusing our attention on the egocentric nature of young children. His term "egocentrism" has sometimes been misinterpreted to mean that young children are selfish, inconsiderate, and want everything for themselves. But this is not the meaning Piaget intended. Egocentrism refers to the child's perception of experience being limitied primarily to a single perspective: his own. A major aspect of cognitive growth relates to this dimension. As the child matures cognitively, his point of view expands, becomes more variable. He becomes increasingly able to consider a situation from various perspectives, to see various alternative interpretations of and solutions to problems, to see another's point of view. *It may be that, in supporting this movement of the child toward a more variable point of view, interaction makes its greatest contribution to cognitive growth.* We succeed in reaching our own communicative goals, largely to the extent to which we are able to take our partner's perspective into account. If my communication goal is to persuade you to do something, my arguments will be more effective if I shape them so as to anticipate the objections you will raise, to stress the factors I think you will favor, to minimize those I think you will oppose—in short, to select and shape a "case" that will be attractive to you *from where you stand.* If I want you to understand an experience I have had, my communicating will be effective largely to the degree to which I am able to take your situation into account, to select events which have relevance and interest from your perspective, to order them in a sequence which is coherent to you, a sequence which provides what you need to know—again, to select and shape a "story" that makes sense and is interesting *from where you stand.* If my goal is to explain to you how to play a game or how to make something, my explanation is successful in terms of how adequately it takes your situation into account, how appropriately I select what you need to know (and only that), and shape it into an orderly, coherent set—orderly, coherent, relevant *from where you stand.* The examples are endless. The point is that as we engage in interaction, we do so always for some purpose(s). One important factor in our success or failure to reach our goals is the extent to which we are able to take the other into account. In interaction there are feedback signals relating to our success as we go along: "Huh?" "Don't get it." "Noooooooooo way!" "Yeah." "So?" "Uh-huh." "Wellllll . . ." "OK" or, most dramatic of all, the loss of the partner's attention when he drops out of the interaction.

It has been pointed out repeatedly that, over time, children become more effective communicators. Presumably this is due in part to their cognitive development in becoming better able to take another's point of view and shape their messages accordingly. But I would argue strongly that children's constant interaction to accomplish communication goals which are important to them powerfully contributes to this dimension of cognitive growth. Engaging in meaningful interaction helps children grow in their ability to take another's view into account, and thus contributes to the growth of mental flexibility. We saw in Section Two that interaction was an important base for language growth. It can be an important base for cognitive growth as well.

Chapter 10

Language in Learning, Teachers, and Children

INTRODUCTION

In this chapter we'll consider three main topics relating to children's use of language for their learning in classrooms: (1) children's curiosity questioning in school, (2) the pressures that the back-to-basics movement exerts against exploratory classroom environments, and (3) characteristics of exploratory classroom environments that support children's questioning.

CHILDREN'S CURIOSITY QUESTIONING IN SCHOOL (DO THEY DO IT?)

If everybody in the world keeps drinking water, are we going to run out of water some day? I don't mean now, I mean years and years from now?

Why is this macaroni on my plate making steam?

What does gravity look like?

Are there more stars in the sky or in a million cans of chicken and stars soup?

People say that no two snowflakes look exactly alike. How do they know that?
How can they tell? How could anybody possibly have looked at every snowflake?

The same nine-year-old who asked these questions at home was observed to
ask very different questions in his classroom:

Do we underline the spelling words?
Do you want us to skip every other line?
Do we write the date on this paper?

Why is his curiosity and the language that expresses it so alive and vital at
home, yet noticeably absent at school where his questions demonstrate an
overriding concern for following the teacher's preferred procedures? How
typical is this child? Unfortunately, my observations of children in elementary
classroom settings suggest that he is the rule rather than the exception. The
main concern of the majority of the elementary level children I observe in
school settings is to do what you are "supposed to do": finish assigned written
work accurately, neatly, in the proper format, and on time.

Some undergraduate education majors who were engaged in field experiences in classrooms ranging from preschool through sixth grade (and including
one Sunday School class), were asked to write down ten successive questions
they heard children ask in their classrooms. (For a related project suggestion,
see number 2 on page 259). These undergraduates did not know why they were
being asked to do this, so presumably they did not select the questions in any
way. Their university instructor had simply told them: "At some time when
you are not doing the teaching in your classroom, say to yourself, 'Now', and
then write down, verbatim, the next ten questions you hear children ask, the
situation in which each question is asked, and the person to whom it is
addressed." The instructor had assigned this question-gathering exercise in
order to get these undergraduates to begin to *listen* to the ways their children
were questioning. This was not intended as a carefully controlled study of
children's classroom questioning; no careful sampling procedures were used,
no interrater reliability was established.[1] Nevertheless, when the resulting
questions were pooled and analyzed, the results were disturbing. The questions
were first divided into three levels: questions asked by pre-school/kindergarten
children, questions asked by primary level children (grades one through three),
and questions asked by intermediate level children (grades four through six).
The questions within each level were then categorized into three groups:[2]

[1]For some controlled studies of children's classroom questioning (relating to dimensions
other than the curiosity/procedural/social distinction used here), see Allender (1969;
1970); Davis (1971); Dodl (1966); Haupt (1966); Ross and Balzar (1975); Torrance (1970;
1972).

[2]Those questions not falling into these three categories were not analyzed further; for
example, questions in dramatic role play situations, questions in which there was insuffi-
cient context to ascertain the speaker's intention, requests for aid, questions seeking repetition for hearing, rhetorical questions.

1. *Curiosity:* a question form functioning mainly to get information about something one wonders about, wants to know about simply to satisfy one's own self. Does not focus on satisfying any outside source.
2. *Procedural:* a question form functioning mainly to get information which will aid one in carrying out a procedure in a way which will be considered acceptable by someone else. Focuses on satisfying an external source; helps one do what one is "supposed" to do.
3. *Social-interactional:* a question form functioning mainly to initiate or maintain or clarify a relationship (for example, an invitation to joint action, a conversation starter, a challenge).

Of the 159 preschool/kindergarten questions analyzed, approximately 45 percent (almost half) were social in nature, approximately 33 percent (one-third) were curiosity questions, and approximately 23 percent (less than one-fourth) were procedural. But the situation changed dramatically at primary level. Here, of a total of 253 questions analyzed, the curiosity questions comprised only 19 percent, and the social only 14 percent, while procedural questions soared to 66 percent (almost two-thirds) of the total. The situation was similar at intermediate level, with 16 percent of the total (116) being curiosity questions, another 16 percent being social, and a staggering 68 percent being procedural. Here are some examples from each level and each question type:[3]

PRESCHOOL/KINDERGARTEN LEVEL

Curiosity:

(Teacher is holding a snake.) What do he like to eat?

(Teacher is outside on a blanket.) How come you took your shoe off?

(To children in a group during play) Where's milk come from?

(To another child) How come you raised your hand and you don't want to do it?

(To an adult observer in the classroom) Is God in cookies?

Procedural:

(During art lesson, to teacher) Can I do it like this?

(During art lesson, to teacher) Do I have to write my name up here?

---

[3]I am deliberately avoiding the problem of defining a question here. At this point, it is sufficient to think of a question as a sentence you would put a question mark at the end of if you saw it written down. I am relying on your intuitive sense of what a question is, though we will see later that interrogative forms (syntactic questions) serve a variety of functions—greeting ("How are you?"); seeking permission ("Can I go next?"); requesting ("Can you get the phone?"); challenging ("Wanna fight?"). We think of questions typically as utterances which seek information. Often they are, but syntactic forms other than interrogatives seek information also (for example, imperatives: "Tell me what you did at school today"; declaratives: "I wonder how you play this game"). The matter of syntactic forms and communicative functions is basic to Section Four.

(During art lesson, to teacher) Is this right?

(During group work, to teacher) What do I do now?

Social-interactional:

(Outside, to another child) Hey, Gabriel. You wanna play this till clean-up time?

(At play dough table, to teacher) See mines?

(After juice, to another child) You like the juice?

(Accusing, during block play, to another child) Are you taking mine?

(At play dough table, to teacher) Know what my mommy buy?

(To student teacher) You know how many I am?

(To student teacher) You didn't know I got my ears pierced, did you?

(Free play, to another child) Andrew, will you talk to me?

(After an argument at art table, to another child) I forgive you, Jenny. Do you forgive me?

PRIMARY GRADE LEVEL

Curiosity:

(All the following, and many more, were asked of a visiting scuba diver who had talked with the children and let them examine his diving equipment.)

Have you seen any sunken British ships?

Do you have a collection of sea shells?

Have you seen any dead people?

Have you ever seen a shark?

What happens if your fin trips on the side of the ship?

Procedural:

(To teacher) Do I gotta put a heading?

(To student teacher) How many pages do I have to read?

(To teacher during art project) Do we have to color it in, teacher?

(To teacher) Miss, I am finished; now what?

(To another child during seatwork time) Is seven times seven fifty?

(To student teacher) Do we have to write one of them stories again?

Social-interactional:

(To another child) Did you watch *MASH* last night?

(To another child, while filling out worksheet) Why don't you sit down beside me, right here?

(To another child) What did you call me!?

(To student teacher) Everybody's angry today, right Miss?

(To another child at recess) What are you doing, you dummy!?

INTERMEDIATE GRADE LEVEL

Curiosity:

(To another child during free play, referring to finger brace) What is this thing any-way? Is it somethin' to put on your finger so it won't break?

(To student teacher) Why aren't you married?

(To adult observer, after seeing a picture of Medusa) How come she's got a head full of snakes?

(To student teacher) Do you get paid for this or something?

Procedural:

(To teacher) Do I put a "j" right here?

(To teacher) Can I go on to the next color of rate builders?

(To student teacher) How many commas is it supposed to have?

(To teacher) Miss, is this right?

Social-interactional:

(To teacher, while looking at book) Want me to show ya' the kind of dog I like?

(To student teacher) You wanna play a little short game?

(To student teacher) Did you know he loves you?

Why would the proportion of procedural questions triple from kinder-garten to intermediate (23 percent to 68 percent), and the proportion of curiosity questions drop by half (33 percent to 16 percent)? It would appear that we are saying to our kindergarten children "Being curious and exploring your environment is appropriate here . . . " but, to our postkindergarten chil-dren we say " . . . but not here."

Needless to say, the "results" of such an informal exercise are at best only suggestive, but they do square with my own observations of children's ques-tioning in elementary school classrooms. Why do I hear so little of the vigorous curiosity questioning that I know the child engages in outside of school, and so much of questioning aimed at making her performance acceptable or correct to someone else? Is the child building a rich theory of the world by asking such questions? Do these questions support her comprehending and learning? Per-haps she is building a theory of how to function without getting into trouble in the classroom, and this will certainly make her school life more pleasant. But why is the environment such that the child's overriding concern is "How do I satisfy others' requirements?" rather than "How does this world I live in work?"

The informal exercise described above had a second part. This involved undergraduate education majors asking school-age children (preschool through grade six) the simple question, "How do you learn in school?" (For a related project suggestion, see number 4 on page 260.)[4] Again, the students did not know why they were being asked to do this. In fact, their university instructor wanted to focus their attention on children's perceptions of what "learning" is in school and, especially, to see whether any of the children questioned would mention their own questioning as a way of learning. We know that children's questioning is an important source of learning outside of school; would children see it as an important source of learning in school?

The results suggested that, although children may be—and in some cases may see themselves as—"why-ers" outside of school, they apparently don't view themselves as "why-ers" in school. Out of a total of eighty-four different responses given to the question ("How do you learn in school?"), only one child, a kindergartner, mentioned questioning, and apparently was thinking of procedural questions: "Ask about it . . . ask the teacher." (Meaning ask the teacher how I should do the work?)

Several responses suggested an active view of learning in school:

K: By looking at things.

3rd: Sometimes I learn from my mind.

4th: I think.

5th: Using my brain.

Some children, especially the younger ones, simply indicated the content of their learning—what they learned, not how:

K: We learn a, b, c, d, e, . . . (to z).

K: I go 1, 2, 3, 4, 5, 6, 7, 8, . . . (to 49).

K: We learn first grade stuff. That's all we do. We learn first grade stuff so we can be good in first grade.

3rd: I do math, cursive, clean the room at the end of school.

3rd: We learn our times, our division. We learn how to talk in school. We learn how to write.

3rd: Learn math, like division . . . learn manners at lunch.

[4]We can learn a great deal about children's learning experiences by simply asking them. If our goal is to understand what the child's school experience is from where *she* stands as *she* lives it, then the child herself would seem to be the most relevant and informative person to ask. Incredibly, however, the child is the one we rarely, if ever, ask. We ask teacher, principal, parent, test score, cumulative folder and, not surprisingly, we receive the perceptions of the teacher, principal, parent . . . etc. But it is the *child's* perceptions of her learning experience that are the most important and, if we ask her for them, we will get them more often than not.

Most of the children asked said they listened to the teacher, and mentioned him or her as the major (or only) source:

K: By my teacher telling myself.

1st: Listening to the teacher. Be real quiet and listen.

2nd: You listen to teachers and then they just teach you something.

2nd: I listen to the teacher and I don't talk much.

3rd: Pay attention. Doing what the teacher says.

3rd: The teacher tells me what to do and I do it (most of the time).

3rd: I listen to the teacher and then she screams at you and if you don't get it she send you to the principal's office.

4th: The teachers tell us stuff. Then most the time we write it down. Or we do a page that has the same stuff on it.

5th: By having the teacher explain.

Many activities were named, especially reading, writing, studying, seeing films, answering questions, doing homework. (One refreshing preschooler mentioned playing!) Several children mentioned "good" behavior:

1st: I work. I do math and reading. Be careful not to get in trouble.

2nd: By not goofing off or playing around.

5th: The teacher being strict. 'Cause if she's not strict, you'll just play around. 'Cause instead of screaming at you she'd giggle at you.

(And how does one categorize this fourth grader's reply: "Find all the short-cuts, and read the instructions two times"?)

The overall impression from the total set of responses was that the majority of the children saw the business of school more as a matter of doing what was assigned than as a matter of exercising their curiosity and initiative and engaging in active searching. The results of these informal exercises and classroom observations suggest that (1) many classrooms beyond kindergarten do not foster children's active curiosity questioning to a significant degree, and (2) many children do not perceive the classroom as an environment where their curiosity questioning is a significant factor in their learning. Many, in fact, perceive their role as a passive one—do as I'm told.

We come back to a basic question. We know that children from a young age learn much through their questioning. Active questioning is their most powerful way to use language as a tool for learning. School is a place intended above all else to foster children's learning. So—it seems a matter of simple logic that school should be a place that encourages children's active questioning, the use of language for learning. Is it such a place? If not, then why not?

BACK TO BASICS
VERSUS EXPLORATORY LEARNING
ENVIRONMENTS
(ARE THEY IN CONFLICT?)

In the past few years, the pressures against encouraging exploration and curiosity questioning have increased. The public demands "accountability," and publishers rally with packaged educational programs that promise it. The public demands higher standardized test scores, and educators respond by revising their curriculum. The public demands back to basics and we respond with a renewed emphasis on children's memorizing multiplication tables; on looking up, writing down, and memorizing dictionary definitions of words that bear little relation to their experience; on identifying parts of speech in sentences no one ever said or ever will, sentences that exist only in exercise clusters in a grammar text. What the public is *not* demanding, and what we therefore have a more difficult time justifying, is that children's own curiosity and resultant expression of it—questioning—be regarded as a top priority item which teachers should provide for and nourish. So what shall we do? Well, we might begin by recognizing the fallacies that are part of the back-to-basics movement.

One fallacy is the notion that educators have abandoned, and now must get back to, a concern that children become competent communicators (especially readers and writers) and mathematicians. I can find no evidence that we have ever abandoned these goals. Which educators have not advocated that our educational institutions turn out young people competent in communication and math? Which educators have suggested that these goals be replaced by others? I know of none. Some educators have suggested that additional goals are important; many educators have suggested alternative ways of helping children to attain communicative and quantitative competence. But I have yet to find the educator(s) who left these goals behind and now must get back to them. Thus back to basics seems to rest on a faulty assumption.

A second problem with the back-to-basics movement is a means-ends confusion. What is often advocated in the name of back to basics is that we return to teaching methods used formerly. Typically this means a heavy emphasis on skills, drills, and the memorization of "rules" and specified clusters of facts. Somehow the skills, drills, rules, and facts become the *ends* in themselves, rather than *means* to the ends of children becoming effective communicators, mathematicians, problem solvers. Too often writing aesthetically pleasing symbols in cursive becomes the goal, eclipsing the real goal—effective written communication, which is the only reason for teaching handwriting in the first place. Handwriting is no more and no less than a means of conveying a message. Drilling the correct spelling of isolated words (typically one bookful each year) often replaces the real goal of effective written communication.

Memorization of phonics rules and applying them to words in lists often replaces the real goal of competent reading—extracting intended language meanings from the printed symbols of connected prose. Practicing handwriting presumably helps one form written symbols more attractively and legibly; it does not, in isolation, help one compose more effectively with words. Practicing specified sets of spelling words may help one spell those and possibly related sets of words correctly, but it does not guarantee more effective written communication (or even that a child will spell those same words correctly in her own writing of connected prose). Memorization of phonics rules may help a child decode lists of phonetically related words, but it will not guarantee a more perceptive, involved, questioning reader.

The goal is not to produce handwriters, spellers of words in lists, spouters of phonics rules. These are, at best, means to the ends of producing effective communicators (readers and writers). When these means cease to be integral parts of the movement toward effective communication, when they become themselves the goals, they become counterproductive and we will surely not produce the more effective readers, writers, and mathematicians that back to basics is demanding.

A third problem is a corollary to the second. Increased emphasis on the learning of rote skills and specified sets of facts means increased emphasis on the use of lower-level cognitive processes. Various educators and psychologists have identified hierarchies of cognitive skills or processes, from lower to higher levels. Though their category schemes are not identical, there are striking similarities among them. Benjamin Bloom's (1956) taxonomy of cognitive objectives is the hierarchy most frequently cited. His categories, from lower- to higher-level processing, include (1) knowledge: the recall of facts, terms, methods, patterns; (2) comprehension: the understanding of ideas which have been communicated; (3) application: the using of some idea or principle in a particular concrete situation; (4) analysis: the breaking of a whole down into its parts (elements, relationships of elements, organization principles); (5) synthesis: the putting together of parts (elements) to form a coherent and interrelated whole; (6) evaluation: the making of judgments (Bloom 1956; Hunkins 1976). There is general agreement among educators and psychologists that lower-level cognitive behavior in the classroom involves students "giving back" the same information that they received, while higher-level cognitive behavior in the classroom involves students going beyond the given information in some way—relating it to something else, reorganizing it, inferring from it, using it as a springboard for creatively solving a new problem. Handwriting, spelling, answering comprehension questions at the end of a reading passage in a basal, memorizing number facts or phonics rules or state capitals, only minimally involve the exercise and development of the child's higher-level cognitive abilities and the language that encodes high-level cognitive processing. As the cognitive task becomes more challenging and more interesting, so, of course, does the language task, the expression of more complex understandings. Surely our goal is to engage children in actively using and further developing their highest-level cognitive and language abilities.

In response to the first back-to-basics problem, the suggestion that we are getting "back to" abandoned goals of producing competent readers, writers, and mathematicians, it would seem that, if in fact we are redefining our goals, it is not by way of abandoning them and substituting new ones, but rather by way of deepening and enriching those we have always upheld:

> We want children who can decode print. But more than that, we want *readers,* children who can and do extract language meanings from printed symbols and respond to those meanings actively, questioningly, analytically, feelingly, creatively. It is important that we not confuse word calling with *reading.*

> We want children who can compute. But more than that, we want *mathematicians,* children who can and do perceive significant quantitative relations and solve new quantitative problems creatively based on their solid understanding of quantitative concepts.

> We want children who can write. But more than that, we want *composers with words,* children who can and do express themselves fluently, relevantly, coherently, clearly, imaginatively, dynamically in speech and writing.

We have never left the "basics" of reading, writing, and arithmetic. It is time to redefine them toward greater depth.

In response to the second problem, the mistaking of means for ends, it is necessary to establish proper perspective. Skills and facts are important. That children be able to form written symbols (handwriting) and arrange sequences of symbols (spelling) on paper so that others can extract the meanings they intend to convey, that they be able to multiply without arranging objects in rows and counting them laboriously—these things are important. But their importance lies in their contribution to the real goals of communicating and problem solving. They are not important for their own sake. Handwriting is less important for making a paper pretty than for making it readable, for helping to make it communicate the author's ideas. When skills do not serve these larger goals, they are no longer justifiable.

Here are two examples of skills taught as ends in themselves, altogether removed from the real goals of more effective communication (reading and writing).

1. E———, a second grader, was a competent reader by any measure: achievement tests placed him well beyond his grade level; he was eager to read to younger children, which he did with fluency and dramatic flair; he spontaneously discussed with others what he was currently reading; his reading sparked many questions and provided him with considerable information; he responded emotiallly as well as intellectually to his reading, feeling his way

into the hurts and happiness of the characters portrayed. He was, in short, an effective reader. His mother was surprised one day when he suddenly announced that he was "no good in reading." When she asked, "Why do you say that?" his answer was, "Because I just can't do long and short vowels. I can read the words, and I can tell Mrs. K———the sound the letter makes, but I don't know which ones to call 'long' and which ones to call 'short.' "

Identifying long and short vowels may be a skill that is a helpful means, for some children, toward being able to decode unfamiliar words and thus toward becoming more independent and flexible readers. But this teacher saw it as an important goal for every child, as an end in itself, even for those children who had attained the goal of independent and flexible reading. However E———was figuring out unfamiliar words, it was clear that he was dealing with them successfully, just as you and I deal successfully with previously unencountered words without consciously applying any rules for long and short vowels. The contribution toward the goal of independent and flexible reading is the only justification for teaching this skill. In and of itself, it is an irrelevant, idle exercise. We want readers, not long and short vowel identifiers.

2. Mrs. A———, G———'s fourth grade spelling teacher, was dedicated to getting every child in her class through the spelling book that year, Parts A, B, C, D, E for every one of the thirty-six weekly lessons. Convinced that she was individualizing instruction, she let the children go as fast or as slow as they liked during the daily spelling period, but there was no question as to what each child was to do during spelling class: whatever exercise came next in the book. The problem for G———came the day Mrs. A——— discovered that the school year was two-thirds over and G———was on Lesson 6. For the remaining third of the year, G———lugged the hated spelling book home each night, spent one hour complaining about spelling and another hour copying, endlessly, the hated words, in cramped, tense, dark, and smudgy handwriting. In answer to his angry, frustrated question, "Why do I have to do this? I already know how to spell the words," his mother could only reply lamely, "Yes, I know you know how to spell these words, but Mrs. A———thinks it's important for you to do this, so you had better do it." And G———finished every exercise, A, B, C, D, E for thirty-six lessons. Mrs. A———had won. Or had she?

Two things are interesting here. First, Mrs. A———and G———both knew that G———was able to spell at least 98 percent of the words in the spelling book at the beginning of the year, and those he didn't know he could have picked up easily in a day or two. Second, never once during the entire year did the children actually write something of their own during spelling that was intended to be read by someone else. Spelling was entirely unrelated to any aspect of written communication. What should have been a means to the end of enhancing one's written communication, became an end in itself, totally divorced from any real communication goal.

Here is a counter example to the above. In this example, children are clearly building skills in the service of more effective communication.

Mrs. L———was interested in helping her second graders become more effective in using language descriptively. One afternoon, she produced a plain brown paper sack and invited each child, one by one, to reach in and pull out an object. The children were intrigued as one surprise item after another came from the sack: a strip of eyelet, a scrunched up bunch of Saran wrap, a clove, a small potato, etc. She had cleared an entire bulletin board so that each child's object and written description of it could go on the bulletin board for all the children to look at as soon as they were done. As the children finished their drafts, they brought them to Mrs. L———, who provided an interested response, appropriate spellings where needed, and a few suggestions for handwriting adjustments that would make it easier for the other children to read the description. Armed with these suggestions and a fresh piece of paper, each child wrote a final version and brought it, with the object, to go up on the bulletin board. As the bulletin board began to fill up with objects and accompanying written descriptions, children gathered to read them, laugh, comment, and eagerly wait for the next one. The written ideas sparked new ideas for the gathered children: What else could you say about a clove, besides that it "looks like a little tree or a squirrel's footprint"? What else could you say about a piece of eyelet, besides that "it is something girls wear; boys don't wear it"? What else could you say about Saran wrap, besides that "it grows in your hand" (when you squeeze it in a fist and then open your hand)?

Handwriting and spelling skills were important to the children in this activity. There was no question in each child's mind but that it was important that the description be written clearly and spelled conventionally *so that the other kids could read it and she could feel proud.* The continuity from the beginning of the activity to its completion left no doubt in anyone's mind about the purpose of what they were doing: "We're all gonna get to read each others'. " And that's exactly what they did. No one lost sight of the communication purpose of the writing.

We teach children the important skills of writing legibly and spelling accurately. Do we teach these clearly in the context of real communication—letters the children are going to send to someone, stories they are writing or observations they are recording for others to read? These skills are important insofar as they enhance communication. Taught as ends in themselves apart from communication goals, they are not justifiable. It is important that we not lose proper means/ends perspective, as some back-to-basics proponents have done.

We currently hear many complaints about poor student performance on college entrance exams in composition, vocabulary, and reading comprehension. This relates directly to the third problem with back to basics, namely, the heavy emphasis on lower-level cognitive processes (recalling, memorizing) rather than on higher-level cognitive processes (applying, analyzing, synthesizing, evaluating). If a young person writes an inadequate composition, it is more likely to be because of a failing in higher-level cognitive processes than in lower-level ones: It is likely to be the result of a failure to perceive and select what is significant and relevant to a topic (evaluate, make judgments); to discern what constitute the important relations in a given area (apply, relate, synthesize); to express them in a way that is well shaped to the reader (organize parts into coherent whole, decenter to take another's view). It is not likely to be the result of a failure to comprehend or remember information, but rather a failure in knowing how to recognize *what,* of the information one has access to, is relevant and significant, and *how* to use it. Endless practice in memorization will not contribute to solving this kind of problem. If a young person performs poorly on a vocabulary test, it is less likely to be because she has not committed enough dictionary definitions to memory (in fact, she may have so overloaded her short-term memory with meaningless definitions, that they have gotten muddied up and mixed with each other), than because her experiencing and theory building and languaging about it are limited. It is inevitable that reading and discussion that involve higher-level cognitive functioning, and thus involve the learner most actively, will build vocabulary. As the child stretches to express her growing understanding, the language necessary to that expression will become hers and will not forsake her under examination pressure, as memorized dictionary definitions that don't relate to real experiencing will tend to do. If a young person's performance on a reading comprehension test is inadequate, it is again not the use of lower level cognitive processes that is to blame. It is not that she is unable to comprehend or recall a set of actions that characters engaged in, but rather that she does not grasp the significance of those actions, fails to pick up subtle implications, can't predict what further actions would be in character, fails to recognize what is "figure" and what is "ground" and how they are related in a given passage. It is not that she does not grasp the basic facts (what happened when and where and to whom), but that she does not know how to *use* them—select, evaluate, apply, analyze, synthesize.

Children's curiosity questioning mainly lives at the upper end of the cognitive range. Look at the nine-year-old's questions that opened this chapter. He recognizes that people need water to drink and always will. Based on that, he predicts that someday the water supply may run out. He observes the phenomenon of steam, and seeks an explanation to account for it. He recognizes that gravity is a reality, but seeks a description of its appearance (probably assuming that it could be seen under a microscope, like many of the things he cannot see with his naked eye). He is aware of manyness, that there are amounts beyond his counting or even his conceptualizing range. Now in his question he seeks to compare and relate amounts that lie in that "beyond." He questions how one establishes a generally accepted fact as a fact—how do people find out things for sure? He is not functioning here at the level of basic comprehension or memory, but at much higher cognitive levels that involve his going beyond what he comprehends and recalls, using his knowledge in new and creative ways.

Pressures for accountability, higher test scores, and back to basics can work for, rather than against, our efforts to provide exploratory, question-generating experiences for our children. In the provision of such experiences we can demonstrate (1) that our goals are consistent with (and go beyond) "basics"—more effective reading, writing, quantitative problem solving; (2) that our teaching develops important skills in meaningful ways, skills in the service of important "basic" goals; and (3) that our teaching emphasizes children's growth at the highest cognitive levels, thereby equipping children with the language and quantitative competence that back to basics seeks.

If we are committed to providing learning environments in which questioning, the child's most important language tool for learning, is encouraged, how shall we go about it?

CLASSROOM ENVIRONMENTS THAT SUPPORT CURIOSITY AND ITS VERBAL EXPRESSION

Below are some excerpts from a science experience in which children were actively involved in using their language in curiosity questioning. It is a situation that few of us would choose to teach in—a televised science lesson using a group of children that the teacher scarcely knew. Yet despite the intrusiveness of TV cameras and lights and personnel, the teacher's divided attention between the children and the TV audience (he makes intermittent comments to the TV audience on the children's activity as it proceeds), and the unfamiliarity of the teacher and the situation for these sixth-grade Mexican-American children, they asked many high-level curiosity questions during this half-hour activity. The excerpts below demonstrate some important characteristics which I believe facilitate children's curiosity questioning. Can you identify some features that seem to you to foster this curiosity questioning? (You might want to do this with one or several other students. You also might want to contrast these excerpts with lessons provided earlier which do *not* encourage children's curiosity questioning.)

> (Six sixth-grade Mexican-American children are on the floor around a large plastic tub of water in which there are five live crayfish. Several pairs of tongs are on the floor. Throughout this activity there was much conversation among the children that I was unable to pick up. Nevertheless, the children's remarks in the excerpts that follow give the flavor of the kind of conversation that was going on. The children's questions are in *italics*. The teacher makes some introductory comments to the TV audience, and then turns to the children and asks them his first question.)

T: So how would you pick up a crayfish?

C: Get them by the back.

T: Sure.

(The children are trying to pick up crayfish and are talking about it as they do so.)

T: Are there any other ways? . . . Can you pick them up with your hands?

Cs: Yes.

T: How would you do that?

C: Do they bite very hard?

T: How would you find out?

C: Let 'em bite you.

T: That's good.

C: Do they bite?

C: Uh-uh (negative). They don't bite.

T: What does that feel like when you're picking him up, S———?

C: Like a rock.

T: Does it feel like a rock?

C: Yeah. With a bunch of little sticks in it.

T: Are they sharp?

C: No.

T: How do you know?

C: 'Cuz I already picked 'em up.

C: He wants to bite.

T: How do you know he wants to bite?

C: He's ready to.

C: But how do you know he wants to bite?

T: Well, can you get him to bite?

C: Could you eat crayfish?

T: Sure. What part of the crayfish do you think you'd eat, E———?

C: Tail?

T: Yeah, the tail. Right. What other animals . . .

C: Lobster.

T: Sure, lobster. Right.

C: Crab.

C: Shrimp.

C: His feet are . . . when I touch 'em, they're real hard.

C: Yuck.

C: They force your finger forward.

C: Is that behind his tail some legs for if these get chopped off or something?

T: Do you think that's what they're for? What other purpose could those legs be for?

C: Well ...

T: Does he swim with those legs?

C: No.

T: Does he *swim?*

C: No.

C: He'd have to if he lives in water.

T: All things live in water swim?

C: No. Some things don't live in water, but they still swim.

C: Clams.

T: Clams. Do clams swim?

C: No.

T: You sure?

C: Yes. They do.

T: Do baby clams swim?

C: Yeah.

T: That's something you might want to investigate.

C: How could you tell which one's a girl or a boy?

T: OK. I'm going to tell you that there are four boys in there and one girl, and you tell me how you can tell them apart.

C: I think this one's a boy.

T: How do you know?

C: He has a little thing sticking out and this one doesn't.

T: Where?

C: It's right there.

C: That one's a girl.

T: (Giving task to two children) Could I ask you if one of you would draw what it looks like from the back and the other one draw what it looks like from the stomach? OK. Good. (T gives Cs magic markers and indicates two large blank sheets of newsprint on bulletin board. The two Cs each take a crayfish and begin to draw.)

T: (To another child) Well, E———. What have you decided about your crayfish here?

C: Yuck.

T: Yuck? What do you mean by that?

C: They don't stay still.

T: That's a good observation, G———.

T: M———, what would you say you're doing with him now ... well, before he fell? What were you doing? What were you doing there when he was crawling on your arm?

C: Observing him?

T: What did you observe him doing?

C: His movement?

T: Sure. Movements. What kind of movements did he have?

T: There you go, S————. (C is getting crayfish to walk on his arm.) Good. What kind of movements would you call that? Good, S————. Watch what M————does. He was having him move in a certain way.

C: Sideways?

T: Does it move sideways?

C: No, back.

C: They walk backwards. A crab will run sideways, but he runs backwards.

C: How much do they weigh?

T: How could you find out how much one weighs?

C: They don't look like they weigh even a pound.

T: It doesn't look like it.

C: What are these other legs for?

T: What do you think those are for?

C: Feelers, or what?

C: It's very interesting.

(Talking about crayfish eating. One child suggests a crayfish eats cheese.)

T: Would you like to try a piece of cheese and see if they eat cheese?

Cs: Yeah. I will.

T: All right. Here, E————. This is cheese. You can try that. See if he'll eat that. This is a piece of chicken. Don't you people eat this food; it's not clean. How could you find out if they eat . . . here's some hamburger, if you'd like to try that.

C: Eat the whole piece of cheese?

T: No, just take a little piece.

C: But where does it eat?

T: I don't know. How would you find out where it eats?

C: (To crayfish) Open your mouth.

C: He can move his eyes in back of him, in front of him, sideways.

T: Good observation, S————. Excellent, excellent.

C: How come it never eats?

C: He ate something.

T: Well, maybe it is eating.

C: When I gave him a little piece of shrimp, he started eating it.

C: He's eating the chicken. He's cutting, like, the fibers.

C: Yeah, he's cutting them.

T: Did he eat anything else besides the chicken?

C: A little bit.

C: It looks like he's going to go for the chicken right now.

C: Liver?

C: Can they eat liver?

T: Can they eat liver, M———? What did you catch yours on? (Reference to child's earlier statement that he had used liver as bait when he went fishing.)[5]

What characteristics of this activity foster the children's exploration and curiosity questioning and might serve as guidelines for us?

1. *The experience is novel, yet the children can relate it to other experiences they have had.* It is sometimes difficult to hit an appropriate balance between the novel and the familiar. Curiosity is apparently stimulated by novelty (Berlyne 1965) rather than by what is quite routine; yet if the experience is too novel—too "far out" from children's experience—they can't relate to it at all and thus don't wonder about it. This science lesson hits that "delicate balance"; the experience is novel in that the children have not actually handled and investigated a live crayfish before, yet it clearly relates to experiences these California children have had fishing, seeing shellfish for sale, buying and eating seafood of different kinds, watching shellfish on the beach. The experience is intriguing, yet it connects with the theories the children are constructing. It can be integrated there; it has the potential for making sense.

2. *The activity invites real involvement through direct experiencing.* A lesson in which the teacher and children had talked about crayfish without crayfish actually being present would have stimulated fewer curiosity questions from the children. Even a lesson in which crayfish were present but the children couldn't touch them would have been less conducive to children's questioning. The direct experiencing in this lesson led to very close observation that triggered some important questions: "Do they bite?" (a question you're especially likely to ask if you're about to pick one up). "Is that behind his tail some legs . . . ?" "How could you tell which one's a girl or a boy?" "How much do they weigh?" "What are these other legs for?" "Where does it eat?" "How come it never eats?" "Can they eat liver?"

3. *The objective of the lesson is to stimulate children's interest and involvement, rather than to pass on a particular body of information.* David Hawkins (1965) talks of the importance of children's "messing about" as they build understanding. This crayfish lesson was designed to provide a messing-about experience. As we all know, the goal we have in mind (or the objective we have written down) for a lesson strongly influences the teaching procedures we use. The goal here was for the children to explore. Therefore, children's moves in an exploratory direction were encouraged.

4. *The group of children involved in the experience was small.* Groups of four to six children tend to work best in such an activity. Groups smaller than four allow for less of an "idea pool," and thus offer less opportunity for

[5]I am indebted to Dr. John Huntsberger, a superb teacher from the University of Texas, for allowing me to use this episode.

children to learn from each other and to trigger each other's questions. When groups get larger than six, they tend to become less interactive and require more in the way of external controls; there is less initiating and responding conversationally, and more raising of hands, being officially recognized, and spouting an opinion; it becomes more of a performer-audience situation and members participate less spontaneously. Different size groups are appropriate for different purposes, of course, but for experiences in which we want to maximize children's interacting in an exploratory, questioning experience, groups of four to six work well.

5. *The experience invites flexibility in student input, rather than following a narrow predetermined course.* In the course of the lesson, children hit on a variety of interesting areas—what crayfish eat, how they move, whether they bite, how males and females differ anatomically, whether people can eat them, what functions the legs serve, how much they weigh. The various interests they indicate through their comments and questions, the teacher follows up on until some children are focusing on and drawing the structure of the crayfish, some are feeding it a variety of foods and observing its response, some are watching and describing the crayfish's movement on their arms. This flexibility provides a richness that will stimulate further questioning and interaction among the children.

What important things does the teacher do to foster the children's curiosity questioning here?

6. *The teacher prepares beforehand for flexibility—multidirectionality.* Clearly this relates to item 5 above: The flexibility in student input didn't just magically happen; the teacher prepared for it.[6] The teacher had thought through and provided for some interesting areas he thought might arise, and was ready with various food items, magic markers, sheets of newsprint, and an appropriate task in response to the sex differences question. But sometimes questions reveal areas of interest that aren't anticipated. What then? In such situations we consider those areas further with children on the spot, and think through some interesting ways to pursue them—which sometimes means gathering necessary materials at that time, sometimes means planning at that time for what is needed and gathering the materials later for use the next day. This, of course, provides the invaluable opportunity for us to plan *with* children, for them to see how we engage and interact in real problem-solving situations. It is important that our preparation equip us to support the children's moving in various directions on the spot, but that it doesn't close us off from following unanticipated directions of interest indicated by the children. We go in with a lot "at the ready," but know that it is only a beginning, that our children

---

[6]See Kohl (1976), especially pages 37–54, for a discussion of unit planning that incorporates this flexibility in the planning stage.

will move in some unexpected directions, and that it will be important for us to support their moves.

7. *The teacher interacts with the children as an interested participant more than as a director or controller.* (Does this remind you of Nelson's "participative but nondirective adult" interactant with young children, discussed in the language acquisition section?) This lesson is a balanced interaction in the sense that all participants, including the teacher, both initiate and respond. The teacher doesn't feel he has to be the one to respond to everything every child says. Often one child responds to another. The children know that their actions, comments, and questions are interesting and of value to the teacher by the ways in which he responds to and uses their contributions and exploratory activities: Sometimes the response is direct praise ("that's good;" "good observation;" "excellent, excellent"); sometimes it is using the child's comment or action as the basis of his next question or suggestion ("What does that feel like when you're picking him up, S———?" "How do you know he wants to bite?" "Yuck? What do you mean by that?" "Can they eat liver, M———? What did you catch yours on?"). Throughout, one has a sense of all group members participating together in an experience which is interesting and enjoyable to them all. Of course, there are many clues to the teacher's interested participation which are evident on the videotape but can't be captured in print—the interest conveyed by his tone of voice; the enjoyment conveyed by his laughter; the involvement signaled by his body language, moving or inclining toward a child, touching a child, establishing and maintaining eye contact. One senses a structure in the experience which evolves from the interested participation of all, including the teacher, rather than a structure set by the teacher's direction.

8. *The teacher conveys an attitude of an ongoing learner, rather than one who is all-knowing.* His talk and his actions suggest that he places a higher priority on learning and discovering in process than on simply demonstrating the knowledge you already possess. It would be easy to simply give information in this situation. But the teacher's attitude is one of ongoing learning. He often leads the children to do the learning, rather than simply telling them things: "How would you do that?" "How would you find out?" "How do you know?" "How do you know he wants to bite?" "That's something you might want to investigate." "I'm going to tell you that there are four boys in there and one girl, and you tell me how you can tell them apart." "What have you decided about your crayfish?" "What did you observe him doing?" "Would you like to try a piece of cheese and see if they eat cheese?" "How would you find out where it eats?" When he does provide information directly, it often serves as the basis for further exploration. It's the ongoingness, the learning in process, which is top priority.

9. *The teacher's questions emphasize higher-level cognitive involvement.*
The teacher's questions invite the children to participate cognitively at higher
levels than the level of rote recall or basic comprehension. The children are
encouraged to observe, compare, apply, hypothesize, predict, test, synthesize.
Higher-level cognitive questions generally encourage greater involvement from
the children, and it is when children are most actively involved mentally that
they use their language most powerfully for learning.

After many years of educational research, we know that (1) the teacher
is the "most important variable" in accounting for the diverse outcomes of
various teaching methods, and (2) models are important in children's development. If questioning, being curious, wondering, searching are learner behaviors we want to encourage, aren't these the very behaviors our children should
see *us* actively engaging in? How do *we*, important models for our children,
go about the business of learning? How often do our children see us figure
things out? How often do our children watch us function in situations where
we don't know what to do, where we don't know the answers? Above all, how
often do they hear us ask a question that we don't already know the answer
to, a question we simply wonder about? Are *we* ever curious and expressive
of it in our interactions with our children?

A significant finding from Donald Graves' (1978) study of classrooms in
England, Scotland, and the U.S. where children were or were not writing,
supports the importance of teacher as doer and active participant or, as Graves
puts it, the teacher as "artisan." Despite wide differences in many characteristics of the teachers in whose classrooms vigorous student writing was going
on, the characteristic of "teacher-as-artisan" was common to them all.

> They had an artisan's view of the universe. There were no final states. Informa-
> tion and material were constantly evolving toward some expression of excellence.
> Compositions, drawings, experiments, mathematical problems were *not wrong,*
> *only unfinished.* This was their stance toward teaching because they either wrote
> themselves, painted, developed photos, or cared for plants. The children were
> aware of teacher crafts since they wrote, drew, painted, or acted with children.
> Teachers enjoyed their craft and wanted to share it. . . . These teachers provided
> time for writing. . . . [They] not only provided time for children, but time for
> themselves to participate in the [writing] process. (Graves 1978, p. 639)

If we want our children to be actively involved in writing as a meaningful part
of their lives, we encourage this by being writers ourselves. If we want our
children to be actively involved in curiosity questioning, we encourage this by
being curiosity questioners ourselves.

I find as I interact with groups of children who are involved in activities,
that the two words which are magic words for me are "I wonder. . . . " "I
wonder how come . . . ," "I wonder why it doesn't . . .," "I wonder what would

happen if you. . . . " For me personally, these two words work; they feel right. Sometimes they stimulate a wondering in a child, something she might not have thought of if I hadn't wondered out loud. Sometimes they don't and I know it's time for me to be quiet and leave the child alone. But at the very least, "I wonder" helps to establish that I am a wondering woman with a head full of intriguing questions, rather than Wonder Woman who has all the solutions. My guess is (and it's only a guess, though the question is a testable one) that those classrooms in which teachers ask a higher proportion of genuine curiosity questions and do a lot of wondering, are those classrooms in which the children ask a higher proportion of curiosity questions too. By overtly demonstrating a wondering attitude, the teacher tells the children, "This classroom is a place for the open expression of curiosity—for questioning to better comprehend and learn."

We let children know what kind of behavior is appropriate in our classrooms in many ways. Some are direct: we tell them in words what we expect. But some are very subtle and doubtless more pervasive and influential—actions which are worth a thousand words: what the child does that we notice and comment on positively, what the child does that makes us smile in a friendly way, what the child says that engages us in conversation, what the child does that moves us to pat her on the shoulder, what the child does that causes us to choose her to lead the lunch line or be emcee for the parents night program. If we value right answers to our questions, we show that, and that's what the children will try for. If we value neat papers, we show that, and that's what our children will try for. If we value written work in a particular format, we show that, and that's what our children will try for. We are telling children all the time, mostly in ways we are not conscious of, what kind of behavior we welcome. You've seen the sign "Mastercharge welcome here." With far more subtle signs we tell children "Completed work sheets welcome here," "Quiet workers welcome here," "Neat workbook pages welcome here," "Correct math exercises welcome here." Do we also tell our children "Active questioning welcome here"? Is active questioning behavior what we model? Is active questioning behavior what we respond to enthusiastically and actively participate in ourselves? No elementary classroom could or should provide *only* exploratory, messing-about kinds of experiences for children. But every classroom can and should provide an atmosphere characterized by a wondering attitude. A teacher who is a learner, an active questioner, provides the surest sign that questioning behavior is appropriate.

Some educators have concerned themselves with designing programs to teach children to ask better questions. Some interesting activities have resulted. But the motivating cause for some of these has missed the boat. The basic assumption in some cases has been that we need to actively teach children to ask better questions. This assumption seriously underestimates children's questioning abilities. Children can and do question effectively—at age two! Our efforts would be better directed toward providing an interactive, questioning environment in which we actively participate, than at providing contrived question-asking games (for example "Ask me everything you can about this picture." or "See if you can guess what I am thinking of by asking me only twenty questions." Obviously if I ask the right question, as any school age child would do in a natural situation, I only need to ask *one* question, not twenty. "What are you thinking of?"). It is a matter of saying to children "Here is a place to keep on doing that thing you do so well and are continually growing in" rather than a matter of saying "Here, let me teach you to question effectively." Nothing stimulates better questioning than experiences which stimulate curiosity and an environment which encourages its expression.

Many of us can remember the many questions that we, as students, never asked because we didn't want to appear stupid in front of our peers. A question said "I don't know something," and the name of the game was to *know,* to have answers—right ones! How was it that we and often our teachers failed to see curiosity questioning as the intelligent behavior it invariably is? A question is the verbalizing of one's recognition that something does not fit one's theory. It arises from seeing a situation in a new way and is the launching pad for consideration at a higher level. The name of the game we play with our children must be different from the one our elementary school teachers played with us. As teachers, we dare not perpetuate the mistaken notion we held as students that curiosity questions signal lack of intelligence. Quite the contrary! Show me your active questioners, and I will show you your active learners.

I am not suggesting here that nothing else ever happen in our classrooms; that all day every day children mess about with creepy-crawlies. But I am suggesting that we approach our teaching with our own sense of wonder still alive, with comments that invite our children to question, with a readiness to respond to children's questions as the exciting, relevant, intellectually alive learning activities they are. It's time to reverse a traditional trend: "For far too long schooling has been a matter of answering questions that children never asked" (Zahorik 1971, p. 360).

INTERACTION REVISITED

It was suggested in the last chapter that interaction contributes significantly to children's comprehending and learning, not just by providing situations for the expression of curiosity, but also by supporting children's focusing of attention, making their understandings more precise, making past experience more retrievable, reinterpreting past experience, and going beyond present personal experience. The classroom implication is as easy to identify as it is difficult to achieve: Our classrooms must be rich interactive environments for children if we intend to maximize their use of language for their learning. Meaning-full communication will be the goal in the many written and oral activities we and/or our children initiate. Remember that it is in meaning-full interaction that children learn to shape their expression for another, to take another's point of view into account. Such interaction supports the move away from their less mature egocentrism, and toward decentering, toward a more variable perspective on experience. This is a major cognitive goal, as well as a major language goal. Whenever we contribute to the one, we contribute to the other as well.

SUMMARY

When children come to school, they are already well able to use their language in their efforts to comprehend and learn. A classroom environment which uses children's language most powerfully for their learning will be one which:

1. fosters children's exploration and active questioning;
2. focuses clearly on children's meaningful communication and problem solving, with skills development activities supporting this focus;
3. encourages languaging and conceptualizing at the higher levels of cognitive processing (applying, analyzing, synthesizing, evaluating) rather than at the lower levels (factual recall);
4. encourages interaction among the children, thus supporting their development toward increased mental flexibility and a more variable point of view;
5. includes a teacher who is an active, ongoing learner in the classroom community.

We can be certain that whenever we support children's comprehending and learning, we support their language growth as well.

SUGGESTED EXERCISES AND PROJECTS

1. *A study of cognitive levels in classroom interaction.* Tape record half an hour of teacher-child interaction (either a teacher with an entire class, or a teacher with a small group of children, or a teacher working with individual children). It is not necessary that the thirty minutes be a continuous, single interaction; in fact, if you choose to tape a teacher with individual children a single continuous interaction of this length would probably be impossible. Transcribe your tape, and analyze it according to Bloom's categories as listed on page 256 (or according to another cognitive hierarchy scheme). What levels of cognitive activity is the teacher inviting the child(ren) to engage in? Can you find similarities in the ways the teacher phrases ques-

tions that relate to each level? Some interesting extensions or variations of this project might include (1) taping and analyzing yourself as teacher (this takes courage but can be very worthwhile); (2) working with a partner or two, with each of you looking at a different teacher in a similar situation (teacher with whole group, or teacher with small group, or teacher with individual children), and then comparing your results in terms of cognitive levels; (3) working with a partner with each of you looking at the same teacher in different situations (one of you studying the teacher with entire group, and the other studying the same teacher's interaction with individual children) and then comparing results in terms of cognitive levels.

2. *A study of children's classroom questions.* In a classroom setting, collect the questions you hear children ask. One way to do this is to write each question on a separate index card, along with any relevant information (situation in which it was asked, to whom it was addressed). This allows for easy sorting and categorizing later. What types of questions are the children asking? Procedural, curiosity, and social-interactional categories, may be helpful ones to use (see p. 250), but don't hesitate to set up your own categories on the basis of the questions you gather. What differences, if any, do you notice between the kinds of questions children are asking each other and the kinds they ask the teacher; between the questions children ask in large group settings and in small group settings; between the questions children ask in formal and in informal settings in the classroom; between the questions asked by children at different grade levels (kindergartners versus third graders)? Do you notice differences in the questions children of the same grade level ask in different classrooms with different teachers? You can probably think of many interesting ways to refine this project to be carried out by two or three people; for example, each one focusing on the children's questioning in different types of activities in the same classroom, or each focusing on the questioning of children with different teachers at the same grade level, or each focusing on children's questioning at a different grade level. Where you find differences, how can you describe these, and, more important, how would you (tentatively) account for them? What in the situation is encouraging or hindering children's questioning of different kinds?

3. *Designing and implementing exploratory experiences.* Working alone or with one or two others, plan and carry out an experience or a series of experiences with children in a classroom setting, in which you deliberately incorporate the nine characteristics which were cited in this chapter as contributing to children's exploration and curiosity questioning. Tape the children as they engage in the experience(s) you have planned. Transcribe your tape and analyze it. To what extent and in what ways did the children

get involved in exploring and expressing this through language? How can you account for this? What new directions did the children think of in their encounter with the experience(s), and how could you help them follow their new-found interests in subsequent experiences? What would you do differently if you were to involve children in this experience or sequence of experiences again? You might want to compare your results here with an analysis of transcribed tapes of children of comparable age engaging in an experience in the same content area (say, a science activity) in some other classroom with a different teacher. Did you hear more of the language of exploration and discovery and curiosity from your children as a result of your having deliberately planned for it? If not, why not? What other factors might be important?

4. *Children's perceptions of school learning.* Ask school children: "How do you learn (things) in school?" Write down their responses verbatim and study them. It is important that the children you ask not think of you as a teacher. It they do, they are likely to give you "teacher-pleasing" replies, so don't use children who know you are (becoming) a teacher. (In fact, you might want to try using a child as the "fieldworker," who asks other children and records their replies.) What you want is honesty—as true as possible a picture of in-school learning as the *children* perceive it. It might be fun to extend this project in various ways: Ask the same children how they learn things *outside* of school, or ask the teachers of the children and maybe the principal also, "How do children learn in your classroom/-school?" Or ask adults how they learned things at school when they were kids and, perhaps, how they learn things now that they are adults. You can see what comparison possibilities there might be here: children's perceptions of learning in and out of school; children's perceptions of school learning and teacher's/principal's perceptions; adults' perceptions of their remembered experience and children's perceptions. You can doubtless think of further ways to extend this and make it more interesting to you. Generally speaking, the greater the variety of children you ask (various ages, various types of school setting), the more interesting your responses are likely to be.

5. *A case study of language in learning.* Study the way one child uses language for learning. A child of any age will do, but choose one who is talkative. (Children who are more quiet are just as likely to be using language in their learning, but for this project you need a child you can *hear.*) Follow this child, either taping or writing bits of his or her interaction with others in typical daily situations (a bit from morning preparation-for-school routine, a bit from breakfast, a bit from the morning car ride to school, a bit from structured class discussion, a bit from informal class activity, a bit from

recess or lunch, a bit from after school play, a bit from evening family time.) Your goal here is to sample the child's interaction in various typical daily situations, and to observe and describe the ways the child uses language for learning throughout the day. Don't let yourself get overwhelmed with masses and masses of taped segments to deal with. Just select representative samples to deal with in depth. It is likely that you will want to enlist the child's parents to help you in taping some of the segments in the home.

6. *A study of language for learning in the classroom.* Working individually or as a small group, tape three or four different types of classroom episodes (for example, teacher with whole group, guest speaker with whole group, aide or parent volunteer with individual child, children working together on a project that involves conversation, teacher or aide or visiting adult with small group of children). Look for instances of children using their language for learning through (1) questioning, (2) focusing attention, (3) making understandings more precise, (4) making understandings more retrievable, (5) reinterpreting past experience, (6) going beyond present personal experience. (It might be helpful for you to review pages 236–245 here.) Transcribe only those portions of the tapes that demonstrate such language use in action. Which of these learning-oriented functions of language occurred most, least, not at all? Why (not)? How might these be encouraged further? Your discussion can take a number of directions, but the major purpose of the activity is to increase your ability to *hear* language for learning when it is going on.

7. *"Your own thing."* Design your own learning experience relating to the ideas in this section, discuss it with your instructor and/or an acquaintance knowledgeable in this area, and execute it.

SUGGESTED FURTHER READINGS

BRITTON, JAMES, *Language and Learning.* London: Penguin Books, 1973.

GARVEY, C., *Play.* Cambridge, Mass.: Harvard University Press, 1977.

ROSEN, CONNIE, and HAROLD ROSEN, *The Language of Primary School Children.* London: Penguin Education for the Schools Council, 1973.

SLOBIN, D. I., *Psycholinguistics* (2nd ed.). Glenview, Ill.: Scott, Foresman and Company, 1979. (Chapter 6)

SMITH, FRANK, *Comprehension and Learning.* New York: Holt, Rinehart and Winston, 1975.

TOUGH, JOAN, *The Development of Meaning.* London: George Allen & Unwin Ltd., 1977.

————.*Focus on Meaning.* London: George Allen & Unwin Ltd., 1974.

Section Four

LANGUAGE USE
IN
SOCIAL CONTEXTS

Chapter 11

Communicative Competence

INTRODUCTION:
EXPLORING COMMUNICATIVE COMPETENCE[1]

We know that as speakers of a language we have linguistic competence, that is, we know a deep system of principles for organizing sentences. These principles enable us to create and to interpret novel sentences in our language. We explored this knowledge of linguistic structure (linguistic competence) in Section One, and we explored its acquisition in children in Section Two.

But our competence in language far exceeds our knowledge of the narrow bounds of linguistic structure. We have *communicative competence* as well as linguistic competence—we know how to interact, how to communicate with one another appropriately in various situations, and how to make sense of what others say and do in communication situations. The business of communicat-

[1]The term "communicative competence" is attributed to Dell Hymes, (1974) a sociolinguist who has been important in describing and stressing the importance of the role of situational factors in communication.

ing is not as simple as it seems. Our conversations are guided by organizational principles just as "out of awareness, yet deeply binding" (Schegloff 1972, p. 347) as those which govern our creation of novel sentences. Virtually every uttered grammatical sentence is, for speaker and hearer, a novel one, but it falls within the set of organizational principles for that language. So virtually every conversation is altogether new for the participants, yet it falls within the set of principles for appropriate and socially interpretable communication. Every conversation rests on underlying principles of organization and sequential order known to the participants.

Just as virtually every child develops linguistic competence, so every child develops communicative competence and, in fact, develops them together. Linguistic competence can be considered a part of communicative competence: In order to communicate adequately, producing and interpreting language appropriate to various social situations, one of the things the conversational participants must be able to do is structure sentences according to the linguistic rules of their language community. But they do far more than this when they communicate. What is the nature of the adult's communicative competence, his knowledge of how communication proceeds and of the complex interaction of speech and social situation? This knowledge is a major aspect of every child's language development. In this chapter we will explore what some important aspects of the adult's communicative competence are and how the child acquires them.

What are some of the underlying rules we, as adults, know for socially appropriate interaction? Put another way, what does our communicative competence (knowledge of appropriate interaction) include, that children ultimately acquire? And if these principles (rules) are unconscious, how do we know they exist at all?

You remember that we were able, in Section One, to recognize some sentences as grammatical—as being in accordance with the structural principles of our language—and others as ungrammatical, not in accordance with those principles. Well, the situation is analogous in the area of our communicative competence: we are able to recognize some talk in conversations as being appropriate, and other talk as being inappropriate.[2] To say that talk is appropriate or inappropriate is to say, among other things, that it either does or does not conform to the expectations we have for how conversation sequences proceed. Let's look at a few examples.

> Two adults are standing in a cafeteria line. The first wants veal cutlet and finds there is none. He turns to the second adult and says, "Every time I come here they seem to be out of the veal cutlet." Now put an asterisk beside every one of

[2]Throughout this discussion, I am assuming that the conversational participants are English speakers with an Anglo cultural background. As specifics of linguistic competence differ from one language community to another, so specifics of communicative competence (rules for appropriate communication behavior) differ from one culture to another.

the following responses that would be inappropriate for the second adult to make.

1. Well have you tried the fish? *That's* awfully good.
2. Tuesday I leave for Chicago.
3. Johnny's mumps are almost gone.
4. Just your luck, huh?
5. I have that problem with their cheesecake.

It is 7:30 A.M. and the phone rings. Adult answers it and says "Hello?" Now put an asterisk beside the following responses that would be inappropriate.

1. Hi, d'I get ya' outta bed?
2. Hello, Tom?
3. How 'bout Saturday?
4. Hello. I'd like to speak with Ms. Johnson please.
5. It's up to 75 now.

There is no structural problem with the sentences you asterisked above. The problem with them is that they do not *fit* at this point in these conversations. Your ability to identify conversational responses that do and do not fit in conversational sequences is evidence of your knowledge of what to expect in conversation. What principles that we know and are drawing on are being violated here? The problem with 2 and 3 in the first example is that they are not topically relevant. The first speaker has initiated a topic and we expect that the subsequent comment will be topically related to it. Topical relevance is a guiding conversational principle for us and we recognize when it is violated. In items 3 and 5 in the second example, the speaker has left the initial greeting ("Hello?") unresponded to. Our expectation with greetings is that they occur in pairs; each partner greets the other (these patterns are particularly conventionalized in telephone conversations). Can you describe what is communicatively inappropriate in the following incidents?

Six-year-old M——— calls up and adult answers phone.
Adult: Hello?
M———: Is G——— there? (G——— is adult's son.)
Adult: No.
M———: Bye.
Fifteen minutes later the phone rings again.
Adult: Hello?
M———: C'n you tell me where he is?

A and B are in a room which is very hot and stuffy. The only window in the room is closed. A says, "Boy, we need some fresh air in here" and walks toward the window with arms outstretched, ready to open it. B says to A, "Would you please open the window?"

In the first example, we know, as M——— apparently does not, that certain relevant information has to be provided before his question "C'n you tell me where he is?" fits. And the interaction between A and B is strange because we share an underlying assumption that we only make a verbal request in a situation where the action wouldn't be likely to occur unless we asked for it. In the incident given, the action (opening the window) is already going to happen so requesting it makes no sense—no communication sense.

Consider one more example. You see a sign "Free Puppy" and go to the door and inquire. The puppy owner brings a reasonable enough looking puppy and says, "He's really adorable. He's so cute—we just love him. He's cuddly and has the cutest way of looking at you. He's friendly and loveable . . . " Why is it that, after a few minutes of this, you find yourself thinking, "I wonder why this fellow is so eager to dump this puppy? It must be a real loser." It is because you have an expectation that a person will respond to your inquiry in a way which is informative, but will not overwhelm you in the amount of talk. If the appropriate amount is exceeded, you suspect some further meaning in the situation. In short, we know when principles of appropriate communication have been violated. We could not be aware of rule violations without "knowing" those rules at some (usually unconscious) level.

Further evidence for the existence and nature of our communicative competence comes from our "repair" of conversational problems when they occur. For example, in our culture we expect a summons to get an answer. When it doesn't, we attempt to repair the conversational breakdown, for example, by repeating the summons louder.

Bill?
(Pause)
BILL? (louder)

It is a guiding principle of conversation that one person speaks at a time. When two people speak at the same time, they fix it up in some way so the conversation can proceed as it should: One speaker stops in midsentence to let the other continue with his turn, or one speaker (or both) may say "Excuse me" and stop talking so the other can continue, or one may say loudly *"I'm not finished,"* meaning "I am the one who is talking now so you be quiet." In any case, the participants typically move to repair the violated principle of one speaker at a time. The opposite of too many speakers at a time is silence —too few speakers at a time (none). You've doubtless noticed how interactants will often fill silences with inane drivel, rather than endure the silence. This is another instance of repair. We know that in conversation slight pauses are acceptable, but periods of silence are not and they make us uncomfortable.

Also, speakers of a language recognize sentences which are communicatively ambiguous, just as they recognize sentences which are structurally or semantically ambiguous (remember "Visiting relatives can be a nuisance"?). Can you find the ambiguity in the accompanying cartoon?

BORN LOSER—By Art Sansom

There is no question at the level of linguistic structure about how to interpret the girl's "You know what's nice about you?" But there are clearly two possible interpretations relating to the communicative intent of the utterance. Is the question to be interpreted as a preface to a compliment (the boy's interpretation), or as an information-seeking utterance (the girl's interpretation)? Here is a single utterance that can serve more than one function in the communication situation.

We also can be sure that we know and use underlying communication principles because we can deliberately alter them to change people's speaking behavior in predictable ways. We probably do this unconsciously more than we realize. For example, if we want a shy child to talk more in conversation with us, we will probably alter our own speaking so as to encourage the child to take more and longer conversational turns. We may use more questions, more open questions, more invitations ("Tell me about ———") than we normally would, and we may do less of taking long turns of information giving.

However, the most dramatic example of the deliberate manipulating of the communication situation to alter speaking behavior that I know of comes from the work of Labov and Robins (Labov 1970a). These researchers, studying the dialect of Harlem preteenagers, got their subjects to produce vigorous interactive and diverse speech in large amounts by manipulating social aspects of the communication situation. "Large friendly white interviewers" interviewing similar subjects in formal settings, have reported these children to be "nonverbal" or, at best, single word mumblers (Berieter and Engelmann 1966). By changing aspects of the social situation, Labov and Robins elicited very different speaking behavior from their subjects. The large friendly white interviewer was replaced by a black one from the neighborhood (Robins) who sat informally on the floor; the "interviewer" had brought along potato chips to make the atmosphere more "party-ish" than "interview-ish"; the "interviewer" talked with a pair of children who were good friends, instead of bringing children in to converse with him one at a time; and the "interviewer" initiated taboo topics into the conversation to show that one could say anything in this situation. In short, the researchers had provided a situation that encouraged conversation in these children. Presto, changeo! "Nonverbal" children were suddenly competing for the floor, jesting, arguing, initiating, and responding with gusto. There was no magic here. The fact that we can deliberately manipulate aspects of the social situation to influence speaking behavior in predictable ways attests to the presence of powerful rules relating social situation and speaking behavior, and to our knowledge of such rules.

Perhaps the most important and the most easily overlooked evidence for our knowledge of principles that guide our communication with others in our language community, is that we constantly communicate with a high degree of success and usually with considerable ease. Communication is a cooperative effort on the part of two or more people. Together, by following the same guiding principles for communication, the participants negotiate conversations, initiating and responding, in patterned, nonrandom ways. This would not be possible if they did not know and use shared rules for appropriate communication behavior.

We have looked at only a few examples here in order to help you explore and begin to feel the reality of your communicative competence. We know that we have a deep knowledge of how to communicate with others appropriately, because (1) we know when communication principles are broken, (2) when they are broken we attempt to repair them, (3) we recognize language situations which are communicatively ambiguous, (4) we are able to deliberately alter situations so as to effect change in participants' speaking behavior, and (5) most important of all, we *communicate* creatively and with a high degree of success. It is no wonder that vigorous study is currently under way of how people communicate with each other in real situations. We have always known that language exists for the purpose of communication. Researchers are attempting to understand and describe both the "context-free" and the "context-sensitive" aspects of communication; that is, both the general overall organizational structure and pattern of communication events (context-free), and also the ways in which people's style of talking changes in response to each particular social situation (context-sensitive) (Sacks, Schegloff, and Jefferson 1974, p. 700). The exciting research of the past several decades has increased our understanding and awareness of many aspects of communication, among them (1) the purposeful nature of language in communication; (2) the underlying principles governing the structure or design of communication events, and (3) the influence of situational factors on the particular talking styles used by the conversational participants. The remainder of this chapter deals with these three aspects of communicative competence and their development in children.

THE PURPOSEFUL NATURE OF LANGUAGE

Communication is purposeful. Every day, as we go about our business and our play, we are doing things through language. We don't simply emit verbal noises; rather, we coax, comfort, cajole, emote, jest, threaten, argue, request, justify, scold, greet, question, challenge, inform, assert, and so on. We use our verbal utterances to express some content, and generally do so in ways which are guided by the principles of linguistic structure in our language. But basic to all our interaction and giving it purpose and shape is a host of communication intentions. These intentions are its reason(s) for being. Our verbal utterances are *forms* (linguistically acceptable expressions of semantic content) expressing diverse communication *functions* (what we accomplish in interaction through the use of language forms).

The form/function distinction is an important one. Obviously in actual communication the two necessarily occur together: We use certain linguistic *forms* to express certain *functions*. But it is instructive to look at form and function separately as components of communicating.[3]

FORM	FUNCTION
(what X is saying)	(what X is doing in the communication by saying it)
X says "I'm sorry"	X is apologizing.
X says "I wasn't listening"	X is explaining (justifying).

[3]See Searle's *Speech Acts* (1970) for an in-depth discussion of speaking as comprised of three components: "utterance acts" (saying morphemes, sentences, etc.) + "propositional acts" (expressing content), + "illocutionary acts" (e.g., promising, stating, questioning, etc.). In the present discussion, Searle's "utterance acts" and "propositional acts" can be thought of as collasped into "form," and his "illocutionary acts" are roughly equivalent to what I am calling "function." You can probably see parallels between Searle's "propositional act" and deep structure (level relating to meaning), and his "utterance act" and surface structure (level relating to expression).

What can you do with these? Study each brief example and complete the function column as indicated.[4] (After completing these fifteen items, you may want to compare your responses with a friend's.)

FORM   *FUNCTION*

1. (Father and ten-year-old daughter
   are standing beside hungry-
   looking dog) Father says,
   "Betsy, have you fed Bruno yet?"   Father is _____-ing.

2. (Impatiently, to noisy third-grade
   class) Teacher says, *"Well, do you
   want to go out for recess or don't
   you?"*   Teacher is _____-ing.

3. (First adult is in room. Second
   adult enters from outside, roasted
   and sweaty) First adult says,
   "Hot, huh?"   First adult is _____-ing.

4. (Twelve-year-old girl, her mother, and
   her friend. Mother has said daughter
   can't go to party that evening)
   Daughter says to her friend, *"Your
   mother is letting you go, isn't she
   Janet?"*   Daughter is_____-ing.

5. (Two adult males on telephone. They
   have already agreed to meet the next
   morning to play golf) One says to
   the other, *"Meet 'ya at 10:00 then."* Adult is _____-ing.

6. (Adult to adult) Adult says, *"C'mon
   over for dinner around 7:00."*   Adult is _____-ing.

7. (Five-foot-tall wife is stretching
   to reach a glass on high kitchen
   shelf. Six-foot husband is standing
   beside her) Wife says, *"Oh, I just
   can't reach it."*   Wife is _____-ing.

8. (Sixteen-year-old girl's boyfriend
   arrives to take her to a movie)
   Girl says, *"Hi."*   Girl is _____-ing.

9. (Mother and eighteen-month-old son)
   Mother says, *"Where's your nose?"*   Mother is _____-ing.

10. (Teacher and first-grade class)
    Teacher says, *"I just can't fool you
    today, can I?"*   Teacher is _____-ing.

[4]Express the function(s) you recognize in whatever way you can. Your particular choice of terms is not important. The format: "X" is ———-ing" is used here simply to focus your attention on the function being an *action*.

11. (Two children) First child says,
    "Knock knock." Second child says,
    "Who's there?"   Children are _____-ing.
12. (Two nine-year-olds on school
    playground) First says, *"Wanna
    fight?!"*   Child is _____-ing.
13. (Mother fixing dinner. Six-year-old
    son enters kitchen) Son says, *"YECH!
    That stinks!"*   Son is _____-ing.
14. (Kindergartner and teacher)
    Kindergartner says, *"Know what?"* Kindergartner is _____-ing.
15. (Family eating dinner at
    restaurant. Thirteen-year-old sister
    tells eleven-year-old brother, "You
    have watermelon all over your shirt.
    You got it all wet.") Brother
    shrugs and says, *"So what's new?"* Brother is _____-ing.

Our responses in conversation indicate that we understand and respond to speakers' intentions, the communication function of utterances, as well as to their forms. Take the first item above as an example. The father is requesting (function) by using an interrogative (question) form. Interrogative forms generally get answers. But if Betsy responded to the form *only,*—if she said "No" (answer) and walked away—her response would be inappropriate. Betsy knows this. Betsy will respond to the father's request function. She may reply

Ooooops, I forgot. I'll do it now.
No, but I'll do it as soon as I finish my math homework.
Nope. We're out of dog food.
No, it's Joey's turn. I fed Bruno yesterday.
Will you please stop bugging me about that!

But whether she agrees to comply with the request, or provides an explanation for not complying, or expresses annoyance at the request, her response will indicate her awareness that the father has made a request. And it is the *request,* the function of the utterance, that she responds to.

Sometimes the verb in a sentence explicitly names the function of the utterance:

To say "I dare you"	is to accomplish the act of	daring
To say "I challenge you"	is to accomplish the act of	challenging
To say "I move that X"	is to accomplish the act of	moving (making a motion)
To say "I second it"	is to accomplish the act of	seconding

To say "I bet five dollars"	is to accomplish the act of	betting
To say "I promise"	is to accomplish the act of	promising
To say "I assert X"	is to accomplish the act of	asserting
To say "I beg you"	is to accomplish the act of	begging
To say "I advocate X"	is to accomplish the act of	advocating
To say "I propose that X"	is to accomplish the act of	proposing
To say "I sentence you . . ."	is to accomplish the act of	sentencing

And what about these: "I now *pronounce* you man and wife," and "And thereto I *plight* thee my troth"—not forms we use often to be sure, but forms in which the verb names the function accomplished by their being uttered. By saying "I now pronounce you man and wife" the state of two people is changed; they become man and wife because they were "pronounced" man and wife. By saying "And thereto I plight thee my troth" a promise is made (a troth is plighted?). More often, however, the forms we use do not explicitly name their function as they accomplish it, but they just as surely carry out diverse functions. For example, I am inviting you to my party regardless of whether I say "I invite you to my party," or "Hey, I'm having a party Friday. Can you come?" Both are utterances which serve to invite; one does so by explicitly naming its purpose, the other does so in another way.[5]   In sum, in our communication we intend to carry out some purpose. When we talk, we don't just *say* things, we *do* things with our words (Austin 1962).

THE STRUCTURE OF COMMUNICATION EVENTS

An interaction is a cooperative activity among two or more people. It proceeds smoothly for the most part because the participants know how conversation works. Interestingly, and frustratingly, though participants "know" how conversation works (that is, are able to negotiate sequences that accomplish their purposes), sociolinguists are still struggling to capture and describe that intuitive knowledge. We have as yet no comprehensive theory of discourse. Different researchers have focused on different aspects of communication structure. In the literature, one encounters different and sometimes conflicting perspectives and can come away with a bits-and-pieces feeling about this work. We still don't know how the various pieces will ultimately fit together to form a comprehensive theory. However, some of the bits and pieces have contributed significant insights in their own right. Some of the pieces important for us here include (1) the study of turn taking in communication events; (2) the positing

[5]Different researchers have categorized language functions in different ways. For a look at some different category schemes, you might want to see Halliday (1973), Jakobson (1960), Tough (1977), Dore (1977), Kinneavy (1971).

of underlying principles that participants adhere to (such as truthfulness, relevance); (3) the positing of situational conditions for the performance of speech acts; and (4) the analysis of communication events in terms of hierarchical structure (larger identifiable units composed of progressively smaller identifiable units).

Turn Taking

Turn taking is a fundamental principle: "turn taking seems a basic form of organization for conversation" (Sacks, Schlegloff, and Jefferson 1974, p. 700). Participants know how to initiate a conversation, take a first turn that begins a turn-taking sequence; they know how to get a turn and how to execute a turn appropriately—how to speak relevantly, informatively, and for an acceptable length of time; they know how to pass a turn to someone else. Together they manage sequences of turns such that one person speaks at a time and there are few (if any) awkward silences, periods with no speakers. Conversational participants are able to introduce new topics at appropriate places in the conversation. They know how to move into and carry out a closing sequence, and when to begin a closing sequence rather than initiate a new conversational topic. This complex knowledge that we generally take for granted is quite remarkable. You can see that, without cooperation and finely coordinated moves among the participants, this complex communication that we routinely engage in every day could not occur. The flow of conversation requires each interactant to move—initiate and respond—appropriately, and typically each interactant does, precisely because he shares with the others an understanding of how turn sequences are executed.

    The necessity for cooperation and shared knowledge of communication rules among conversationalists is especially obvious in what some researchers have called the "adjacency pair," conversational exchanges that typically (though not always) have two parts, such as greeting-greeting, question-answer, offer-acceptance/refusal. It can be disconcerting when in conversation we give the first part of a pair and our conversational partner does not respond with the second part. In fact this is sometimes deliberately done in an effort to tease or annoy, as, for example, when one child asks another child a question and the second child repeats it as part of the age old I'm-going-to-repeat-everything-you-say game instead of responding, as expected, with an answer.

Underlying Principles

Grice has pointed out some "maxims" that are part of the set of cooperative principles of conversation that speakers adhere to (Grice 1975). One of these is the "quantity" maxim: "Make your [conversational] contribution as informative as is required (for the current purposes of the exchange)," but "Do not make your contribution more informative than is required" (p. 45). This relates to the free puppy example given earlier; we expect speakers to provide information in their turn, but overdoing it (violating the quantity rule) may make us suspect some further, hidden meaning.

Grice also suggests a "quality" maxim: "Do not say what you believe to be false," and "Do not say that for which you lack adequate evidence" (p. 46). We assume that we and our conversational partners are speaking the truth unless some indication is given to the contrary—for example, telling a joke or deliberately exaggerating for effect or using metaphor or being ironic. In all these cases it is usually clear that we are suspending the "truth" principle, often from the situational context itself, but sometimes from indications we give verbally (like using our voices in special ways). When we or our partner talk about things for which we lack adequate evidence (gossip?), we may mark this verbally in some way, as in, "Well, I didn't actually see this, but Rhonda said that Glenn, ... " Bates gives this example of how we interpret conversation in a special way when it violates the truth principle.

> If I have just come home from walking through a torrential rain and my spouse says to me *You look terrific,* we both know that the utterance is not true. Because the sentence is false, and we both know it to be false, and because we assume that there is a conversational rule against blatant falsehoods, the sentence serves in this context as an ironic statement that I am soaking wet and look horrible. When the truth maxim is deliberately violated, we ascribe some special meaning to the speaker's utterance. (Bates 1976, p. 28)

A third maxim is that speakers will be relevant in their contributions. In the earlier examples you identified some responses that were inappropriate in that they were irrelevant at that point in the conservation. Here is another example demonstrating the strong influence the principle relevance exerts as we interpret conversationalists' meanings.

> ... a woman at a bus stop says to me *Do you know what time it is?* There is a conversational rule which says that speakers do not request irrelevant information from their listeners, and I know that my own knowledge of the time is in itself irrelevant to the stranger waiting for a bus. I therefore conclude from this clear violation that the woman wants more than she has actually requested. I cannot simply answer *Yes I do know.* I must also add *It is 4:30.* (Bates 1976, p. 28)

As with the quantity and quality (truth) principles, so with the relevance principle: When the principle is violated in conversation, we "read" more and other meanings into the situation; we assume that more is implied than is explicitly verbalized.

Grice's final maxim deals with the conversationalist's manner of speaking. We expect participants to be clear and comprehensible when they talk. If they are not, we repair the problem with devices such as inserting questions or requests for clarification: "*Who* was it who said that?" "Don't you mean a Rabbit, not a Dasher?" or even "Wait a minute. You've lost me. Go back over it again."

Situational Conditions
for Performance of Speech Acts

In his study of speech acts, Searle has contributed significantly in bringing to our attention some additional underlying conditions that speakers know about conversation, but generally take for granted (Searle 1975, p. 71). Searle has dealt explicitly with the speech acts of requesting and of promising. Conditions that speakers know (but don't consciously know that they know) relating to the making of a request include (1) that the one to whom the request is directed is able to perform the requested action (I will not request a three-year-old to reach something for me that is on a high shelf); (2) that the one making the request does in fact want the requested act to be carried out (a truth or "sincerity condition"); (3) that the requester will indicate the future act to be carried out by the requestee; and (4) that the utterance of the request, whatever its form (Would ja get me some water? I need a glass of water. Hand me that glass of water, will ya?) counts as an attempt by the requester to get the requestee to perform the requested act. We never think about these conditions consciously when we make a request or perform a requested action, but our behavior is predicated on these conditions, accepted by both requester and requestee.

Comparable conditions underlie the act of promising: (1) that the speaker (promiser) is able to do what he is promising and that the promised act is desired by the hearer (I will not promise to buy you a Porsche because I am unable to, and I will not promise to demolish your present car because that is an act you do not desire; I may, however, promise to bake cookies for your party, an act which I am able to perform and which I have reason to believe you would find desirable); (2) that the speaker in fact intends to carry out the promised act ("sincerity condition" for promising); (3) that the speaker will indicate the promised act that is to be carried out; (4) that the utterance of the promise actually counts as the speaker's undertaking of the obligation to perform the promised act.

Hierarchical Structure in Conversation

Some researchers have studied conversations as entities having hierarchical structure. They have suggested that, just as a sentence can be described as a hierarchical structure composed of identifiable subparts or components, so a conversation can be described as a hierarchical structure of identifiable components (Garvey, Baldwin, and Dickstein 1971). Here the basic unit to be described structurally is not the sentence, but the communication event—a conversation, an interview, a telephone call, a discussion, a classroom lesson. One promising suggestion is that at least some communication events can be described as having several *stages:* an orientation stage, a task conduct stage, and a closing stage. Telephone calls offer the perfect example here. Typically when someone calls us, we begin by engaging in talk which gets us interacting, establishes rapport, but does not contribute to the real business of the call: "Well, how've ya been?" "Haven't talked with you for a long time." "How're the kids?" "Yeah, been really busy lately." "Have ya seen————recently?" "Gee I was just thinking about you the other day." We know this is not the business of the call, but is an important preliminary stage. Without it, the call would seem rude or brusk, but if it goes on too long we sometimes find ourselves thinking, "I wonder what he's calling about" or "I wish she'd hurry and get to the point; I don't have all day." We usually know when we enter the next stage, the task conduct stage, because it is usually marked in the conversation. For example, there may be a slight pause and then the caller might say, "Well what I'm really calling about is . . ." or "I'm calling to ask you a favor." Notice, it is the caller, not the receiver, who initiates this stage. It would be very rude for the receiver to ask, "Well, what are you calling about?" (unless, of course, the participants were very familiar with one another and the receiver said this in a joking way—the joke being that the receiver has broken a communication convention that they both know). When the business has been taken care of, the participants move into a closing stage. Like the orientation stage, the closing usually contributes nothing directly to our conducting the business at hand, yet without it the conversation would seem rude somehow: "Gee, it's really been good talking to you." "We've got to get together sometime." "Say 'hi' to————for me next time you see her." "Good luck in your exams." "Have a good trip."

According to this suggested analysis, each stage is composed of identifiable *chunks* or sequences of conversation focusing on a particular topic. Within each chunk there are clear *exchanges* (or sequences of exchanges) between the conversational partners, that is, conversational turns that are closely linked as, for example, a question and answer and response sequence (A: "Think you'll be able to come?" B: "I'll sure try." A: "Good. *Do.* "). And of course in each exchange or exchange group, one can identify each partner's speaking turn, the individual utterance or *event.* Just as we can have embedded sentences (a sentence within a sentence), so we can have embedded exchange sequences (a sequence within a sequence) as in the following example:

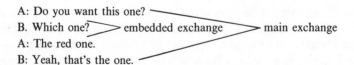

A: Do you want this one?
B. Which one?————> embedded exchange————> main exchange
A: The red one.
B: Yeah, that's the one.

Some sociolinguists posit an important further unit—the *move*—typically an utterance stretch (though possibly a nonverbal signal) accomplishing a certain purpose in the discourse; the *move* is what gets accomplished. Some events (speaking turns) will include several utterance stretches, each contributing to the discourse in a different way. For example, in the sequence above, B's last turn (event) might have been "Yeah, that's the one. Now wanna see what I can do with this?" If so, this event would consist of two moves, the first a response to a preceding question, and the second an initiation of a new conversational focus.

This is only one way to look at the structure of communication events hierarchically, but it is a suggestive way. Different sociolinguists have defined and labeled discourse units in somewhat different ways, but they seem to agree that

> It seems reasonable to assume that communications, like less extensive stretches of linguistic material such as clauses, may exhibit internal structure, that is, may be composed of hierarchical units whose arrangement can be specified. (Garvey, Baldwin, and Dickstein 1971, p. 1)

Discourse as a Dynamic Event

The study of conversations as structured entities has underscored the fact that the actual experience of discourse is a dynamic one. The structure of the communication evolves as the participants interact, as they initiate and respond. Only after the fact, the completed interaction process, can one look back at the conversation and study it as a product with a given structure. A game analogy is frequently used to capture the dynamic reality of communication. A conversation, like a game, involves a series of moves by participants. In a game there is some sort of turn-taking mechanism, and each move is influenced by preceding moves and exerts influence on successive ones. So in a conversation. The moves in games and in communication events occur in accordance with some set of rules (conventions, guiding principles) known to the participants, but within that guiding rule framework the specific nature and shape of the interaction which evolves is unique.

Various types of communication events have been identified and studied: convergent communication, the situation in which one partner knows the solution to a problem (the knower) and must convey to the partner (the doer) how to reach the solution (as, for example, when the knower gives the doer directions for getting somewhere) (Garvey and Baldwin 1970); argument (Brenneis and Lein 1977); instruction (Cook-Gumperz 1977); therapeutic discourse (Labov and Fanshel 1977); joke telling (Sacks 1974); teacher-led lesson (Sinclair and Coulthard 1975). Evident in all these types is a describable pattern of hierarchical structure (though the various researchers have described it somewhat differently), and also a dynamic sequence of moves carried out in accordance with discourse rules understood by the participants.

This discussion barely scratches the surface of what we are beginning to understand about a speaker's communicative competence as it relates to the overall organizational structure or design of communication events. Typically we are very casual about talk. It would not be at all unusual for any of us to respond to the question "What were you and X doing?" by saying, "Oh we were jes' talkin' 'bout this an' that." But "jes talkin' 'bout this an' that" is a remarkably complex, mutually and sensitively coordinated sequence of appropriate moves. Jes' talkin' 'bout this an' that may be the most complex and intricate game we ever play, in spite of its being so effortless and often so pleasurable.

THE VARIATION IN SPEAKING STYLES IN CONVERSATION

"It ain't what cha say, it's the way how cha say it," as the old song puts it. What's the difference between identifying someone as a "janitor" or as a "sanitation engineer"? What's the difference between calling something "unpleasant" and calling it "the pits," or between calling someone "unstable" and calling him "wifty"? Is being "blotto" the same as being "inebriated"? The differences here have social significance; that is, their use is sensitive to the social context. In some situations one form would be appropriate, in other situations another form would be.

We all control a range of speaking styles. Some sociolinguists are studying what some of the specific factors of situations are that influence our choice of which speaking style to use. That is, they are trying to discover more about the speaker's underlying knowledge relating to the context-sensitive nature of communication. You can begin to explore this yourself by considering the following pairs of sentences from Williams, Hopper, and Natalicio's book *The Sounds of Children* (1977). For each member of the pair, suggest a situation (or several) in which it would be appropriate (for example speaker, person or group spoken to, purpose, setting). (You may want to do this with several other people. You may find that you come up with a variety of situations for each utterance depending in part on the way the words are spoken—tone of voice, accompanying gestures, and facial expressions.)

No way I'm gonna do that.
I'd rather not do that.

I beg your pardon?
Huh?

Bye-bye.
Good-bye.

Shall we go?
Let's get out of here.

What do you want?
May I help you?

May I have your attention please?
Shut up and listen. (pp. 64–65)

The changes we make in our talking style in different situations are not just changes in word choice. Our syntactic forms and our pronunciations are sensitive to various social factors also. In general we are more likely to use passive constructions in more formal situations (especially in writing). Speaking in a large meeting, with the purpose of recalling to the group an action taken at a previous meeting, we would be likely to say, "You may remember that, at least week's meeting, it was moved that. . . ." But in telling a close friend about the action in casual conversation, we'd be more likely to use the active forms: "Remember last week X moved that we. . . ." And, as we saw in the previous section, if our conversational partner is a young child, we will tend to shorten and simplify our sentences. The forms we pronounce as "why don't you" and "I'm going to" when we are conversing with our new school superintendent at a reception, are likely to become "wyoncha" and "I'm gonna" when we're in blue jeans stretched out on the floor of our living room in front of a cozy fire, talking with spouse or close friend while munching on Fritos. We use our voices differently too, talking louder in some situations and more quietly in others, sometimes using a wider intonation range and sometimes a more restricted one, often conveying a special meaning—sarcasm, mockery, cynicism, irritation—by using a special tone of voice.

Nonverbal aspects of our communication vary from situation to situation too, though these are aspects of communication that we understand less well. The ways in which we do (or don't) establish and maintain eye contact when we converse, the physical distance we establish and how we incline toward or away from our partner in conversation, our use of touch (whom do we touch and how and when in conversation?), our facial expression and use of gesture —these are only a few of many nonverbal aspects of communication that alter with the social situation we are in. Many teachers use touch a great deal when they interact with their children. We can generally recognize when the touching conveys impatience, affection, or restraint. We have much to learn about nonverbal aspects of communication. Usually we are unaware of these aspects of communication altogether. However, sometimes we are aware that verbal and nonverbal signals are in conflict. For example, a teacher may grab and restrain a student impatiently, all the while talking in a "honeyed" tone of voice, or in an oversteady voice that tries to convey (between clenched teeth) a calm and control that the teacher does not feel. Our awareness of conflicting or inappropriate nonverbal signals suggests that these aspects of our communication are, like the verbal aspects, nonrandom and rule governed. If we know when a rule has been broken (that is, recognize when one behaves in a way which is counter to our expectations), then clearly we have knowledge of some rules or guiding principles for that behavior, however unconscious that knowledge may be. A college student once described one of her professors to me by saying, "She always tells us that she really wants us to actively participate in class and really get involved in discussion. But then, as soon as we begin to say something, she looks nervously at her watch." The student had zeroed in on a clear conflict between the verbal and nonverbal messages that professor was giving. Our unconscious knowledge of appropriate nonverbal behavior is one more aspect of our language knowledge that humorists have exploited.

© King Features Syndicate, Inc. 1977

Unconsciously, automatically, we slip in and out of various communication styles, adapting our speech and gesture so that they are appropriate to each social situation. We are generally no more aware of the various styles we are shifting in and out of so facilely than we are aware of the linguistic structure of the utterances we endlessly create. An example of this lack of awareness of the styles we use is the following from an adult English speaker learning Spanish. The authors of his text had translated an informal Spanish sentence with an English sentence that included "gonna." When the student encountered one of the textbook authors who was involved in doing some of the teaching for the class, the student pointed out the "gonna" translation and suggested that they must be teaching the students "substandard" Spanish if the equivalent English translations were so "substandard" as to include "gonna." The author/teacher protested that "gonna" was not substandard English but, indeed was a form he himself used all the time. The student replied adamantly, "Well I don't. And I'm not gonna start now!" The author/teacher reports, "The effect was electric. His embarrassment at being caught was aggravated by the amused laughter of his classmates" (Bowen 1966, p. 45). For the first time, perhaps, the student heard what he actually said, not what he thought he said.

As with this student, so with ourselves. Only occasionally does our stylistic use come to the level of our conscious awareness. One such time is when we use an inappropriate style in a given situation. This is usually embarrassing and often we become flustered and/or apologetic as in the following example. A second-grade teacher had been working very hard at trying to break the habit some of her children were in, of not listening to instructions of any kind. She had firmly resolved that every time she gave an instruction she would follow a pattern of first alerting the children to the fact that she was going to give an instruction, then give the instruction clearly and respond to any questions regarding it, and then under no circumstances would she repeat the instruction for the ever-present few who requested it over and over again. She was trying very hard to follow this firm resolve, and often heard herself say to a child, "———, I told you that already and I'm not going to tell you again. You'll have to figure it out the best you can." After dinner one evening, her husband asked her a question about something they had previously discussed. She turned to him and said in a "schoolmarmish" voice, "I've told you that already and I'm not going to tell you again." Of course he replied, with justifiable annoyance, "I am *not* a second grader!" a response which showed his clear recognition that she had used an identifiable and inappropriate style in talking with him. Her own embarrassment and mumbled apology attested to the same recognition on her part. She had clearly violated some principles of appropriate language use for that situation, principles that both she and her husband knew.

We also become consciously aware of varying our language style in different situations when we, or someone we are listening to, suddenly and dramatically shift from one style to another. Consider the teenage girl engaged in a fight with her younger brother: (sarcastically) "Oh *sure!* You weren't in my room while I was out! Then how come my records are all messed up and my jeans are on the floor? You're always . . ." (Phone rings. Sudden shift as she answers it and says in a neutral voice) "Hello?" then sweetly, "Oh hi, Paul" and an animated conversation continues. Some cartoonists have noted similar events.

© King Features Syndicate, Inc. 1978

Or consider children's use of language in a role play situation. Their use of language to negotiate the play ("You be the mommy and I'll be the little girl, OK? And pretend you just came back from the store and you find me all covered with mud") is clearly distinguishable from their use of language in the assigned roles.

Our stylistic range includes written as well as spoken channels. We expect, use, and interpret a variety of written syles. We expect a biology text to "sound" different from a poem and we respond to each on its own terms. The business letters we write and receive use a style quite different from that which we use when we write to a friend. And what about the old high school yearbook? It would be unthinkable to write the truth: "I don't know you very well, but as much as I know you, you seem OK. I have no particular reason to think you're a loser or really terrific. You seem to be kind of regular." or "I've known you a long time and you're average." *Every* high schooler knows better than to do this; *every* high schooler has a language style appropriate for writing in yearbooks.

Let's sum up for a moment. Our communicative competence includes knowing how to adapt our language appropriately for various situations; our communication is context sensitive. We all control a range of communication styles. Without even thinking about it, we choose among the words, syntactic structures, phonological devices and even gestures that we control, those which are appropriate to each situation we are in. And although our choices are not conscious ones, we know that they are nonrandom and rule governed, because we and our conversational partners know when those guiding principles of appropriate speaking are broken.

Just what are those aspects of communication contexts that so strongly influence the ways we speak on different occasions? You identified some when you responded to the exercise pairs on pages 292–93, and the Labov and Robins example suggests some more. First, who are the participants in a communication event and what is their relation to one another? Age will make a difference here. The language style that teenagers use in conversation with their peers will differ from the style they use in talking with a younger child (as in a babysitting situation), or with someone older (a friend's mother or father). How familiar are the participants with one another? Are they friends, family members, neighbors, or are they relative strangers who just happened to arrive at the same meeting early or sit beside each other on a bus or stand next to each other in a cafeteria line? What is the relative status of the participants? Are they fellow students, playmates, or colleagues, with comparable status? Or is there a status imbalance—an older child tutoring a younger one, a boss talking with a subordinate, a teacher conversing with a student, or a school superintendent with a teacher? Clearly these aspects are not always distinct. Variables of age and status often overlap (older tends to have more status), as do age and familiarity (often greater familiarity among age mates), or status and familiarity (often greater familiarity with someone of similar status).

One intriguing feature that exerts a very strong influence and overlaps with several of the above is the shared background of the participants in a communication event. If the participants know each other very well, they can assume so much background knowledge and thus leave so much unspoken, that the outside observer might either not understand the interaction at all, or else might misinterpret it, perhaps taking at face value what the participants understand to be sarcasm or jest or mockery. Consider this example.

A mother who was driving a carpool of elementary school children pulled up in front of the last rider's house and honked. The rider, an eleven-year-old girl, walked to the car. As she opened the car door, the following conversation took place between her and a nine-year old girl already in the car:

Nine-year-old: How long?

Eleven-year-old: Ummmmm, I think till Wednesday. Maybe, if I'm good today she might cut it shorter. I might get just, you know, today. (Both laugh.) But . . .

Nine-year-old: Did she mean nobody over there too?

Eleven-year-old: Well, I thought she didn't say "You couldn't play with anybody." She said, you know, "You cannot leave the house," and I thought, so OK, I didn't leave the house. And I invited you over and she goes "Um . . . that wasn't part of the deal."[6]

It is not until this point that the outsider begins to be aware that these two girls (who have not seen or talked to each other for twenty-four hours) are talking about the older child's punishment by her mother. It was an exchange that made no sense to the others in the car, but the shared background of the two participants made it perfectly clear to them.

The setting in which a communication occurs also influences language usage. The time and place will make a difference; people will speak differently at an afternoon picnic in the park, at a Sunday morning church service, and at a fashionably late dinner party. The type of speaking event makes a difference too. The fact that we use different terms to label various types of speaking events suggests that we think of speaking events differently. We call some speaking events "meetings," some "services," some "debates," some "interviews," some "bull sessions," etc. Each occasion has its own set of speaking conventions and the participants know (unconsciously) what they are.

Setting also includes the number of people present and/or involved. The talk in a group of three or four is likely to be a "conversation" or a "discussion," while the talk in a group of thirty or forty is likely to be a "presentation." The public or private nature of the interaction may influence the language; we

---

[6]I am grateful to Kay Walther for this example from her data.

would expect language that is not meant to be overheard to differ from that which is intended to be heard by many people. The formality level of a situation (which obviously overlaps with other aspects of setting) influences the language of the participants also. The tone or spirit of the communication is important, too; how do the participants interpret the event? Is it serious, perfunctory, playful? You can see, perhaps, that aspects of setting overlap with each other, and overlap with who the participants are as well.

The channel of the communication influences the language style also. By "channel" here I mean written versus oral. Stylistic conventions governing written expression are different from those governing oral expression. Also, our purposes in communicating are different and each purpose guides the language choices we make. We talk differently when we comfort, persuade, argue, inform, instruct, entertain, and so on. The topic we are discussing exerts its influence also. Recently I might have experienced a vacation trip to Hawaii, the death of a friend, and intense study for an upcoming economics exam. The nature of these topics, the very events themselves, would influence the way I told you about each one.

The aspects of social situation discussed here are only a few of many that we are sensitive to and adapt to when we talk. Clearly our communicative competence, "the knowledge that underlies socially appropriate speech" (Ervin-Tripp 1977, p. 6), is at least as complex as our linguistic competence.

> Inter-individual communication requires more than mastery of the rules of a sound system, of a grammatical system and of a system of meanings. The player in the communication game must identify his opponent (or interlocuter), assess the objective of the game, weigh the various circumstances of the situation such as the location, presence of observers, etc., and he must know the ground rules, i.e., who is responsible for the moves in the game, how the moves are sequenced, and what constitutes a violation of the rules. The player then continuously adapts his performance to take into account these diverse and complex factors. Most players who belong to the same community learn to adjust their performance that is, make appropriate choices of linguistic form and content, in very similar ways. (Garvey and Baldwin 1970, p. 1)

SUMMARY

As sociolinguists continue their vigorous research we will learn more about (1) the various functions we use our language for, (2) the structure, dynamics, and underlying assumptions of communication events, and (3) the diverse speaking styles we use and the factors influencing this diverse usage. As you might guess, language acquisition researchers are keenly interested in children's development of communicative competence: How do children acquire communicative competence? How do they develop a range of language functions and various forms for conveying each? How do they learn the rules of the communication game and how to move appropriately in a conversation? How do they learn to shape their language to each situation?

Once again we look to the interactive environment which provides the child with information about how language is used, as well as about how language is structured.

THE DEVELOPMENT OF
COMMUNICATIVE COMPETENCE
IN AN INTERACTIVE ENVIRONMENT

Forms and Functions

It has been suggested that "a major difficulty for children" in their acquisition of language is the lack of fit between form and function (Coulthard 1977). As pointed out earlier, a single function, for example requesting an action, can be accomplished by a variety of forms. For example:

an imperative	Get me a drink.
an imbedded imperative	Would 'ja get me a drink.
a need statement	I need a drink.
an interrogative	Do you have a drink handy?
a statement	Tennis sure does make ya' thirsty.
	(Based on Ervin-Tripp 1977)

On the other hand, one form can be used to express a variety of functions. Take interrogatives, for example:

challenge	Oh yeah! Wanna' bet?
threaten	Want a punch in the nose?
entertain	What do you get when you cross a——— and a———?
seek information	What time is it?
invite	Why don't you come over for lunch tomororow?
request action	Can you reach the salt?
initiate conversation	Ya' know what?
greet	How ya' doing?

Consider the various functions conveyed by the interrogatives in the accompanying cartoon.

Whether or not this lack of a one-to-one correspondence between form and function constitutes "a major problem" for language-acquiring children, it is clear that form/function relations are a vital feature of the language they must learn. The language environment provides them with plenty of data.

In the following conversation between a mother and her one-year-old son as they play ball, you can see that the mother's language is serving many different purposes. She "is doing things with words." What different functions can you identify? (The child's responses are transcribed here in a very informal way. You'll notice that some of his responses seem very close to English words that would be appropriate to the situation, and others bear almost no resemblance to English words at all, though the mother generally treats his responses as if they are the appropriate words; for example, she responds to his "eh bah" as if the child really had said "Mickey Mouse," the response she is seeking.)

> *M:* Where'd that ball go?
>
> *C:* uguh
>
> *M:* Where'd it go?
>
> *C:* oguh
>
> *M:* D'ya have it? There it is. (Pause) D'ya wanna play catch?
>
> *C:* kesh
>
> *M:* Catch the ball.
>
> *C:* gah
>
> *M:* Oh, what a throw!
>
> *C:* ebaw
>
> *M:* Here's the ball. Catch.
>
> *C:* wuu guh
>
> *M:* Are your pants wet? (Touches child's pants to find out.)
>
> *C:* kesh kesh

M: Catch.

C: guh

M: Ooooohhhhh.

C: eduh baw

M: Here's the ball.

C: bawh

M: Oh, good catch!

C: uh

M: Want me to take your hat off?

C: bawh

M: A———, let me take your hat off. (Pause while M takes child's hat off.) Let's look at what's on your hat. D'ya see all those animals that M——— and D———were talkin' about? See?

C: yuh

M: Who's that?

C: duk

M: That's a dog (as if repeating what child said). Who's this?

C: eh bah (high-low intonation)

M: That's Minnie Mouse? (as if what child had said). And who's this?

C: ba bah (low-high intonation)

M: Donald Duck? (as if what child had said). And who's this?

C: eh bah (high-low intonation)

M: Mickey Mouse (as if repeating child). Mickey . . . (waits for child to repeat) . . . Mouse. And who's that?

C: duk

M: A dog (as if repeating child). Who's this?

C: gee goh

M: Minnie Mouse?

C: thusuh giddy go   giddy gish?

M: A who? (as if asking child to repeat meaningful utterance)

C: bawh   kesh

M: Welllllllll?

C: ge dula ell

M: Are you gonna tell me "well"?

C: bawh

M: Bow-wow, chuh. Hit me right in the eye ball.[7]

Through a variety of linguistic forms and actions and gestures, the mother initiates and maintains interaction, she informs, she expresses and explains, she

[7] I am indebted to Ben Blount for this episode.

praises, she alerts, she invites the child to action, she "tests" him, she seeks information ("Are your pants wet?" plus her action), she entertains or plays with language (see last utterance), she provides social formulas ("Thank you"), she requests action ("A———, let me take your hat off," that is, come here and be still) and verbal repetition ("Are you gonna tell me 'well'?"). Given this rich kind of interactive environment—people communicating with the child using a variety of forms to express a variety of functions—the child figures out how conversation works in both its context-free and context-sensitive aspects. He uses this developing knowledge to guide his own communication behavior, continually hypothesizing, testing, and revising his hypotheses as he continues to get more data. Remember, the language structure (form)/language use (function) distinction is one we impose as a convenience to ourselves in trying to study a vast and unwieldy topic—language. But the distinction has no basis in the child's (or our own) experiencing of language. Forms and functions are all of a piece, quite an inseparable wholeness for the child as he interacts with others.

> What is common to every use of language is that it is meaningful, contextualized, and in the broadest sense social; this is brought home very clearly to the child, in the course of his day-to-day experience. The child is surrounded by language, but not in the form of grammars and dictionaries, or of randomly chosen words and sentences, or of undirected monologue. What he encounters is "text," or language in use: sequences of language articulated each within itself and with the situation in which it occurs. Such sequences are purposive—though very varied in purpose—and have an evident social significance. The child's awareness of language cannot be isolated from his awareness of language function. . . . (Halliday 1973, p. 20)

Children's earliest language serves diverse functions (as do their prelinguistic expressive behaviors). It is fascinating that even when children's linguistic means of expression are limited to single word utterances, those single word utterances, according to Dore, serve at least the following recognizable functions: labeling, repeating, answering, requesting an action, requesting an answer, calling, greeting, protesting, practicing (Dore 1975, p. 31). The child's word(s), intonation contour, nonlinguistic behavior, and the immediate context, taken together, make possible the (tentative) identification of these diverse early functions in children's speech. And from his observations of a child from nine to eighteen months of age, Halliday has identified the following set of language functions (in order of their emergence) as those "functions in which a child first learns to mean" (Halliday 1977, p. 37): (1) instrumental or "I want" through which the child's material needs are met; (2) regulatory or "Do as I tell you" through which the child gets others to do what he wants them to; (3) interactional or "me and you" through which the child moves into or maintains an interaction with someone else; (4) personal or "here I come " through which the child expresses his uniqueness and self-awareness; (5) heuristic or "tell me why?" through which the child explores the environment; (6) imaginative or "let's pretend" through which the child creates his own environment; and, emerging somewhat later (around two years) (7) informative or "I've got something to tell you" through which the child conveys information to someone. And Joan Tough has observed the following functions in the language of three-year-olds: directive function including directing self and directing others; interpretative function including reporting on present and past experiences, and also reasoning; projective function including predicting, empathetic, and imaginating; and relational function including self-maintaining and interactional (based on Tough 1977, pp. 68–69). Though different researchers categorize children's language functions in somewhat different ways, it is absolutely clear that from the time that children "have words" they are "doing things with words." It is also clear that an important part of children's language growth that continues through the elementary school years is (1) the adding of new functions to their range, and (2) the adding of new means for expressing each function. Initially, children use a limited set of linguistic forms to express a limited set of functions; ultimately, they use a diverse set of linguistic forms to express a wide range of functions.

> Children have to build up structure and function at the same time. As they learn more about structure, they acquire more devices with which to convey different functions. And as they learn more about function, they extend the uses to which different structures can be put. But even at age seven or eight, children still have a long way to go. Acquiring a language is a long and complicated process. (Clark and Clark 1977, p. 373)

Communication Structure

As children's social experience expands, their interactions will necessarily encompass a wider range of types of communication events. It is likely that, on entering elementary school, children will have had substantial experience in some kinds of discourse (for example, argument, question-answer sequences). Further, some moves in discourse will be very familiar (children's use of "Know what?" as a conversation starter). Remember that conversational turn taking begins in infants even before identifiable words emerge and that mothers do everything they can to engage their prelinguistic infants actively in conversation. Mothers assure that their interactions with their babies are conversation-like by passing the conversational turn to the baby as much as possible (so there is alternation of turns), and then interpreting anything that occupies the baby's turn (burps, gurgles) as coherent and relevant to the ongoing conversation.

It is interesting to note what happens when an adult is not a participant to take the major responsibility for assuring conversation-ness. One researcher has studied the tape recorded predawn conversations of her twin sons from age two years and nine months to three years and eight months (Keenan 1974; Keenan and Klein 1975), and found them to be truly conversational in nature: turn-taking sequences in which each turn related to the partner's previous one and influenced the next. Before age three, many of the exchange sequences (about one-third) were sound play; that is, one twin's turn would involve a nonsense sound sequence and the second twin would then incorporate that sound sequence in his next turn, sometimes repeating it, sometimes modifying it. It is significant that, without an adult present to take major responsibility for making the dialogue follow conversational norms, these very young children's interactions followed basic conversational conventions of turn taking, coherence (sequences of related exchanges), and relevance (each successive utterance relating to the preceding one).

Consider the following three excerpts from the interactions of preschool children, slightly older than Keenan's twins (three- and four-year-olds). Identify every instance you can find of the participants demonstrating their awareness of discourse structure and dynamics: their engaging in a sequence of moves, each one responsive to preceding moves and influencing succeeding ones, and all occurring within a rule-governed framework.

Mark: That's my red car John.

John: But it isn't really.

Mark: Well—I was playing with it—I had it first.

John: Oh—well—which shall I have then? I'm going to have the blue one and I'm going to race it.

Mark: Mine's racing too—round it goes.

John: Push your car faster Mark, like this. Wow—wow—mine's going fast as anything —as anything and fast as a train.

Mark: Mine's going fast as a rocket—whoosh.

John: Watch out Mark—my car's coming fast—I think there'll be a crash—make yours come to mine.

Mark: Yes there will be a big crash—mine's coming—watch out—brr—there—there crash.

John: Oh an accident, an accident—my car's on fire.

Mark: Fetch the fire engine—the cars are burning all up.

John: And the people are getting all burnt up too.

C-1: Guess when my birthday is.

C-2: The 4th of June.

C-1: No.

C-2: The 16th of September.

C-1: No.

C-2: The 3rd of November.

C-1: No way.

C-2: I give up.

C-1: In March. (She begins to draw on the desk top.)

C-2: Look what you did, T————. Miss S————, T———— drew on the table.

C-1: Stop, you're dumb.

C-2: You called me dumb, dummy.

C-1: Ha ha ha ha ha. Look what I made.

C-2: Ha ha ha ha ha. That isn't pretty.

C-1: Ha ha ha ha ha. That isn't pretty.

C-2: Ha ha ha ha ha. (C-1 leaves)[8]

(C-1 and C-2 below are playing, and their interaction occurs in an entirely playful manner.)

C-1: I will turn the light off.

C-2: I will turn the light on.

C-1: And I will put you into the garbage can.

C-2: I will put you into the garbage can.

C-1: And I will go somewhere else.

C-2: I'll go somewhere else, where you can't find me.

C-1: Uh-uh (meaning no). I know how ta run . . . and fight.

C-2: Me too . . . and I'll run and jump over you.[9]

In each of these episodes the children use language interactively. Each child takes the partner's moves into account and shapes his or her own accordingly. The children are moving in these communication games in ways that give evidence of their being members of the same community, playing the same games governed by similar rules.

Our knowledge in this area of children's growth is in its infancy. But we do know that, during the elementary school years, children will participate in new types of communication events, perhaps structured group discussions, meetings, debates, teacher-controlled large group lessons. They will also refine and expand their knowledge of familiar types of communication events (say, informal conversations) through their continuing participation in them. In the activity of meaningful interaction, they will further develop underlying conversational principles that will make them more effective conversational partners.

[8]I am grateful to Cynthia Postel for this example from her data.
[9]I am grateful to Genevieve Kerr for this example from her data.

Appropriate Speaking Styles

> Linguistic theory treats . . . the child's acquisition of the ability to produce, understand, and discriminate any and all of the grammatical sentences of a language. A child from whom any and all of the grammatical sentences of a language might come with equal likelihood would be of course a social monster. With the social matrix in which it acquires a system of grammar a child acquires also a system of its use, regarding persons, places, purposes, other modes of communication, etc.—all the components of communicative events. . . . (Hymes 1974, p. 75)

As the child's social world expands, his exposure to more varied styles of socially appropriate speech also necessarily expands. The infant's social world is somewhat narrow, including home and family and family friends, perhaps a limited number of caregivers, and probably some friendly strangers with whom to interact on outings or in the supermarket. The speech of the people interacting with and around him is appropriate to this limited range of contexts. The two-year-old's social world probably expands to include neighborhood children and their families, members of a play group perhaps, more experience in other settings (other children's homes, Sunday School, local playgrounds, public library, shopping centers). The four-year-old's social world is wider still, possibly including a substantial period of time in nursery school or day care settings. And of course the six-year-old's social world includes a school experience which daily brings contact with many children from various backgrounds, a variety of adults (teachers, aides, classroom visitors, school personnel, parent volunteers), and a variety of settings (playground, library, classroom, cafeteria, field trips) and interaction groups (twosomes, small groups, classroom group). Communication is an important part of all these situations. As the child grows, he is exposed to and participates in an ever widening range of social situations which vary in the many dimensions which influence our language use: age, familiarity, status of the participants; number of participants; time and place; type of communication event; formality level of the interaction; the spirit of the interaction; the channel, topic, purpose of the communication. As the child's data base for appropriate stylistic variation expands, his hypotheses about this aspect of language expand also, and we find his language becoming "more widely adapted" to diverse situations. He is a "little sociolinguist" as well as a "little linguist": Given rich interaction experience he discerns underlying regularities for adapting speech to fit the social situation.

We can say little at this time about the specifics of the sequence of acquisition of stylistic varsatility. We are at an early stage in our investigations of this aspect of children's language growth. But we do know that this is an aspect of children's language development that continues actively over a long period of time, at least through the elementary school years. However, it is impressive to note the solid start that most children have made by the time they come to elementary school. Consider how the language style of the following five-year-old boy, E, alters as he talks to his five-year-old friend, his mother, and his infant sister.

(Two five-year olds eating lunch.)

E: Do you like pickles?

B: What?

E: Do you like pickles on your hamburger?

B: Pickles?

E: Yes.

B: Yes.

E: Not me. My mommy took 'em off.

(Now they are playing.)

B: I need a big block like that.

E: Here—because you can use those medium ones.

B: Okay, now.

E: Hey, look at this! My trailer's gonna park in here with my truck.

B: So is mine.

E: I need some medium ones (blocks). These are mine, right? Here, you need these? You have to put it just like mine. You see how I put it there?

B: How? Where are the mediums?

E: You see, there are a lot of mediums.

B: I don't have enough blocks.

E: You don't? Oh my gosh! Here's a little one. Now look! Look how many cars I have!

(E is talking with his mother about the tape recorder.)

E: What is that star? (Refers to the microphone on the tape recorder.)

M: What is what?

E: The star.

M: Where? Right there?

E: Yes.

M: That's the microphone.

E: It is?

M: Uh-huh. Isn't that neat?

E: But if people are far away from it, how will they talk through it, and will it still be loud?

M: Yes, because this little dial over here can make it louder or not over here. So that's what we have to do.

E: Where's our other tape recorder what we used to have—ours?

M: A long time ago?

E: Yes.

M: I don't know.

E: Can we ask Daddy? He might have took it somewhere.

M: Maybe. We'll have to find out.

E: Now?

M: Not now.

E: If he doesn't know where it is, then you know what we are just going to do?

M: What?

E: Buy another one, and it's gonna be mine!

(E is talking with his infant sister.)

E: You are my beautiful M————. You're a beautiful bye, you're a beautiful bye. I will get you somewhere else. Beautiful pie, beautiful pie. Beautiful girl. M————, how are you doing? Yes, you're beautiful. They are records in there. Do you know what records are? Do you know? Do you know what this is for? They are things what we listen to. Did you know that? M————, records are the things what we listen to with our ears. (Baby babbles)

E: M————, hi there! M———— da-da-da! Da-da-da-da-ya-ya-da-da-da-da! Say "da-da," M————. (Sings) Hello, sweetie pie. We'll put some fancy socks on and you will look so pretty, my little M————. (Baby coos)

E: M————, how are you doing this morning? That's my beautiful pie, that's a beautiful bye, right, M————? This is a sweel li'l girl. (Baby whines)

E: . . . Don't cry, my sweetie baby girl. Don't cry, sweet as apple pie. (Sings) I like you, my sweetie pie, pretty girl. Do you want to go to school, sister? It's a beautiful day outside.[10]

IN CONCLUSION

Currently we know more about both the sequence and the processes of a child's acquisition of linguistic competence than we know about his acquisition of communicative competence. We are hindered in part by not having a comprehensive and coherent theory of communication at this time. But from the research available thus far, we can with confidence assert at least the following:

1. Children acquire linguistic and communicative competence simultaneously; they do not learn language structure and *then* learn how to use it, but rather are engaged in purposeful interactive speech from the outset. Linguistic competence is a part of children's communicative competence.

2. The communicative competence that children develop includes the use and interpretation of (a) language serving various purposes through use of various forms, (b) language which exhibits hierarchical structure and move

[10]I am grateful to Debbie Strasmick for these examples from her data.

sequences appropriate to various types of communication events, and which accords with underlying conversational maxims; (c) language which is variously adapted to be socially appropriate.

3. Children acquire communicative competence (like linguistic competence) in an interactive environment, by engaging in meaningful communication.

4. Children are active in this aspect of their language growth, hypothesizing, testing, revising in light of the feedback they receive.

In a few years we will know much more about children's acquisition of communicative competence, as this is the area which is currently getting perhaps the most attention of all in child language acquisition research. But for now, it is supremely important that we—especially as teachers—understand that "communicating and learning to communicate always go hand in hand" (Labov and Fanshel 1977, p. 20).

Chapter 12

Communicative Competence, Teachers, and Children

INTRODUCTION

... What children use language for in school must be "operations" and not "dummy runs." They must continue to use it to make sense of the world: they must *practice* language in the sense in which a doctor "practices" medicine and a lawyer "practices" law, and not in the sense in which a juggler "practices" a new trick before he performs it. (Britton 1972, p. 130)

We come now to consider the dimensions of children's language growth which the school can contribute to most powerfully of all: children's growth as effective and versatile communicators. Now those very aspects of the classroom which we tend to bemoan—the large numbers of people involved and the great diversity of abilities, needs, background, and interests among them —become our staunchest allies. In this chapter we will focus on the classroom environment and consider (1) some possibilities for developing children's language functions (using three functions as examples: narration, explanation, personal expression); (2) some ways of incorporating situational diversity in the child's interaction experience (using three variables as examples: age, status, familiarity of interaction partners); (3) some possible sources of ideas for rich interaction experiences; (4) the place of real communication experiences versus skills development; and (5) some final thoughts about classroom talk.

We begin this chapter with what we know. We know:

What our goal is: (1) That the child shall be able, in speech and in writing, to express herself clearly, interestingly, relevantly, fluently across a wide range of communication functions and situations, and (2) that the child shall be able, in her listening and reading, to interpret and respond effectively to the functionally and situationally diverse expressions of others.

That the young child has a long way to go toward reaching this goal.

> The speaker must be able to direct the listener's attention, to take account of his knowledge and expectations; the speaker must have means for surprising, impressing, playing up to or putting down his interlocutor; he must have linguistic means of expressing relations of status and affiliation between himself and his conversational partner. (Slobin 1975, p. 4)

> Will [the child] be able to order information so that the listener knows what he needs to know at each point in an exposition? . . . Can he maintain a consistent point of view when he wants to and change when he wants to do that? Can he shift styles to suit different sorts of decoders? Can he find a metaphor that captures the essentials of an entire intellectual structure? *None of these skills is entailed in grammatical knowledge. None of them is well developed in early childhood.* (Brown 1968, pp. vi–vii; italics added)

That the child develops communicative competence through discerning rules underlying the diverse interaction contexts which she observes and in which she participates ("practices" in Britton's sense, as the lawyer and doctor "practice" their trades, by engaging in them).

In sum, we know something about where the child is going (the goal), where she is now, and how she will move toward the goal, namely, through active participation in functionally and situationally diverse interaction experiences which she considers purposeful. Such experiences allow for hypothesis building, testing, and revising in the light of continuous feedback. The time is right: the child's communicative development is going on vigorously from preschool through elementary years. The place is right: A classroom can offer functionally and situationally diverse meaningful interaction inside and outside its four walls. In fact, given a teacher who is sensitive and aware of how a child's communication abilities develop, the school can provide a richer diversity of interactive experience than the child's home or neighborhood. It

remains, then, for us to translate this knowledge into interactive experiences
for our children.

FUNCTION

We begin again with a child who is the active learner, the little sociolinguist
figuring out how the spoken and the written language are used appropriately
and powerfully for various functions. Given an environment which offers the
child many opportunities for "practicing" (engaging in) language used in
various ways and for various purposes, we know that she will expand her
repertoire of language functions as well as the forms she uses in the expression
of each.[1]

For illustrative purposes, I am selecting three different ways of using
language that we know we would like each child to develop. For each one I
am suggesting a few experiences that many children find involving and purposeful. The intention is neither to produce a comprehensive set of language
uses that we would hope a child's repertoire would ultimately include, nor
provide a complete set of activities that all children should engage in to become
effective users of language for particular purposes. *To plan communication for
any children apart from the children themselves, without their active participation and without reference to their natural interests and concerns, is to miss the
whole point.* My intention is, rather, to discuss three uses of language that we
engage in all the time in many different ways (narrative, informing/explaining,
personal), by way of focusing attention on the range of uses our (and our
children's) language includes; and to provide a few examples of classroom
activities relating to each language use, that some children have engaged in
meaningfully. Consider these examples nothing more than a jumping-off point
for your own thinking about your children's language in the classroom. Think
of them as simply one side of the barest beginning of a brainstorming session.
Remember that it is your ensuing part in the brainstorming session that is
indispensable; it is *you* who know your own children and what they're into,
and this is the only viable base for a "language program."

Narrate

We want children to be able to tell (or follow the telling of) a "story," a series
of related events, either real or imagined, in an orderly time sequence. As

[1]I am ignoring here a distinction that some scholars have maintained between the communication goal and the means of achieving it; for example, Kinneavy's (1971) distinction
between "aims" and "modes," and Tough's (1977) distinction between "functions" and
"uses."

adults, we use language in this way a great deal: "I had the worst dream last night. I dreamed I was. . . ." "I was reading in the paper just yesterday that the police finally caught up with X. At first they had thought . . . so they had . . . but then they found out that . . . so they had to . . ." "You probably don't remember the time you fell on broken glass and we had to take you to the hospital. You were only little then. You see, you had been out playing in your sandbox. . . ." "Saw a great movie yesterday. It was about a. . . ." "Once upon a time. . . ." "Dear Sir: Three weeks ago I requested from you. . . . One week later I was informed that. . . ."

Our narrating serves different purposes. Sometimes we narrate in order to inform someone of something; sometimes by way of persuading someone to change a course of action; sometimes for pure enjoyment. But whatever the ultimate purpose this use of language is serving, narrating effectively involves at least:

1. *Selecting content appropriately* in terms of the listener's (reader's) knowledge and interest. You know how frustrating it is when someone relates an incident most of which you have heard before, or belabors points in a story which you already know, or talks at great length about points which are just not very interesting to you. It is equally frustrating when the narrator doesn't provide information you need to make sense of what is being said, assuming a background which you don't have.

2. *Foregrounding and backgrounding.* People interested in visual perception sometimes talk of "figure" and "ground" in pictures. So in narrative. Certain events are major in carrying the momentum of the story. Others provide background or supporting detail, but are clearly subordinate to the main line of action. It can be very trying to listen to someone relate an experience when that person treats the unimportant details as if they were equal in importance to the main events ("So then I bumped into Jim. You know Jim Maxwell, Mary's brother? The one who used to sell shoes but decided that was really a dead end so he went back to school and started taking courses in engineering. He finally took over the family business. . . .") The narrator who does not treat "ground" as subordinate sometimes gets derailed from the story line altogether and you find yourself thinking, "Would you just please get on with the story!" The momentum of the story has drowned in a sea of unimportant, sometimes even unrelated, detail.

3. *Conveying a chronological sequence of events.* Consider the frustration you feel when the narrator keeps backing up to insert important preceding information that's been left out ("Oh yeah, I forgot to tell you that before that she had told her brother. . . .") This does not mean that the telling must proceed in a linear string, first event, then second event, and so on. Flashback and other techniques can be very effective as we all know. But the telling, whatever the techniques used, must make the order of events apparent to the listener/reader.

4. *Using a variety of linguistic means.* (How many times have your children told you those monotonous "and then . . . and then . . . and then . . . and then . . ." stories?)

It is easy enough to bathe children in narrative experiences so that they will become more adept at incorporating these four aspects of effective narration in their own *production.* But immersing children in such a narrative bath is also the surest way to develop their ability to *interpret* narration. Children's literature offers the most obvious rich resource for narrative. We would contribute greatly to our children's ability to read and to their love of reading, as well as to their narrative bath, if we provided a half-hour period every day without fail, for children's self-chosen reading. We provide the time, the place, the model, and the materials. The place—are there cozy, inviting corners available where children curl up with their books? Are there some carpeted areas where children can stretch out? Are there inviting places for reading outside of our classroom? Are the children permitted to go to the library for their reading time, or to sit outside on the grass under a tree on a nice day? The model—do we read too? Do our children see us "get into" books of our choice? Do they see that this reading time is a special and highly prized time of our day—for *reading*, not for grading papers or arranging materials for an art activity? The materials—they need to be abundant and diverse so that children really do have choices for their reading. Obvious sources are school and public libraries. Inexpensive paperback editions of fine works abound and are an excellent investment to your ongoing classroom library. Combining your resources with, or trading off with, those of another class doubles the materials available to all the children. Fader's idea is still a good one: Give each child a paperback that *belongs* to him or her, that can be traded with another child, and so, many traded books keep circulating (Fader and McNeil 1968). More and more we are coming to realize that comics are a valuable resource: *Asterix, Tin-Tin, Bugs Bunny* are nothing if not narratives—related happenings in a time sequence. You may want to include wordless storybooks and books accompanied by cassette tapes for those of your children who are not yet able to read independently even at a beginning level, but who can tell stories for picture sequences and can follow stories in books as they listen to someone else read them on tape.

One of the richest resources of all is, of course, children's own writing, much of which is narrative. *Kids* magazine, children's writing available through Teachers and Writers Collaborative, and of course collections put out by commercial publishers are readily available. *Children like to read the works of other children.* (If you doubt this, try the following experiment. Make available five issues of *Highlights,* an attractive magazine written by adults for children, and five issues of *Kids,* an attractive magazine written by children for children. See which gets the most use.)

The most powerful resource of all is the writings of your own children.

Over time this can become a substantial part of your class library. Children's work should be valued, preserved, and, above all, made available for other children to read. A plastic spiral binding is very inexpensive and laminating equipment for front and back covers is available at many schools. Thus, collecting your children's work into "real books" is a simple and inexpensive matter and can happen continuously in a natural and informal way. You simply need to keep the materials available—bindings, paper, and, of course, an atmosphere that encourages written communication.

The crucial thing about the self-chosen reading period is that the children really be free to choose what and how they will read during this time. This means changing materials each week—not all of them, of course, but those that seem to have served their purpose—so that the children really do have choices. This also means resisting the temptation to say to a child who is endlessly reading the same type of material, "Why don't you read a different kind of book for a change? Why here's an interesting biography. You haven't read biography for a long time." You may want to do this at some point, *but not during the child's free reading period.* Some fifth graders may read every single Nancy Drew ever written before they move on (just like some adults do with Agatha Christie novels.) Some second or third graders will go through every *Tin-Tin* and then go back to the beginning and read through them all again! And many children will read through all their favorite Dr. Seuss books that you thought they had left years earlier. But for this sacred half hour, that is their privilege. Most important of all, if the child is to be truly *free* in this reading time, there will be no test to take, no comprehension questions to answer, no book reports to write or present, no stars or brownie points of any kind awarded, no subtle competition gimmicks, no possibility of failure (see Holt 1969). (How much would you and I read for enjoyment, if we knew that we were going to be examined at the end of each book via tedious comprehension questions, being required to write about the funniest incident or "the part I liked best"? The experience of reading a book is our own, pleasant and personal. So it should be for our children.) Will the children talk about what they are reading? Undoubtedly, just as you and I do when we really "get into" a book, but they will do it because they want to (the right reason), not because we force them to (the wrong reason).[2]

Another important area of your children's narrative bath will probably be stories read or told to them. There are so many possibilities here:

1. Taped stories on cassettes with three or four copies of the storybook available. You can easily tape five stories a week yourself, and in no time you've got a substantial tape library going for a listening center. It is fascinating to

---

[2]It is my belief that such a half-hour period every day of every week of the school year, would do more to foster children's reading skill than half an hour of daily phonics drills, reading aloud from basals, answering comprehension questions from basals, or doing word recognition drills.

get other story readers on tape also, various parents or other adults, representing various speaking styles and dialects, some teenagers you know, your own children (those you have heard read the particular story and whom you know read it effectively. I don't think we gain anything by inflicting on children the bumbling, ineffective oral reading of others, including ourselves!)

2. Professional records and tapes. These are readily available from school and public library—stories, story songs, ballads, fables, folk tales, etc.

3. Reading/telling aloud. This never gets old, in any culture or in any generation, provided that it is done well, of course, and the story is one worth reading or telling. Do you always read stories to your children, or do you sometimes tell them? Do you invite classroom visitors to read or tell stories —parents, grandparents, friends, your principal? Do children get to read or tell stories to each other in pairs? Do they get to go and read or tell stories to children in younger classes? Do they get to be read or told stories by children they admire in older classes?

4. Telling real episodes. Do you ever tell your children episodes from your own past experience? My experience has been that many children are fascinated with the personal incidents their teachers tell. (It's sometimes a real revelation to young children to learn that the teacher currently has a life outside of the classroom, and that she was once a child and even, on occasion, got in trouble.)

5. Filmed versions of favorite stories.

6. Do you and your children ever just turn off all the lights on a gray gloomy day and tell ghost stories?

Most of the ideas so far are what Ashton-Warner (1963) might call the children's "breathing in" part of actively engaging in narrative. What about the "breathing out," the children's creating and expressing of their own narratives? Most children need no help or urging to get started with an original story. But there are many ways to give a bit of a boost when and if a child needs it:

1. Wordless storybooks for which the child provides the story (e.g., Mercer Mayer's *Bubble Bubble,* a great favorite here).

2. Film strips for which the child (or group of children) provides the story.

3. Picture stories of various kinds: for example, sets of photos that children arrange in a sequence and then tell a story for,[3] or sets of pictures children cut from magazines and put in an envelope for other children to arrange and make up a story for.

4. Creating variations on story songs (somebody other than the fox could go out on a night that was other than chilly).

---

[3] *Interaction* (Moffett 1973a) offers fine sets. You can provide your own and/or have some of your own photography enthusiasts do so, of course.

5. Creative drama. An area for children to use in dramatizing their own and others' stories or realistic incidents should be available for all children at least through grade six, possibly with suggestive, flexible costume pieces and props. (I know eighth graders who participate in creative drama in their classes with complete abandon and delight.) Sometimes puppets will be helpful too. Remember, puppets don't need to be elaborate cloth or paper maché items. Anything can be a puppet—a face drawn on the pad of your thumb with ball point pen, a popsicle stick or wooden clothes pin, a small paper bag, a large grocery sack with holes for arms and eyes makes a child a human "puppet." (I have watched table forks spontaneously become puppets for children as they ate lunch.)

6. Playreading and writing (on tape with sound effects? sometimes). The most elaborate created narrative I know of produced by school children came from a group of sixth grad ̣rs. They made up a story about a difficult new child in the classroom, based on a real experience they had had that year. Their final creation involved a series of slides they had taken, as groups of children acted out segments of the story, accompanied by a tape of children playing the parts in the dramatized version they had written, and also including musical background selections for some of the slides. (As you might guess, narrative was one of *many* language uses involved in the children's languaging as they worked on this production for several months. Their goal was the creation of a powerful story. In order to accomplish this, they had to communicate with each other in many ways.)

Both the "breathing in" and "breathing out" activities here have included more fantasy situations than real ones. And, of course, using language for entertainment (narrative as literature) is valid. But it is important not to overlook the many rich real contexts in which children's narrative abilities can develop. In fact, although as adults we probably narrate more real situations than imagined ones, as teachers it is the imagined ones we tend to encourage in the children almost to the exclusion of the real. Here are a final few ideas to right the fantasy/real balance:

1. The collection of first-hand narratives (from important people in the community? from community members from diverse ethnic backgrounds? from parents and grandparents—which might have to be done long distance using cassette tapes—to help children better understand their own roots?).

2. Children's writing (over time, probably) of their own autobiographies. (Remember the inexpensive plastic spiral binding which allows for the addition and rearrangement of pages!) This might include snapshots as well as writing, and will probably include important early incidents that the children have been told about as well as those they remember.

3. Reading materials—biography, autobiography, newspaper.

4. Class newspaper/book. This can be in a variety of formats: personal or class news articles posted on the bulletin board in a "Recent Events of

Interest" section, articles taped on sheets of newsprint that are newspaper size, articles reporting special class experiences collected into a book, etc.

5. Picture stories with Polaroid. Class experiences can be nicely captured and preserved as a sequence of Polaroid pictures with commentary (on tape, in scrapbook form, on bulletin board with different children's written versions of the same pictured events, etc.).

6. Most important, probably, and often the most neglected, is the child telling you, an interested, caring listener and responder, what is going on in her life from day to day.

These are only a few possible ideas to get your own ideas going for your children's narrative bath. You will have many more ideas and your children more still. The main point is that like all uses of language, narrative is *real.* Speakers of every language the world over narrate because human beings want to tell each other events that actually have happened as well as events that have "happened" in fantasy, someone's or some group's creation. In your classroom (as elsewhere), the child's reasons for engaging in narration are real ones—sheer enjoyment, sharing, collecting desired information. The child never need engage in a narrative experience "because the teacher said I had to."

If the teacher, you, aren't saying "you have to," what are you doing? You are providing a variety of activities for your children to "practice" narrating in; you are interacting with them as you move about among individuals and groups as a participant and especially as an interested listener; and you are helping the children to implement their ideas for their further activities.

Should you ever do any deliberate shaping of a child's narrative? I think so, but ever so sensitively and only when you are sure of your relationship with the child in question. Suppose a second grader of yours is excitedly telling you an "and then and then and then" story. You might try something like this: "Oh, Cathy! This is too good to miss. Let's get it on tape." Then simply push the button on your ever ready (literally) cassette tape recorder and just respond as an interested listener while the child tells it all the way through. Then, "Cathy, that's a story I know the other children would be interested in too." Let's write it out and get it up on the bulletin board where everybody can read it." Then play it back, sentence chunk by sentence chunk, with you and child modifying the original single sentence into several sentences "so the kids will understand it when they read it," and you typing (or writing) it sentence by sentence. Then it goes directly on the bulletin board in the "Recent Happenings of Interest" area (or wherever you put the children's current written materials for public sharing).

There are several important principles here. One is that you have preserved the *child's* story, and you have preserved it as an item of great value. It is most important not to overhaul the story or tamper with it so that it is your story and not the child's. Secondly, although you have contributed slightly to the story's form, your focus and indeed the only reason for your input at all, has been your own genuine interest and your desire to make the child's meaning available to the other children. It is crucial that form be always and only dealt with in the interest of conveying meaning. Thirdly, you have not interfered with the momentum of the child's story; she has told it from beginning to end and you have expressed your appreciation for her tale in your response. Only then do you go back to parts as you replay it on tape in order to get it into written form. (We tell children it is rude to interrupt. We must be careful of interrupting them also.) And finally, you have provided a real example of what writing is for. We write something down in order to communicate it to a wider audience, and often to make it into a "thing" that we can work over, smooth, polish. And out of your typewriter has come just that, a communication for many children, that was revised slightly so as to convey the message more understandably. It is not important in this instance that the child has not written it out in her own handwriting (though second graders will often do this with shorter compositions, of course). A second grader's capacity for telling an incident far outruns her ability for writing one down. If we limit her use of narrative to what she can write on paper, her use of language for effective narration will simply have to be put on ice for several years until her transcribing abilities catch up with her oral composition abilities.

Explain/Inform

We know that we want children to be able to put something that they understand into words in such a way that their listener(s) and/or reader(s) will understand it also; and to be able to seek and interpret effectively the explanations of others in speech and writing.

As with other language functions, explaining is something we engage in frequently. Just consider the explanations you provide, seek, and interpret each day relating to such diverse topics as why the car won't run, what's happened to your friends' faltering marriage, why the checkbook doesn't balance, the rationale underlying a particular math text series, how your new blender functions to accomplish all those culinary miracles described in the accompanying booklet, what the nature of your illness is, how it's possible that there's any such thing as infinity when (as that sharp student is quick to point out) "you can always have one more."

As with narrative, effective explanation involves at least:

1. *Selecting appropriate content* for the listener's (reader's) knowledge and interest. One important aspect of this is whether you explain something *at all.* Probably every one of us has at least one acquaintance who insists on explaining to us at length some phenomenon which is fascinating to her but which we do not care about. Yet the speaker expounds excitedly, completely

oblivious to the obvious signals we are giving (yawns, glances at our watch, minimal responses, active attempts to change the subject) that we are not interested. On other occasions we do want explanatory information on a given topic, but the giver provides the explanation in a way which is inappropriate for us—doctors who explain our illness in a way that only they and their AMA colleagues would understand, or the meteorologists who tell us far more about the weather than we care to know.

2. *Foregrounding and backgrounding.* In explanation, the purpose is to inform others of the structure, relations, and processes of something they don't know about. The structure, relations, and processes are figure. When an explainer's supporting examples (ground) take over and become the main purpose, instead of serving to clarify the basic principles and relations, we get that frustrated feeling of "OK, OK. Just get on with the explanation." An effective explanation incorporates enough, but not too many, relevant examples whose relationship to the main principles or processes remains clear and subordinate.

3. *Ordering material clearly.* The information must be so organized and presented that the structure (for example, the anatomy of a crayfish), or relations (cause-effect as in illness where the doctor relates causes and symptoms), or processes (such as steps in developing film or doing origami) be clear and complete. Whether the explanation of structure moves from top to bottom, or inside to outside, whether the explanation of cause and effect moves from cause to effect or from effect to cause, is a matter of choice. What is crucial is that the information be presented in a series of bits such that they build coherently to form, ultimately, a comprehensible whole.

4. *Using a variety of linguistic means.* An explanation is likely to be more effective if it it is not simply a series of factual statements, but involves various devices that help to relate it to the listener's knowledge and interest, such as an apt metaphor or several vivid examples.

The matter of tone used in explanation can be, I think, a bit tricky. There is often a built in status differential in a situation in which one person explains something to another. The "knower" in a knower-nonknower relationship may be in a touchy position. She must convey the necessary information without seeming to put the listener down or herself up. In speaking or in writing, the explainer's tone is equally insulting if condescending or "cute." You know how annoying it is in a one-to-one relationship, in which you are the nonknower, to be lectured at rather than conversed with. Tone might be something to be particularly aware of in our relations with our children, as we are likely to often be knowers in knower-nonknower situations. It is very different to explain something to someone in a way that conveys that that someone is a person whose intelligence you respect and who just happens not to know a particular thing, and to explain something to someone as if you considered that person not very bright. You and I know the difference when other adults explain things to us. Our children know the difference when we explain things to them.

The most typical classroom instructional interaction pattern is teacher asks question and child answers it. Whether in a one-to-one, small group, or whole group situation, when we ask a child "How did you arrive at that answer?" or "How do you know that————?" or "Why do you suppose that ————?" we are asking the child to use language to explain something which she understands. We might paraphrase these requests as "Use your language to explain how you arrived at that answer, to explain how you know that X, to explain why you suppose that Y."

Typically the situations in which children inform/explain to us are of two different types. In the first and probably the most frequent, we ask children to explain something to us so that we can get some insight into their understanding. This is a way of using language that is special to the classroom. Underlying normal (outside of classroom) conversation, there is a basic condition we adhere to—that one asks for information because one sincerely wants to know that information, that is, one doesn't know it already. If I ask you "What time is it?" you and I both assume that I don't already know; if I ask my garage mechanic "Why is my car making that grinding noise?" we both assume that I really don't know why and that I want to have that information. But if I ask a child in a classroom, "Mark, how could I find out which set has more members?" it is not because I myself do not know how to find out which of two sets has more members. Mark and I both know that in this classroom context, the usual operating condition of asking for information which I don't already know is suspended. Mark and I both know that I am seeking information about Mark's understanding of how to determine which of two sets has more members. Notice, however, that we are both engaging in language for explaining/informing. The explanation Mark is constructing and expressing is a math concept and process for verifying; the explanation I am extracting from Mark's language is what is the nature of his understanding of this math concept and procedures for verifying.

The second type of situation in which children explain things to us is the one which more accurately reflects "real" (nonclassroom) conversation, namely, the situation in which we really don't know the information or explanation that we explicitly seek in our question. Let's take an example. Suppose five of your fourth graders decided they'd like to start a regular program for presenting a story to a kindergarten class each day for two weeks. They've been working on this project for several days. They've talked with the kindergarten teacher to see if she'd like them to do this, they've arranged with you and the kindergarten teacher for a particular daily time block for presenting and also for scheduling their own practice and preparation sessions. They've dealt with the problem of what stories to present: They've talked with the kindergarten teacher about the children's favorites and which have and haven't been read to them this year; they've talked with school and local librarians to find out which books seem to be the current favorites of five- and six-year-olds; they've looked over a catalogue and a few new children's books the public librarian has given them; they've recalled their own kindergarten favorites and talked with classmates about what their favorites were when they were in kindergarten. They've decided to present the selected stories in different ways—one person reading aloud, several people reading in parts (for a poetry session), dramatizing one story, presenting another with puppets, telling several short folk tales (instead of reading them) while another group member shows the pictures on the overhead projector. They've arranged for who will do what in each presentation, and for how they'll provide suggestions for one another in their practice sessions.

All this has involved a lot of languaging—talking, listening, reading, writing—for various purposes. Throughout all this, you've been somewhat in the background. You're aware of how their plans are gelling in a general way; you've responded to their ideas with enthusiasm when they've told you about them; you have provided realistic limits when they were moving in directions that weren't feasible ("You know, since it's only a half-day kindergarten and the teacher has a lot of things for the children to do in that time, you'll have to think in terms of twenty-minute presentations each day. Maybe it would be a good idea to time each one when you practice it to be sure you're close to the twenty-minute mark.") You've probably thrown in a suggestion or two to carry the children's ideas further ("You know, it might be fun to tape your presentations and leave the tapes with the children as a start for their own tape library."). But there comes a point at which you need to know in more than a general way what their plans are. Now you sit down with them for the purpose of having them inform you about things you don't already know: what their planned procedure and schedule will be, what stories and poems they've finally chosen and why, what their plans are for each presentation. Here they are explaining to you what they have been doing, what they plan to do and why, because you really don't know. Situations like these, in which teacher and children confer and in which the children are the knowers and explainers/informers and the teacher is the nonknower, are extremely valuable. They tend to be frequent in classrooms where the teacher feels that an important aspect of the job is to support and extend the children's initiatives and ongoing plans for their learning experiences. In this situation in which you, the teacher, are the learner, the children have the invaluable opportunity of watching you learn, seeing how you listen, analyze, question relevantly, request information, synthesize what they are telling you. ("Let me make sure I have it straight so far. You feel it's important for little children to——so you're going to——. What about——? What are you going to do if——?")[4]

---

[4]As Carole Edelsky reminds me and I remind you, we carry our teacher status with us in all our interactions with children. Even when we are nonknowers and our children explain to us, we all know that the final approval for the children's plans is ours. Thus in interactions like the one described here, there is an element of "approval seeking" as well as "explaining/informing" on the children's part.

Of course much of children's textbook material is explanatory and informative in nature, whether the explanation deals with a mathematical process, the structure of social organization of an African tribe, or the human body's use of food. We sometimes think of this kind of language as being boring, and something we have to force on children because they wouldn't engage in it otherwise. But clearly this is not the case. We all know children who pour over auto manuals. We know that children are eager to talk or write about personal hobbies and interests, which involves language heavy in explaining/informing. Consider the following titles of explanatory/informing type articles from *Kids* magazine: "How to Make a Moon Goon" (Number 9), "Water, Our Lifeline in Danger: Water pollution" (Number 4), "How to Make Rubbings" (Number 7), "Countdown to Extinction" (Number 8), "How I Made My Movie" (Number 7), "Making Giant Totem Poles" (Number 10), "Life With a Boa Constrictor" (Number 14), "What's it Really Like to be a Twin" (Number 14), "The Wonderful World of Shells" (Number 15), "Sun Blackout July 10" (Number 15), "My Pet Raccoon" (Number 17). Not only did children choose voluntarily to write on these topics, but child editors selected them for publication in the magazine, presumably because they found these articles interesting and thought other children would too.

Children working together on some project of importance to them inform each other a great deal. Each has a special contribution to make to the project; each must keep the others informed about what she is doing and how and why, and how that part fits in with the others. Each child must also respond to the information provided by other group members.

Children can be important learning resources for one another. Informing and explaining to each other is natural. However, a word of caution is in order. It concerns the assignment and presentation of reports. We are all familiar with the situation in which the teacher assigns each child a topic to write a report on (for example, each child writes about a different North American Indian group), and then, when the reports are done, each child reads the report to the entire class. A sixth grader who had been through this experience recently reminded me of how painful this can be for some children, and how boring it may be for others. This child had been instructed to write a report about an Indian group he was totally uninterested in. The writing was a hated and seemingly interminable chore. The reading of reports by class members dragged on monotonously day after day for ten days. As luck would have it, his report came the tenth and last day. (During the ten days he had frequently expressed his dread of presenting his report.) Feeling terribly embarrassed at having to stand up in front of his peer group (the very people he wanted most to impress favorably) and deliver what he knew to be a boring report, he tried to liven it up a bit and cover his embarrassment by injecting some humorous comments. The teacher misinterpreted his humorous remarks as his mocking the customs of the group he was reporting on, and he received a failing grade.

The grade was by far the least painful aspect of the experience. He said to me, through tears, "I don't think a teacher has the right to make you get up in front of your friends and make a fool of yourself." Though I tried to point out that it hadn't been his teacher's intention to do that, I couldn't disagree with his point, especially remembering so vividly similar embarrassing report experiences from my own grade school days.

How could the situation have been different? First, what was the child writing about? Was it something he chose to write about and saw some purpose in writing about? The previous *Kids* examples indicate that writing informational/explanatory material can be of genuine interest to children, both to those who write it and to those who read it. But it is crucial that the children gather and express information that is of real interest to them, and that they want to share with others.

Second, was the best approach having the child read the report to the entire class, who were being forced to "listen" (that is, to sit still and be quiet —which is not at all the same thing as *listening*)? There is all the difference in the world between making an experience available to someone, and forcing it on someone. Making experiences available to children is likely to be enriching; forcing experiences on children is likely to be self-defeating. Let's suppose that several children had written about topics that were of interest to them. How could their informative work have been made available to others without being forced on them? A display format of some sort might have been useful: a bulletin board area or a table displaying the child's written material, perhaps some interesting books that she had found during the writing, some books with paper-clipped pages where interesting pictures could be found, any models or related art work that she might have done, a cassette tape on which she had read/told a relevant folk tale or provided explanatory comment relating to the selected pictures or to her art work. Providing areas where children can make available to other children what they are researching, and providing opportunity for children to explore those works of others which they choose to explore, will facilitate children's learning from the work of their classmates. What we need to aim for is more in the way of following children's interests, and less in the way of coercing them to follow ours.

Much of explanation is the how-to-do-it type, steps in a process. Children are "practicing" explanation every time they read, write, listen to, or tell someone else how to play a particular game, how to construct a model, how to make chocolate chip cookies, how to make a kite. Our tendency is to give instructions for these activities to all the children at once. But we provide an important opportunity for our children to explain if we give instructions to only one or two children who then explain to one or two other children who then explain to one or two other children. . . . If a child who knows how to play a particular game wants to play that game with a friend who does not know how to play it, the "knower" will use language purposefully to explain the game to the friend, and the friend will interpret the instructions and provide immediate and clear feedback as to the success of the first child's explanation. And remember, you can be an important example of a learner if you share with your children your own experience of figuring out from the written instructions how to use a new piece of classroom equipment, or how to play a new game, or how to prepare for a new gerbil. How do you gather and use explanatory material? It's valuable for your children to see.

Personal Expression

We know that we want children to be able to express personal feelings and opinions in ways that make it possible for others to understand "where they are coming from," and also to be able to respond to, to feel into, the personal expressions of others. It would be impossible to underestimate the importance of language growth in this function. As the child's sense of self and her awareness of others continue to develop, and as she experiences new depths and heights of feeling (fear, joy, awe, frustration, humor, sympathy, anger), her language grows to find more adequate ways of expressing these feelings. At the very least, the child's personal use of language (1) supports her building of self-identity, (2) supports her growing understanding of the feelings of others, and (3) provides a solid base for the appreciation of great literature, which requires the ability to feel into other selves. Despite the increasing social pressures toward a more academically oriented curriculum (Bring up those standard test scores! Start formal reading instruction in kindergarten!), there is some evidence that we are becoming more aware of the importance of children's development of personal expression and response. It is no longer surprising to walk into a third grade and find a group of children sitting on the floor with their teacher, discussing personal fearful experiences with an honesty that would have been unusual ten years ago.

Some excellent children's literature is available to feed this personal understanding and expression. Children's fiction specifically focusing on children's feelings abounds and often helps to move children into their own personal expression of experience.[5] In fact, all excellent fiction, whether or not its specific purpose is to deal with some difficult emotional experience common

[5]See, for example, Kraus' *Leo the Late Bloomer* (1971); Viorst's *Alexander and the Terrible, Horrible, No Good, Very Bad Day* (1972); Anglund's books—*Love Is a Special Way of Feeling* (1960), *Look Out the Window* (1959), *A Friend Is Someone Who likes You* (1958); Steptoe's *Stevie* (1969); Blume's *Are You There God; It's Me, Margaret* (1970), and *Tales of a Fourth Grade Nothing* (1972). In the area of children's nonfiction, I have known Eda LeShan's *What Makes Me Feel This Way* (1972) to help some children understand their feelings and find ways to articulate them.

to most children, presents characters who are *real* and thus experience a range of feelings. In reading/hearing such works, children are having the invaluable experience of feeling into another's life.

Much of children's own expression and interaction in this personal function will be intended to be read or heard by others (though sometimes the source will remain unidentified). Children writing for other children in *Kids* came up with regularly appearing "Dear Dr. Loker" and "Don't You Hate . . ." sections. Here are a few samples:

Dear Dr. Loker:

I have just moved. And it is hard to find a friend because I am shy. What should I do? Signed, Shy. (Number 17)

Dear Dr. Loker:

In school I am no good in math. I try and try to do it, but I just can't do it right. Do you have a good solution? I sure do need it. Your friend, Math-Whiffer. (Number 7)

Dear Dr. Loker:

I have three brothers and no sisters. That can be a real problem! They always beat up on me but I never get revenge on them. How can I? Signed, Revenge. (Number 10)

Don't You Hate . . .

Being bawled out for something your friend did (Number 11)

Kids that copy your papers (Number 9)

When your mother "screams" at you (Number 9)

When your parents treat you like a child, even though your'e [sic] five (Number 9)

Forgetting your lines in a school play right in front of the whole P.T.A. (Number 10)

On Christmas getting excited over a lot of presents for you, but finding out it was nothing you wanted (Number 10)

When your mother sends you to school with a rain coat on, and no one else in the world is wearing a raincoat . . . and then it gets sunny (Number 10)

It's easy enough to provide a "Dear————" box or bulletin board area, and a box or area where children can put their responses. A "Don't You Hate . . ." caption on an empty bulletin board will elicit a lively response from some children.

Sometimes you might want to provide a very involving item intended to evoke personal responses from your children—perhaps a sensory item for younger children (such as, slime), or an emotional or ideational item for older children (an inflammatory editorial or article relating to serious ethical or moral conflict, perhaps). Your purpose here is to stimulate individual personal expression and response. Perhaps you'll write down what your young children say and make it available for others to read (or hear you read). Other times the expression and response may take the form of conversation or debate. Older children may be moved to write their personal responses for others to read. But whatever the form, the purpose is the same: a personal expression (emotion or opinion) and/or response to someone else's.

Poetry is a rich resource for language in the personal function. Exposure to a wide range of personal poetic expressions conveyed in various forms is important here. Poetry written by children, especially by your own children, speaks meaningfully to children. We often forget that poetry is all around us. Our children often talk poetry; we can simply write down, exactly, snatches of their own talk—a line here, a line there—if our ears are tuned to hear the poetry in their talk. A group poem can provide a rich means for sharing personal expression relating to a particular experience or idea.

On a Walk Today . . .
I found a smooth white pebble—a bright spot in a patch of mud. (Jamie)
I found some moss that feels soft when I rub it on my cheek. (Tim)
I found an orange and black speckled butterfly wing. (Celia)
And I found a baby leaf, the size of my thumb nail. (Jody)

Treasures in our pockets.

It's important not to equate poetry with rhymed and metered verse. Much of the poetry we love—from Dr. Seuss to Shakespearean sonnets—is rhymed and metered. Much of it is richly beautiful; much of it is simply hilarious great good fun. But much of poetry, especially children's poetry, does not and should not have to conform to strict formal constraints. Even young children seem so naturally to provide the vivid word picture, the unique personal expression that captures an individual perception. Preserve it! It is a poem in its own right. If we provide exposure only to jingles in the name of "poetry," we will find our children substituting fat cats wearing hats and sitting on mats for real personal expression. This was brought home to me all too vividly once when a group of my second graders had gotten completely "into" a delightful collection of rhymed verse. We had all been enjoying this immensely for a week or so, when K———, one of the most perceptive and eloquent seven-year-olds I have ever known, brought me up short. From early in the year she had quite steadily and effortlessly been writing free verse. Recording her observations and experiences poetically seemed as natural to her as breathing. Suddenly she completely abandoned her true poetic voice, and began coming up with nothing but doggerel, for example, "Good things happen when you help [from a Red Cross poster on the classroom door]. It may be only a dog with a yelp." I realized with alarm that I had been failing to provide a rich range of poetry types and styles for the children to interact with. I had for too long given the children a concentrated dose of only one kind of verse.

Much of our personal use of language is intensely private. Conversation between friends is often a private matter. Our children may engage in this a great deal in school, but often they are forced to do so surreptitiously; often private personal conversation is not sanctioned in the classroom. We would do well, I think, to legitimize it, to support this as a valid and welcome interaction activity. A "Conversation Corner" might help. An area so labeled and demarked by a carpet scrap would do, to be recognized as a place for private conversation among friends.

Diary keeping is perhaps the most private and intensely personal writing activity of all. It is imperative that we respect the children's privacy here. The child's diary writing is not for our eyes unless the child specifically asks us to read it. Then more than at any other time, we must remember that what the child has chosen to share with us is a meaning, not a form; we respond to the meaning *only* and are careful not to see spelling errors or immature grammatical constructions. There are many ways to support and encourage this important means of personal expression. One is by simply providing time for it. A simple diary makes a lovely Christmas or un-Christmas or un-birthday gift for each child. Basically it's a bunch of blank pages, after all, but made special in some way—a blank cover front and back for the child to decorate in a personal way and you to laminate? Or a cover you have personalized with a snapshot you have taken of the child? A personal note from you inside the front cover? Your own word picture description of the child to accompany your diary gift? A plastic spiral binding makes the diary a "real book," of course, but regular brass fasteners do just fine.

To me, one of the most intriguing types of personal writing that children seem to engage in so naturally is note passing. I find it interesting that we try so hard to stamp out this activity that is written personal communication at its very best! That it is so resistant to our stamping out efforts should tell us how meaningful this activity is to our children. Note passing is alive and well —thriving—in most of the classrooms I visit. And it should be! It involves everything we would ask of a communication experience: It is purposeful and relevant communication for the child; it is language used for a valid function (personal); it receives relevant and immediate feedback in the response of the receiver. Why then, do we pounce with such zeal on the note being passed from hand to hand under the desks and across the aisles? Usually so that the children can get back to their assigned task, which is often one that engages their interests and language abilities far less—a worksheet involving comprehension questions on a reading assignment, a spelling exercise, a "language arts" exercise on verb forms or parts of speech or sentence types. (I have been amazed at the high level of personal writing in many of the note-passing series my own three children have kept and have let me read. I have found vivid imagery and sophisticated wit and humor that these children rarely attained in assigned writing tasks. One such series involved lengthy personal ritual insults, written in the style the teacher had taught them was used by Eskimos, clear evidence that these children had grasped far more from the Eskimo study than the teacher dreamed!) So why don't we use note passing, legitimize it?[5] A personal mail envelope on every desk might do and the understanding that getting up and going over to another child's desk to deliver a letter was OK, just like going to sharpen a pencil or get a drink. I know one teacher of young children who uses a carpenter's apron with great ingenuity, regularly putting a surprise in each pocket for her young charges. Carpenter's aprons are easily made (by your children, perhaps?) and each pocket can be a mail pocket for a different child. You can doubtless think of more and better ideas than these, but the point is to capitalize on children's real use of an important language function, rather than to punish it.

Do your children ever see you engaging in personal writing? Do you do any diary writing in class, or sometimes write a line or two of poetry? Do you express personal feelings and responses verbally, out where the children can hear them? Do your children hear/see you respond sensitively to the personal expressions you read or hear? Your own use of this function (as all functions) is important to your children's communication growth.

One obvious way that your children might see you engage in personal language is by your writing them notes—quickies, even one-liners, that you dash off as the spirit moves you.

You're sure grinning a lot today. Do you have some special secret?

Sorry if I jumped on you pretty hard this morning, but—
    I meant what I said
    And I said what I meant.
    You're driving me up the wall today
    One hundred percent!
Let's talk for a minute in the Conversation Corner after lunch about how we can get through the afternoon better.

Thanks for helping to comfort Celia. I know you made her feel better.

I think—I just think maybe you have a new friend today. Am I right?

[5]A word of caution. I don't know how much of the joy of note passing comes from the fact that it's forbidden. If making it "above board" lessens its desirability for children, then let's just ignore it and let it thrive.

How do you think up so many unique ideas? Your idea about———was an interesting and valuable contribution to your group's discussion this morning.

Dear Jess,
  This is a hint!
  There once was a student named Jess,
  Whose desk was a terrible mess
      By the end of the day
      He'd cleared it away
  And now his teacher nags less.
  Today, Jess?!

It's unique, it's personal, it's your thoughts and perceptions and feelings spilling over into writing in a way that's natural and comfortable and fun for you. If your children see that this is an easy and natural way of expressing for you, it's likely to become an easier way of expressing for them too.

Narrating, explaining/informing, expressing personal feelings and opinions—these are obviously just a few of many uses we make of our language and will encourage in our children. These are the three I have chosen to discuss at some length because they are different enough from one another to reflect the wide range of language use. But whatever the uses chosen as examples for discussion, the basic principles would remain the same. Using language effectively:

1. involves both receptive and productive abilities (interpreting and responding to the writing and speech of others as well as expressing in speech and writing);
2. involves developing an awareness of another's perspective and shaping expression appropriately for the listener/reader; or interpreting the language of others from the producer's perspective;
3. develops through the active involvement of children figuring out through using language in meaningful interaction, how they can make language work effectively—how they can accomplish what they want to accomplish with words.

SITUATION

We use language always for some purpose(s) and always in some situation. It is through interaction in a wide variety of social contexts that the child's language becomes a more widely adapted communication instrument. We have identified a few of the many situational variables that influence the talking style we use on a given occasion (for example, the age of the conversational participants, their respective status, the topic of conversation, the time and place.) How can we deliberately incorporate a diverse range of these variables in the communication experiences we provide for our school children? We will attempt to answer this question by discussing in an exploratory way several selected situational dimensions, much as we did in the previous portion on language uses. My hope is that you will be spurred to consider ways you can incorporate within your classrooms other aspects of social situations not discussed here, as well as additional ways to incorporate those discussed. Remember that the goal here is to involve the children as fully as possible in real communication experiences that are maximally diverse situationally. The hypotheses that children build, test, and revise will grow to account for the ways speech and writing are adapted to these diverse social situations. Let's take age, status, and familiarity as examples, remembering that they are only three among many, and that, like all situational variables, they often overlap.

Age

We tend to think of a classroom as a giant peer group. It is, and this is doubtless important. But it can be much more, especially for language. My mind runs immediately to the grandparent generation and the rich contribution the older members of our community can make to our children's growth as competent communicators. One school I know instituted Grandparents Week. It was exciting to watch grandparents participate in the children's school activities and to see new "cross age" friendships grow up on the playground or at lunch. When we talk about a friendship, we are talking about a relationship in which language plays a vital role. A friendship is a languageship. More and more I find myself wondering why we in education have so little used people of retirement age in our classrooms. Why have we so quickly forgotten the rich educational resource "the older generation" was not so long ago when we were a more rooted, less mobile people, and several generations of one family lived in one home or neighborhood? This potential resource is greater now than it has ever been. The number of vigorous, interesting, and highly skilled retired people is steadily growing. Many of them are eager to contribute to the community in ways that the demands of their steady jobs had previously made impossible. Many of them care about children and their growth. We have failed to see the potential contribution of this virtually untapped resource.

Sometimes we have used older people as resources for specific projects, for instance, as primary sources in a unit on local history. One kindergarten studying lullabies from around the world relied heavily on local grandmothers (many of whom had strong European ties, and many more of whom were fuzzy on their ancestry but knew plenty of non-American lullabies). But why limit our children's classroom interaction with older people to a special week or to special units or to blood relations? Older people can contribute much in our classrooms—talking with (listening to?) individual children, sharing personal experiences and interests with the children in an informal way, reading/telling stories and listening to children read stories individually, helping with small group projects that need some overseeing (cooking experiences, perhaps), but most important of all, just being friends who come by to visit and participate because they enjoy it. My experience has been that these friendships are as enriching to the adult as to the child.

Younger children offer another important source of relationships. Just as we rarely involve older people in our classrooms, so we rarely involve preschoolers in elementary classrooms. But what about the younger brothers and sisters of our children? Couldn't we work out times that they would be welcome in our classrooms so that our children could build meaningful relationships and languageships "downward"? (And think of the important languaging that would be involved as our children planned for activities that would be interesting and involving to younger children.)

We have always known that younger children often look up to older ones. We can use this. Involving fifth graders significantly in second-grade classrooms helps children at both age levels; the fifth grader gets an ego boost, and the second grader gets a new hero or heroine. Language is at its best in a relationship which is mutually satisfying. We are using older children more and more as tutors for younger ones, and this is good. How can we use our intermediate level children more as classroom aides, as story tellers/readers, with small groups or individuals, as friends who stop by to visit or who join the younger children for picnic lunches on nice days, as walking partners for the younger children when they go on local field trips, as helpers for younger children working on projects that place heavy demands on their reading and writing abilities? And of course, whatever a fifth grader can be to a second grader, the second grader can be to a kindergartner.

The relationships between children and their peers, children and older people, children and younger children will be different. The language that lives in and fosters these relationships will be different also. And that's what we want!

Status

When older children interact with younger ones, the older ones usually hold the position of higher status. But what provisions do we make for their interactions with people of higher status than theirs? (I know adults in their forties and fifties who are so nervous about interacting with people of higher status, that they avoid such interactions at all costs. Our children needn't grow up to be like this!) Do we do as much as we might by way of inviting school board members, city government officials, the principal to come and visit, to have lunch with us, to participate in our activities for a day? Having started relationships through these visits, do we then make return visits?

Do our children have many opportunities for interacting in writing with people of higher status? If they wonder why an author "made the story end sad" do they write and ask him or her? If they have questions relating to actions taken by city, state, or federal government officials, do they write or call up and ask for explanations? If they are concerned by these actions, do they write to explain the implications they feel the actions will have for them when they are adults? Or to point out the ways these decisions affect children? If the decisions are made by local officials, do they make an appointment to discuss their concerns with them, either at school or at the official's office? If their local newspaper discontinues a favorite comic strip, do they write to protest? Our children should know that those who hold high status positions are usually only a telephone call or a postage stamp away.

Interviewing activities offer endless possibilities for interacting with people of different status precisely because you can interview *anyone* about *anything*. Taped interviews are sometimes best because they can be conducted individually or in a small group and then made available to everyone in the class.

It's fascinating to watch children of all ages in dramatic play as they assume high-status roles and role play interactions in various status relationships. They play with various language styles, deliberately changing style when they are queen or subject, teacher or pupil, boss or employee, parent or child. Such play is an important support for the children's growing ability to express and to interpret language expressions of role relationships, one of many reasons that role play should be an ever present opportunity in *every* elementary and preschool classroom. (No, sixth graders are not "too big" for this! They love it!)

Familiarity

A shared background of experience is the basis of familiarity. To say that a friend is more familiar to us and the grocery store cashier is less familiar to us, is to say that we share a greater background of experience with the friend than we do with the grocery store cashier. We may talk to both. Our talk will reflect our greater familiarity with the friend and our lesser familiarity with the cashier.

In an interactive classroom, teacher and children steadily build a rich background of shared experience during the year. Sensitive teachers know how important it is to get a picture of each child outside of school as well as inside. That's why we encourage children to talk about outside interests, hobbies, concerns; that's why we try to establish contact with the child's parents and, where possible, visit the child at home. In becoming more familiar with our children's lives, we are expanding our interaction range with each child beyond the confines of what we do together in school.

It is important to us that we know our children as people, not just as students. Yet we seem less concerned that our children know us as people, not just as teachers. I was struck one day by how limited children's views of their teachers can be, when I walked my five-year-old daughter up the walk to her kindergarten class and she asked me, "Where does Miss J——— (the teacher) keep her pajamas? And where is her bed?" I suddenly realized that she had no concept of Miss J——— apart from school, and assumed that Miss J——— lived there. As it happened, several weeks later Miss J——— invited her class to her home for part of the morning and for lunch. She showed them her home, her interests—the books she was reading, the dress she was making, the art work she had collected. She had them prepare the lunch in her kitchen. They played with her dog, ate lunch on the floor of the living room, cleaned up, went for a walk (Lucky for Miss J———, she lived on a California beach!). It was an important shared experience for both teacher and children, and opened new areas of communication. Miss J——— and her children had more to talk about because they were more familiar with each other as friends, rather than simply in teacher-student roles.

We help to extend our children's language when we make provision for interaction with people with whom they are less familiar also. Communicating effectively with someone with whom we share little background of experience often requires greater explicitness for we can't assume the listener will know what we're talking about in the way that a friend does. Bringing "outsiders" into the classroom is valuable, whether as "guest speakers" or as "consultants" to work on a specific project with a group of children, or just as interested visitors. Providing for interaction with children from other schools can be helpful also. I have known same-grade children from different schools to get together for lunch and to exchange jump rope rhymes and hand clap games. The actual visit was preceded by exchanges of letters and was followed by a return visit—and then several more as the children found other areas of common interest.

Negotiating with outsiders about field trips, both prior to and during the field trip, provides many real reasons for the children to communicate with people they know less well. We tend to assume that it is for us to arrange field trips for our children, and the value to them begins when they board the bus or start the walk. But this is not so, especially for language. Much of the value for our children is in their planning and followup—requesting information, selecting places to visit and persuading others of the value of their choice, arranging (by phone? by letter?) for the trip itself, communicating with other classes the advantages and disadvantages of such a trip, how other groups might modify the arrangements (based on their experience).

Again the point is the range of communication experiences we provide. As children's social experience becomes more diverse, so does their language. We want the children's language use to include styles appropriate to interaction with people familiar and with people unfamiliar to them. We can provide for this if we decide to. Language arts, the art of producing and interpreting language effectively in spoken and written forms, is everywhere and always; it is not something that happens during a particular time of day. If we're providing truly interactional environments for children, they are languaging all day long, with each other, with outsiders, with you, with others, with themselves.

SOURCES

Where do meaningful interaction experiences originate? Some will come from your own ideas. Understanding something about what constitutes effective communication (the goal) and knowing your own children and their interests as you do, you will think of many valid and engaging experiences for them. This is an important source. But obviously you can't be an endless fountain of creative and interesting experiences, nor would you want to be. If you were the only source, you would be cheating your children out of being sources— initiators of interactive activities they want to engage in. You are one source, but each of your children is one source also. By including your children as important sources, your "source pool" increases from one to twenty-five or so. Surely it is a major function of ours as teachers to help our children implement and extend their own ideas for activities.

Another source is other children. Materials like *Kids* magazine and child-written materials made available through Teachers and Writers Collaborative and other organizations and publishers, allow us to listen to what children are communicating with each other about, and how they choose to do it. What other children are into might be of potential interest to our children also.

We can also tune in to the ideas of other adults who understand what language is about, who are creative, who are sensitive to children, and who have had substantial experience with children. Some of these are teachers in our own schools; others are teachers who have made their ideas available through their writing (for example, Kohl, Holt, Moffett and Wagner).

Finally, we can look to commercially available materials designed to foster meaningful communication in speech and writing. But be warned: more often than not, these will not be designated as "Language Arts" or "Language

Development" materials. Some excellent science materials are a case in point. The *Essence* program (1975), and the *Elementary School Sciences Program* (1976) materials encourage real interaction as does no language arts textbook series that I know of. Language arts texts tend to focus on language for its own sake, to put it under a microscope and examine and analyze and label it. The science programs mentioned do not do this, but rather use language for real communication goals. *Interaction* (Moffett 1973a) is one set of language materials that actually does, as its name implies, foster oral and written interaction.

Hopefully you will draw on all these sources. Whatever the source, what is important is that

1. interaction experiences be purposeful and involving to the child
2. interaction experiences be many and diverse functionally and situationally
3. interaction experiences provide feedback—response—in a communication context.

With these ideas in mind, you might want to look again at the burning issues activity briefly described on pages 218–219. Does this experience meet the criteria: real purpose? functional and situational diversity? communication feedback? How? You might also want to examine the same experience from a more traditional perspective. We have traditionally designated four kinds of activities as "language arts": listening, speaking, reading, writing. (I have considered these as channels in one's languaging.) Are the burning issues children having meaningful experiences in these four traditional "arts"? How?

COMMUNICATION/SKILLS

The thrust of this chapter has been in providing richer and more authentic communication experience for children. "Skills," as such, have scarcely been mentioned. This is for two reasons.

First, ideally (as has been suggested) skills are developed within the context of authentic communication experiences. These experiences necessarily involve reading and writing of many kinds. We provide exercises (in spelling or phonics) as additional supports for the real interaction experiences the child is engaging in, but never allow them to replace, supersede, or obscure the real communication purposes those exercises serve.

Second, skills-oriented materials already exist in abundance. It may be that you feel apprehensive about moving toward a more interactional, child-responsive curriculum. By definition, a "language curriculum" that "responds to what the child is trying to do" and builds out from children's real interests and concerns, lacks the comfortable security of a preset, filed away sequence of assignments. It is likely that you will move slowly (for your sake and your children's), gradually incorporating more experiences that come from the children and involve their interaction—written and oral—with each other and with many people outside the classroom. Over time perhaps you'll move from "special projects" involving a few children, toward a variety of ongoing projects involving more children. Over time perhaps you'll move from allotting an odd twenty minutes of "free time" to child-initiated, designed, and executed activities, toward allotting more of your real language program time to these activities. Gradually these activities will become your curriculum, rather than extra appendages to it. In the meantime, you'll perhaps depend more heavily on traditional spelling, language arts, and reading texts and worksheets. Even after you feel comfortable with a "language program" that is more communication oriented and less skills oriented, you will still make judicious use of selected items from traditional materials as supplemental supports. Supposing you become aware that Robert is getting a number of ie/ei words in his "Spelling Words From My Writing" notebook. You'll want to pull out the several relevant spelling exercises from the ie/ei section of whatever speller from whatever grade book: "Robert, a lot of people mix up these tricky ie/ei words. I found some spelling exercises for you on that very thing. Do these and see if you can't take care of that ie/ei business once and for all." Or you become aware that Brenda, in her writing, often doesn't punctuate at sentence boundaries. So you pull out the appropriate punctuation cassette from the *Interaction* materials, and get her started. But the point is, these supporting skills materials already exist in great amounts. What I believe are in much shorter supply, are suggestions for teachers relating to how they might make their classroom environments more purposefully interactive, and thus more conducive to children's ongoing growth in effective communicating, as they continue to develop in both producing and interpreting oral and written forms of language.

SOME TALK ABOUT TALKING
(OR, UP ON THE SOAP BOX AGAIN)

In some ways tradition works against those of us who want interactive, talky, environments for our children. It is interesting that traditionally many teachers who have all along sincerely professed an intense concern for children's oral language development, punish children more for talking in school than for any other single "offense." More children miss recess, stay after school, have their seat moved to an isolated area of the classroom, write paragraphs about what constitutes good (quiet?) behavior, for their "offenses" relating to talking, than for any other "misbehavior" including a host of various deliberate and calculated unkindnesses. The "offender" talked when she "should have been working" ("Stop talking and do your work;" maybe some talking *is* her work). She talked too loud ("———, I can hear your voice above everyone else's"). She talked in the wrong place ("We don't talk in the halls"). She talked about the wrong thing ("We're talking about social studies now, not about what you are going to do after school"). She talked to the wrong person ("———, you're supposed to be working with Jenny now; Susan isn't in your group"). She talked without raising her hand and being recognized first ("Did I call on you? I don't remember seeing your hand up!" or "I called on David. Is your name David?"). She talked too much ("Margaret, can't you *ever* be quiet and just listen!").

Am I suggesting here that there should be no constraints on talking in the classroom? *Absolutely not.* I am suggesting, rather, that we be sure that our restrictions are in line with the very definite talking constraints that already exist in the society which our classrooms supposedly reflect, many of which constraints the young child is already aware of. Consider:

1. *Talking when working.* There are kinds of work that are enhanced by a quiet atmosphere. But in the "real world" much of our work involves talk. I know we provide for work requiring silence. Do we provide adequately for work that talk is a vital part of?

2. *Talking when one should be listening.* Remember that conversational turn taking is learned early. Its roots are in mother-infant interaction. Turn taking makes sense to children. It is part of their sociolinguistic understanding. But if *all* turn taking involves teacher to child 1, teacher to child 2 . . . teacher to child 28, this means that for every fifty-six turns(twenty-eight for the teacher and twenty eight for the children, assuming one turn for each child), the child has only *one.* One out of fifty-six is hardly a reasonable proportion and does not correspond to many kinds of social encounter outside the classroom. Are our questions always in the context of whole group "discussions"? Are classroom interactions always teacher-directed and teacher-centered? Also, we need to ask ourselves what it is that we are requiring the child to be quiet and listen to. In the "real world" there is usually a reason to listen, and when there isn't a reason, we stop listening. We listen to find out something we don't already know, or to establish a caring relationship with someone else. But in school the child is often supposed to listen to other children read (usually bumblingly) a passage from a story she has already read. Why? She is supposed to listen to other children answer the teacher's questions designed to find out whether the children have learned the facts the teacher hopes they have learned. Why should we expect a child to listen to this? Put another way, why are we surprised that the child only "listens" in these situations through greater or lesser coercion: "Listen so you'll know where we are when I call on you," or "If I catch you not listening again, you'll have to miss recess." Would you or I *"listen"* if we were in the child's place? Maybe I should rephrase that: *Did* you and I listen when we were in similar situations as students in elementary school or even in college? Listening to someone read poorly a passage

which you have already read and in many cases found only minimally interesting anyway, could only be described as a colossal bore. That children don't *listen* in these situations is surely a tribute to their intelligence and demonstrates that they know what reading aloud is for: namely, for conveying new and interesting information, or for enjoying fine literature together, or for using language for the valid function of entertainment.

All too often when we tell children to "listen," what we actually mean is "Don't talk and keep minimally aware of what's going on so you'll be ready to perform when your turn comes." (You and I were very good at this as elementary school students. In classes where our teachers went systematically around the room calling on each child in turn, we got very good at counting how many children were left before the teacher got to us, and at anticipating what question we would have to answer or what passage we would have to read. Remember? This made it unnecessary for us to listen to the intervening stuff. And woe to us when we found we had counted wrong or the teacher suddenly changed tactics!) We often make listening a negative thing, refraining from talking. But listening, real listening, is far too important to be treated this way. Real listening requires mental activity, the processing of new information, the integrating of new information into one's existing cognitive structure, the encounter with the new idea that triggers a new question one never had before. This active process is *listening*.

3. *Talking too loud.* Another early and real learning about talking is that there are some places where one talks quietly and other places where one doesn't. One whispers in church and in libraries, one talks in a moderate voice at the dinner table, one talks loudly in an outdoor game where the participants are widely separated. The question we need to ask ourselves is only if our volume requests are reasonable. Children know that there are good times and reasons for quiet voices; this is *not* a new idea to children when they come to school. But loud voices are appropriate on the playground, and moderate voices, not whispers, are appropriate in group work or in the cafeteria.

When many children talk at once in moderate voices (in the cafeteria, say), the overall noise level will be, must be, significant (just as it is at a cocktail party where we never ask people to quiet down). It is important, and at first difficult, when the overall volume level is up (as in a class where children are all working and talking in groups simultaneously) to learn to hear the difference between simple *noise,* and the sound of meaningful verbal interaction.

4. *Talking in the wrong place.* Examine where children can and can't talk. In many schools I visit, the cafeteria is the "wrong place," yet we value mealtime conversation in our homes. Are all areas of the classroom the wrong place? I visit many classes where there is no right place for talking. If we sit down and actually list the right and wrong places for talking, and find more wrong places than right ones, we need to look again and do some revising. If the child's only right time for talking in the classroom is "After you have

finished your work you can go to a center and play a game with a friend," then children who never finish their work (and every classroom has them) never get to talk with their friends, and they may be the very children who need it most.

5. *Talking about the wrong thing.* Children need to learn to be relevant. But some wondering aloud about fringe areas to the discussion may lead to relating one area to another. Do we sometimes restrict too narrowly what is "on the subject"? Are we sometimes worried by laughter when children are supposed to be working on a social studies project? Why? In terms of real talk in the real world, don't we inject humorous remarks or tell related anecdotes while we work jointly toward some serious goal? And if our children are, in our view, continually "off the subject" perhaps we need to reexamine the subject itself: Is it one that is of genuine interest to the children in the first place? Children are generally pretty good at staying on topics or tasks that are of interest to them.

6. *Talking to the wrong person.* Who is this "wrong person"? It is the "wrong person" from the teacher's point of view, but clearly not from the child's or the child wouldn't be talking with this person. Children elicit conversation for purposes that are real to them, and carry on these conversations with the appropriate people, just as you and I do. If we have children working in groups on some kind of project, and a child from one group is consistently going to another group to interact with someone there, we need to ask what the basis for our grouping was. Were the children grouped with people they wanted to talk and work with? Are the children talking about something else? If so, what is it? Obviously it is something that, at that moment for those children, is more important than our purposes. We need to know what the children's important purpose is at that point so that we can respond to it. It is where the children's purpose is that the more powerful opportunity for their learning is. Is there some way we can focus on that purpose? Now? Later? How can we provide for these children who have sought each other out to work together? Our reaction should be "Aha, here's a real interest and a real relationship—the real bases for meaningful communication. Where can we go with this?"

7. *Talking without raising one's hand.* Again, turn-taking conventions are well understood by children. Such conventions are especially necessary in large groups. Notice that we have well-established formalized conventions for turn-taking in adult meetings and other large group settings. But do we have too much of large group in our classrooms? How much of our typical social encounter in the real world is large group meetings where these formalized conventions are required? (One evening at dinner I asked, "Who would like some more peas?" and out of habit, my daughter's hand flew up.) Another question: Do we require the hand-raising-teacher-recognizing convention the same way of everyone? I suspect not. I remember a nine-year-old describing to me the usual situation in teacher-led whole group discussions in her classroom. The two children whom she described the teacher as treating very

differently, were two children whom I knew and had observed in class: Tracy —tiny, bright, very talkative, "cute" in every way, with two bouncing pony-tails, self-confident, outgoing; and Thomas—large, friendless, whiney and ba-byish, emotionally troubled, receiving significant psychiatric help outside of school. (On one visit I had watched him kick and hit the teacher during a violent emotional outburst.) My nine-year-old friend told me, "When we have class discussions, Tracy just says her ideas right out without even raising her hand, and Miss B——— says, 'That's an interesting idea, Tracy.' But when-ever Thomas says his ideas out, Miss B——— says, in an angry voice, 'Thomas, I didn't see *your* hand up' or 'Did I call on you, Thomas? I've told you before, don't talk until I call on you.' "

8. *Talking too much.* I think immediately of Cazden teaching in a combined first, second, and third grade, wistfully wishing out loud "for a key to turn Greg on and off"—mostly off (Cazden 1975). Every teacher who draws breath on this planet has been there, and many times! We would only want to be sure that we provide plenty of opportunities for acceptable talk within our classrooms.

All teachers need to have noise levels that they are comfortable with. Probably this is different for each one of us, and certainly it is different for various types of activities. That's fine; that is reality and we live with that. But we do need to ask ourselves whether and in what ways we are being held to the typical silence dominated situations we knew as elementary school stu-dents, and how we can assure that our classrooms reflect and encourage the kinds of interaction that are appropriate in the larger society of which our children are members.

We have come a long way in our understanding of language and its growth in children. In the early 1960s a prevalent view was that the child possessed an innate "language acquisition device" which was set into action when the child encountered language in the environment, and which carried the child through a largely preset course. Now we know better. We know that acquiring a language means learning to *communicate,* not just learning lan-guage structure, and that children learn this in an interactive environment. "Surely it has been true all along that the only real 'language acquisition device' is the whole child growing up in a social world" (Bates 1976, p. xii). A classroom peopled with whole children (and teachers) all growing in an interactive environment can contribute powerfully to that "language acquisi-tion device." School can be a very special place for children's language growth.

SUGGESTED EXERCISES AND PROJECTS

1. *Language functions exercise.* Alone or with several friends, study the fol-lowing conversations involving children from three to ten years old. Iden-tify the various functions the children are using in each interaction. You

may find Halliday's categories (pp. 302–3), or Tough's categories (p. 303), helpful, or you may choose to "call it like you see it," without any preconceived category scheme.

Adult and three-year-old.

A: What are the babies doing? Your baby dolls.

C: Shhhh ... they are sleeping (low voice).

A: They are sleeping, so we cannot talk loud. OK, so why don't we go to ... Pull the other chair. (Pretending to have breakfast.) OK, let's have some breakfast.

C: Put your coffee right here (on little table).

A: Well, let's have a good breakfast. What do you want?

Ten-year-old and adult riding in car on the way to school.

C: Hey look! They're flying in a V. (Refers to birds.)

A: Yeah, birds often fly in formation like that.

C: Why?

A: Instinct. Which doesn't really tell you anything, of course.

C: (laughs)

Four-year-old and adult.

C: Do you wanna know why I'm sucking on my thumb?

A: Why are you sucking on your thumb, Rebecca?

C: 'Cuz I got a hurt on it.

A: How did you hurt your finger?

C: I don't know.

Ten-year-old at dinner table with his family.

C: (looking at steam coming from plate of hot macaroni from dumped over aluminum foil dish). Why is it making steam?

A-1: 'Cuz it's hot.

C: Yeah, but why is it making steam?

A-2: Because it has moisture in it and it's evaporating. Like when you boil water and it makes steam.

C: Oh. So that's why, when you heat things up over and over again they get so dry. If you heat an egg up again and again, it gets like rubber.

Adult and friend sitting in a booth at a restaurant. Aquarium next to booth. Three-year-old comes to look at fish and starts conversation with two adults.

C: I never seen big fishes like them. Did y'all?

A: No, we didn't.

C: Look at them big fishes. Them are angel fishes. Ahhhh. Them are pretty.

Eight-year-old and her father.

C: Look over there!

A: Where?

C: In the corner! There is a spider!

A: (turning around) Where?

C: April Fool
Go to school
Tell your teacher
That you're a fool.

Several four-year-olds.

C-1: Everybody get on the bus. Here we go. (She sits on a bookcase which serves as the bus.) Somebody get on the bus!

C-2: OK. We're on the bus ready to go off on the bus. We're ready on the bus. (Other children get on the "bus" also.)

C-3: OK.

C-2: OK.

C-4: OK. (Giggles)

C-2: OK. (Giggles)

C-3: OK. (Giggles)

C-2: Kay, kay, kay, kay. We're going now.

C-3: OK. Honk, honk, honk, honk.

Four-year-old and mother in supermarket.

C: I want some candy.

A: You may have gum but not any candy.

C: I want candy!

A: No, no candy.

C: I want that gum.

A: OK (gives child gum).

C: Let me have it. I want life savers, Momma (pointing).

A: The doctor says you can't have candy. You've got gum.

C: Open it. (A pours out gum pieces.) I want one more.

Nine-year-old doing chalk picture at table with several friends in classroom.

C: Yech!!!Phew!!! I *hate* workin' with chalk. It's irritating!

Four fourth-grade girls are sitting at table, trying to get going on a writing assignment in which they are to use metaphoric language to describe owls in a picture. (Mrs. K——is their teacher.)

C-1: Mrs. K——, how could you really say an owl's like anything else?

T: I'll give you one we had last week. "He's as thin as a rail."

C-1: But he's *not* thin.

T: But maybe part of him reminds you of something else.

C-2: Maybe he's square as a box.

T: Right! Good. His body's as square as a box. You compare (inaudible). (T leaves group.)

C-3: You should call him Blockhead.

C-?: His foot is as thin as a worm.

C-?: He's fatter than his wife.

C-?: Oh I wish we didn't have to do this!

C-?: Oh I know! The ugly one looks like V———. (V——— is one of the four girls.) (Laughter)

C-?: His face is triangular.

C-?: He's thinner than a worm. (Laughter) That's a good one.

C-?: How 'bout "He is as smart as an owl?"

C-?: Who is?

C-?: You.

C-?: He's as wise as a pig.

C-?: He's as pink as a pig's rump.

Adult holding infant. Two-and-a-half-year-old approaches.

C: Let me see the baby.

A: You may see her, but please be careful with her.

C: Look at her little feet and tiny toes. Can she wear shoes?

A: Yes, she can wear shoes if her mother wants her to.

C: Look, she can blink and stick out her tongue.

A: She can do a lot of things you can do.

C: She cries a lot but I don't, because I'm not a baby.

Five-year-old and teacher are looking at fish tank.

C: They're eating it. Look.

C: They must be hungry.

C: Will they grow fat if they eat a lot?

A: I expect so.

C: Will they get bigger and bigger?

A: Do you think they will?

C: Yes, they'll get bigger and fatter until they're as big as *that.*

Ten-year-old and adult.

C: Why do you go to school?

A: To learn things. Like how to read and how to write and how to work with numbers.

C: Yeah, but you could learn that anyway.

A: It's true you can learn in other ways too, but if people didn't go to school, some of them would learn those things, but some wouldn't. We have schools so everyone can have the chance to learn.

C: Yeah, but when will we ever use those things?

A: Well, I'd sure hate not to know how to read. I use that every day.

C: But when will we ever use things like finding the factors of a fraction and things like that? (A slight pause and he changed to new topic.)

2. *Child observation: interests.* Observe one child in school for one morning or afternoon (or, if possible, for one day), especially focusing on signs of interest. (a) List five interests of that child, (b) describe the particular behavior(s) of that child that demonstrated each interest you have listed, (c) suggest several possible interaction experiences that the teacher might provide for each interest. (Any or all of this project could be done by two or three people. For example, three people might observe a different child each and list interests, and then combine for a brainstorming session for part c. Or two or three people might observe the same child and combine their findings for parts a, b, and c.)

3. *"Language function environment" study.* Working individually or as a group, do a "case study" of one child that focuses on his or her "language function environment." First select typical portions of the child's day (you may need to talk with the child's mother to get this information), and then get a language sample from each portion—morning school preparation routine, breakfast, car pool ride to school, whole group teacher-directed lesson, small group discussion in class, recess, lunch, afterschool play, dinner, evening conversation with family members. It is helpful to get taped samples and then transcribe them for study. However, for some activities (such as recess), it is impossible to keep the child in taping range without highly sophisticated equipment, so a written record would have to suffice. Also, some activities might best be taped by the child's mother (morning routines, dinner) so you might want to leave a tape recorder and several cassette tapes with her. When you have gathered and transcribed your language samples, study them for the purpose of identifying and describing the range of language functions the child is using in his or her interactions with others. Your goal is to describe the child's typical daily language function environment. (If you do this project individually, you might want to limit yourself to four or five different situations and about half an hour of taped interaction from each. If you work as a group, you can gather, transcribe, and analyze more conversation from more situations, of course. Remember that transcribing tapes is very time consuming. Keep the project scaled to a feasible size so that the major part of your creative energy goes into insightful analysis and description, rather than into transcribing time.)

4. *Child observation: classroom interaction.* Individually or as a group, observe a selected child in his or her school experience for one morning or afternoon (or one day, if possible), keeping a written record of the child's interactions,

the people involved in each, the time and place of each, the nature of the activity, the topics discussed, the formality level, etc. Then analyze your record for the purpose of describing the range of situational variables in the child's typical interaction experience in a school day. Include such information as: age, status, degree of familiarity of interaction partner(s); the time and place of the interactions; the number of participants in the interactions; the formality level, tone, type of activity, topical focuses of the interactions; the channel of the interactions. When you have analyzed and described the child's school interaction experience in this way, suggest ways of expanding that experience to include more situational diversity. For example, you may find that the written channel is rarely used for interaction (but only for exercises), or that the child has little or no opportunity to interact with people who are relatively unfamiliar to him/her, or with people of lower status. How might interaction experiences in these areas be strengthened?[6]

5. *Repeated language experience study.* Record a child engaging in the same language activity three times, and analyze and describe how the child's language changes over the three times. Some activities you might want to try are: (a) the child teaches another child to play a new game (three different children in turn); (b) the child tells another individual or group of children about his or her hobby display (three different children or three different groups); (c) the child tells a story for a wordless storybook to three different small groups of younger children.

6. *Adult-present and adult-absent child interaction study.* In a home or a school setting, tape record a group of children engaging in an activity when an adult is and is not present. What differences do you notice in the children's language in the two situations? In what they talk about? In how they talk? (One university student did this in a nursery school setting with four year olds. She placed the tape recorder near the children's play dough table with the microphone suspended above the center of the table. She left the equipment there—sometimes on and sometimes off—for several weeks before she started collecting the tapes she was intending to analyze. By then the children had become oblivious to the tape recorder, which seemed to be just another piece of furniture. The children went on with their play dough activity and their conversation in a completely natural way. The student taped for several days, just pushing the record button and *leaving the area* from time to time. Parent volunteers drifted in and out of the play dough area as usual. Thus it was possible to compare the children's language in adult-present and adult-absent situations that were very natural,

[6]Note: Items 3 and 4 involve various aspects of home, school, function, situation of a child's interaction. You might want to design some other project for study involving modifications or combinations of these.

and in which the children's activity was the same. Because the area was small, the microphone close, and the number of children limited (by the activity itself), it was possible to pick up almost everything that was said —which is not always the case when taping children in classroom settings.)[7]

7. *Language experience in the "content" areas.* If you are a teacher or are a student involved in a teaching field experience, collect your social studies, science, and math lesson plans for a week (a semester if your teaching in these areas is limited). Viewing these as plans for language experiences *(which they are)*, identify all the (a) language functions and (b) situational variables which these lesson plans engage your children in. What special language opportunities do these lessons provide? How could they be extended?

8. *Adult as "function model."* If you are a teacher or a student teacher, record samples of your own classroom languaging with your children. Then transcribe your samples and study them to see which language functions you do and do not "model" for your children; that is, which functions they do or do not see you actually engage in (in speech, in writing). Try to think of ways that you can increase your range. (If you are not involved in teaching children yourself, you might want to observe the "function modeling" of another classroom teacher.)

9. *Classroom language functions study.* Tape children and teacher (yourself, if possible) languaging in various types of classroom activities—in a whole group teacher-led social studies lesson, in a small group session with no teacher present, at a center, at free play, at lunch. Transcribe and analyze your taped samples to see whether the activities provided daily involve the children in as wide a range of language functions as possible. Do they provide opportunities for children to narrate, to report observations, to explain or inform, to justify, to persuade, to evaluate, to entertain, to establish and maintain social rapport, to express feelings, to question, to imagine, etc.? What language functions seem to be dominant in each type of activity? Why? How could the activity types be modified or expanded to provide opportunities for a wider range of language functions among the children?

10. *"Knower-doer" communication study.* View the film *Shared Nomenclature* (see "Suggested Further Readings and Resources" below). Then conduct the same (or a similar) experience using three pairs of subjects: ages four

---

[7]I am indebted to Victoria Perry for this description of a successful way of executing this study.

to six, ages eight to ten, and adult. Tape record the experience and transcribe your tape. Discuss and compare the performance of the subject pairs, including their descriptions of the block designs, their descriptions of the placement of the blocks, and aspects of the interaction between each pair.

11. *Wordless storybook.* Tape record three children from different grade levels telling a story based on the same wordless book. (Mercer Mayer's *Bubble Bubble* is a great favorite.) Transcribe your tape. Analyze the three story tellings, comparing and contrasting them on such dimensions as sentence length, syntactic complexity, semantic complexity, fluency, elaboration (inclusion of detail), explicitness. (This suggestion is based on Fisher and Terry 1977, p. 74.)

12. *"Your own thing."* Design your own learning experience relating to the ideas in this section, discuss it with your instructor and/or an acquaintance knowledgeable in this area, and execute it.

SUGGESTED FURTHER READINGS AND RESOURCES

Some interesting works relating to communication include:

BRITTON, J., *Language and Learning.* Harmondsworth, England: Pelican Books, 1972.

COULTHARD, M., *An Introduction to Discourse Analysis.* London: Longman, Inc., 1977.

HALLIDAY, M. A. K., "Relevant Models of Language." In M. A. K. Halliday, *Explorations in the Functions of Language,* pp. 9–21. London: Edward Arnold, 1973.

HYMES, D., "Models of the Interaction of Language and Social Life." In *Directions in Sociolinguistics: The Ethnography of Communication,* eds. J. Gumperz and D. Hymes. New York: Holt, Rinehart and Winston, 1972.

Some interesting works focusing on children's languaging in school settings include:

GORDON, J. W., *My Country School Diary.* New York: Dell Publishing Co, Inc., 1970.

GRAVES, D. H., "We Won't Let Them Write," *Language Arts,* 55, no. 5 (May 1978).

HOFFMAN, M., *Vermont Diary.* New York: Teachers and Writers, 1978.

LEE, D., and J. B. RUBIN, *Children and Language.* New York: Wadsworth Publishing Co., Inc., 1979.

MOFFETT, J., and B. J. WAGNER, *Student-Centered Language Arts and Reading, K-13. A Handbook* (2nd ed.). Boston: Houghton Mifflin Company, 1976.

ROSEN, C., and H. ROSEN, *The Language of Primary School Children.* London: Penguin Education for the Schools Council, 1973.

TOUGH, J., *The Development of Meaning.* London: George Allen & Unwin Ltd., 1977.

————,*Focus on Meaning.* London: George Allen & Unwin Ltd., 1974.

A film relating to language in the classroom that might be of interest is:

Oral Language Development: Views of Five Teachers. Agency for Instructional Television, 1111 West 17th Street, Bloomington, Indiana 47401.

Another film of interest, focusing on children's development of language over time is:

Shared Nomenclature. Ohio State University. Film Lab Service, Inc., 4019 Prospect Avenue, Cleveland, Ohio 44103.

Section Five

LANGUAGE VARIATION

Chapter 13

Dialect Variation

"I knowed you wasn't Oklahomy folks. You talk queer kinda. That ain't no blame, you understan'. Ever'body says words different . . . Arkansas folks says 'em different, and Oklahomy folks says 'em different. And we seen a lady from Massachusetts, an' she said 'em differentest of all. Couldn' hardly make out what she was sayin'. " (Steinbeck, *Grapes of Wrath*)

REGIONAL AND SOCIAL DIALECTS

Folks from Oklahoma, Massachusetts, Arkansas "say [English] words different"; and so do folks from Alabama, Oregon, and Arizona. And what about folks from England, Scotland, Australia, or the millions of folks for whom English is a second language in India, Kenya, Saudi-Arabia? They all "say words different," yet we would agree that they are all speaking English. If we can "make out what people are sayin'," but their way of speaking calls attention to itself and we are as aware of how they are speaking as we are of what they mean, then we say they are speaking a different dialect of the language.

Some dialect differences will be in the pronunciation of words: while we take *vit-* (rhymes with "bite") -amin pills, many Britishers take *vit-* (rhymes with "bit") -amin pills. And many people from England work in science la-*bor* -a-trees, follow time *shed*-jules, and wrap their left-overs in al-yew-*min*-i-um. And while some of us object to "grea*s*y" (with /s/) French fries, others of us complain about "grea/z/y" ones.

Some differences will be in the words and word combinations used. Some of us eat hoagies, others eat submarine sandwiches. Some of us fry our eggs in a skillet, others in a frying pan, and others in a spider. Some of us eat green peppers while others of us eat bell peppers. Some of us order "donuts" and get something cakey; others of us order "donuts" and get something puffy. Some of us wish on chicken wish bones, and others of us wish on pulley bones. And some of us eat (or know people who eat) cottage cheese, pot cheese, farmer cheese, or even smearcase—and we're all eating the same thing. While some of us "are able to" do something, others of us "might (maht) could" do it. And from a Texas first grade comes this example. The teacher is giving the class instructions as they take a standardized multiple choice test which involves circling pictures.

T: Draw a circle around the picture of someone getting ready to take a bath.

C: Is that the same as "fixin' to"?

The differences discussed so far are all geographically based. People from one geographical region will speak differently from people from another region. The more widely separated they are and the less contact they have with one another, the more distinct their dialects tend to be. Geographical regions are rarely clearly demarked; neither are dialectal "regions." Nevertheless, the general notion of regional dialects is helpful.

We often identify other people as "speaking with an accent," yet sometimes fail to realize that we also "have an accent," that is, we too speak a distinct regional variety of the language. Sometimes this is called to our attention when we travel to a different area and people living in that area will recognize our speech as nonlocal. You'll fall into casual conversation with a post office clerk or bus driver in the area you're visiting and he'll suddenly ask, "Where're you from?" and when you've answered, he'll say, "Well, I knew you didn't sound like you came from around here." But notice, too, that the longer you stay in the new area—say, if you move there—the more your speech takes on the characteristics of that region, the more you blend in language-wise.

You've probably heard people speak of "the standard dialect" or "standard English." This is a notion that gives trouble as (1) "standard" is so variously defined, and (2) the term suggests that there is some preferred "correct" variety of English and deviations from this variety are inferior. But we know that no dialect is inherently superior to or more "correct" than any other; each variety of English (or any langauge) is simply an alternate way of expressing meanings, no more or less effective than any other. As for defining "standard English," some of the favorite definitions are: "Standard English is a dialect that doesn't call attention to itself," or "Standard English is the kind of English Walter Cronkite (or some other national newscaster) speaks." (One definition that is infrequently stated but may in fact be the most common is: "Standard English is English as I speak it.") You can see what the problems are here. *Every* dialect of English "calls attention to itself" in some situation. Walter Cronkite's speech calls attention to itself in Boston or Alabama. Thus the notion of a "regional standard" dialect (rather than just a standard for the language in general) seems to better reflect the situation of dialect diversity in that it recognizes that there are many identifiable varieties of English (or any language), and that they are all valid linguistic systems. Think of a regional standard as that language variety spoken by the majority of adults in the community—the language as you hear it on the bus, on local radio stations, in local department stores, in your doctor's office, at PTA meetings. Of course, no two people speak a language *exactly* the same, but the speech of the majority of adults in any region will be more alike than different.

We tend to have preconceived attitudes toward different regional dialects and the people who speak them, though these attitudes are usually unconscious. They are the result of many factors in our backgrounds—how much contact we have had with speakers of a particular dialect, what the nature of that contact has been. We hear (and perhaps even make) comments like: "His speech is so *quaint*." "She sounds so *provincial*." "I love to listen to him talk; he sounds so *charming* and *genteel*." "She has such a *high-flown* way of talking—a little *stuck up*. Oh, it sounds very *intelligent* and all, but she makes me a little bit nervous." "I guess he's bright enough but he talks so *slow* and *lazy-like* with a sort of a drawl." Initially these attitudes about particular dialect varieties tend to color our impressions of the people who speak these varieties; we see the *speaker* as well as the speech style, as quaint, provincial, genteel, stuck up, intelligent, slow, lazy. However, in the case of regional dialects we can usually manage to get past these initial impressions. Jimmy Carter speaks differently from Walter Cronkite and so did John F. Kennedy, but we don't think of them as quaint, lazy, unintelligent, or whatever because of their dialects. For the most part we can, in time, accept regional dialects and their speakers; for the most part, regional dialects "ain't no blame, you understan'."

However, this is generally not the case with social dialects. A social dialect is a way of speaking which is closely associated with a particular social group. As with regional dialects, various social dialects develop and are perpetuated because of distance between the speakers of the different varieties. However, that distance is geographic distance in the one case, but social distance in the other. Both types of distance limit interaction between dialect groups and thus reinforce each group's distinct language system. Typically that dialect spoken by the more powerful social group in an area is more prestigious. Notice that that more socially prestigious dialect is not more expressive, or more cognitively powerful, or more abstract, or more anything else. Different dialects are simply different expression systems for conveying meaning. No dialect is inherently better or worse than any other. Each dialect serves the intellectual and social purposes of its speakers with full adequacy and effectiveness. But dialects spoken by social groups which hold less of the power and prestige within a society, tend to be regarded by the larger society (and often by themselves) as inferior ways of speaking. In fact, these less prestigious dialects are often not regarded as intact linguistic systems (which they are) but rather as error-ridden, garbled, inadequate attempts of a group of people to speak a regional standard dialect (which they are not). A speaker of a less socially prestigious dialect of English will often not be heard as speaking a valid, rule-governed variety of English, but rather as trying unsuccessfully to speak a more prestigious variety. Those semantic, syntactic, and phonological aspects of his dialect which are different from the regional standard are regarded as "mistakes," rather than as linguistic forms which result from a different set of language rules than the standard dialect employs. In short, what is in fact a *different* linguistic system from the regional standard, comes to be mistakenly heard as *deficient*.

Nowhere has this been more true in American society than in the case of what has come to be known as "Black English." It may be that with regional dialects there "ain't no blame." But in the case of the dialect Black English, there has been considerable "blame" and profound misunderstanding that has had serious negative consequences for many Black English-dominant children in our schools. For that reason and because the majority of elementary teachers will at some time teach Black English-dominant children, we will look further at Black English.

FEATURES OF BLACK ENGLISH

First of all, what is it, this so-called Black English? Is it a dialect all black people speak? Is it a dialect only black people speak? Do people who speak Black English speak only Black English? The answer to all three questions is *no*—which makes one wonder how adequate the term Black English is for the dialect in question. Black English is perhaps best described as an identifiable set of syntactic, phonological, semantic, and performance features which frequently occur in the speech of many urban Afro-Americans. Many black people do not speak Black English (hereafter BE) at all; for example, Nigerians educated at Oxford University in England, or people living in the Caribbean.

We don't hear Barbara Jordan or Andrew Young speak BE in public speeches or interviews (though it may be their linguistic versatility is such that fluent BE is a part of their linguistic range). Many, probably most, Americans who are not Afro-Americans frequently include BE features in their repertoire. For example, deletion of the last consonant of a word ending in a consonant cluster (saying "la*s*" for "la*st*," or "fi*n*" for "fi*nd*"), pronunciation of "going," "waiting," and "having" as "goin'," "waitin'," "havin'," or pronunciation of "about," "important," or "suppose" as " 'bout," " 'portant," " 'spose" are features typically associated with BE. But most Americans use these forms in alternation with other forms, depending on the social situation they are in. And this alternation of forms is very much present in the speech of most Afro-Americans who are fluent in BE. Often, the BE speaker's total range includes BE and standard English (understood as regional standard English, hereafter SE) alternative forms. It is part of his communicative competence that he will often choose one form rather than another in a given situation. Black English, then, is a sort of nickname for a dialect included in the language range of many urban Afro-Americans, but not spoken by *all* blacks, *only* blacks, or *always* by those blacks who do use it.

What are some of the language features that we can identify as part of BE? It's important that we consider some of the most prevalent ones not because these features are important in and of themselves, but because it is crucial that we, as teachers, hear these features in the speech of our children, as the regular, rule-governed expression of a particular linguistic system rather than as "mistakes" that we need to erradicate. First, some prevalent pronunciation features that *some* BE speakers (though not *only* BE speakers) *sometimes* use:

1. *Final consonant sounds*, especially when they are part of a consonant cluster, will frequently be deleted. This means that for some children, the words "men," "mend," and "meant" may all be homonyms (sound alikes), all pronounced /mVn/. The words "six" (/sVks/) and "sick" (/sVk/) may be sound-alikes, both pronounced like "sick" for the same reason, namely, the /s/ dropping out of the final /ks/ consonant cluster in "six." (Remember, we are talking as always about sounds, not about spellings.) "Bowl" and "bold" may be homonyms for some BE-speaking children (like "know/no" or "there/-their" for some SE speakers), and so on. When, in reading, we ask a child whether two words are "sound-alikes," we might do well to listen to the child's pronunciation of the two words before we evaluate his response to our question. The child's sound-alikes and ours may be different.

A particularly interesting situation arises when the final consonant which is deleted is one of the following: /t/, /d/, /s/, /z/. Can you see why? In SE, these four sounds often express syntactic information: past tense ("walk*ed*" /t/ or "crie*d*" /d/), plural ("ball*s*" /z/ or "bat*s*" /s/), possessive ("Johnny's" /z/ or "Janet's" /s/), third person singular subject of a verb ("walks" /s/ or "cries" /z/). We sometimes hear people say of a BE-speaking child who says

$$\text{She} \left\{ \begin{array}{c} \text{cry} \\ \text{walk} \end{array} \right\} \text{yestiddy.}$$

that this child "doesn't have an understanding of time, doesn't differentiate between what happens in the present and what happened in the past." But clearly this is absurd. There are verb forms for the SE speaker that have a single form for present and past. We would not think of questioning the SE speaker's knowledge of present and past because he says "I *put* my books on my desk every day" and "I *put* my books on the desk yesterday." The case is similar with plural. We sometimes hear people comment that BE-speaking children "don't know the difference between one and more than one" because they say "one cent" and also "five cent." But again, comparable examples exist in SE where the speaker expresses both the singular and plural with the same form —"one sheep" and "five sheep," or "a fish" and "several fish." Both SE and BE include instances where a single verb form expresses past and present, or a single noun form expresses singular and plural. The particular nouns and verbs that work this way are simply a slightly different set in each dialect, but the speaker's linguistic knowledge in each case is the same.

2. *The consonant sounds /l/ and /r/ are frequently not pronounced* or else pronounced very lightly in the middle or at the ends of words. We might hear a BE-dominant child say something like "Mah schoo teachuh she hep me wif mah wok." Again, the child who deletes /l/ and /r/ sounds medially and/or finally may have different homonyms than the teacher, e.g., "hep" and "help"; "sore" and "saw"; "whole," "hole," and "hoe"; "toe" and "toll"; and "carrot" and "cat" all may be homonym sets for some BE-speaking children. Can you tell how each set would be pronounced?

3. *The "th" sounds* show interesting variation also. Remember that there are two "th" sounds, a voiced one like the first sound in "*th*y," and a voiceless one like the first sound in "*th*igh." The sound /d/ often occurs in BE at the beginning of words that SE speakers would start with the voiced "th." Thus words that an SE speaker would usually pronounce as "this," "that," "these," "then," "them," "the," some BE speakers would pronounce with /d/ as the first sound (as would speakers of various other dialects, of course). This is a pronunciation feature that, for some mysterious reason, is sometimes heard as ignorant or illiterate. Attitudes toward others' dialects can be insidious and dangerous. In fact, substitution of BE initial /d/ for SE initial voiced "th" is simply a regular pronunciation feature. There is no more reason to hear "dem"

as ignorant than there would be to hear "them" as the ignorant substitution of voiced "th" for initial /d/. In the middle of words, voiced "th" becomes /v/ for some BE speakers; thus SE "bro*th*er" might become BE "bro*v*ah."

Voiceless "th" as in "*th*ing" and "*th*ank" for SE speakers, may be pronounced as /t/ at the beginning of words by some BE speakers. In the middle of words we sometimes hear /f/ as a BE variant of voiceless "th" as in "nu*f*in" ("nothing"). And in word final position we are likely to hear BE speakers pronounce /f/ where the SE speaker would use voiceless "th." Thus "dea*th*" and "deaf," "Ru*th*" and "roof," and "wi*th*" and "whiff" might be sound-alike pairs for some BE speakers, each ending in /f/. (Interestingly, the word "with" is pronounced "wid" instead of "wif" by some BE speakers.)

4. We sometimes hear it said that *BE speakers "drop the g" in progressive verb forms* like "walking," "coming," "going," "thinking." Here is a sound-spelling confusion. There is no /g/ sound in these verb forms, only the alphabet letter "g" in their spelling; in fact, the "ng" spelling combination represents a single sound, / ŋ / as in the last sound of "ki*ng*." The pronunciation feature being referred to here, and one which is common in the speech of many people other than BE speakers, is the substitution of one nasal sound (/n/), for another / ŋ /, thus yielding verb forms that are often misleadingly represented in print as "walkin'," "comin'," "goin'," "thinkin'." Our traditional spelling representation suggests, mistakenly, that something has been left out. In fact, one sound has been substituted for another.

5. *Some BE speakers tend to use "a" before words beginning with consonant or vowel sounds*—"a box," "a apple," "a egg"—while SE speakers use "an" to precede words beginning with vowel sounds. Stress in some words occurs differently for some SE and BE speakers also; the words usually pronounced "ho*tel*" or "po-*lice*" by an SE speaker may be pronounced "*ho*-tel" or "*po*-lice" by a BE speaker. Sometimes multisyllable words beginning with an unstressed syllable get reduced in BE by deletion of the first syllable. Thus "important" may become "portant," "suppose" may become "pose" or "spose." One word that often stands alone in BE, not as part of a general pattern but just as a particular case, is the word "ask." Often this word is pronounced as "axe" by BE speakers, that is, the final two consonant sounds are reversed ("ask" /Vsk/ becomes "axe" /Vks/).

For some obscure reason, the syntactic differences between BE and regional standard dialects are often more jarring to teachers' ears than the pronunciation differences. One of the most disconcerting to many teachers is the expression of negative more than once in a sentence. Sentences like "I ain't got no pencil" are likely to be censured, corrected, or met with responses like "Well, if you 'ain't got no pencil' then you must have a pencil—if it 'ain't the case that you have no pencil, then you really do have one." The simple fact is that BE is a dialect whose rule system permits inclusion of more than one negative element in a sentence. It's interesting that multiple negatives are so abhorrent to some SE speakers, though they use multiple negatives themselves, but do so in different types of sentences and are unaware that they do it. Sentences like "It is not impossible that they'll still make it" contain two negative elements (can you find them?), yet would be regarded as quite OK by most SE speakers. And what about sentences including "any": "I don't want any." Clearly "any" is a negative element, for in the affirmative case the SE speaker would use "some": "I want some." (And of course the SE speaker has no difficulty accepting the fact that French speakers express negative twice per sentence, placing *ne* before the verb and *pas* after it.) Obviously the issue is not one of whether one "should" express negative once or more than once per sentence. Both BE and SE use multiple negative in some cases; however, their rule systems differ in which types of structures they are used in, and in just what the negative elements will be.

It's interesting that in the case of BE negative, some SE speakers will, out of ignorance of the BE rule system, criticize BE for expressing a meaning —negative—*more than once* in a sentence, yet these same SE speakers will also criticize BE for expressing *only once* in a sentence, some elements that SE expresses more than once in a sentence. In each of the following three SE sentences, one syntactic meaning is expressed twice. Can you find it in each one?

> She is going now.
> I have three blocks.
> He rides his bike to work every day.

In the first, the syntactic information that the action of going is in process at the time of speaking, is indicated by the "is" before the verb and also by the "-ing" at the end of the verb. In the second, plurality is indicated by the "three" preceding the noun and also by the /s/ added to the end of the noun. And in the third sentence, the fact that the subject is a third person singular, is indicated both by the pronoun "he" and also by the addition of /z/ to the verb "ride." Here we have three examples of SE expressing syntactic information more than once in a sentence, a situation comparable to the BE speaker's expression of negative more than once per sentence. These same three sentences in BE would be cases where each element might be expressed only once. In BE these sentences could be

> She going now.
> I have three block.
> He ride his bike to work every day.

In short, some syntactic information will be expressed more than once per sentence in BE and only once per sentence in SE, and vice versa. The rules of each system simply delineate a different set of particular structures for each case. But "there ain't no blame, you understan'," just different rule systems operating.

(Some linguists account for the "three block" and "he ride" cases in BE by the pronunciation regularity discussed above, of deleting the final consonant: ride/z/ becomes ride, block/s/ becomes block. Others see these as the result of the operation of syntactic rules. In either case, these phenomena are systematic and rule governed.)

The pervasive third person singular pattern (he go, she have, Mama say) is only one of the interesting patterns relating to verbs in BE. In some cases where the SE speaker uses a variety of verb forms, a BE speaker may choose one verb form and stick to it. The BE speaker may use "have" or "go" whatever the person and number of the subject (I have/go, he have/go, they have/go), whereas the SE speaker uses both "have" and "has" or "go" and "goes" depending on the subject. With irregular past tense forms a BE speaker will sometimes use the present tense form for both present and past. For example:

he say . . .
yesterday she come . . .
he get . . .
she run . . .

whereas most SE speakers would use the special irregular past tense forms "said," "came," "got," and "ran" in these cases. Many BE speakers use a single form of the verb "be" across a variety of situations (as main verb and as auxiliary, as present and past tense) whereas the SE speaker would use different forms. Thus the following would all be possible in the speech of some BE speakers.

She *be* busy now. (Main verb)
They *be* busy now. (Main verb)
She *be* coming tomorrow. (Auxiliary)
They *be* coming tomorrow. (Auxiliary)

Sometimes another form than "be," such as, "was," or "is," is used in various situations. In any case, an SE speaker should not be surprised by this BE reduction of SE "am" "is" "are" "was" "were," to one or two of these forms used throughout all "be" situations.

One very helpful rule is: "If it's contractable in SE, it's deletable in BE." Consider the following SE sentences:

She will come at 6:00. (She'll)

She is coming at 6:00. (She's)
She will be coming at 6:00. (She'll)
She has gone. (She's)
She had gone. (She'd)

The contractable elements here can be deleted in BE. Thus we may get:

She come at 6:00.
She coming at 6:00.
She be coming at 6:00.
She gone.
She gone.

But notice, what can't be contracted in SE can't be deleted in BE. Consider the following pair. The "be" in the first is contractable (therefore deletable in BE), and the other is not.

I know where he is going. (I know where *he's* going becomes I know where he going)
I know where he is. (Cannot become I know where *he's* and therefore cannot become I know where he.)

In BE we can get "I know where he going," but never "I know where he."

Pronouns are interesting in BE also. We sometimes hear the forms "mines" (counterpart of SE "mine") and "hisself/theirself" (counterpart of SE "himself/themselves"). These forms seem to "regularize" an SE paradigm. Consider the SE possessive set: "they're your*s*, hi*s*, her*s*, our*s*, their*s*" but "they're *mine*." In BE, the " mine" case works like the others and becomes "mine*s*" rather than being an exception to the pattern as in SE. Consider also the SE set "*my*self, *your*self(ves), *her*self, *our*selves," but "*him*-(not *his*) -self" and "*them*-(not *their*)-selves." Again in BE there's a tendency toward regularization and we may hear "He did it all by hisself" or "They did it all by theirself."

BE speakers frequently use pronoun apposition. Don't be frightened by the term. The concept is simple as you'll see from these examples:

Miz Jones, *she* always be sayin' . . .
Randy, *he* say dat.
Daniella, *she* be sick today.

It's sort of a double subject in a sentence; a noun subject followed by the appropriate pronoun. There are also cases where SE "there" is expressed as "it" in BE.

SE: There's a door by the window.
BE: It's a door by the window.
SE: There's some children in here.
BE: It's some children in here.

A final syntactic feature of BE that is prevalent enough to deserve mention here is the expression of conditional. SE conditional sentences like

She asked him *if he wanted to go.*
She asked him *if he went.*

are expressed by some BE speakers as

She axe him *do he want to go.*
She axe him *did he go.*

This discussion of pronunciation and syntactic features frequently heard in the speech of BE speakers has just touched on a limited set of particularly prevalent features of BE.[1] Remember these features do not occur in the speech of *all* Afro-Americans, nor do they occur *only* in the speech of Afro-Americans, nor do they occur *always* in the speech of someone fluent in BE. What is important for us is to hear the BE forms our children use as regular features of a different dialect than SE, rather than as a poor attempt to speak SE. BE speakers are not speaking SE; they are speaking something else, a valid systematic something else called BE. In her autobiography Maya Angelou says:

> My education and that of my Black associates were quite different from the education of our white schoolmates. In the classroom we all learned past participles, but in the streets and in our homes the Blacks learned to drop *s*'s from plurals and suffixes from past-tense verbs. We were alert to the gap separating the written word from the colloquial. We learned to slide out of one language and into another without being conscious of the effort. At school, in a given situation, we might respond with "That's not unusual." But in the street, meeting the same situation, we easily said, "It be's like that sometimes." (Angelou 1973, p. 191)

With this brief discussion of some important BE features behind you, consider the talk of the following kindergarten children. Both episodes were taped without the children's knowledge and without an adult present in the immediate area. The episodes were recorded in two different kindergarten classrooms. See which BE features you can identify in these conversations. From the first class:

[1]For a more complete and detailed discussion of pronunciation and syntactic features of BE see Baratz (1969); Fasold and Wolfram (1970); Labov (1969; 1970a, b); Dillard (1972).

C-1: Nobody gonna mess wid mah dawg. Whoever mess wid mah dawg gonna, they gonna git bite—bit.

C-2: Whoever mess wid mah dawg gonna git bit.

C-3: Whoever mess wid mah dawg gonna git bit on da boody.

C-2: Whoever mess wid mah aintie (aunty) dawg, what . . .

C-1: My aintie, my aintie dawg, boy, boy Midnight tear you up.

C-2: My aintie got a doberman picher, boy.

C-1: My aintie do too, boy. She, she, las, las time she thought dere was a robber in in da garage. Boy, Midnight tore 'im up. It was one in da garage.

C-3: What?

C-1: A robber.

C-4: A robbery.

C-1: Boy, Midnight came aftuh 'im an RRRRRRRRRR, Arf - arf - arf - oh-oh-oh-oh.

C-1: Look at D———.

C-2: Dat a wig?

C-3: Nuh-uh. Dat's mah real haih. Ain't no wig.

C-2: Dat ain't no wig.

C-2: It's you wig.

C-1: Cain't ya'll see da real hair stickin' on her?

C-4: M———, dat a wig.

C-1: Naw.

C-4: Sure ain't.

C-1: I see dat. I see dat hair stickin' on.

C-5: It's you Afro.

C-1: It's you Afro. Let me see it (refers to picture card). Let me see it.

C-2: I'll keep if'n it ain't nobody's.

C-1: Dat's a mama. Dat's a mama. She gonna be a mama. She gonna be a mama, D——— (C-2 pulls on C-3's wig).

C-3: Stop!

C-2: I be seein' if it be a wig.[2]

From the second class:

(playing with dolls)

C-1: My baby, she cryin'.

C-2: I'm goin' gi' huh some foo (food).

C-3: (Talking to a doll) Lil' boy you better shut yo mouf an' git up dere and eat, boy fo' you git hit on da head.

C-1: Dat's V———'s baby.

[2]I am indebted to Brenda Cone for these excerpts from her data.

C-2: You better leave my baby 'lone.

C-3: He keep cryin'.

C-2: Oh, o- o- o- o- o, dat's my chillin in dere.

C-3: I'm fixin ta eah egg. Um, yum, yum.

C-2: We fixin' ta eah. Gots ta come on.

C-1: I is.

C-3: I'm gittin' my own lunch.

C-1: What cha gonna do wit your own lunch?

(Now they are playing with toy cars.)

C-1: Tol' ya dat's woner bug, he rollin' by hisself, ain't he? Woner bug, he a bad lil ol cah. He be catchin' all up wit you. Cause I . . .

C-2: Bettah watch out, boy!

C-1: Woner bug, he'll 'tack dat cah, righ'?

C-3: Um-uh. Woner bug is *mean*!

C-1: He'll be mean ta . . .

C-2: A-o-o-o-o he fixin' to dribe (drive) hisself. Rum—m-m-m.

C-3: Git 'way from baby wit dat cah, gir'. My baby, she, she want dat cah.

C-1: Dat's my baby's bottle. I put some milk in here fo mah baby.

C-2: Here dat kine (kind). You bettah hush you mout.

C-1: Leabe her 'lone. She sleepin'.[3]

Many of the familiar BE features are here—consonant deletion, single verb form for different tense and number situations, consonant substitution, deletion of initial unstressed syllable, pronoun apposition, multiple negative, deletion of contractable elements, "hisself," substitution of "it" for "there" ("It was one in da garage"). How did you interpret the child's "Woner bug is *mean!*" in the second class? The term "mean" (probably more like "meeeeeeeeeean") expresses admiration. The term "bad" in BE is also a complimentary one. It is high praise to say of someone "He baaaaaaaaaad!" One often encounters this pattern of using a term in BE with a meaning opposite to its meaning in SE. Also we find vocabulary items in BE that are entirely unique to that dialect and culture. For example, many SE speakers would not know what it means to "climb fool's hill," a reference to adolescents' going through a carefree period of life when they are not expected to be very responsible.

But some of the most striking aspects of BE don't relate to pronunciation, syntax, or vocabulary but rather to the diverse, vigorous, dynamic ways its speakers use BE in communication in public, on the street. Abrahams (1974) distinguishes between "house talk" and "street talk." It is possible to

---

[3]I am indebted to Lenora Burkhart for these excerpts from her data.

(and most blacks do) identify a variety of playful and artful, often highly stylized, communication events that young men on the street engage in. (The names given to various communication events differ from one community and one time to another: rapping, signifying, jiving, shucking, playing the dozens. But though the names differ, the same events are recognizable across Afro-American communities.) It is largely by performing effectively in these street interactions that a young man establishes his reputation. These different communication events are characterized by both particular verbal devices and nonverbal devices—stance, movement, etc. Abrahams feels one can identify a basic continuum

> . . . from talk in which information is the focus, to the most stylized, in which more concern is shown for the artful patterning of the utterance than the message. With the former the style is buried in favor of the message; the interaction to be effective must seem relatively spontaneous. With the latter, the message is subordinated . . . while the intensity and effectiveness of presentation become most important. Between these are interactions in which stylized devices are introduced—and call attention to themselves—but in which message remains as important as style. (Abrahams 1974, pp. 251–52)

It's clear from the autobiographical writings of Afro-Americans that children are very much aware of this lively verbal street culture, though as young children they don't actively participate in it.

> The street is where young bloods get their education. I learned how to talk on the street, not from reading about Dick and Jane going to school. . . . The teacher would test our vocabulary every week, but we knew the vocabulary we needed. (From H. R. Brown, quoted in Abrahams 1974, p. 244)

Black English is more than a distinctive set of linguistic structures. It is also a distinctive array of verbal performance events that are an important part of the verbal culture of many of our Afro-American children.[4]

MYTHS

A number of myths have for a long time surrounded the BE-dominant child. Because these myths continue to interfere with many teachers' effective interaction with their BE-speaking children, it is important to consider these myths here. One group of myths has to do with the children's language; another group has to do with the children's cultural background; a third group

---

[4]For further information relating to these verbal performance styles ("street talk" and "house talk,") you might want to see Abrahams (1974; 1976); Labov (1970a); Ward (1971); Mitchell-Kernan (1969).

has to do with the children's cognitive abilities. But all three groups of myths share a common basic assumption: They all see the children and their backgrounds as deficient. Let's look at these myths closely, for they are insidious, pervasive, and damaging to our relationship with children, and thus ultimately detrimental to children's learning.

Language Myths

We have been told many negative things about BE-speaking children's language by people (especially educators and educational psychologists) who are not linguists and do not understand BE as a linguistic system relating sounds and meanings. To the degree that BE is not like SE, it has been considered *sub*standard by some, that is, not as "good" a way of speaking as SE. What we now know to be a systematic dialect (BE) has not always been regarded as an organized entity at all, but has often been seen as imperfect and bumbling attempts of children to speak SE. We have been told that BE is slang, that it is informal speech, that it is dull, repetitive, and unimaginative, that it is a nonlogical mode of expression, that it is lazy speech, that it is characterized by poor syntactic structure, and that BE speaking children's language development is delayed. Bereiter and Englemann conclude that the speech of lower socioeconomic BE-speaking children

> ... seems to consist not of distinct words, as does the speech of middle-class children of the same age, but rather of whole phrases or sentences that function like giant words ... that cannot be taken apart by the child and re-combined; they cannot be transformed from statements to questions, from imperatives to declaratives, and so on. Instead of saying "He's a big dog," the deprived child says "He bih daw." (1966, p. 34)

They also conclude that "langauge for the disadvantaged child seems to be an aspect of social behavior which is not of vital importance" (1966, p. 42).

A veritable army of language-oriented researchers did battle in the 1960s with these notions of linguistic deficit. Linguists, sociolinguists, and anthropologists studied BE, its historical development, and the ways it is used by its speakers. They gathered data in natural settings and provided descriptions of the linguistic structure and the communicative functioning of BE. Some of their work was particularly dramatic. Labov and Robins, by varying the social context of the interaction, elicited lively, forceful interaction from teen-agers and preteenagers in Harlem—young people who had been called nonverbal (see earlier discussion, p. 281). Other researchers (Abrahams, Mitchell-Kernan, Labov) collecting data from inside BE-speaking communities, have made us aware of the communicative power and versatility of BE verbal performance. They have brought to our attention a host of communicative performance events that are an important part of street life.

An early study done by Joan Baratz (discussed in Baratz, 1969) documented the presence of a valid and distinct BE dialect in the language of many Washington, D.C. school children. Baratz devised a sentence repetition test including a BE version and SE version of each of fifteen sentences, yielding a total of thirty sentences. One sentence was "Does Deborah like to play with the girl that sits next to her in school?" and another was "Do Deborah like to play wid da girl that sit next to her at school?" Another was "I asked Tom if he wanted to go to the picture that was playing at the Howard," and another was "I aks Tom do he wanna go to the picture that be playin' at the Howard" (pp. 102–3). The subjects in the study were thirty Anglo children (fifteen third graders and fifteen fifth graders) from a low-middle-income community near Washington, D.C., and thirty black children (fifteen third graders and fifteen fifth graders) from an all black inner-city school in Washington, D.C. The sentences were presented in a random sequence on tape to each child, and after hearing the model sentence once, the child was to repeat it.

Not surprisingly, the Anglo children did better than the black children in repeating the SE sentences, and the black children did better than the Anglo children in repeating the BE sentences. What was particularly significant was the ways in which each group tended to alter the model sentences that were not in their own dialect, when they "repeated" them. Not unlike Slobin and Welsh's "Echo," they produced a version which retained the original meaning but was expressed in their own dominant system; the BE speakers tended to "black English-ize" the SE sentences, while the SE speakers tended to standardize the BE sentences. Thus the "errors" made by each group were not some unsystematic mishmash, but rather a predictable "translation" of the sentences in the unfamiliar code into a more familiar version. These results provided clear evidence of the operation of two distinct and rule-governed dialect systems in the speech of the subjects, one system dominant for the one group, and a different system dominant for the other.

Contrary to the 1960s notions of linguistic deficit espoused by many educators and educational psychologists, those researchers who intensively and systematically studied the role of language in communities where BE was prevalent found a culture in which language flourished, in which there was dynamic performance, in which the "man of words"—the Martin Luther Kings and the street corner gang leaders—held sway largely because of their language power. Looking at the members of BE-speaking communities interacting within their community, researchers did not find the single word mumbler children that educational psychologists had written about in their descriptions of BE-dominant children who had been observed and interviewed in classrooms and in laboratory settings.

Culture Myths

During the 1960s we were told many negative things about BE-speaking children's cultural background. The picture painted was one of chaos reigning where a culture ought to be. Much was made of the fact that in many homes the father was not present and the mother worked. The conclusion was that the children were pretty much neglected and did not receive adequate psychological and emotional support, and that there was no adult present to talk with the children, which was said to be why the children "had no language" when they came to school. We were told that the children received little or no "stimulation" in their homes, had few interesting toys. Interestingly, when researchers began to actually go into urban black communities they found many people interacting in children's homes—a variety of people coming, going, often staying a while. There was in fact a great deal of stimulation and activity, many people and things for the children to interact with. At this point, we were told that the "problem" with urban black children's background wasn't that there was *too little* stimulation; rather the problem was that there was *too much* stimulation and therefore the children couldn't focus their attention on any particular thing and learn from it. We were told these environments were "noisy" and therefore not well suited to learning. In retrospect, this sudden 180-degree turnabout is remarkable. Surely one must be suspicious on purely theoretical grounds, when some observed behavior is " explained" by "reasons" which are diametrically opposed: not enough stimulation/too much stimulation.

As in the case of the language deficit myths, so in the case of the culture deficit myths. Educators and educational psychologists saw behaviors which followed different norms from their own middle-class patterns, and they assumed those behaviors to be deficient insofar as they differed from their own accepted behavioral norms.

Fortunately, some anthropologically-oriented researchers have pointed out some of the important differences between the structure and organizational patterns of urban black culture and of Anglo middle-class culture. One of the most important is a difference we frequently find in family structure. In Anglo middle-class culture, the nuclear family is the typical pattern: mother, father, and child(ren) born to them. (This is undergoing significant change now with the increase in various competing family patterns such as blended families and one-parent families). But in many other societies of the world, urban black among them, one finds a prevalent pattern of extended family structure in which one's own family consists not only of mother, father, brothers and sisters, but also of grandparents, aunts, uncles, cousins (both close and distant), as well. One cares about and has responsibilities toward all of these. The child from such a family does indeed have psychological and emotional support and a great deal of interaction. But whereas most of this support for the middle-class Anglo child will come from mother and father, for some urban black children that support will come from a variety of sources—all of them "family" in an extended family structure.

The difference in family structure is just one example of a cultural pattern of difference between urban black culture and Anglo middle-class culture that has been seriously misunderstood (some others will be discussed in the next chapter). It is one of many instances where Anglo middle-class educators saw an environment which was different from their own and from the pattern they accepted as the "norm" (*norm*al) and concluded that that environment was deficient, patternless, chaotic, (ab*norm*al). It was not until researchers stopped asking the question "How is this environment different from the 'normal/right one' (that is, always defining "normal" as mainstream middle-class environment)?" and started asking the question "what are the systematic organizing principles for human behavior operating within this community?" that we began to better understand the richly diverse experiential background that many of our BE-dominant children come from, on its own terms, instead of in relation to some *other* cultural norms.

Cognition Myths

It is only a small step from claiming that children's language and cultural background are impoverished, to claiming that they are lacking in cognitive abilities. Again it was during the 1960s, when Head Start programs were at their peak, that cognitive deficiency myths flourished. Well-intentioned educators felt that BE-dominant children from urban backgrounds had come from impoverished cultural environments and that their language was under-developed. They assumed that, since children's experiential and linguistic background were basic to their learning and since both were "deficient," that the children's cognitive abilities were underdeveloped. They rushed in with almost religious zeal to save these children, to develop adequate cognitive abilities where they thought only inadequate ones existed. There was, and perhaps still is, a fundamental confusion between "cognitive, intellectual ability" and "good performance on school achievement measures." Although many educators thought they were making children more academically oriented, they were in fact making them more middle class, better performers on traditional mainstream school achievement measures. Comments about these children's "inability to think abstractly" and about their "learning deficits" (resulting from their cultural and linguistic deficits) were typical in the 1960s and are still with us.

It seems incredible that these deficiency notions so totally dominated educational thinking as recently as the late 1960s, and more incredible still that they are prevalent even now. We know that every environment that offers people and things for children to interact with is a rich learning environment for young active learners, explorers, discoverers. BE-dominant children have such a learning environment. We know that every culture socializes its children to behave in ways that are appropriate within that group. BE-dominant children have learned to behave in ways that are appropriate within their culture. We know that members of every community interact with children in a wide range of ways and for diverse purposes, and that the children figure out the language of those interactions that they engage in—they speak the language of their community. BE-speaking children have done precisely this. They come to school with the background and the abilities and the tools that are the stuff of valid and effective ongoing learning. What has been deficient all along has not been BE-dominant children's language, culture, or cognition, but rather our inadequate understanding of these areas.

THE MYTHS LIVE ON

We would not spend so much time discussing these deficiency myths if they were only a matter of historical interest, something dead and gone. Unfortunately they are not gone. They plague us still. We still hear deficiency attitudes expressed. Today in our schools we still find teaching materials flourishing that are based on deficit assumptions.

The Distar materials, perhaps the most striking example, are the outgrowth of Bereiter and Engelmann's earlier work described in *Teaching Disadvantaged Children in the Preschool.* Though the program is not used only with BE-dominant children, the impetus for its development came from the "deficits" attributed to "disadvantaged" populations. Drills like the following are clearly aimed at substituting SE for BE, though the authors apparently feel that they are teaching the child *language.* (What is italicized in the following is the teacher's speech, written in blue lower case in the original. The remainder tells the teacher what to do as she talks.)

> *Let's find out if you can really listen.*
> *Note:* Pronounce *sss* as *zzzz.*
> a. *My turn. I'll tell you if I hold up fingerssss or finger. Listen carefully.*
> Hold up two fingers. *Fingerssss.*
> Hold up three fingers. *Fingerssss.*
> Hold up your index finger. *Finger.*
> Hold up four fingers. *Fingerssss.*
> Hold up your little finger. *Finger.*
> b. *Your Turn. Tell me if I hold up fingerssss or a finger.* (Book B, p. 19)
>
> *Now we are going to name some objects. Listen carefully.*
> a. Point to the apple.

My turn. What is this? An apple. Listen again. What is this? An apple.
b. *Say it with me. What is this?* Touch.
Respond with the children. *An Apple. Again.* Touch. *An Apple.*
Repeat *b* until all children are saying *an apple.*
c. *All by yourselves. What is this?* Touch. *An apple. Again. What is this?* Touch. *An apple.* Repeat *c* until all children are saying *an apple.* (Book A, p. 56)

The materials are based on the assumptions (1) that many children do not have adequate language to function in school, (2) that they do not have the mental resources to learn the language necessary to function in school, (3) that expressing a meaning in a dialect other than SE is equivalent to lacking the meaning, (4) that one learns both concepts and how to express them by engaging in drills requiring fixed choral responses to fixed questions. But we know (1) that children's language abilities are well developed by age five, whatever the dialect in which they express themselves; (2) that children have powerful processing abilities for further developing their language range, both in structure and in use (to extend their communicative competence in an interactive environment); (3) that one can express *any* meanings in *any* dialect; (4) that children learn through their own active experiencing and their interaction with others in creative, individual ways. In the face of this knowledge, it seems remarkable that this deficit approach has managed to survive, let alone thrive. Such materials are based on serious misconceptions about what language is, and how children acquire and use it, as well as on deficit assumptions about children's conceptual and linguistic abilities. But it seems to me that these materials not only assume that children are deficient, they also assume that teachers are deficient. You've doubtless encountered teaching materials lauded as being "teacher proof." The Distar materials are a good example. They tell teachers every word to say, how to move their hands to get all the children to respond at exactly the same time (and in exactly the same way), how to point, how to touch. For example, here are the "touching" instructions.

TOUCHING

At the end of the one-second interval move your finger quickly away from the page and then quickly and decisively touch the page just below the picture.
The instant your finger touches the page the children should respond. Look at a low-performing child in the group. See if he or she is responding.
Keep on touching the picture for the duration of the children's response. Drop your finger when they finish responding. (Teacher's Guide, p. 13)

Besides being insulting, it is surely a mistaken notion that "teacher-proofing" materials is a virtue. It is teachers, not materials, who know and interact with their children sensitively, responsively. It is in this real interaction, rather than in the robot execution of nonlanguage drills, that children's language grows.

We need to ask why in the face of solid research on BE and on the culture and cognitive abilities of its speakers, these mistaken language, culture and cognitive deficiency notions persist and even serve as the basis of some educational programs. There are probably many partial explanations. One may be that it simply takes a long time for research findings to make their way into the general public and longer still for educational materials to be published which reflect newer knowledge. Probably the more significant reason for the persistence of these myths has to do with deep-rooted attitudes. One of these attitudes (mentioned earlier) is the pathology attitude toward education. Many educators see their job as finding out what's wrong with children (diagnosing the illness) and then eradicating it (prescription and treatment). This attitude toward teaching is compatible with deficit interpretations of the behavior of those Afro-American children whose behavior patterns are different from those the teacher expects. The diagnosis is that those areas of functioning which differ from the teacher's expectations are "problems" and the treatment is that these "problem behaviors" will be replaced by more middle-class behavior. Another attitude which interferes with the eradication of our deficit misinterpretations is the negative attitude which pervades the society at large. Our BE-dominant children typically come from a social group which even today does not enjoy a position of high prestige.

What is hopeful is that attitudes are changing, and education is feeling the change. It's interesting that the range of attitudes from strongly-negative toward BE and Afro-American culture, all the way to strongly-positive, are held by Afro-Americans as well as by Anglo-Americans. Cazden, Bryant, and Tillman (1972) collected interviews with parents, teachers, and community leaders from the urban black area of Boston (Roxbury). It would be hard to find a more negative attitude toward BE than one parent's "Get rid of it [BE]. Throw it away. Tell the kids, 'Hey, don't speak that junk. Forget it' " (p. 74), or to find more positive attitudes than teachers' "I think Black language relates. You know, it really gets to the point." Or " . . . their [black people's] language is part of their Blackness. And until, if ever, the whole Black society changes their way of speech, it'll be taking something from them [to get rid of BE]" (pp. 76–77).

The position of BE and the misguided notions about those who speak it hold for many other social dialects as well. However, as these groups have become prouder of their own unique history and more eager to assert and express their own identity, the society at large has become more aware. Some writers have contrasted the "melting pot" and "salad bowl" views of our ethnically diverse populations. We seem to be witnessing a move from melting pot thinking toward salad bowl thinking—a move from a desire that all ethnic groups blend into the mainstream and become some homogenized substance, toward a desire that all groups maintain their distinctness and thus contribute uniquely toward a richer, more diverse social whole. All of us, but most of all our school children, whatever their background, can only benefit from such a widened interaction of language and life styles. Their cognitive and langauge growth can only be enhanced by an ever broader range of experience and interaction.

Chapter 14

Black English, Teachers, and Children

HOME-SCHOOL MISMATCH

It has been noted repeatedly that BE-dominant children (as well as children from some other ethnic minority backgrounds) perform less well on standard school achievement measures than do mainstream middle-class children. Generally their achievement test scores are lower, their report card grades are lower, and many read below grade level. The obvious question is *why*. The myths of the 1960s told us it was because something was wrong with urban Afro-American children: Their language and cultural background were deficient and had resulted in underdeveloped cognitive abilities. We know now this is not the case. BE-speaking children in fact come to us with a well-developed system of language structure and language use. They come to us from a culture in which they have been "bathed in verbal stimulation from morning till night" (Labov 1970a, p. 11); have been surrounded by, interacted with, cared about by many people of all ages; have developed a complex code of appropriate social behavior. They come to us with substantial experience in accepting high-level responsibilities (the care of younger siblings, food purchase and preparation), and engaging in real problem solving. In short, these children bring to school a linguistic, social, and cognitive background of experiences which constitute a powerful base for continuing linguistic, social, and cognitive growth. This is what we see when we look at our BE-speaking children.

What do we see when we look at the school? We generally see an institution which is designed for mainstream children and which does not understand or fit the BE-speaking child's situation very well. Our public schools have traditionally been very middle class in their educational goals and methods, in their assessment measures, in their assumptions about children's backgrounds (what they have been, but even more what they "should" have been), in their expectations of how children will and "should" behave, and in their values, what they consider good or worthy. The school is typically an institution that perpetuates and actively reinforces mainstream values and behaviors. The majority of teachers whether black or white (or Chicano or Navajo or . . .) value mainstream behavior in their own lives, unconsciously model that behavior, and consciously try to teach children what they believe to be best. The result of this tends to be an institution that attempts to make its children as mainstream as possible.

There is nothing inherently wrong with middle-class culture and values, any more than there is anything inherently wrong with any other subculture and value system. But there is something very wrong with an institution that purports to foster the intellectual and social growth of *all* its children, but in fact understands and supports the growth of only *some.* Teachers commit themselves to trying to teach all children effectively—Mexican-American, German-American, Chinese-American, Native-American, Anglo-American, Afro-American. Our purpose, I believe, is to help children become more powerful independent learners, more creative problem solvers, more effective interactants in their social dealings with others; to help them develop more alternatives for and control over their lives. Our purpose, I believe, is *not* to make children more mainstream in their values, aspirations, and behavior.

It would seem to go without saying that children whose background more nearly matches the values and expectations of the school (that is, the children for whom the school is designed) stand in a better position to achieve within that institution, on that institution's terms, than children from some other background. The closer the match between the child and the school, the better the child's chance to achieve in school. But the *mis*-match between child and school is very great in the case of some of our children, particularly some of our Afro-American, BE-dominant students. It is this mismatch that, to a considerable degree, accounts for the noted lower achievement scores of non-mainstream children in our mainstream oriented schools. Let's look at a few of these areas of mismatch between the school and some of our Afro-American children.

Position of Written
versus Oral Language Channels[1]

Mainstream children generally come to school eager to learn to read, in fact, many of them come already able to read to some degree. Their parents have surrounded them with written materials, and have read aloud to them from the time they were toddlers. The written word itself is accorded special status and the child is repeatedly told that she will learn to read it, to understand the wonderful mysteries when she goes to school. The child's teacher reinforces this. Most primary level teachers see their single most important task as teaching their children to crack the written code. More hours of the school week in grades one and two are devoted specifically to the teaching of reading and writing than to any other area. Many mainstream children who come into this setting are already primed and ready for this; they already are in awe of the written word and are eager to master code cracking skills relating to it.

This eagerness to learn to read is common to many Afro-American children also. But for some of them it has been the spoken word, the skillful verbal performance, that has reigned supreme before they enter school. It is the adept, adroit verbal performer who commands respect in many communities. Abrahams distinguishes between words as things or products (the written word, fixed, fossilized, permanent—so cherished by middle-class culture), and words as process or devices to be used in verbal performances (so highly valued in many Afro-American communities).

Surely both are important. We would want all our children to be facile in their oral languaging (fluent and skillful narrators, persuaders, entertainers), and also in their written languaging (fluent and skillful producers and interpreters of the written language). We should work to develop both. Every child's oral language is an important base for reading and writing. A child from a culture that highly prizes effective and versatile oral languaging stands in an excellent position for the continuation of language growth into written channels.

The increase in teachers' use of language experience approaches in children's early reading shows our growing awareness of the importance of children's own oral language in the process of learning to read. This approach may be especially important for those children for whom the spoken word has been of primary importance, those children who will "bridge into" an understanding of written words as "things" rather than process, happenings.

---

[1]The mismatch discussion that follows is based on a variety of readings and personal interactions that have shaped my thinking. Though I can't identify the separate contributions and thus give proper credit to the original source of each idea, I know that Roger Abrahams' writings and informal conversations have been important. I acknowledge him here. Keep in mind that the areas of mismatch discussed in this chapter do not apply to *all* BE-dominant children or to *only* BE-dominant children.

Ashton-Warner's (1963) techniques with the New Zealand Maori children she taught may have relevance here. She was confronted with the task of moving children from a primarily oral culture into written materials, in fact, into basals about well-behaved English children from a culture altogether removed from their own experiences. She began by engaging them vigorously in the telling of lively stories and relating incidents from their experience, endlessly immersing them in interaction that was alive and meaningful for them, consciously and deliberately surrounding them with words, words, words. It was a small step to begin writing the words down, not just any old words, but the "biggies"—those the children gave her from deep within themselves, words the children used in their eager relating of often frightening or angry personal events.

First words must have an intense meaning.
First words must be already part of the dynamic life.
First books must be made of the stuff of the child himself, whatever and wherever the child. (p. 28)

With small cards of sturdy paper and magic marker in hand, she would ask each child, "What word do you want?" She wrote the selected word on the card and gave it to the child. It now *belonged* to that child, a word as thing; the written word *was* the ghost or bomb or jet. With an accumulation of these, the child was gradually able to write fuller experience stories on the chalkboard area designated as her space. These stories were a kind of first "basal"—the child's own words, her own experiences in writing. It was an effective bridging from words as devices in oral performances to words as *things.*

Dictated stories that individual children watch you write or type serve a similar function: They relate the familiar oral language and the transformation of that into an unfamiliar symbol system, helping children to see that both the oral and the written symbols encode their meanings. Sometimes the dictated stories are on tape, but the child watches you translate her meanings into another symbol system as she watches you write or type them from the tape. The story is hers—she performed it and you have put in permanent form what was her own happening.

The *Interaction* tapes offer a beautiful variety of dialect readings (regional and social) with accompanying sets of storybooks and poetry books for groups of children to follow as they listen to the tape. This is a wonderful way of demonstrating that diverse dialect forms are valued and that all relate to written symbolization. None of us is dependent on our school's purchasing the *Interaction* materials, for we can provide the same kinds of materials ourselves simply by having friends, parents, acquaintances who speak different dialects, tape stories and poems that the children can listen to in groups as they follow the original in print.

Signs and ads effectively bridge the way from oral to written language for some children. Thus one child's first reading book might consist of pictures and words "Buick," "Mercury," "Datsun," "Dodge," "Volkswagen." One child I know came up with an interesting variation on the activity you have probably seen, in which the child lies down on brown wrapping paper and another person traces around him or her and then the life-sized version of the child is cut out. This particular child, after cutting out her traced "self," cut out words from magazines that told about herself and she pasted them onto her cutout—written words that "told" her feelings, thoughts, likes, physical characteristics. For children who don't yet recognize the words they want when they see them in print, we can provide them on small cards for activities such as this one. What matters is that meanings which have importance to children be the ones we put in print for them.

One word of caution: It's important that we who prize the written word so highly not see the child's oral language as valid only insofar as it is a springboard to the written word, but rather that we value it and continue to assure its development in its own right. We sometimes tend to neglect the oral language channels for the sake of written ones.

Children's own language, whatever their background, is more advanced, more interesting, and more vigorous than the pablum served up in most beginning basals. The more we can use the children's own language as the stuff of their reading and writing, the more effective language users—in oral and written channels—the children will become. BE-dominant children, like *all* children, have an alive and vital language system. There is no better starting place for learning to read and write.

To summarize, it is important to recognize that our children come from different places in regard to an understanding and appreciation of oral and written forms of language. Some come from backgrounds in which oral forms are most valued; others from backgrounds in which written forms are. But this means that both groups have a significant contribution to make; each can shine in some language area. The ideal classroom will be one in which children come from diverse backgrounds, thus assuring that we, as teachers, will not neglect but will use and further children's growth across both oral and written channels of language. It's important for us to discover and get in step with "where each child is coming from" in her attitude toward oral and written forms of language so that we can use it effectively in expanding her languaging.

Role of Peers and Adults as Information Sources

Mainstream children tend to come to school from backgrounds in which adults have been the primary information source. Adults are appealed to as the final intellectual authorities, the ones who know the answers. And adults inform children (whether they ask for it or not) and informally "test" them from the early days of the naming game ("What's this a picture of? Can you find the picture of the kitty? Where's the kitty?")—all questions designed to demonstrate to the adult that the child has learned certain things. Very like school teachers' questions, you'll notice. And indeed the assumption that the adult is the major source of information and tests you on that information frequently fits in very well with the school situation. There the adult, teacher in this case, is the major source of information which he or she dispenses and tests regularly. If you want to know something, ask the teacher, and if the teacher is giving you some information whether you asked for it or not, try to take it in, as you will probably be held accountable for it later.

But some of our children, many of them urban Afro-Americans, come from backgrounds where other children, particularly those somewhat older (older siblings, cousins, neighbors) have been especially important information sources. This may be a pattern that matches the school less well as most schools are set up now. But the point is, it needn't be a mismatching pattern. Expanding the use we make of peers and older children in our classrooms as information sources can aid all our children, and serve to lessen the mismatch between school and home for many children. Peer and cross-age interaction is a powerful learning base. It is important for children who come from a background in which adults are seen as all-knowing to expand their range of significant information sources to include other children. Likewise, it is important for children who have relied heavily on peers as information sources to extend their range to include adults as people to interact with intellectually. Again it's a matter of understanding where the child is coming from in her experience and understanding of whom to engage with in interaction for learning. All children come to school with many years of information seeking behind them. Different patterns of information seeking may have been emphasized for children from different backgrounds. It is for us to recognize the differences, to understand that all information-seeking patterns are valid for children's learning, and to attempt to extend the children's range of information sources. For many classrooms this will mean relying more on small group interaction under informal and often unobtrusive (but aware) teacher guidance, and less on teacher-directed whole group instruction, so as to establish more of a balance of different types of learning interactions. It may also mean increased use of cross-age interaction.

Role of Competition versus Cooperation

Much that we do in school tends to encourage competition among children in their work. Children compete for the number of As on report cards, for the number of spelling words correct on Friday's test, to be the last one left standing in the spelling bee, for reading the most "free reading" books and getting the most stars, for moving into a higher level reading book, for working ahead in the math workbook. Their school work is a highly individual and competitive venture. In many situations the child is to "do your own work" and cooperation is "cheating." Let's face it, mainstream culture encourages competition, and prizes individual achievement and, for better or for worse, our schools tend to reflect this cultural value. The child who comes to school eager to "shine"—to stand out from among the others—is well suited for this. (I am reminded of the first school day of a kindergarten friend of mine. The mothers had been invited to visit for the children's first morning. When the teacher called the children to sit on the rug, my little friend scurried over and sat up in an abnormally straight and rigid posture, behavior which was very puzzling to her mother, until the child explained, in a stage whisper that carried across the room, "I'm going to get an A!" Neighborhood children had initiated her well in their games of playing school. Sitting on the rug was not to be taken lightly!)

But competition of this kind is not the norm for many of our children. There are many subcultures that value cooperation in work. Many see work as a time for helping each other, while they regard play as a situation where one demonstrates individual prowess. Afro-American verbal gaming is one such situation. Here the individual performance is all-important. Clearly the child who comes to kindergarten primed to get an A for performing teacher-assigned tasks better than the other children fits in more easily with the school's expectations than the child who sees work as an essentially cooperative venture, something we help each other with.

One wonders whether the competitive nature of classrooms hasn't been overdone; whether we have sacrificed teaching and learning to testing as the major goal. Do we want our children to choose and read a particular library book because it is interesting and enjoyable to them, or because it will get them another star on the chart or because it has more pages than someone else's or because it has impressively small print? Do we want our children to spell words conventionally so they can get As in Friday's test, or so that their writing will be more readily understood by those who read it? Many more of my college students come to talk with me during office hours about their course grades than about their learning. They are mostly public school products. Thirteen years of public school has contributed to this ordering of priorities, placing "getting an A" above grappling with significant ideas.

Again, a greater inclusion of group *work* in our classrooms both extends the competitor's repertoire of work situations, and provides a better match with the backgrounds of some of our children. Our competitive-work-oriented and our cooperative-work-oriented children have much to learn from each other. The range of work contexts can be extended for all. Let's just try to realize that different children come from different places with regard to their understanding of competition and cooperation and the situations in which each is appropriate.

Nature of Adult-Child Interaction

It is not unusual to hear an Anglo middle-class teacher say of an Afro-American child in her class, "When I talk to her, she doesn't even look at me and just won't answer. She just stands there looking at the floor and at the very most manages to mumble 'yes ma'am.' " Sometimes the teacher will interpret the child's avoidance of eye contact as evidence of sneakiness or sly behavior. This is a most unfortunate misinterpretation and can have serious consequences for the teacher's relationship with the child. In many cases, these children are behaving in a way they have been taught demonstrates appropriate respect and deference toward adults. If the behavior that children intend as respectful, teachers see as sneaky, we have a mismatch of major proportions.

There is a pattern within some black communities in which an important part of the adult's role in an adult-child interaction is to instill appropriate social behavior in the child (telling the child what to do and how to behave, chiding the child for inappropriate behavior). The child's role is to express respect, to accept with deference the adult's behavioral dictates. Making eye contact is considered hostile, aggressive, challenging to authority, whereas eye avertance conveys a respectful attitude. You can see the kinds of problems that can arise when the child who is used to this deference pattern confronts a teacher who expects the child to establish eye contact ("You look at me when I'm talking to you!") and in some cases to explain what has happened. The child's mumbled "Yes ma'am" or silence may be interpreted by the teacher as rude behavior and may reinforce the label "nonverbal" for this child. The challenge is for us to try to understand what the child's behavior means *from the child's point of view;* that is the only valid starting point.

Because adult-child relations for some of our children are primarily authority interactions rather than intellectual or social back-and-forth exchanges, we can assume it will take time for these children to add new types of adult-child interaction patterns to their range in the school setting. At first, a child may only be able to relate to the teacher as an authority figure. It's important that we understand this as the respectful socially acceptable behavior the child intends. Initially the child's intellectual and social dialoging may come primarily from peer interaction, so it's important to make ample provision for this. But in time, you can perhaps move from being on the periphery of peer group interactions to being an occasional participant; here the child interacts with you in a sense, but still from a solid and primary peer interactive base of support. In time, if sensitively handled (which basically means knowing when to leave the child or peer group alone), the child may begin to extend interactions with you beyond the original authority-deference relationship into more social and intellectual areas of exchange.

Understand that what is happening is that additional interaction contexts are being added to the child's repertoire. These patterns are not replacing the adult-child appropriate behaviors the child already understands, for these home-based patterns are of crucial importance in many areas of the child's life. You are simply extending the child's behavior range to include patterns that are appropriate to some settings outside of the home.

Passive versus Participative Audience

If you've ever attended a black church service, you know the meaning of the phrase "participative audience." Audience members respond to the leader's exhortations and questions with shouted "Amens" and "Hallelujahs." And so it is with many types of performer-audience situations in some black communities. The audience is actively and expressively *there,* with the speaker, responding verbally all the way. This active verbal audience involvement indicates that the performer is an effective one. A passive, silent audience would indicate the opposite, that the speaker had not captured and inspired the audience.

Kochman (1969) has pointed out how different this audience participation is from the expected audience behavior in the classroom. The most prevalent type of teaching episode in many classrooms is a performer-audience pattern; the teacher performs and the children are the audience. It is for them to appear attentive (which essentially means to be quiet until called on to verbalize). Appropriate mainstream audience behavior, whether in church service or classroom, is to remain quiet and passive. The mainstream child who comes to school steeped in this pattern fits in easily with the teacher's expectations. But the child whose notion of appropriate large group audience behavior follows a more active, verbally participative pattern, may behave according to that pattern and be mislabeled as "hyperactive," "noisy," "undisciplined," "unruly." D———, a black fourth grader in a class I observed over several months is an example. D——— was a child I noticed immediately, as any observer would have. He was bright and confident, highly interactive, aware of everything going on around him, and above all, articulate and expressive (constantly) of his observations. This last proved to be his downfall with his classroom teacher. During the first month of my weekly observations, I watched the teacher's frustration with D——— steadily increase: "D———, I didn't call on you. I called on ———. Is your name ———? How many times do I have to tell you to raise your hand? D———, is that your voice I hear again? If I want your opinions I'll ask for them." By the second month, D——— spent as much time alone for disciplinary reasons (in the hall, in the office, missing recess) as he spent with the other children. Into the second month, the corporal punishment began. But the situation between D———

corporal punishment began. But the situation between D—— and his teacher was not the "fault" of either one so much as it was a *mismatch* of expected behaviors which became compounded over time: the teacher saw D——'s overt expressiveness in the group setting as unruly and as a challenge to her authority and control. D—— saw the teacher as being against him ("You always takin' up fuh ev'body else. How come you nevuh take up fuh me?") and all her actions reinforced his interpretation. Couldn't the situation have been different? If the teacher had better understood where D—— was coming from, what his understanding was of how one behaves —participates verbally—in large group situations, perhaps his behavior would not have been so threatening or have seemed so aggressive and challenging. Perhaps the teacher could have dealt with D—— as friend rather than foe, helped D—— to add to his range a new audience behavior pattern which is appropriate for certain situations, while providing ample opportunity for D—— to interact with peer groups and while capitalizing on the remarkable insights he contributed to whole group discussions: "D——, your idea is a good one and I want everyone to hear it. Hold on a minute until —— is finished talking and then we can all listen to your idea."

Family Structure and Responsibility

Throughout our society, family patterns are becoming more variable. As blended families, one-parent families, and other nonnuclear patterns become less exceptional, it may be that the extended family structure pattern common in many urban black communities will be easier for mainstream society to understand and accept. It's important for us to know and accept our children's family patterns. Who, in the child's home, provides psychological and emotional support, who loves the child, who cares most about the child's intellectual and social growth? What kind of growth do they see as important? Home visits can be helpful here. Whom do we send notes home to? Have "parent" conferences with? Whom does the child make Christmas gifts for?

In the extended family structure that many of our Afro-American children come from, they have often accepted substantial responsibilities for the smooth-functioning of the home that are not usually executed by children so young from middle-class families. It is not unusual for a five-year-old girl to be an important caregiver for her two-year old brother or cousin, to go to the store to buy food, to help fix dinner. Yet this same child, on coming to school, may be treated as one who has only accepted trivial (if any) responsibilities at home; she is given inconsequential tasks like leading the lunch line—and then told they are important responsibilities. If we are more aware of the substantial responsibilities some of our children are accustomed to accepting and derive feelings of competence and worth from executing, we can perhaps use these abilities better in school. Perhaps these children could perform some of the responsibilities we now delegate to aides and parent volunteers. There is real work to be done in the running of the classroom relating to care and preparation of supplies and equipment. For children who have derived much of their feeling of self-worth from recognizing the real contribution they make at home in carrying out significant tasks, we might both provide continuity for the child (closer match between home and school) in carrying on this responsible behavior, and also reinforce the child's feeling of self-worth and pride in making a contribution to the smooth functioning of the classroom. And of course, the cross-age interaction is a natural place for ensuring continuity. The five-year-old who cares for the two-year-old can readily be the second grader who helps care for and teach kindergartners. Needless to say, the more we use a child's contribution, the more we show we value it; and the more we value the child's contribution, the more comfortable, friendly and *good* a place the classroom is for him or her. The child comes from "*my* home"—mine because I help to make it what it is; the same child can come to "*my* class"—mine for the same reason, because of the significant contribution I make to it.

The home-school mismatches discussed here are only a few. Notice however, that they all involve interaction in some way: adult-child and child-child interaction patterns; interaction in oral and written channels; interaction in large group and small group; interaction in work settings and play settings. If our classrooms are to be interactive environments for children's language to grow in, then these dimensions of interactive mismatch are crucial. The child needs to know: What are the special purposes served by written and oral aspects of language and how can I become a powerful communicator—producer and interpreter—in both? What information sources are available and how can I effectively interact with them for my learning? How can I learn from children? From adults? In what situations do I interact competitively with others and when do I interact cooperatively? When do I try to excell individually and when do I work with others to achieve a common goal? How should I interact with classroom adults, especially the teacher in a one-to-one situation? Am I expected to be silent and behave as the teacher tells me? Am I expected to interact verbally? About social things? About curiosity questions I have—my wonderings about the world? How am I to interact as a member of a large group where the teacher is performing? Do I sit quietly? Do I participate? If so, how? When? At home I do a lot of things to keep the place going well. What can I do here to look after things?

These are all questions relating to the large question: How shall I use language and communicate with others in school? As teachers we can perhaps be more aware of these areas of mismatch for some children: We can (1) recognize mismatch when we see it and more accurately interpret the meaning of the child's behavior, (2) lessen the mismatch for the child by incorporating teaching methods better suited to the child's background experience, (3) gradually extend the child's repertoire to include new behaviors appropriate to new situations, (4) use the child's well-established behaviors as starting points for extending—through interaction—the behavioral range of those children whose behavior patterns match the school's already and are pretty much limited to that.

READING

Children's learning to read has always been a primary concern of the school. It is not surprising that the reading instruction of BE-dominant children has gained particular attention because (1) educators are aware that BE does not closely match the SE typical in basals, and (2) BE-dominant children's reading achievement scores tend to be lower than the reading scores of SE-dominant children. Several approaches to teaching BE-dominant children to read have been advocated. The one which is probably the most frequent, and so obvious that we overlook it, is to give BE-speaking children the SE basal and insist that the children orally call the words one by one, exactly as they appear on the printed page. Thus, if the basal says, "Cathy is going too" and the BE-dominant child reads this as "Cathy, she be goin' too," or "Cathy goin' too," the reading is considered incorrect. The child is asked to go back and reread the sentence "more carefully." The teacher might say, "She? I don't have any 'she' in my book." or "Look again. You've left something out. (Pointing to "is") What's this little word here?" The problem with this approach, it seems to me, is that the child *was* reading and the teacher is requiring the child to replace that reading with *word calling*. If reading is, as current psycholinguistic research suggests, a process of relating one's language meanings to printed symbols, then BE-dominant children who would say and who orally read "Cathy is going too" as "Cathy she be goin' too" are doing precisely that. These children have gotten their language meaning from the printed symbols. Requiring children to call off the words exactly as printed asks them to ignore their language meanings and instead call word sequences that do not convey their language meanings. This is substituting word calling for reading. Further, it seems to me that we want to develop children who are skilled in extracting meanings from strings of printed symbols, rather than children who are good at focusing on and naming each individual word in a sequence. Thus when a child "takes in" and interprets meaningfully a printed string (as the child has done if she verbalizes her own dialectal rendering of the message conveyed in the sentence), the child is demonstrating more advanced reading behavior, closer to the ultimate goal. We ask the child to regress if we ask her to drop down to focusing on single words. This is self-defeating, as it interferes with the goal of getting meaning from longer printed sequences. We do not want to encourage word-by-word fixation. (My own personal concern is that too heavy emphasis on oral rather than silent reading with any child encourages single word fixation that may interfere with the child's development of reading fluency.)[2]

Heated debates about effective methods of teaching all children to read have been with us for quite some time and will doubtless continue—phonics versus sight word, "lap method" versus "ladders of skills," emphasis on oral reading versus emphasis on silent reading, strict adherence to basals or heavier reliance on language experience approaches. But through all this, three basic principles seem to emerge that are true to what we know about children, learning, and language—all of which are involved in children learning to read (a language-based process).

The first is that children, in learning to read, as in their learning of other langauge processes (figuring out of meaning-expression relations and how to use them), are active and individual learners. Children, given rich and diverse opportunities to interact with and through printed symbols, will use their own figuring out mechanisms to crack the written code. They did it with the oral language; they will to a considerable extent do it with the written language. Children, earlier, were bathed in diverse verbal interactions in situations which were meaning-full. Given this rich data base they figured out the sound-meaning relations in various situations. I think these same abilities can work for children figuring out print-meaning relationships also. Providing a "print" bath as well as, and often closely related to, a verbal one, can be helpful. It will provide a variety of materials for children to use (signs, magazines, letters we and others write to our children and they write to each other, popular lyrics on record jackets, storybooks, basals, class writing—poems, stories, children's own books of dictated stories and/or single experience stories, taped stories with books for the children to follow as they listen) so that a child may select and use, in her own way, materials and approaches that match her way of making sense out of this aspect of her world. Again we assume a child is an active learner who makes sense out of the world in her own way—by observing, listening, questioning, trial and error. Providing for a variety of types of printed matter, and a variety of ways for children to relate to it, will give us a chance to see how (and when) the child prefers to approach the task of cracking the printed code, and then we will be able to, as Smith recommends, "Respond to what the child is trying to do."

The second basic principle is that reading is a process of deriving meaning. "Deriving meaning" is less a matter of taking meaning out of something, in this case printed symbols, than it is a matter of putting meaning *in*. It is because children already have a solid meaning store built of past experience

---

[2]For a beginning consideration of other reading approaches for BE-dominant children, see Dale (1976), pp. 287–94; and Baratz and Shuy (1969).

that they are able to imbue the printed black squiggles on the page with meaning at all. In an important sense, children already know what the printed symbols will say. This is why children read "new words" better in running text than in isolated lists. In the one case, they draw on their own meanings; in the second case they are unable to.

A third principle follows from the second. There is no language more meaningful to children than their own. The more we rely on capturing the children's own experiencing and expressing it through symbols, the better.

Because BE-dominant children come to us with a rich experiential and verbal background, the possibility of reading success is as great for them as for other children. We have active learners; we have children with a rich and diverse meaning store; we have children with meaningful experiences that we can encode as printed symbols. To assure the children's success we may need to be more aware of the way written and verbal language forms are viewed in their culture, of the ways the children expect to interact with us and with the other children, of the ways they expect to cooperate with other children in reading tasks. Armed with this increased awareness, we may be better able to interpret what our children are trying to do, and thus respond to it more relevantly for their learning.

A FINAL QUESTION

Teachers often ask, "If my children speak only BE, shouldn't I teach them SE instead? After all, when they grow up they'll never be able to get good jobs if they don't speak SE."

Again, think of all children as having a range of speaking styles. That range is constantly expanding as the individual's social contacts expand and diversify. BE-dominant children typically understand SE: usually the TV set, the teacher, and the movies bombard them with it. As children's interaction base expands, their language repertoire expands also (as we saw earlier when we considered children's development of communicative competence in diverse social situations). Children add new speaking styles to their range as they interact with new people in new types of settings. The answer then, is to increase every child's opportunities for diverse meaningful social interaction. This is where language lives. This is every bit as true of SE-dominant children as it is of BE-dominant children. As discussed in the previous section, the school has the potential for providing a richer base of diverse meaningful interactive opportunities than any other place.

The broader the child's language range, the more social situations she will be able to interact in comfortably. What is important in the case of all children is that their home language be valued and encouraged. To say *no* to a child's language is to say *no* to the child. Children's language is born and fostered in the context of the most important relationships and interactions of their entire lives. Their home language will continue to be an integral part of their deepest meanings and relations, those of home and community. That language is more appropriate to the maintaining and furthering of those most important relationships than any other language system could ever be. We must never tamper with that precious entity, inextricably tied up with the child's own sense of identity. Every child's language grows beyond this home language, incorporating new features and adapting to a wider range of situations. We can contribute significantly to that expansion. But ours is not to supplant the child's one language system (the most important) with another.

ASHES TO ASHES

In closing, here is a portion of a conversation between a university reading tutor and a fourth grade BE-dominant child who is having trouble with reading. Can you find in this conversation any support for the language, cultural, or cognitive deprivation myths we heard so much about in the 1960s to "explain" this child's low reading achievement?

C: I pick some dewberries and some plums and I ate 'em up. But firs my daddy . . . my daddy made some dewberries. He put some dewberries and bashed 'em up and den put a couple o' milk and den a couple o' sugar and den mash it down and they turn purple and I ate it all up; my brother messed in it.

A: He messed in it? How'd he do that?

C: He go (makes noise and accompanying gestures to demonstrate).

A: Oh, he just got and played in it?

C: Uh huh.

A: Where'd you get your dewberries?

C: Uh, we picked 'em down ta our our grammaw house . . . we go (demonstrates) . . . and den he throwed dem dewberries in the truck and I had to get (inaudible) I had to pick 'em (inaudible) he missed.

A: He did?

C: Uh huh.

A: What else'd you do down at your grandmother's at Easter?

C: Uhmmmm . . .

A: Did y'all go to church?

C: We went to church. And my mama went, went to work.

A: She did? She had to work?

C: Uh huh. But everyday we haf to go ovah Co' Madabee's. I *hate* dat.

A: You have to go where?

C: Ovah Co' Madabee's. She keeps ma ... she keeps ma brothah and ma sistah when I don' have ta go ta school. And when I have to go ta school, she don't keep me, but when I don't ... when I when I have to ... when I when I don' have to go ta school, den she have to keep me too. So I don' like huh.

A: How come?

C: Because she won' let us bring our bikes over dere n' ride.

A: Oh.

C: So all we has to do is jes' sit aroun' and *wait* and *wait* and *wait*; den when we get home we play wid our Play-doh, go boomp (demonstrates). I'm gonna bring my Play-doh if it's all right wid you.

A: You're gonna bring your Play-doh to school?

C: Uh huh.

A: Well, you'd have to ask Ms. ——— first, probably.

C: OK.

C: Now, I I killed two hairy worms, dat makes six all together. My sistah say "Ahhhhh". And den he, and den he got crawlin', I went ... I was walkin' over dere and he go POW, and I stepped on it.

A: Oh, wow, was he ...?

C: He was a-ah, honey we yelled and that juice went sliiiiidin' all out.

A: Yuk!! Oooh!

C: It was a green caterpillah but he look like a hairy worm but he didn't have no hair up on him. And den I, I put it in a in a cup and I kep' it. It was on a flower at firs' and I got it off, my cousin picked it up and we kep' on playin' wid it and den I wan I wanted ta bring it ta schoo' but it die and we went ashes ta ashes an' dus' ta dus'.

Again the familiar dialect features are here: the deleted final consonants, the basic verb used for third person singular ("My sistah say"), the multiple negative ("He didn' have no hair up on him"). But do we hear anything of language deficit? Quite the opposite! We hear a rule-governed expression of linguistic structure, but more than that, we hear an incredibly effective language user. This "woman of words" performs with extreme skill—persuasive, descriptive, expressive, entertaining, and with a real flair for literary closure. Using language is a well developed art for this child.

What about cultural deficit? Do we find any support for that? Again the answer is a resounding *no*. The child's daily life is filled with a group of caring people to interact with—parents, siblings, cousins, grandmother, adult sitter, teacher, university tutor. Is there "cultural deficit" in the daily experiences of picking dewberries and plums with one's family at grandmaw's house, in going to church, in riding bikes, in playing with Play-doh, in collecting caterpillars? Who could question this as a rich experiential base for the child's cognitive growth?

But what about cognitive deficiency? After all, the child is having "difficulty" with reading and we often connect the two. (How often have you heard teachers make comments like these: "She's very bright. Only in second grade and reads on a fourth grade level" or "She's kind of slow—in second grade and only in the first preprimer.") I hear no cognitive deficit in this conversation. I hear, rather, a child who is eager and curious, is impatient when her exploratory activities are curtailed, collects and examines specimens, solves problems (what to do with a dead caterpillar). All this going for her—remarkable language skill, rich experiential background, curious and active intelligence—and yet low achievement in the matter of relating language meanings to printed symbols. We can only raise some questions here as to why.

1. Has this child's language found a welcome place in school? Has it been regarded as a valid expression system—not corrected but responded to with interest?
2. Did her own experience encoded in her own language expression serve as an important base for her reading, or was she early subjected to printed symbols encoding what in terms of her experience was meaninglessness?
3. Has she been comfortable and proud in her school experience? Have her nonmainstream behaviors been understood and accepted on their own terms? Has she been able to make a worthwhile contribution in this place?
4. Has her background been viewed and used as a valid base for continuing intellectual and social growth?
5. Has her lively curiosity and its expression been provided for?
6. Have her teachers understood "where she was coming from" and what she was "trying to do" so that they could "respond to what [this] child [was] trying to do"?

I don't know the answers to these questions in the case of this child; we can only ask and wonder.

Chapter 15

Different Languages, Teachers, and Children

"Why, Huck doan' de French people talk de same way we does?"

"No, Jim, you couldn't understand a word they said—not a single word—"

"Well, now, I be ding-busted! How do dat come?"

"I don't know, but it's so. I got some of their jabber out of a book. S'pose a man was to come to you and say Polly-voo-franzy. What would you think?"

"I wouldn't think nuffin, I'd take en bust him over de head—dat is, if he warn't white. . . ."

"Shucks, it ain't calling you anything. It's only saying, do you know how to talk French?"

"Well, den, why couldn't he say it?"

"Why he *is* a-saying it. That's a Frenchman's *way* of saying it."

"Well, it's a blame ridicklous way, en I doan' want to hear no mo' bout it. Dey ain't no sense in it." (Twain, *Huckleberry Finn*)

INTRODUCTION

Sometimes linguists define different languages as "mutually unintelligible" systems; Huck expresses this idea more simply; if you "couldn't understand a word they said—not a single word—" you would know that you and "they" were speakers of different languages.

We laugh at Jim's naivete in the above conversation, and yet we know that a great deal of naivete abounds among more "sophisticated" folks than Jim where different languages are concerned. Have you ever heard someone say that a certain language is "more expressive" or "more poetic" or "more difficult" or "more analytical" or "more abstract" than some other? Think a minute. Languages are simply expressive systems for their speakers to use to communicate in. The language—every language—does whatever its speakers want it to. Every language serves poetic, analytical, social, and cognitive purposes because its speakers are poetic, analytical, social, cognitive beings. If some languages were in fact more difficult than others, how could we explain the fact that children acquire different first languages by about the same age? It is true that there is considerable individual variation in rate of acquisition from child to child, but the variation is *not* from language to language; Chinese-speaking children do not as a group take longer to learn Chinese than German-speaking children take to learn German, nor do Swahili speakers take longer to learn Swahili than Portuguese speakers take to learn Portuguese. As with different dialects, so with different languages: Each is a rule-governed system for relating sounds and meanings and serves adequately all the purposes its speakers put it to. No language is inherently more difficult, or more logical, or superior, or inferior to any other. However, as in the case of dialect differences, in a society in which several languages are spoken and the speakers of the one exercise less control in that society (if they are poor, hold fewer political positions, hold fewer prestigious jobs), that language and its speakers may be stigmatized and regarded as less "good." Understand, this has nothing to do with the language, but rather with the misguided attitudes of people toward that language. French is a fully intact language system. Parisians know this, but people in Montreal, Quebec or areas of Maine may regard French and French speakers in their area as "inferior," because as a group they are socially less powerful in that region. And so it is with many languages our school children and their families speak. Spanish may be regarded one way in Spain, Mexico, or Puerto Rico, but a different way in New York, Texas, or California. Tagalog may be regarded differently in the Philippines and in Portland, Oregon, and Japanese regarded differently in Japan and on the California coast. These differences do not have to do with the language in question, but with deep-rooted and often unconscious attitudes toward the people who speak them.

As our classrooms become socially, ethnically, and racially more diverse, many more of us as teachers have opportunities to work with children speaking different dialects of English. But some of us even have the opportunity to work with children who speak different languages as well. For those fortunate teachers, the possibility exists for their children's language range to expand to include not only stylistic and dialectal variation, but to include more than one language as well.

Traditionally, American public schools have fostered the melting pot approach, mentioned in the last chapter. Nowhere has this been more evident than in the school's concern that all children who enter school with a home language other than English learn to read and write in English. Traditionally, English has been the sole medium of instruction for all school children, regardless of whether they were monolingual speakers of Navajo, Spanish, German, Swedish, or Chinese. Nowhere has the move toward salad bowl thinking become more evident, perhaps, than in the more recent state and federally legislated dictates that children whose dominant language is not English shall receive instruction in their own language as well as expanding their range to include English. But there is a great gap between the federal voice saying "Children who come to school dominant in a language other than English shall receive instruction in both their home language and in English," and educators actually devising and implementing bilingual programs in our schools. Currently there are more questions than answers regarding bilingual education, and the various programs that call themselves "bilingual" reflect these questions: How shall we identify the child who is monolingual in language X or dominant in language X? How much instruction should be given in each language? Should the amount of instruction be the same in each of the languages or should there be more of one than the other? Should the amounts change as the child moves to a higher grade? How? Or should some subjects be taught entirely in one language and other subjects entirely in another? Should children learn to read and write in their home language or just learn to read and write in English? How shall the parents' desires be taken into account? What do we do with children whose parents do not want their children to be instructed in the home language? What can we do to assure that, in this society in which English is the dominant and prestigious language, children will acquire English *in addition to* their home language, rather than *in place of* it; how can we assure that the children not lose their home language?

In this chapter we will focus on two distinct views of (1) the second language learning *task* (what does second language learning involve?); (2) the second language *learner* (what does the learner bring to the task and how does he use it?), and (3) the role of the second language *environment* (what can the environment contribute to second language learning?). Then we will reconsider these two distinct views of the second language learning task, learner, and environment in light of some important recent research. And finally we'll consider some classroom implications for second language learning suggested by that recent research.

TWO VIEWS

Below are two episodes involving a teacher and several children. These episodes are vastly different, yet both purport to help second grade Spanish-dominant children acquire English as their second language. It seems incredible that two such diametrically opposed approaches can be thought to serve the same ultimate goal. The two approaches are based on different assumptions about the three basic ingredients: the task, the learner, and the environment. Study the two episodes carefully and, if possible, discuss your observations with several other students. You will probably want to begin by simply identifying (listing? describing?) the differences between the two episodes. Then try to characterize the underlying assumptions each approach reflects about (1) the nature of the task (what is involved in acquiring a second language? what is it that the learner has to learn?); (2) the nature of the learner and the learner's abilities (what abilities does the learner bring to the second language learning task? how does the learner use these abilities?), (3) the nature of an environment conducive to the child's learning (what kind of situations should we try to provide that will aid the learner in acquiring the second language?).

EPISODE 1

(Two children are saying a poem.)

T: Are they saying words, class?

C (Class): Yes, they are saying words.

T: Now, ask me, "Are they saying words?"

C: Are they saying words?

T: Yes, they are saying words.

T: Aren't they saying words?

C: Yes, they are saying words.

T: Group 1 ask Group 2, "Aren't they saying words?"

G: Aren't they saying words?

G: Yes, they are saying words.

T: Is language made of words, class?

C: Yes, language is made or [sic] words.

T: Isn't.

G: Isn't language made of words?

G: Yes, language is made of words.

T: Is language made of sounds, class?

C: Yes, language is made of sounds.

T: Isn't. (Pointing at Group 1)

G: Isn't language made of sounds? (Looking at Group 2)

G Yes, language is made of sounds.

(Drill continues through "sentences," "ideas," "rules," "meaning.") (Southwest Educational Development Laboratory, *Oral Language,* Book 3, pp. 53–54)

T: I tasted the lemon. Passive.

C: The lemon was tasted by me.

T: She tasted the candy. Passive.

C: The candy was tasted by her.

T: I heard the bells. Passive.

C: The bells were heard by me.

T: The boys touched the horse. Passive.

C: The horse was touched by the boys.

T: The cat smelled the fish. Passive.

C: The fish was smelled by the cat. (Southwest Educational Development Laboratory, *Oral Language,* Book 2, pp. 39–40)

T: Class, ask [Juan/Maria], "How do you feel?"

C: How do you feel?

P: (individual pupil): I feel [fine/good/well].

T: Class, ask [him/her] "Are you happy?"

C: Are you happy?

P: Yes, I am.

T: Ask [him/her], "Do you need to lie down?"

C: Do you need to lie down?

P: No, I don't need to lie down.

T: Ask [him/her], "Do you need food?"

C: Do you need food?

P: No, I don't need food.

T: Class, ask [him/her], "What do you need?"

C: What do you need?

P: I don't need anything.

C: How do you feel?

P: I feel [fine/good/well].

C: Are you happy?

P: Yes, I am.

C: Do you need to see the nurse?

P: No, I don't need to see the nurse.

C: What do you need?

P: I don't need anything.

C: How do you feel?

P: I feel [find/good/well].

C: Are you happy?

P: Yes, I am.

C: Do you need to get warm?

P: No, I don't need to get warm.

C: Do you need to go to sleep?

P: No, I don't need to go to sleep.

C: What do you need?

P: I don't need anything (Southwest Educational Development Laboratory, *Oral Language,* Book 1, pp. 77–78).

EPISODE 2[1]

(The children and teacher are looking at a film strip of *Put Me in the Zoo* and discussing the pictures.)

C-1: The dog is walking. The dog is going to the zoom.

C-2: No. It is *zoo, zoo* not zoom.

C-1: Zoo.

T: Right. The dog is going into the zoo. Why is he going into the zoo, C-2?

C-2: To see the animals.

Cs: Animal.

T: Very good, C-2.

T: What are the men doing here?

C-1, C-4: Cut the hair.

T: The man is cutting the hair.

T: What is the dog doing now?

C-5: He is looking. Laughing.

C-3: He is laughing and looking at something.

T: What do you think that something is?

C-3: A lion.

T: Good thought. True. What is the other man in the back doing?

C-2: Eating the fish to the . . .

Cs: Giving the fish to the. . . . Feeding the fish to the . . .

T: Seal.

Cs: Seal. (Relieved to know the word in order to finish the sentence.)

T: Giving the fish to the seal. Feeding the fish to the seal.

C-1: The men . . . no . . . the zoo men . . . see the dog.

[1] I am grateful to Michelle Hewlett-Gomez for this episode

T: Why are they looking at the dog?

C-4: (Answers in Spanish and asks for translation.)

T: Because he is sticking out his tongue.

C-4: Because he is sticking out his tongue.

C-2: (Says his idea in Spanish and asks for translation.)

T: Yes, because he is not supposed to be there. Very good, C-2.

C-3: Because the dog don't belong there.

T: Right, because the dog doesn't belong there. What is that thing there?

C-1: The girl and the boy is look at the dog.

C-6: And the man . . . the two man . . .

C-4: . . . is looking the dog.

C-1: And the boy and the girl is eat popcorn.

T: Yes, the boy and girl are looking at the dog. The boy and the girl are eating popcorn.

T: Why is the dog sad?

C-4: Because he out the zoo.

T: Because he is out of the zoo. Very good thinking, C-4. What about here?

C-3: The dog is very happy because he have blue circles. Blue light.

T: Light blue circles. Right. Blue circles.

C-1: Falling down the popcorn.

C-3: Come falling down the popcorn.

C-4: Come down the popcorn.

T: Yes, the popcorn is falling out of the box. They turned the box upside down.

T: What's happening here?

C-5: Blue circles.

C-2: No, purple circles.

T: Right, they are purple circles. C-4, tell us . . .

C-4: The dog have circle red.

C-5: Purple circles.

C-2: The dog has red circles, green circles, purple circles, and blue circles.

C-3: The dog has light blue circles. And the boy and the girl is happy. And the dog is happy. The dog have all the colors . . . all kinds of colors.

C-1: The dog has just a . . . (asks for translation of Spanish *poco*) . . . few circles . . . The dog has few circles.

T: Yes, the dog does have a few red circles. He does not have a lot like he did before.

C-4: The girl have circle red. The boy have circle red. The shirt . . . the hair . . . the hair . . . the dress . . . the box . . . has red circles.

T: Very good. They all have red circles.

C-5: The tree have circle red.

Cs: Red circles.

T: Right. The tree has red circles.

C-1: The girl and the boy don't have red circles. The tree don't have too red circles.

T: Nothing has red circles. Good.

T: What happened here?

C-3: The dog is playing with little circles red.

T: Little red circles, right.

C-3: Red circles little.

C-1: Little circles red. Little red circles.

C-2: Little red circles.

T: Yes. Little tiny red circles.

Views of the Task

Underlying the first sample above (exemplifying what is often called the "audiolingual" method) is the assumption that the learner's major task is to make the structures of the second language matters of unconscious, automatic habits; the major focus is on mastery of utterance form. In contrast, underlying the second sample is the assumption that the goal is communicative competence; that the learner be able and want to communicate with speakers of the second language. Remember that linguistic competence, the acquisition of linguistic structure, can be regarded as one component of communicative competence. In order to be understood in a language, one must eventually select and organize language elements in the ways that speakers of that language do it.

Advocates of the first approach would probably say that the communication goal is important but that the child can't use the language in communication until he *has* the language, that is until he controls its structure. Once he has mastered this, he will use it in communication situations. Advocates of the second approach feel that, as with first language acquisition, such separation of structure and use is impossible; all language for the first language learner is "contextualized"; that is, it is language used in a communication context. They feel that that is the nature of the system the second language learner must acquire also.

It's easy to identify items in the first sample which demonstrate the assumption that acquisition of structure is the learner's primary task. The drills are designed to make language structures maximally obvious to the learner (Are they verb-ing X? Yes, they are verb-ing X. Aren't they verb-ing X? or Is X made of Y? Yes, X is made of Y. Isn't X made of Y?). It does not matter that the sentences themselves are communicatively empty or absurd. "The bell was heard by me" is not only a sentence that no native English speaker *has* ever said in a natural situation; it is a sentence that no native English speaker *would* say, for the passive construction simply would not be used in a situation where one heard a bell ring and later related that information. However, the sentence serves to demonstrate the structural relation between active and passive sentences, and this is what is considered most important. In a real conversation, on finding out that you were feeling fine, I would not proceed to ask questions intended to discover your nonexistent problem and help you solve it (do you need to lie down/see the nurse/ get warm/go to sleep). But the drill provides controlled practice of specific structures and is therefore considered helpful.

Also underlying the first approach is a strong belief that acquiring a language is acquiring a set of habits which become more firmly entrenched through practice. It is assumed that the second language learner has already mastered a set of first language habits (semantic, syntactic, phonological) and that where these differ from the patterns of the second language, they will interfere with the learning of the second language. The learner will tend to impose the habits of his first language on the patterns of the second. Therefore, a major job for the second language learner is to practice the patterns of the second language, especially those which are different from the first, so that second language habits will become automatic. In contrast, the second approach above sees the learner's task as a more cognitive one, namely, to discern the underlying regularities (both structural and social) of the second language as it is used around and (especially) with him in interaction.

In summary, the first approach assumes the learner's task is to make the structural patterns (especially syntactic) of the second language automatic habits, and then he will be able to use them in talking with people who speak the second language. The second approach assumes the learner's task is to learn how the new language is used by its speakers, and that he will learn the structure as well as the communicative appropriateness of utterances together in interactive contexts.

Views of the Learner

Advocates of both approaches above acknowledge that the language learner already basically controls one language. But whereas advocates of the second approach see this as an advantage in some important ways, advocates of the first approach see this as being largely a disadvantage. The purported disadvantage is that the learner has well-entrenched language habits that will interfere with establishing new habits appropriate in the second language. Encountering a new linguistic form in the second language, the learner is likely to impose the nearest equivalent from the first language. For example, in Spanish the adjective follows the noun it modifies rather than preceding it as is generally the case in English. Thus the Spanish speaker learning English is likely to talk of the "circle purple" rather than of the "purple circle," making the second language structure conform to the first. The Spanish speaker's "I have hunger" might occur as a direct translation from first language to second.

The advantages that the proponents of the second approach see in the fact that the learner has already acquired one language are (1) that he does not need to develop basic concepts and understandings about the world as he did in learning the first language—he already has these and mainly needs to develop a new expression system (which of course includes some reorganization of semantic domains), and (2) that he has had solid experience in using cognitive processes well suited for language learning (as evidenced by the fact that he has successfully learned one language) and these same well-developed cognitive processes are basic to the acquisition of an additional language. While the first approach focuses on children's previous practice of particular forms (semantic, syntactic, phonological) specific to that language, the second approach focuses on children's process "practice" (engaging in), their "practice" in using cognitive processes basic to the learning of any language. Thus the first view sees well-practiced *specific content*—forms and patterns—interfering with the mastery of new specific forms and patterns, while the second view sees the development of more *general processes* of language learning as aiding further language learning.

Proponents of the first approach see the learner as one who must practice new forms required by the new language. The more practice he has in using new forms correctly, the more firmly they will be entrenched and the more likely he will be to continue to use these correct forms. Thus a great deal of practice in error-free responding will be the learner's major occupation. Group response increases the number of times the learner gets to practice saying particular forms exemplifying new language patterns. Reinforcement for the second language forms he uses will help to establish the new language habits. (You can probably see the behaviorist orientation here.)

Proponents of the second approach see it as the learner's job to engage in interaction which will provide natural language samples for the child to exercise his language-figuring-out abilities on. The "reinforcement" the child receives will be responses to the meanings he conveys, not to the forms he uses. As he did when he acquired his first language, he will make hypotheses about how the new language operates, and will test and revise these in interactive contexts.

In summary then, according to proponents of the first approach, what the learner *brings* to the second language learning task is a set of first language habits and forms which will in many instances interfere with the habits and forms the second language requires; what the learner *does* is intensely practice the new language forms until they become unconscious, habitual ways of responding. According to proponents of the second approach, what the learner *brings* to the second language learning task is a well-developed conceptual base and a set of well-developed cognitive processes for figuring out how a language works; what the learner *does* is interact with speakers of the new language and make, test, and revise hypotheses about how their language is structured and how it is used.

Views of the Environment

Each approach above is a different way of providing a situation intended to help the learners (as they are characterized) to accomplish the task (as it is characterized). Different views of the learners and their task result in different approaches to helping them accomplish that task. Thus, those favoring the first approach provide an environmental situation in which the children's attention is carefully directed to the patterns of the new language, which provides large amounts of practice in error-free responding, which corrects—immediately—all errors of form. Structured drill becomes a major activity; the "audiolingual" approach is to listen to a pattern ("audio") and say it and others like it ("lingual"). Those favoring the second approach provide an environmental situation in which the children are immersed in interactive experiences which involve diverse forms embedded in diverse communicative contexts, and in which the children are responded to and interacted with according to the meanings they are conveying (rather than on the basis of the correctness of the forms they are using). Conversation with the children about things they are doing and are interested in becomes a major activity.

Two Views: A Pulling Together

The two contrasting views discussed here are sometimes called the *interference* view and the *creative construction* view. The interference view and its well-developed audiolingual methodology has been with us for a long time. It has been basic to adult second language learning programs—for foreign students in American universities or high school students in Commonwealth countries (Kenya, India, Nigeria) learning English as a second language. It has also been basic to high school foreign language programs in the United States in which students learn some French, German, or Spanish as a college entrance requirement, but with little intention of really using that language in communication with native speakers. It also is probably the most prevalent view and methodology encountered in bilingual education programs in American elementary schools today.

The interference view is rooted in observations of errors learners make as they acquire the second language. Many of these errors appear to be the result of learners trying to make the new language structures (semantic, syntactic, phonological) conform to those they already know from their first language. Lacking a particular structure in the second language, learners will use the nearest equivalent from the first language. The audiolingual methodology based on the interference view was a logical outgrowth which took shape and steadily gained prominence during the past several decades when behaviorist approaches to learning were prevalent. Also, a view of learning which identifies (possible) "trouble spots" (points of interference or difference between the first language and the second) and provides ways of either avoiding or remedying them (audiolingual drills) is of course likely to flourish in an educational milieu in which teachers see their job as diagnosing and treating children's problems. The audiolingual method provides ways of diagnosing (potential) problems and treating them. Thus the interference view and its resultant audiolingual methodology took shape and gained ground as the result of a composite of factors including (1) observations of second language learners' errors (especially by adult learners), (2) the prevalence of a compatible behavioristic theory of learning—what learning is (building habits) and how one does it (practice), and (3) the presence of a compatible educational philosophy of diagnose, prescribe, treat.

The creative construction view maintains that children acquire a second language as they do a first, namely, by discerning the underlying rules of language structure and use in the language surrounding them, and continually hypothesizing, testing, and revising in the light of subsequent interaction. They "creatively construct" novel sentences on the basis of the rule system they are building. This view is more recent than the interference view, so recent in fact that it is stretching the point a bit to suggest that it really has a developed methodology. This view has grown out of our observations and insights relating to young children's acquisition of a first language. Whereas the interference view originated from observations of *adult* learners in *second* (and foreign) language situations, the creative construction view originated from observations of *child* learners in *first* language situations. As we came to know more about the sequences and processes of first language acquisition, some researchers began to ask whether the sequence and processes of second language learning by young children might not be similar. Early research has indeed revealed some similarities. Researchers (Dulay and Burt 1974a, b, c; Milon 1974) have identified some general similarities in sequence of acquisition by children learning English as a first language and children learning English as a second language, and also between children from different first language backgrounds (for example, Spanish and Chinese) learning English as a second language. The sequential acquisition of the fourteen grammatical morphemes identified by Brown, and the sequential development of stages in acquisition of negation as identified by Klima and Bellugi-Klima (see chapter 6), have been observed in children learning English as a second language, and some significant similarities have been found. However, sequential differences have also been found. In their excitement at having found significant similarities, researchers have sometimes glossed over the differences. The sequence evidence does not suggest a strong hypothesis that children's acquisition of a second language follows *the same* sequence of stages that children's learning of that language as a first language follows, but it does support a weaker version of the hypothesis, suggesting that there is similarity in the sequence, and that *one* factor operating may be a simpler to more complex sequence inherent in the language itself.

More impressive than the research looking at similarities in sequence of acquisition is the research relating to similarities in the acquisition processes first and second language learning children seem to be using. Here we find some rather compelling similarities between first and second language learning. For example, we find children moving in the second language as they did in the first, from shorter utterances composed of heavy content items toward longer utterances including more "ivy"—inflections, articles, etc. We find the children's longer utterances including elaboration of a term, as is the case with first language learners. We find the familiar overgeneralization—the early regularizing of exceptional forms in the language. We also see overextension of terms so that initially a child's word denoting a category will include members that, for the native adult speaker, would belong to other categories. We see children refine both the overgeneralized syntactic cases and the overextended vocabulary items over time, as is the case with first language learners.

In studying four- to nine-year-old English monolingual children acquiring French as their second language while living in France, Ervin-Tripp (1974) found that

> . . . the functions of early sentences, and their form, their semantic redundancy, their reliance on ease of short term memory, their overgeneralization of lexical forms, their use of simple order strategies all were similar to processes we have seen in first language acquisition. In broad outline then, the conclusion is tenable that first and second language learning is similar in natural situations. (Ervin-Tripp 1974, p. 126)

Also we find that some imitated fixed routine expressions are present at an early stage in both first and second language acquisition, and that over time these expressions become analyzed as rule-governed structures. It seems that, in a natural interactive environment, young second language learners are in some important ways using their language acquisition strategies and processes that served them so well in learning the first language: They are little linguists, discerning and utilizing the underlying principles that relate meanings and their expression and use in this language.

While both views—interference and creative construction—have contributed to the picture of second language learning, each has erred by being oversimplistic and narrowly focused. It is as if the proponents of each view have asked the question "Is second language learning the same as first language learning or is it different from first language learning?" The interference group have answered, "It is basically different," and then have focused their attention on the differences (in language A you say————but in language B you say————). The creative construction group have answered, "It is basically the same," and then have focused their attention almost exclusively on the similarities and ignored some important differences. It is time to recast the question, to take it out of its either-or form, and ask the richer question, "How are first and second language learning similar and how are they different for young children?" Fortunately for us, Lily Wong Fillmore (1976) has done just this in her intensive study of five Spanish monolingual children, five to seven years old, acquiring English as their second language. Since this is the most thorough and insightful study to date on non-English-speaking school children's acquisition of English as their second language, I will rely heavily on her findings in the remainder of this chapter.

Each of the five monolingual Spanish children in the study was paired with an English speaking friend.[2] The five pairs of children were in a bilingual school in which half of their instruction was given in Spanish and half in English, with Spanish-dominant and English-dominant children in classrooms together. There was no explicit instruction in either language as a second language; both languages were used as mediums of instruction for all the children. Fillmore followed the Spanish monolingual children's development of English during the course of one school year. One type of data in her study was the children's performance on a structured sentence-producing task administered at regular intervals during the year (giving each child a model sentence for a pictured action and then requiring the child to describe the remaining pictured actions). These data yielded very little information about how the children were going about the job of acquiring the second language, and also very little about their level of progress—how much they had acquired and how adept they were at functioning in the new language. But the second type of data yielded an abundance of rich information about how the individual children were proceeding with their learning of English. The second and major type of data consisted of tape recordings and accompanying observational records of weekly sessions for each Spanish/English pair of friends in a well-equipped playroom. Only the observer and the two children were present in the room for each weekly play session.

[2]The one exception here was a child whose partner was bilingual.

The Task Reconsidered

What is it that second language learners must learn? They have to

> ... figure out how the sound system of the new language is organized, how units of meaning are organized into words, by what principles these words are put together to form sentences, how these sentences can be used appropriately in given settings, and in what ways meanings can be conveyed in the new language and culture. (Fillmore 1976, p. 634)

This sounds remarkably similar to the first language learner's task, namely, to develop communicative competence—the ability to use and interpret well-structured sentences appropriately in various social settings. It also sounds like an enormous task: In Fillmore's words "The [second language] learner has everything to learn ..." (p. 634). But does he? There are some aspects of the first language learner's task that the second language learner's task does *not* include.

Second language learners must learn how to express meanings and how to interpret the expressions of others, but they don't have to develop those basic meanings in the first place as first language learners do. Their task, unlike the first language learners', does not include prerequisite maturational development, development of perceptual control, or muscular control. They already possess the ability to sort out, remember, and produce signals. In short, though their task is an enormous one, they already have the prerequisite understandings and mechanisms to begin cracking the new code; they don't have to develop these as first language learners do.

The Learner Reconsidered

Let's start with Fillmore's conclusion: " ... the process of second language acquisition is not completely different from first language acquisition, but they are not entirely alike either" (p. 51).

First of all, what does the second language learner *bring* to his task? As mentioned already, he brings increased experience and understanding, including knowledge of a first language. Learning the second language

> ... is facilitated in some ways by the added age and experience in the case of the second language learner, and possibly inhibited in some ways by his knowledge of a first language. Prior knowledge of a first language may predispose the learner to look for familiar ways of expressing in the new language meanings he

is accustomed to expressing in his first language. He will be inclined to make the kinds of distinctions in the new language—perhaps inappropriately—that were relevant in his first. (Fillmore 1976, p.55)

The learner also brings certain attitudes toward the second language and its speakers as well as toward his own language and culture. These attitudes are an important factor in the child's success in learning the second language. The learner who is positively predisposed toward the second language and culture is more motivated to become like its speakers, and is likely to experience greater success in second language acquisition than is the learner who has negative feelings about the second language, its speakers, and their culture.[3] Also, the learner who feels strongly positive toward speakers of the second language is more likely to actively seek interaction with them, and this interaction is the basic "stuff" of his second language learning. Notice that there is an important difference here between the first and second language situation. It doesn't make much sense to talk about the first language learner's "attitude" toward the first language and its speakers. The young child becomes more of a participating member of his community as he acquires language. There is not the posibility of deciding whether or not he chooses to identify with this group. It is his only group. He simply develops as a more social human being, with increased social skills, one of which is language. To be able to interact and to be like *the* group (his only group) is to speak its language. But the second language learner already belongs to a social group, is a fully participating member of it including speaking its language. Only at this point at which the child has an awareness of different social/language groups does it make sense to talk about his having positive or negative attitudes toward them.

The second language learner brings to this learning task (as to others) certain individual characteristic learning preferences or styles. One is reminded here of Nelson's one- to two-year-old first language learners, some of whom preferred an observational or comprehension strategy, others a productive strategy, still others a questioning strategy. In Fillmore's study the five subjects demonstrated wide variation in their approaches to the learning. At one end of the continuum was a subject who produced almost no English for the first six weeks of the study and then suddenly began to speak in English a lot and to do so with considerable skill, demonstrating that he had been actively noticing and remembering all along in his own way. At the other end of the continuum was five-year-old Nora who appears to have talked her way nonstop in English from the first moment of the study to the last.

Closely related to learning preference or style (for example, to observe, to produce), and perhaps inseparable from it, is one's own personality, one's ways of relating to others socially. Fillmore's study demonstrated that this has

---

[3]For further study relating to attitude and its relation to second language learning see Gardner and Lambert (1972).

special significance for second language learning in that individual children's abilities and inclinations to interact with English-speaking children, largely determined how much interaction, and therefore how much language data, the learners were getting. For young children acquiring their first language, this personality factor seems less important. Others will interact with them no matter what they do. Not so for second language learners. They must have the skill and desire to initiate and maintain interactions with second language speakers in order to get the language samples they need. They must be socially effective and active in their own learning.

In summary, second language learners bring to the learning task increased age and experience, certain attitudes toward their own and toward the target language and culture, their own preferred learning style, and their own unique personality.

What does the second language learner *do* in accomplishing his task? Fillmore identified three stages in second language acquisition (overlapping and not clearly demarked, of course) which seemed to motivate and guide the learners' strategies. The three stages are perhaps best characterized as evolving concerns of the learner. Briefly, the learner's earliest concern (first stage) was to establish social relationships with speakers of the second language; his next concern (second stage) was to communicate content, messages to second language speakers; and the final concern (third stage) was to be correct in speaking the second language. In the first stage, when the learner was intent on establishing social relations, he would often engage in activities with second language speakers that were more "interactional" than "informational" (p. 659), relying heavily on fixed verbal formulas (such as "You know what?" "Guess what!" "You know what dese doing?" "Shaddup your mouth," "Oh goody," "This is mine," "Stupid"). The learner in this stage also relied on nonverbal communication, and on learning key words—labels—that would be useful in the interaction situations of the immediate environment. In the second stage, when the learner became more concerned about communicating messages, he began to create more novel sentences, moving away from socially useful intact formulas toward new combinations including parts of those formulas and some acquired lexical items. During this stage there was more mixing of languages; the child seemed intent on getting his message across using whatever means he had. It was in the third stage that the learner worked on the finer points of correct form—the incorporation of grammatical devices and refinements that made his speech more "native-like."

This suggested sequence is an interesting one and feels familiar from first language acquisition. The learner's initial thrust toward relating socially recalls Bruner's and Snow's studies of mother-infant interaction. That prelinguistic interaction might well be characterized as "more interactional than informational." However, in the early mother-infant interaction, the concern for establishing a social relationship seems to be more the mother's than the learner's. With Fillmore's subjects, the concern was primarily the learner's.

It is possible that Fillmore's second stage, a concern for communicating in whatever ways one is able, is an apt description of a next stage for the first language learner also. Think back to children's one-word and early combinatory speech. It is clear that children's utterances *do* communicate, and it is reasonable to suppose children mean for them to. As in the case of Fillmore's subjects, we also see first language children making the most of whatever limited linguistic means they have. And, certainly, first language learners' speech becomes "more correct" over time; from initial utterances composed of rudimentary content items in short combinations, children move toward the incorporation of refinements, grammatical niceties and complexities. It is certainly a move toward correctness in speaking the first language.

Fillmore's three stages—establish social relations, communicate, be correct—go a long way toward accounting for her subjects' sequence of linguistic strategies. The learners initially built up an extensive repertoire of formulas, "language which functioned wholly or partly as unanalyzed, fixed or automatic units for the speaker" (p. 295). Remember, the first concern was to establish social relations. How better to do this than by being able to provide the right expression in the right social context: "Can I have one of these?" "I wanna do it," "And one for me and one for you." "Can I be the X?" "Ready, (get) set, go." These formulas served an important early social function. Gradually the learners began to analyze (unconsciously) the elements of the formulas and elements began to be freed from the intact formula. Though the formulas remained intact in those social situations in which they were appropriate as formulas, elements of the formulas began to occur elsewhere in the children's speech. Various combinations of elements became possible, thus enhancing the children's communication, their major concern of the second stage. Eventually the children's speech became "productive"—they produced sentences created by a rule system governing elements and their combinations. Fillmore describes this move from formulaic to productive speech:

> ... phrase-sized units which function as formulas for the learner are indeed among the first things learned in the new language, and it is through the analyses of these units that the learner eventually figures out the form and meaning of the component parts. What the learner derives from the analysis of formulas already in his own speech repertory are grammatical rules, and these rules, which form the bases for productive speech, gradually free him from his early dependence on formulaic speech. (p. 300)

First language research has maintained that children's earliest language is primarily productive, that is, rule governed. Though fixed imitated expressions occur, first language research has suggested that these play an insignificant role in children's acquisition of linguistic structure. It may be that Fillmore's work showing early formulaic expression to be of crucial importance to the second language learner will encourage a reexamination of the role of formulas in first language acquisition. As for now, we can be sure that they play a significant role in second language learning for young children.

Fillmore characterizes a set of five cognitive strategies and a set of three social strategies that her second language learners seemed to be using. She deliberately states them as operating principles similar to Slobin's operating principles for first language learners (see chapter 7). Here are the cognitive strategies she identifies.

1. *Assume that what people are saying is directly relevant to the situation at hand, or to what they or you are experiencing. Metastrategy: guess* (p. 634). The children in this study had ample opportunity to use this strategy in their classroom experience and they did. In the children's classrooms, the teachers followed a predictable daily routine and the language of this routine was predictable also—signaling the end of one activity or the initiation of another, giving directions or suggestions, etc. The children were able to relate the predictable language to the predictable situation, and "Because they paid attention to contextual cues, the children were able to function as if they understood what was going on in the classroom long before they understood the language used in it" (p. 637). One important factor enabling these children to make maximum use of this language-situation relating strategy was that they were active participants in the language-full situations rather than mere observers of the situations:

> . . . they were centrally involved in the activities in which the language was used, rather than merely observing others using it . . . (p. 638). Being a participant in the situations in which language is used is essential, since it gives the learner a better chance of knowing what the social situation is than if he were only an observer. (p. 639)

2. *Get some expressions you understand, and start talking* (p. 639). The early and extensive use of formulaic expressions discussed above was common to all five children in Fillmore's study. She maintains that this strategy of acquiring speech formulas was crucial in the children's acquisition of the second language, for (a) these formulas enabled the children to start speaking —interacting verbally with others—before they knew how the language was structured, and thus they were able to get "data" from the speakers of the second language; and (b) these formulas were the basic language data on which the children's linguistic analyses were eventually performed.

3. *Look for recurring parts in the formulas you know* (p. 644). The children in this study, remember, gradually freed "recurring parts" (elements, constituents) from the original intact formulas. Here is an example of one

child's (Nora's) gradual "freeing" of "how" from her original formula "How do you do dese?" (based on pp. 647-48). At first Nora used this question often but always and only in this fixed form. After awhile she began to add elements to this fixed frame:

	little tortillas?
How do you do dese	in English?
	September por mañana?

Then the part of her sentences following "you" began to show variation from the original fixed "do dese," yielding sentences like

	like to be a cookie cutter?
How do you	make the flower?
	gonna make these?

or sentences with "did" instead of "do"

	lost it?
How did you	make it?

Then she began to vary her sentences after the do/did/does, with the "you" no longer necessary in the developing frame.

How did	dese work?
How do	cut it?
How does	this color is?

And finally Nora freed "how" from the original formula, using it in sentences like

Because when I call him, how I put the number?
How you make it?
How will take off paste?

Though these last sentences may sound no more native-like than Nora's original formula "How do you do dese," you can see that they represent a tremendous advance in her figuring out the structure of the new language and how to use it flexibly to convey her own meanings.

4. *Make the most of what you've got* (p. 649). Evidence for the children's use of this strategy comes from their semantic overextensions (use of "sangwish" to refer to all food, "no good" extended to mean "dead," and "gotcha" extended to mean "kill") as well as their overuse of acquired expressions which

they would sprinkle about generously in their conversations whether they were appropriate or not ("if we want" or "already" got attached to many sentences where they helped make the child sound fluent, but were semantically empty). One child's "Wha' happen?" and "Wha'sa matter?" served to ask all questions he had in mind.

> . . . the children managed to get by with as little English as they did because they made the greatest use of what they had learned—and in the early part of the acquisition period, what they had learned was largely formulaic. (p. 654)

5. *Work on big things; save the details for later* (p. 655). Details like auxiliary elements and verb inflections came later in the children's productive speech (that is, analyzed language produced by rule rather than unanalyzed formulaic expression). Their earlier productive (analyzed) speech relied heavily on basic verb forms and word order. By the end of the period of this study, only one of the children had reached the point of sorting out the various English verb inflections, but it was clear the others were moving in that direction.

Some of these cognitive strategies seem to operate for first language learners as well as for second language learners. As we saw earlier, in acquiring a first language, children rely heavily on deriving language meaning from situational context and are very active participants in the situation. Like Fillmore's subjects, first language learners assume that the language and the situation in which it occurs are directly related (first cognitive strategy). Fillmore's third cognitive strategy ("Look for recurring parts in the formulas you know.") seems relevant to first language acquisition too, though perhaps with some modification. First language learners certainly seem tuned in to recurrent items in the speech others use around and with them. It is hard to think where children's early "key," "car," "clock," would come from if not as noticed separable (recurrent) elements of verbal strings they hear. But whereas Fillmore suggests that for second language learners these recurrent parts are in the formulas they "know" (that they use in interaction), for first language learners these may be more from the speech of others and from sensorimotor activity than from their own limited verbal repertoire.

Fillmore's fourth and fifth cognitive strategies we have also seen clearly in first language acquisition: "Make the most of what you've got" and "Work on big things; save the details for later." It is precisely because first language acquirers are making the most of their limited linguistic devices that intriguing sentences occur like "Everything is not to break, just plates and cups." And children's early work on big things and later work on refinements is apparent in many aspects of their generally predictable acquisition sequence: moving from sentences composed of heavy content items only to sentences which incorporate articles and prepositions; moving from uninflected to inflected noun and verb forms; moving from overgeneralized syntactic forms to adult-like exceptional forms.

It is the second cognitive strategy ("Get some expressions you understand, and start talking") that is harder to relate to first language acquisition for two reasons. First, many first language learners are not early talkers. They do not use an early "productive strategy" (Nelson 1973), yet their language acquisition does not appear to be less adequate than that of more talkative children. "Start talking" seems to be a more important strategy for second language learners for social reasons, than for first language learners who are interacted with verbally whether they talk a lot or not. Second, this strategy rests on second language learners' heavy reliance on formulas initially. First language acquisition research to date has minimized the importance of unanalyzed formulas for first language learners' acquisition of linguistic structure (the aspect of language acquisition most studied). It may be that subsequent research will show early formulas to play a more important role for first language learners socially and cognitively than has been demonstrated so far. However, at this time the indications are that they have special importance for second language learners.

Fillmore suggests three social strategies used by her second language learners. You can see how closely they relate to and provide motivation for the cognitive strategies:

1. *Join a group and act as if you understand what's going on, even if you don't* (p. 667).

2. *Give the impression—with a few well-chosen words—that you can speak the language* (p. 669).

3. *Count on your friends for help* (p. 688).

And here is where the major difference apparently occurs between what first language learners must do to learn the language, and what second language learners must do. Second language learners bear a major responsibility for initiating and maintaining social interaction with those who speak the second language. It is this interacting that will enable them to learn the language. Yet without having skill in the language already, they seem to be in an extremely difficult position for assuring this necessary interaction.

In contrast, think of first language learners. Mother and other caring adults bend over backwards in every conceivable way to provide and sustain interaction: taking both roles in a conversation when the child does not respond; interpreting inappropriate or nonexistent responses as present and communicatively acceptable; interpreting incomprehensible verbal responses as comprehensible, random noise making as semantically meaningful speech, and nonverbal responses as explicit verbal ones. Mother does everything possible to assure conversation-ness even when the child (as an infant) is very limited as a conversational partner.

But second language learners, though they too are limited as "conversational partners" must be social activists. Thus these social strategies have special significance for them. The first strategy is important because, in order to be included in the conversations of the speakers of the second language, those speakers have to believe that the learners understand them. The speakers will believe this if the learners do appropriately what the others in the group do. The children in Fillmore's study watched and copied the second language speakers' actions closely, thus giving the impression that they understood the language of the situations.

In connection with the second social strategy Fillmore says:

> If the desire to join a social group whose language the learner does not speak is the social motivation for using contextual information to figure out what people are saying, then the desire to maintain contact and to sustain social relations with members of the group is the motivation for the acquisition of formulaic speech. (p. 669)

The children's "formulaic speech" comprised the "few well-chosen words" of the second social strategy. In order to continue interaction opportunities, second language learners must convince the group that they speak (as well as understand) the language. And the second language speakers in this study were convinced, frequently commenting that the learner understood English, or getting annoyed with the learner for not saying something in English, assuming that the learner was in fact able to and simply chose not to. By using useful interactional formulas liberally, the language learners were able to be active verbal participants in a variety of social situations and thus get clues to how the language is used appropriately and get feedback relating to the appropriateness of their language use. Fillmore helpfully categorizes these formulas (pp. 672–81) as attention callers (like "Oh Teacher" or "Hey Stupid"); name exchanges (like "What's your name?" or "I'm/She's———."); greetings and leave takings (like "Take care!" "I see you," or "I gotta go"); politeness routines (like "I'm sorry," or "Thanks"); language management (like "I don' understand you," or "I don't speak English," or "How do you do this in English?"); conversation management (like "You know what?" or " . . . , OK?" or "What is it mean?" or "You shaddup"); comments and exclamations (like "Man!" or "Oh crazy!" or "All right, you guys!"); questions (like "Who has the X?" or "Can I have one?" or "You wanna play?"); response to comments or questions (like "I know," or "OK," or "I don't care!" or "uh-huh"); commands and requests or attention callers (like "Lemme see," or "Hey look," or "Knock it off"); presentatives and parallel talk (like "Here it is," or "This go here/there/somewhere else," or "One more"); play management (like "Me first," or "My turn?" or "I'm not playing"); story-telling routines (like "Once upon a time . . . "); explanations (like "Because X," or "Because, that's why"); "wannas" and "wannits" (like "I wanna get these," or "I don' wanna do nothing"); and miscellaneous (like "Get the Anacin!" or "Time to clean up"). Equipped with even just a few formulas from most of these categories, children, if they make the most of them, can get along in a variety of interaction situations. And that's just what Fillmore's subjects did. Because the learners were making like they were speakers of English by using social formulas liberally in socially appropriate ways, the English-speaking children continued to speak with them in English and thus the crucial interaction with speakers of the language continued and expanded.

The English-speaking friends that the learners "counted on for help" aided the language learners in many ways. Obviously they provided the second language in interaction contexts. They believed that the Spanish-speaking children were learning English and so they kept the interaction coming. They provided encouragement, and made every effort to understand what the learner was trying to say in English.

To summarize, we can say that child second language learners move through a sequence of stages of concerns (establish relationships, communicate meanings, be correct) which motivate and influence their learning strategies. They rely heavily on formulaic speech initially, building up a repertoire that serves them well socially as they seek and maintain interaction with speakers of the second language, and also serves them well cognitively as the basic linguistic material that they will gradually analyze as they construct an underlying system of rules for productive speech. They employ identifiable operational cognitive strategies, most of which appear to have modified counterparts in first language acquisition, but they also employ identifiable social strategies special to the second langauge learning situation which enable them to interact with speakers of the second language so that they may learn it.

The Environment Reconsidered

The environment in which the children of Fillmore's study were observed was a playroom in which each subject played with one English-speaking friend (and sometimes with the observer who was always present).[4] Obviously this was only a small part of each child's total second language environment which included classroom, lunch room, playground, neighborhood, etc. However, close study of this part of the environment suggests certain aspects which made it helpful for the children's learning of English. First of all, the English-speaking friends' language input is interesting. The friends modified their language much as adults do for children acquiring their first language. Their

[4]One subject's friend was bilingual and the playroom interactions involved as much Spanish as English.

sentences tended to be syntactically simpler, though well formed and natural at the same time. They provided a lot of repetition and paraphrase, and limited their choice of vocabulary. Their language focused mainly on the immediate situation, thus providing the perfect situation for the child's use of the first cognitive strategy: situation-language relation strategy. The English-speaking friends frequently provided nonverbal supports for their talk—gestures, sound effects, demonstrations. They also alerted the learner when their speech was for him by using some attention getters ("Hey———, watch this"). As the learners became more competent speakers of English, the friends' language became more complex. Thus the partner was providing the perfect language sample—always beyond the learner's current level, yet usable; beyond the learner's complete grasp, yet within his reach. The friends focused on the meanings the learners were conveying, rather than on the forms they were using. When they corrected the learner, it was for content, not for form:

> ... it seems that the friends were able to accept gross problems with structure without comment, and were generally able to figure out what the learners were saying no matter how little their sentences resembled English ones. The friends occasionally rephrased and repeated the learners' sentences by way of verifying their own interpretations, or sometimes they simply made no comment; but no one ... ever corrected the learners on the structures they used. There were, however, corrections of fact. (p. 702)

Most important, the linguistic input was *contextualized*. What were the contexts? The setting here was a playroom with many different kinds of toys (inviting participation in many different interaction situations), a second language learner, and a target language speaker who was a friend chosen by the learner. What is a friend if not someone you *want* to interact with? Thus the learner had an appropriate partner for interaction. But the pair also were in a setting that invited interaction. In the playroom were materials for many activities including various games—quiet games like concentration and active games like marbles—and dramatic play. The play setting provided for active participation in a situation including language. It provided a variety of activities requiring cooperation between learner and partner. It provided a "buffered" situation in which learners could explore and experiment with language without negative consequences (such as a teacher who would correct nonnative forms). It provided situations in which learners could make like speakers of the language without yet being speakers, by using whatever appropriate formulas they had plus following clearly indicated action sequences, thus encouraging the friends to keep interacting with them in English.

> In the context of play, it is possible for children to learn a lot of language. It is ideally suited for language learning since it permits interaction without requiring much true verbal communication, and it provides an opportunity for the learner to hear many well contextualized utterances which are formulaic in nature and therefore fairly easy to learn (p. 111).

What the environment did *not* include for the children in this study, was formal language instruction. Spanish and English were used as mediums of instruction in equal amounts in these children's classrooms. This seems a crucial point, given the fact that all five learners made impressive gains in their use of English during the year. Currently audiolingual methods of second language instruction prevail in bilingual programs in many areas. The assumption is that we will help children in the new language by focusing their attention on language forms which they will acquire as comfortable habits and then be able to use socially. However, the results of this study indicate that (1) children's communication— language *use—precedes* their acquisition of language structure; they care about and engage in interacting first and only subsequently care about and engage in working out correct forms; they begin with formulaic expressions but they do " . . . not learn the meanings of the component parts at first; rather, [they learn] under what conditions particular expressions can appropriately be spoken and what they can do for [them] (p. 723); (2) children's move toward greater correctness occurs within natural meaning focused interaction contexts, not within a sequenced curriculum based on formal language drill. Again the parallel with first language acquisition is striking; young children communicate first, and then, over time, always in the context of meaningful interaction, move toward adult-like forms.

Thus some of the aspects of the environment that seem to promote children's acquisition of an additional language include the provision of a natural language sample which is tailored and responsive to the learner; meaningfully contextualized language rather than drill; ample opportunity for the learner to actively participate in and initiate a variety of interaction situations; freedom to try out the language—to experiment with it and in it—in interactions focused on meanings rather than on forms.

CLASSROOM IMPLICATIONS

What does all of this mean for us as teachers as we try to provide environments which will maximally facilitate our children's development of more than one language? Some of the implications are obvious from the preceding reconsideration of the second language learning environment. It seems that our seven major conclusions relating to children's acquisition of their first language at the end of Section Two (pp. 198–200 and chapter 8) have relevance once again, some of them in special ways in the second language situation.

1. *The development of the second language is a continuous process for children.* Children move predictably from more formulaic to more productive speech as their major concerns change from an eagerness (1) to establish relationships with others, (2) to communicating messages, (3) to speaking correctly.

2. *The development of the second language is rooted in the child's cognitive growth.* The child comes with a well-developed "theory of the world in his head" and plenty of practice in actively figuring out language. Now he uses identifiable cognitive strategies as he figures out the use and (then) the structure of the new language.

3. *The child is the active party in his learning of the second language.* We see this even more dramatically in children's second language acquisition than in their first, because here they are not only "cognitive activists," attacking the "language problem" according to their own learning preferences, but they are the "social activists" as well, initiating and maintaining interaction with second language speakers so as to learn to communicate with them in their language.

All this suggests that:

4. *A classroom environment which is compatible with the child's way of learning the second language will be helpful.* This means a classroom which provides ample opportunity for children to (1) *participate actively,* (2) in *meaningful situations* (such as play), (3) with *speakers of the second language,* (4) who are *friends,* that is, whom they choose to interact with. We know that children use cognitive and social strategies in learning the second language. They must have this kind of interactive environment in which to use these strategies. We may have to build in such activities, deliberately provide for them. We cannot sit back and assume that English and non-English speakers will naturally seek each other out to interact with, especially at the beginning. It's easier to work or play with someone who speaks your own language, and often children will choose partners from their own language group. But for some part of each school day, we can establish that children work and play in cross-language pairs. And of course, if this part of the day should just "happen" to include the richest, most diverse, and most interesting free and open-ended activities we have to offer, well, so much the better for the children's cross-language friendships (which, remember, are languageships also).

5. *A classroom environment which is responsive to the second language learner will be helpful.* At the very least this means that we will be sensitive enough to tailor our language for his concern stage and for his understanding; we will relate to him socially through all possible verbal and nonverbal means, initially providing many formulas which are clear in context. We will respond to his communication efforts—*whatever their form*—as *communications,* not as imperfect expressions. And most of all, we'll assure lots of child-child interaction, since children seem so adept at naturally, intuitively, shaping their language and actions for the learner's benefit.

6. *A classroom environment which focuses on the second language learner's meaning rather than on his form is helpful.* Given the audiolingual background of second language instruction that many classroom teachers have come out of, this one is difficult. We must believe, and act on our belief, that

children will learn the forms of the second language, but not as the result of attention being drawn to those forms. As for first language learners, it is in the environment which accepts and encourages communication of meanings that children will in time shape their second language speech to be more like the speech of the second language speakers around them.

7. *A classroom environment which provides rich diversity of verbal and nonverbal experience is helpful for the second language learner.* This diversity is especially important for second language learners. They have much to learn about language in context, so the contexts they get to participate in must be many and diverse. Further, they bear much responsibility for initiating and maintaining the social interactions that provide them with contextualized language samples, and this at a time when their second language skills are limited. We help them by providing a variety of activities to choose among. It may be that, at any given time, some activities are easier for a given child to socialize in. Perhaps he has a more abundant supply of useful formulas for one situation than another. Activities he can succeed in socially must be available, as well as the freedom to choose them. Also, a diverse environment offers maximum opportunities for exploring and experimenting with how the language works in various situations. Experimentation—being able to try language out in a situation to see how it goes—is helpful, and a diverse environment provides for this. Finally, we know that we are dealing with learners who differ enormously in their ways of going about second language learning. Though general cognitive and social strategies are evident in the learning of all of them, the specific ways in which they carry out these strategies are unique to each learner. What individual learners like to do, how they choose to do it, what they notice, how they use the noticings, their personality styles, their learning styles, their social styles, will differ from one child to the next. Only a deliberately diverse environment can provide for our diverse learners.

In Fillmore's study, the diversity of the personalities and general approaches to the second language learning task were particularly fascinating. Again a pattern emerges that we have seen before of wide individual variation within a predictable general pattern. The general sequence and strategies of her second language learners were similar, but the difference in rate of learning was considerable among her subjects and related to a composite of factors unique to each learner. Seven-year-old Juan, who made the slowest progress in English during the year, and five-year-old Nora, who made the most rapid progress, offer a striking contrast. Juan's personality style was one which worked against rapid learning of the second language. Juan was

> ... extremely tentative about trying things out ... and needed to be coaxed to use what he knew. With prompting and encouragement, he would say what was asked, but no more.... Juan was not a child who took many chances, but he was keen and observant and he seemed to notice everything going on around him ... (Fillmore 1976, p. 144)

He liked to have control over things and was hesitant about using English with others until he had good control.

> Most of all, he was reluctant to interact with individuals who did not speak the same language he did—and thus cut himself off from potential input without which he could not learn the language. Because he avoided those who might have provided him with input, and most of all because he tended to avoid using the language until he had control over it, he did not acquire the varied expressions which would have permitted him to perform the analysis needed for rapid mastery. (p. 341)

Nora, on the other hand, jumped into English with real abandon, eager to communicate in whatever way she could. She actively sought interaction with English speakers, and then chose to engage in the very activities that "involved almost constant verbalization—play-acting, arguing, complaining, gossiping, and general chit-chatting" (p. 573). Nora picked up many formulas and useful ones—those that were general and that involved interaction (such as "Do you wanna play?"). Interestingly, she started analyzing the formula almost immediately: That is, while she would continue to use it intact in situations where it "belonged," she would early use parts of the formula elsewhere in her speech also. She was extremely flexible in her approach, assuming (unconsciously) that items comprising the formulas had other possibilities. Juan, however, tended to hold onto the formulas longer as intact "correct" units.

> It seemed that the more Nora knew, the faster she learned. Her development might be regarded as a kind of linguistic "capitalism" at work—once she had some language to play around with, or to "invest," she was in a position to gain even more. One of the mechanisms in Nora's rapid development was her inclination to put into immediate use whatever she learned, practicing and experimenting with it in her speech. (p. 522)

What is most important here is that all the children of the study, whatever their personality style, will in time learn English; they will simply learn it in different ways and at different rates. This is as it should be. It is not for us to tamper with our children's unique personality and learning styles, but only to provide for them.

It would be impossible to overemphasize the importance of play in children's second language learning. As teachers we tend to lug around with us a puritanical notion that work is what responsible people ought to be doing, and play is what we allow as a concession or a bribe when (if ever) the work is done. After all, we want the children we teach to be "responsible." But as Fillmore has pointed out, play is an ideal environment for second language learning because it maximizes the opportunity for the crucial ingredients to children's language growth: contextualized language that is easily understood, active participation in language-filled situations, the accumulation of useful formulas, establishing and maintaining of social relations, the opportunity to experiment. Perhaps our consciences would be salved if, in our lesson plan books, instead of writing "play period" we wrote "second language development period."

Also, it seems that a reconsideration of structured language drill is in order. Fillmore's findings cast doubt on the efficacy of structured formal language drill. Such drill seems to be out of step with the learner's concerns and strategies. It would be better to increase children's interaction experiences with second language speakers than to engage these children in formal drill. If we assume that the more children engage in something the better they get at doing it, and that the goal of second language acquisition is to communicate in the second language, then we would expect more experience in communicating to produce better communicators, while we would expect more experience in drilling to produce better drillers. Also it may be that emphasis on drill encourages an inflexibility which works against learning the second language. It was Nora's flexibility that enabled her to experiment with the parts of her formulas early in the game. Audiolingual drills discourage this experimentation, encouraging, instead, error-free response using fixed expressions. Thus these drills work counter to children's social concerns and also to their use of strategies that would help them learn the second language rapidly.

Finally, it is important to reconsider a trend we find in many bilingual programs to teach separately the children who are dominant in each language. There is currently a great concern among educators for appropriate tests for assessing language dominance. One important reason to determine language dominance, apparently, is to then group the children according to their dominant language and teach them separately. We call this "meeting the needs of the individual child." But clearly to keep the speakers of the two languages apart is to lose our strongest ally for second language learning: cross-language interaction among children. Also, if non-English speakers interact only with non-English speakers, they will develop a special, nonnative version of English.

This does not mean that the children should never be separated by language dominance for instruction. In the case of non-English dominant children, it might be well for their instruction in major areas (reading and math) to be in their first language, at least initially, and for English-dominant children's instruction in these areas to be in English. But for significant portions of the day, it would seem advisable for the language groups to be deliberately mixed and put into real interactive situations.

A FINAL UNRESOLVED CONCERN

Little has been said here about English-speaking children's acquisition of a second language. Based on Fillmore's study, there is little to say. It didn't happen. Though the English speaking friends of the subjects were in the same half-English, half-Spanish classrooms as the subjects themselves, though they had ample opportunity to interact with Spanish-speaking children in activities in the playroom and in the classroom, though they had at least one special Spanish-speaking friend (the partner in the study), in short, though they had a rich opportunity to learn Spanish, they *didn't* except for picking up a few lexical items here and there. This is in striking contrast to the Spanish-speaking children of the study who were, after nine short months, well on their way to being fluent English speakers (one even having attained skill comparable to many of her six-year-old English-speaking peers). This one-way language learning situation is not atypical.

> . . . in any language contact situation where individuals speak different languages, it is seldom the case that the learning goes both ways—at least it is hardly ever symmetrical. (Fillmore 1976, p. 12).

Why? Apparently because society exerts pressure on the members of the non-dominant language group to conform to the language of the dominant group. "Children . . . are aware of pressure to conform to community linguistic norms" (p. 13), and the "norm" in this case was English. In the classroom setting, despite deliberate attempts to encourage two-way bilingualism, it is apparently difficult to offset strong societal pressures. It is disturbing that these pressures interfere with English-speaking children's acquisition of a second language.

Far more disturbing, however, is the evidence suggesting that more rapid gains in acquiring English as a second language often correlate with loss of one's first language and culture; children's move toward English language and culture may at the same time be a move away from their own, rather than the acquisition of an additional system to their own. Juan, the child in Fillmore's study who was the slowest to learn English, was the child who clearly preferred and hung onto his first language and culture (for example, he sought only the company of Spanish-speaking children). Nora was Juan's opposite in this study. She was by far the most rapid learner of English and was obviously eager to participate as a member of Anglo culture. She chose to play mainly with English-speaking children though she had access to many Spanish-speaking children in school; she often became annoyed when her bilingual friends spoke in Spanish rather than in English when they played together; and she explicitly rejected the Spanish pronunciation of her name—all signs of accepting one language and culture at the expense of another. Perhaps the most serious question facing bilingual educators is how to keep the *bi-* in "bilingual" and "bicultural," for non-English speaking children. Fillmore leaves us with this haunting concern in the case of Nora.

The signs were . . . that she was . . . rejecting that part of her which was Spanish-speaking. If this is true, then perhaps she paid a high price to achieve that rapid development. (p. 577)

SUGGESTED PROJECTS

1. *Interviews with educators: BE.* Tape a sample (approximately ten minutes) of one or several BE-dominant children in as natural a situation as possible. Design a set of informal interview questions to ask educators representing different groups—student teachers, classroom teachers, school principals, classroom aides, college education professors. For each person you interview, first play the taped sample (you might want to provide a transcript as well, to help the interviewee follow and then recall the sample), and then tape your interview with the person. You might want to ask some questions relating to the child's background such as "Just from hearing this small sample, would you feel able to make any tentative guesses about this child's home background? What kinds of experiences do you think she might have had prior to coming to school? What might her family be like?" You might want to ask some questions about the interviewee's perceptions of the child's school experience: "Would you expect that this child might have found any particular areas of adjustment to school difficult when the child first arrived? How? Why? Would you be willing to make any guesses about what this child may be strong in or weak in in school? How would you expect this child to perform socially in school—in relations with peers? in relations with adults? Why? What sort of educational program would you want to provide for this child? Why?"

These are only a few suggestions to get your thinking started. What you want to see is what kinds of attitudes and knowledge the educators hold relating to BE-dominant children. It is important that you not force the interviewees into biased responses. You want to phrase your questions in such a way as to allow for responses like "Just listening to ten minutes of a little girl talking on tape I couldn't possibly tell you what she'd be good at or poor at in school." This kind of comment would tell you a great deal about the attitudes held by the interviewee. You might want to follow such a comment with a question like "What kind of information *would* you need to make such a guess?"

Analyze your taped interviews. Do you see any similarities within groups and differences between groups? What are they? Or do you find similar attitudes and suggestions across groups? Or is there no particular pattern, but simply an interesting range of responses? Describe the patterns, similarities, differences, etc.

2. *Interviews with educators: Bilingual.* Adapt suggestion 1 to focus on language difference (rather than dialect difference) by taping a child or children whose first language is not English. Be sure to include some native speakers of the child's dominant language in your interviewee group. You might want to see whether interviewee responses differ in any significant and interesting way between the native speakers of the child's first language and the native speakers of English. (I am assuming that English is the child's second language, though this project could be done with an English-dominant child acquiring another language.)

You can doubtless see ways of doing suggestions 1 or 2 with several friends working together—for example each of you interviewing a different group of educators and then listening to each other's taped interviews and discussing them together.

3. *A study of preferred educational approaches to ESL (English as a second language).* Prepare a brief description of a mythical school child in your class—maybe six or seven years old, who speaks a language other than English: family background, language background, personality, special abilities and interests observed. Present your description to various educators (as in above projects). Then present a variety of second language oriented experiences and get the educator to discuss the (de)merits of each for use with the child you have described. You might also want to have the educator rank the activities from most to least effective. It might be particularly helpful to work as a group on this project so as to come up with an interesting range of suggested activities initially. (Your results can't possibly be any more interesting than the range of possible activities you suggest.) You may want to include some typical audiolingual drill type activities, some typical whole group teacher-directed lesson types, some structured independent types (seatwork, work sheet, and workbook exercises), some small group (about five in a group) project type (perhaps one more structured and one less structured), some free activities like talking with other children on the playground or at lunch, some play activities in which children are paired with friends from the second language group (after Fillmore). Try to vary the suggested activities along these dimensions: (1) the degree of imposed structure, (2) the number and language background of people involved, (3) the meaning-full-ness—interestingness (versus form-full-ness). Again, taping your discussions with the educators you interview might be the most helpful way to capture and preserve their ideas. See whether, for each activity selected as helpful, you can infer what the respondent's assumptions are about how a young child acquires a second language. For example, if a respondent suggests thirty minutes a day of audiolingual drill "so the child will learn to not make so many mistakes and say things backwards" you might assume the respondent considers language learning largely a matter of establishing correct habits. If the respondent says "Well, I'd want the child to have plenty of time to just talk and play with friends who speak the second

language" you might assume the respondent sees second language learning as largely a social communication process.

4. *Bidialectal sentence Repetition Test.* Have a bidialectal (BE and SE) speaker tape record Joan Baratz' Bidialectal Sentence Repetition Test (Baratz 1969, pp. 102–4), leaving ample space on the tape after each model sentence, for a child to repeat the model sentence. Then have three to five BE-dominant children and three to five SE-dominant children take the test, preferably without you or any other adult present. This will involve two tape recorders, one on which the model sentences are played, and one that is recording the taped model sentences *and* the child's repetitions of them. Then analyze the differences between the children's repetitions and the model sentences.

5. *Analysis of black English sample.* Tape record and transcribe thirty minutes of language from a BE-speaking child or group of children. Analyze and discuss the dialectal features in your transcript.

6. *Social interaction for second language learning.* Collect thirty minutes of language from a child who is learning a second language, when he or she is engaged in an informal play activity with one or several children who speak the child's second language (the language being learned). An ideal situation would be the housekeeping or dramatic play area of a classroom. Your data collection will have to include both a tape recording and your own supplemental handwritten observational notes as the interaction proceeds. (Of course videotape would be ideal if you have access to it and can arrange a situation in which the equipment is minimally intrusive.) Your goal is to observe and describe (1) how the child uses language and other means to become and remain part of the social group. For example, does the child use some pat formulas in the second language ("Hi" "Can I play?" "Me too")? Does the child watch and copy the actions of the others (if one child picks up a dish and pretends to wash it does the subject child do the same)? Does the child use whatever devices he or she has in the second language to express new ideas? How? Does the child pantomime? What? How? (2) How do the other children adapt their behavior for the child's benefit. Do they use simpler structures and vocabulary? Do they repeat and/or paraphrase? Do they accompany their words with extra gestures that help to make their meanings clear? Do they ever guide the child physically through an appropriate action sequence?

7. *Language switching.* If you have access to a bilingual child, do a short case study to see how the child uses each of his or her two languages. This will involve gathering data on the child both at home and at school, so you will want to be sure you have the parents' support for your study. Your study will not involve taping and transcribing, but will be observational and descriptive in nature. You will "follow" the child through one day (possibly the parents will need to fill you in on the child's morning routines before school, and on the evening or bedtime routines). What topics does the child use each language to discuss? With which different persons does the child use each language? In

what settings does the child use each language? What seems to influence the switch from one language to another? In what situations are both languages used—switched within a single conversation or even within a single sentence? In what situations does the child reply in a language other than the one he was addressed in?

8. *Your own questions.* Discuss in depth any questions and wonderings you now have about language—what it is, how it is learned, and how it is used.

9. *"Your own thing."* Design your own learning experience relating to the ideas in this section, discuss it with your instructor and/or an acquaintance knowledgeable in this area, and execute it.

SUGGESTED FURTHER READINGS

Some interesting and readable works relating to Black English and/or black culture include:

ABRAHAMS, R. D., *Talking Black.* Rowley, Mass.: Newbury House Publishers, 1976.

BARATZ, J. C., and R. W. SHUY (eds.), *Teaching Black Children to Read.* Arlington, Va.: Center for Applied Linguistics, 1969.

LABOV, W., "The Logic of Nonstandard English," in *Report of the Twentieth Annual Round Table Meeting on Linguistics and Language Study,* ed. J. Alatis. Washington, D. C.: Georgetown University Press, 1970. Also reprinted in *Language and Poverty,* ed. F. Williams. Chicago: Marxham Publishing Company, 1970.

MITCHELL-KERNAN, C., *Language Behavior in a Black Urban Community,* working paper no. 23. Berkeley, California, 1971.

WARD, M. C., *Them Children: A Study of Language Learning.* New York: Holt, Rinehart and Winston, Inc., 1971.

A powerful autobiography of a black woman is:

ANGELOU, M. *I Know Why the Caged Bird Sings.* New York: Bantam Books, Inc., 1973.

Some helpful works relating to child second language learning and bilingualism include:

BURT, M. K., and H. C. DULAY (eds.), *New Directions in Second Language Learning, Teaching and Bilingual Education.* Washington, D. C.: Teachers of English to Speakers of Other Languages, 1975.

DIL, A. (ed.), *Language, Psychology and Culture: Essays by Wallace E. Lambert.* Stanford, Calif.: Stanford University Press, 1972.

FILLMORE, L. W., *The Second Time Around: Cognitive and Social Strategies in Second Language Acquisition.* Ph.D. dissertation, Stanford University, Stanford, Calif. 1976.

A personal account by a teacher of children in another culture is:
ASHTON-WARNER, S., *Teacher.* Middlesex, England: Penguin Books, 1963.

Several useful collections of articles focusing on the educational situation (especially language) of American children from various ethnic backgrounds include:
ABRAHAMS, R. D., and R. C. TROIKE (eds.), *Language and Cultural Diversity in American Education.* Englewood Cliffs, N. J.: Prentice-Hall, Inc., 1972.
CAZDEN, C., V. JOHN, and D. HYMES (eds.), *Functions of Language in the Classroom.* New York: Columbia University Teachers College, New York: 1972.
The Florida Foreign Language Reporter, 7, no. 1, (1969); 8, nos. 1 and 2 (1970); 9, nos. 1 and 2, (1971); 10, nos. 1 and 2 (1972); 11, nos. 1 and 2 (1973).

A fascinating film of black children's playground games is:
Pizza Pizza Daddy-O, University of California, Extension Media Center, Berkeley, California 94720.

References

ABRAHAMS, R. D., *Talking Black.* Rowley, Mass.: Newbury House Publishers, Inc., 1976.

———, "Black Talking on the Streets," in *Explorations in the Ethnography of Speaking,* eds. R. Bauman and J. Sherzer. London: Cambridge University Press, 1974.

———, (ed.), *Jump-Rope Rhymes: A Dictionary.* Austin, Texas and London: Published for the American Folklore Society, 1969.

———, and R. C. TROIKE (eds.), *Language and Cultural Diversity in American Education.* Englewood Cliffs, N.J.: Prentice-Hall, Inc., 1972.

ALLENDER, J. S., "Some Determinants of Inquiry Activity in Elementary School Children," *Journal of Educational Psychology,* 61, no. 3 (1970), 220–25.

———, "A Study of Inquiry Activity in Elementary School Children," *AERA,* 6 (1969), 543–58.

ANGELOU, MAYA, *I Know Why the Caged Bird Sings.* New York: Bantam Books, Inc., 1973.

ANGLUND, J. W., *Love is a Special Way of Feeling.* New York: Harcourt Brace Jovanovich, Inc., 1960.

————, *Look Out the Window*. New York: Harcourt Brace Jovanovich, Inc., 1959.

————, *A Friend Is Someone Who Likes You*. New York: Harcourt Brace Jovanovich, Inc., 1958.

ASHTON-WARNER, S., *Teacher*. Middlesex, England: Penguin Books, 1963.

AUSTIN, J. L., *How To Do Things With Words*. Oxford, England: Oxford University Press, 1962.

BAR-ADON, A., and W. LEOPOLD, *Child Language: A Book of Readings*. Englewood Cliffs, N.J.: Prentice-Hall, Inc., 1971.

BARATZ, JOAN, "Teaching Reading in a Negro School," in *Teaching Black Children to Read*, eds. J. Baratz and R. Shuy. Arlington, Va.: Center for Applied Linguistics, 1969.

————, and R. Shuy (eds.), *Teaching Black Children to Read*. Arlington, Va.: Center for Applied Linguistics, 1969.

BATES, ELIZABETH, *Language and Context: The Acquisition of Pragmatics*. New York: Academic Press, Inc., 1976.

BEHR, M., Project for the Mathematical Development of Children. Florida State University, Johnston Building, Tallahassee, Florida 32306.

BELLUGI, U., "Simplification in Children's Language," in *Language Acquisition: Models and Methods*, eds. R. Huxley and E. Ingram. New York: Academic Press, Inc., 1971.

BEREITER, C., and S. ENGELMANN, *Teaching Disadvantaged Children in the Preschool*. Englewood Cliffs, N. J.: Prentice-Hall, Inc., 1966.

BERKO, J., and R. BROWN, "Psycholinguistic Research Methods," in *Handbook of Research Methods in Child Development*, ed. P. H. Mussen. New York: John Wiley & Sons, Inc., 1960.

BERKO GLEASON, J., "The Child's Learning of English Morphology," in *Child Language: A Book of Readings*, eds. A. Bar-Adon and W. Leopold. Englewood Cliffs, N.J.: Prentice-Hall, Inc., 1971.

————, and S. WEINTRAUB, "The Acquisition of Routines in Child Language," *Language and Society*, 5 (1976), 129–36.

BERLYNE, D. E., "Curiosity and Education," in *Learning and the Educational Process*, ed. J. D. Krumboltz. Chicago: Rand-McNally & Company, 1965.

BLOOM, BENJAMIN S., *Taxonomy of Educational Objectives, Handbook 1: The Cognitive Domain*. New York: David McKay Co., Inc., 1956.

BLOOM, L., "Language Development Review," in *Review of Child Development Research (vol. 4)*, ed. F. D. Horowitz. Chicago: The University of Chicago Press, 1975.

————, *Language Development: Form and Function in Emerging Grammars*. Cambridge, Mass.: The MIT Press, 1970.

BLOUNT, B., and E. PADGUG, "Mother and Father Speech: Distribution of Parental Speech Features in English and Spanish," in *Papers and Reports on Child Language Development*. Stanford, Calif.: Stanford University, no. 12, December 1976.

BLUME, J., *Tales of a Fourth Grade Nothing*. New York: E. P. Dutton, 1972.

————, *Are You There God? It's Me, Margaret.* New York: Dell Publishing Co., Inc., 1970.

BOWEN, J. DONALD, "English Usage and Language Learning Among the Navajo," in *Workpapers in Teaching English as a Second Language,* 2 (June 1966). Los Angeles: University of California.

BOWERMAN, M., *Early Syntactic Development.* Cambridge, England: Cambridge University Press, 1973.

BRAINE, M. D. S., "On Two Types of Models of the Internalization of Grammars," in *The Ontogenesis of Grammar,* ed. D. Slobin. New York: Academic Press, Inc., 1971.

BRENNEIS, D., and L. LEIN, " 'You Fruithead': A Sociolinguistic Approach to Children's Dispute Settlement," in *Child Discourse,* eds. S. Ervin-Tripp and C. Mitchell-Kernan. New York: Academic Press, Inc., 1977.

BRITTON, J., *Language and Learning.* Hammondsworth, England: Pelican Books, 1973.

BROWN, R., *A First Language.* Cambridge, Mass.: Harvard University Press, copyright © 1973.

————, "Introduction," in J. Moffett, *Teaching the Universe of Discourse.* Boston: Houghton Mifflin Company, 1968.

————, C. CAZDEN, and U. BELLUGI-KLIMA, "The Child's Grammar from I to III," in *Child Language: A Book of Readings,* eds. A. Bar-Adon and W. Leopold. Englewood Cliffs, N.J.: Prentice-Hall, Inc., 1971.

BROWN, R., and C. FRASER, "The Acquisition of Syntax," in *The Acquisition of Language,* eds. U. Bellugi and R. Brown. Chicago: The University of Chicago Press, 1964.

BROWN, R. W., and E. H. LENNEBERG, "A Study in Language and Cognition," *Journal of Abnormal and Social Psychology,* 49 (1954), 454–62.

BRUNER, J. S. "The Ontogenesis of Speech Acts," *Journal of Child Language,* 2, no. 1 (April 1975).

————, "From Communication to Language," *Cognition,* 3, no. 3 (1974–75).

————, *Toward A Theory of Instruction.* New York: W. W. Norton & Co., Inc., 1968.

————, "The Course of Cognitive Growth," *American Psychologist,* 19 (1964), 1–15.

CAMPBELL, R., and J. LINDFORS, *Insights Into English Structure: A Programmed Course.* Englewood Cliffs, N.J.: Prentice-Hall, Inc., 1969.

CARMICHAEL, L., H. P. HOGAN, and A. A. WALTER, "An Experimental Study of the Effects of Language on the Reproduction of Visually Received Form," *Journal of Experimental Psychology,* 15 (1932), 73–86.

CAZDEN, C. B., "How Knowledge about Language Helps the Classroom Teacher—or Does It: A Personal Account," *Urban Review,* 9 (1976), 74–91.

————, "Classroom Teaching Relived," *Harvard Graduate School of Education Association Bulletin,* 19, no. 3 (Spring/Summer 1975).

————, B. H. BRYANT, and M. A. TILLMAN, "Making It and Going Home: The Attitudes of Black People Toward Language Acquisition," in *Language in Early Childhood Education,* ed. C. B. Cazden. Washington,

D.C.: National Association for the Education of Young Children, 1972.

CAZDEN, C., V. JOHN, and D. HYMES (eds.), *Functions of Language in the Classroom.* New York: Columbia University Teachers College, 1972.

CERF, B., *Book of Laughs.* New York: Beginner Books, Inc., 1959.

CHOMSKY, C., *The Acquisition of Syntax in Children from 5 to 10.* Research Monograph No. 57. Cambridge, Mass.: The MIT Press, 1969.

CHOMSKY, N., *Aspects of the Theory of Syntax.* Cambridge, Mass.: The MIT Press, 1965.

———, "Current Issues in Linguistic Theory," in *The Structure of Language,* eds. J. Fodor and J. Katz. Englewood Cliffs, N. J.: Prentice-Hall, Inc., 1964.

———, "A Review of B. F. Skinner's *Verbal Behavior,*" *Language,* 35, no. 1 (1959), 26–58.

CHUKOVSKY, KORNEI, *From Two to Five,* trans. and ed. Miriam Morton. Berkeley: University of California Press, 1968.

CLARK, E. V., "Some Aspects of the Conceptual Basis for First Language Acquisition," in *Language Perspectives—Acquisition, Retardation, and Intervention,* eds. R. L. Schiefelbusch and L. L. Lloyd. Baltimore: University Park Press, © 1974 University Park Press, Baltimore.

———, "What's in a Word: On the Child's Acquisition of Semantics in His First Language," in *Cognitive Development and the Acquisition of Language,* ed. T. Moore. New York: Academic Press, Inc., 1973.

———, Review of *The Acquisition of Syntax in Children from 5 to 10* by C. Chomsky. Research Monograph No. 57. Cambridge, Mass.: The MIT Press, 1969. In *Language,* 47 (1971), 742–49.

CLARK, H., "The Primitive Nature of Children's Relational Concepts," in *Cognition and the Development of Language,* ed. J. Hayes. New York: John Wiley & Sons, Inc., 1970.

———, and E. V. CLARK, *Psychology and Language.* New York: Harcourt Brace Jovanovich, Inc., 1977.

CLARK, R., "What's the Use of Imitation?" *Journal of Child Language,* 4, no. 3 (1977), 341–58.

COOK-GUMPERZ, J., "Situated Instructions: Language Socialization of School Age Children," in *Child Discourse,* eds. S. Ervin-Tripp and C. Mitchell-Kernan. New York: Academic Press, Inc., 1977.

COULTHARD, MALCOLM, *An Introduction to Discourse Analysis.* London: Longman, Inc., 1977.

CROSS, T., "Some Relationships Between Motherese and Linguistic Level in Accelerated Children," *Papers and Reports on Child Language Development,* Stanford University, Stanford, Calif., no. 10, 1975.

DALE, P. S., *Language Development: Structure and Function* (2nd ed.). New York: Holt, Rinehart and Winston, Inc., 1976.

DAVIS, R. M. S., "A Study of the Relationship Between Pupil Questions and Selected Variables," *Dissertation Abstracts,* 31A (1971), 5027–28.

DIL, A. (ed.), *Language, Psychology and Culture: Essays by Wallace E. Lambert.* Stanford, Calif.: Stanford University Press, 1972.

DILLARD, J. L., *Black English.* New York: Random House, Inc., 1972.

DODL, N. R., "Questioning Behavior of Elementary Classroom Groups," *California Journal for Instructional Improvement* (October 1966), 167–79.

DONALDSON, M., and G. BALFOUR. "Less is More: A Study of Language Comprehension in Children," *British Journal of Psychology,* 59 (1968), 461–72.

———, and R. WALES, "On the Acquisition of Some Relational Terms," in *Cognition and the Development of Language,* ed. J. Hayes. New York: John Wiley & Sons, Inc., 1970.

DORE, JOHN, " 'Oh Them Sheriff': A Pragmatic Analysis of Children's Responses to Questions," in *Child Discourse,* eds. S. Ervin-Tripp and C. Mitchell-Kernan. New York: Academic Press, Inc., 1977.

———, "Holophrases, Speech Acts and Language Universals," *Journal of Child Language,* 2, no. 1 (April 1975), 21–40.

DULAY, H. C., and M. K. BURT, "Errors and Strategies in Child Second Language Acquisition," *TESOL Quarterly,* 8, no. 2 (June 1974), 129–36. a

———, "Natural Sequences in Child Second Language Acquisition," *Language Learning,* 24, no. 1 (June 1974), 37–53. b

———, "A New Perspective on the Creative Construction Process in Child Second Language Acquisition," *Language Learning,* 24, no. 2 (December 1974), 253–78. c

The Elementary School Sciences Program. Developed by the Biological Sciences Curriculum Study, Boulder, Colorado. Philadelphia: J. B. Lippincott Company, 1976.

ENGELMANN, SIEGFRIED, and JEAN OSBORN, *Distar Language I* (2nd ed.). Chicago: Science Research Associates, Inc., 1976.

ERVIN, S. M., "Imitation and Structural Change in Children's Language," in *New Directions in the Study of Language,* ed. E. Lenneberg. Cambridge, Mass.: The MIT Press, 1964.

ERVIN-TRIPP, S., "Wait for Me, Roller Skate!" in *Child Discourse,* eds. S. Ervin-Tripp and C. Mitchell-Kernan. New York: Academic Press, 1977.

———, "Is Second Language Learning Like the First," *TESOL Quarterly,* 8, no. 2 (June 1974), 111–127.

———, "Discourse Agreement: How Children Answer Questions," in *Cognition and the Development of Language,* ed. J. R. Hayes. John Wiley & Sons, Inc. 1970.

Essence. Produced by the Environmental Studies for Urban Youth Projects, sponsored by the American Geological Institute. Copyright 1975 by the American Geological Institute. Reading, Mass.: Addison-Wesley Publishing Co., Inc.

FADER, D. N., and E. B. MCNEIL, *Hooked on Books: Program and Proof.* New York: Berkeley Publishing Corporation, 1968.

FASOLD, R. W., and W. WOLFRAM, "Some Linguistic Features of Negro Dialect," in *Teaching Standard English in the Inner City,* eds. R. W.

Fasold and R. W. Shuy. Arlington, Va.: Center for Applied Linguistics, 1970.

FERGUSON, C., "Baby Talk as a Simplified Register," *Papers and Reports on Child Language Development.* Stanford University, Stanford, Calif., no. 9 (1975).

――――, "Baby Talk in Six Languages," *American Anthropologist,* 66 (no. 6, pt. 2), (1964), 103–14.

FILLMORE, C., "The Case for Case," in *Universals in Linguistic Theory,* eds. E. Bach and R. T. Harms. New York: Holt, Rinehart and Winston, Inc., 1968.

FILLMORE, L. W., The Second Time Around: Cognitive and Social Strategies in Second Language Acquisition. Ph.D. dissertation. Stanford University, Stanford, Calif., 1976.

FISHER, C., and A. TERRY, *Children's Language and the Language Arts.* New York: McGraw-Hill Book Company, 1977.

FLAVELL, J. H., *Cognitive Development.* Englewood Cliffs, N.J.: Prentice-Hall, Inc., 1977.

The Florida Foreign Language Reporter, 7, no. 1 (1969); 8, nos. 1 and 2 (1970); 9, nos. 1 and 2 (1971); 10, nos. 1 and 2 (1972); 11, nos. 1 and 2 (1973).

FLEMING, JOYCE DUDNEY, "Field Report: The State of The Apes," *Psychology Today,* 7, no. 8 (January 1974), 31ff.

FRIJDA, N. H., and J. P. VAN de GEER, "Codability and Recognition: An Experiment with Facial Expressions," *Acta Psychologia,* 18, no. 5 (1961), 360–67.

FROMKIN, V., and R. RODMAN, *An Introduction to Language.* New York: Holt, Rinehart and Winston, Inc., 1974.

FULLER, FRANCES F., "Concerns of Teachers: A Developmental Conceptualization," *American Educational Research Journal,* 6, no. 2 (March 1969), 207–26.

GARDNER, R. C., and W. E. LAMBERT, *Attitudes and Motivations in Second Language Learning.* Rowley, Mass.: Newbury House Publishers, Inc., 1972.

GARVEY, C., "Requests and Responses in Children's Speech," *Journal of Child Language,* 2, no. 1 (1975), 41–63.

――――, *Play.* Cambridge, Mass.: Harvard University Press, 1977.

――――, and T. BALDWIN, *Studies in Convergent Communication: Analysis of Verbal Interaction.* Baltimore: John Hopkins Center for the Study of Social Organization of Schools. Report No, 88, 1970. ERIC ED 045 647.

――――, and E. DICKSTEIN, "A Structural Approach to the Study of Convergent Communication," paper presented at AERA, 1971. ERIC ED 056 555.

GINSBURG, H., and S. OPPER, *Piaget's Theory of Intellectual Development* (2nd ed.). Englewood Cliffs, N.J.: Prentice-Hall, Inc., 1979.

GORDON, J. W., *My Country School Diary.* New York: Dell Publishing Co., Inc., 1970.

GRAVES, DONALD, "We Won't Let Them Write," *Language Arts,* 55, no. 5 (May 1978) 635–40.

GREENFIELD, P. M., L. C. REICH, and R. R. OLVER, "On Culture and Equivalence: II," in *Studies in Cognitive Growth,* eds. J. S. Bruner and others. New York: John Wiley & Sons, Inc., 1967.

GRICE, N. P., "Logic and Conversation," in *Syntax and Semantics: Volume 3: Speech Acts,* eds. P. Cole and J. Morgan. New York: Academic Press, Inc., 1975.

GWYNNE, F., *The King Who Rained.* New York: Windmill Books, 1970.

HALLIDAY, M. A. K., *Learning How to Mean.* New York: Elsevier North-Holland, Inc., 1977.

———, *Explorations in the Functions of Language.* London: Edward Arnold, 1973.

HAND, JOHN S., WAYNE HARSH, JAMES W. NEY, and HAROLD G. SHANE, *Adventures in English: Experiences in Language* (2nd ed.). Palo Alto, Calif.: Laidlaw Brothers Publishers, 1975.

HAUPT, DOROTHY, *Relationships Between Children's Questions and Nursery School Teachers' Responses.* Detroit, Mich.: Wayne State University, 1966. ERIC ED 046 507.

HAWKINS, DAVID, "Messing About in Science," *Science and Children,* 2, no. 5 (February 1965).

Highlights. 2300 W. Fifth Street, Columbus, Ohio 43216.

HOFFMAN, M., *Vermont Diary.* New York: Teachers and Writers, 1978.

HOLT, J., *What Do I Do Monday?* New York: E. P. Dutton, 1970.

———, *How Children Learn.* New York: Pitman Publishing Corporation, 1967.

———, "Making Children Hate Reading," in *The Underachieving School.* New York: Dell Publishing Co., Inc., 1969.

HOPPER, R., and R. NAREMORE, *Children's Speech: A Practical Introduction to Communication Development.* New York: Harper & Row Publishers, Inc., 1973.

HUNKINS, FRANCIS P., *Involving Students in Questioning.* Boston: Allyn & Bacon, Inc., 1976.

HYMES, DELL, *Foundations of Sociolinguistics: An Ethnographic Approach.* Philadelphia: University of Pennsylvania Press, 1974.

———, "Introduction," in *Functions of Language in the Classroom,* eds. C. Cazden, V. John, and D. Hymes. New York: Columbia University Teachers College Press, 1972a.

———, "Models of the Interaction of Language and Social Life," in *Directions in Sociolinguistics: The Ethnography of Communication,* eds. J. Gumperz and D. Hymes. New York: Holt, Rinehart and Winston, Inc., 1972b.

INGRAM, D., "The Acquisition of Questions and Its Relation to Cognitive Development in Normal and Linguistically Deviant Children: A Pilot Study," Stanford University, Stanford, Calif., *Papers and Reports on Child Language Development* 4 (April 1970).

JAKOBSON, ROMAN, "Linguistics and Poetics," in *Style in Language,* ed. T.

A. Sebeok. New York: Published jointly by the Technology Press of MIT and John Wiley & Sons, Inc., 1960.

KEENAN, ELINOR O., "Conversational Competence in Children," *Journal of Child Language,* 1, no. 2 (1974).

———, and E. KLEIN, "Coherence in Children's Discourse," *Journal of Psycholinguistic Research,* 4, no. 4 (1975), 365–80.

Kids Magazine. Childpub Management Corp., 747 Third Ave., New York, N.Y. 10017.

KINNEAVY, JAMES L., *A Theory of Discourse.* Englewood Cliffs, N.J.: Prentice-Hall, Inc., 1971.

KLIMA, E. S., and U. BELLUGI-KLIMA, "Syntactic Regularities in the Speech of Children," in *Child Language: A Book of Readings,* eds. A. Bar-Adon and W. Leopold. Englewood Cliffs, N.J.: Prentice-Hall, Inc., 1971.

KOCHMAN, T., "Culture and Communication: Implications for Black English in the Classroom," in *Linguistic-Cultural Differences and American Education,* eds. A. Aarons, B. Gordon, and W. Stewart. *The Florida Foreign Language Reporter,* 7, no. 1 (1969), p. 89.

KOHL, H., *On Teaching.* New York: Schocken Books, Inc., 1976.

———, *The Open Classroom.* New York: A New York Review Book, distributed by Vintage Books, A Division of Random House, Inc., 1969.

KRASHEN, STEPHEN D., "Lateralization, Language Learning, and the Cricitical Period: Some New Evidence," *Language Learning,* 23, no. 1 (1973), 63–74.

KRAUS, ROBERT, *Leo, the Late Bloomer.* New York: Thomas Y. Crowell Company, Inc., 1971.

LABOV, W., "The Logic of Nonstandard English," in *Report of the Twentieth Annual Round Table Meeting on Linguistics and Language Study,* ed. J. Alatis. Washington, D.C.: Georgetown University Press, 1970a. Also reprinted in F. Williams (ed.), *Language and Poverty.* Chicago: Markham Publishing Company, 1970a.

———, *The Study of Nonstandard English.* Published by the National Council of Teachers of English by special arrangement with the Center for Applied Linguistics, Arlington, Va., 1970b.

———, "Some Sources of Reading Problems for Negro Speakers of Nonstandard English," in *Teaching Black Children to Read,* ed. J. C. Baratz and R. W. Shuy. Arlington, Va.: Center for Applied Linguistics, 1969.

———, and DAVID FANSHEL, *Therapeutic Discourse.* New York: Academic Press, Inc., 1977.

LANGACKER, R., *Language and Its Structure.* New York: Harcourt Brace Jovanovich, Inc., 1973.

LEE, D., and J. B. RUBIN, *Children and Language.* New York: Wadsworth Publishing Co. Inc., 1979.

LENNEBERG, E. H., *Biological Foundations of Language.* New York: John Wiley & Sons, Inc., 1967.

———, "The Capacity for Language Acquisition," in *The Structure of Language,* eds. J. A. Fodor and J. J. Katz. Englewood Cliffs, N.J.: Prentice-Hall, Inc., 1964.

LeSHAN, EDA J., *What Makes Me Feel This Way*. New York: Macmillan, Inc., 1972.

LIMBER, JOHN, "The Genesis of Complex Sentences," in *Cognitive Development and the Acquisition of Language*, ed. Timothy Moore. New York: Academic Press, Inc., 1973.

LUNDSTEEN, SARA W., *Children Learn to Communicate*. Englewood Cliffs, N.J: Prentice-Hall, Inc., 1976.

MACNAMARA, J., "Review of C. Chomsky, *The Acquisition of Syntax in Children from 5 to 10*," *General Linguistics*, 10 (1970), 164–72. (Research Monograph No. 57, Cambridge, Mass.: The MIT press, 1970).

McNEILL, D., *The Acquisition of Language*. New York: Harper & Row, Publishers, Inc., 1970.

———, "Developmental Psycholinguistics," in *The Genesis of Language*, eds. F. Smith, and G. Miller. Cambridge, Mass.: The MIT Press, 1966.

MARATSOS, M. P., "How Preschool Children Understand Missing Complement Subjects," *Child Development*, 45 (1974), 700–706.

MAYER, M., *Bubble Bubble*. New York: Parents' Magazine Press, 1973.

MILON, J. P., "The Development of Negation in English by a Second Language Learner," *TESOL Quarterly*, 8, no. 2 (June 1974), 137–43.

MILLER, G., "Some Preliminaries to Psycholinguistics," *American Psychologist*, 20, no. 1 (January 1960).

MILNE, A. A., *Winnie-the-Pooh*. © 1956 by A. A. Milne. New York: E. P. Dutton, 1956.

MITCHELL-KERNAN, C., Language Behavior in a Black Urban Community. Ph.D. Dissertation. Working paper no. 23, Language-Behavior Research Laboratory, October 1969.

MOFFETT, JAMES (ed.), *Interaction: A Student-Centered Language Arts and Reading Program*. Boston: Houghton Mifflin Company, 1973. a

———, *A Student-Centered Language Arts Curriculum, Grades K-6: A Handbook for Teachers*. Boston.: Houghton Mifflin Company, 1973. b

———, and B. J. WAGNER, *Student-Centered Language Arts and Reading, K-13: A Handbook (2nd ed.)* Boston: Houghton Mifflin Company, 1976.

NELSON, KATHERINE, *Structure and Strategy in Learning to Talk*. Chicago: The University of Chicago Press, Monographs of the Society for Research in Child Development, Serial No. 149, 1973.

NELSON, KEITH C., GAYE CARSKADDON, and JOHN D. BONVILLIAN, "Syntax Acquisition: Impact of Experimental Variation in Adult Verbal Interaction with the Child," *Child Development*, 44 (1973), 497–504.

The New Roget's Thesaurus, ed. N. Lewis. New York: G. P. Putnam's Sons, 1964.

OPIE, IONA, and PETER OPIE, eds., *Children's Games in Street and Playground*. Oxford, England: Clarendon Press, 1969.

———, (eds.), *Lore and Language of School Children*. Oxford, England: Oxford University Press, 1959.

Oral Language Development: Views of Five Teachers. Agency for Instructional Television, 1111 West 17th St., Bloomington, Indiana 47401.

PARISH, P., *Amelia Bedelia*. New York: Harper & Row, Publishers, Inc., 1963.

PARISI, D. and F. ANTINUCCI, *Essentials of Grammar,* trans. E. Bates. New York: Academic Press, Inc., 1976.

PIAGET, J., *Six Psychological Studies.* New York: Random House, Inc., 1967.

Pizza Pizza Daddy-O, University of California, Extension Media Center, Berkeley, California 94720.

POSTAL, PAUL M., "Linguistic Novelty and the Problem of Grammar," in *English Transformational Grammar,* eds. R. Jacobs and P. Rosenbaum. Waltham, Mass.: Xerox College Publishing, 1968.

REED, D., and J. SAWYER, "Linguistic Considerations in Reading Disability," in *Language and Reading: An Interdisciplinary Approach,* ed. D. Gunderson. Arlington, Va.: Center for Applied Linguistics, 1970.

ROBINSON, W. P., "Social Factors and Language Development in Primary School Children," in *Language Acquisition: Models and Methods,* eds. R. Huxley and E. Ingram. New York: Academic Press, Inc., 1971.

ROSEN, CONNIE, and HAROLD ROSEN, *The Language of Primary School Children.* London: Penguin Education for the Schools Council, 1973.

ROSS, HILDY S., and RITA H. BALZAR, "Determinants and Consequences of Children's Questions," *Child Development,* 46 (1975), 536–39.

SACHS, J., "Talking About the There and Then: The Emergence of Displaced Reference in Parent-Child Discourse," *Papers and Reports on Child Language Development,* Stanford University, Stanford, Calif., no. 13, August (1977).

———, and J. DEVIN, "Young Children's Use of Age-Appropriate Speech Styles in Social Interaction and Role-Playing," *Journal of Child Language,* 3, no. 1 (1976), 81–98.

SACKS, HARVEY, "An Analysis of the Course of a Joke's Telling in Conversation," in *Explorations in the Ethnography of Speaking,* eds. R. Bauman and J. Sherzer. Cambridge, England: Cambridge University Press, 1974.

———, E. SCHEGLOFF, and G. JEFFERSON, "A Simplest Systematics for the Organization of Turn-Taking for Conversation," *Language,* 50 (1974), 696–735.

SAPIR, EDWARD, "Language," in *Culture, Language and Personality,* ed. D. G. Mandelbaum. Berkeley: University of California Press, 1956.

———, "The Status of Linguistics as a Science," in *Selected Writings of Edward Sapir in Language, Culture, and Personality,* ed. D. G. Mandelbaum. Berkeley: University of California Press, 1949.

SAVIĆ, S., "Aspects of Adult-Child Communication: The Problem of Question Acquisition," *Journal of Child Language* 2 (1975), 251–60.

SAXE, J. G., "The Blind Men and the Elephant," in *New Nation English: Book Five (B),* ed. E. Akaduh. London: Nelson, 1968.

SCHEGLOFF, EMANUEL, "Sequencing in Conversational Openings," in *Directions in Sociolinguistics,* eds. J. Gumperz and D. Hymes. New York: Holt, Rinehart and Winston, Inc., 1972.

SEARLE, J., "Indirect Speech Acts," in *Syntax and Semantics: Volume 3: Speech Acts,* eds. P. Cole and J. Morgan. New York: Academic Press, Inc., 1975.

————, *Speech Acts.* Cambridge, England: Cambridge University Press, 1970.

SELDEN, G., *Cricket in Times Square.* New York: Ariel, 1960.

Shared Nomenclature, Ohio State University, Film Lab Service, Inc., 4019 Prospect Ave., Cleveland, Ohio 44103.

SHATZ, M., and R. GELMAN, *The Development of Communication Skills: Modifications in the Speech of Young Children as a Function of Listener.* Monograph of the Society for Research in Child Development. Serial no. 152, vol. 38, no. 5 (1973).

SINCLAIR, J. McH., and R. M. COULTHARD, *Towards an Analysis of Discourse: The English Used by Teachers and Pupils.* London: Oxford University Press, 1975.

SINCLAIR-DEZWART, H., "Language Acquisition and Cognitive Development," in *Cognitive Development and the Acquisition of Language,* ed. T. E. Moore. New York: Academic Press, Inc., 1973.

SKINNER, B. F., *Verbal Behavior.* Englewood Cliffs, N.J.: Prentice-Hall, Inc., 1957.

SLOBIN, D. I., "The More It Changes . . .: On Understanding Language by Watching It Move Through Time," *Papers and Reports on Child Language Development,* 10 (September 1975), Stanford, Calif., Stanford University.

————, "Cognitive Prerequisites for the Development of Grammar," in *Studies of Child Language Development,* eds. C. A. Ferguson and D. I. Slobin. New York: Holt, Rinehart and Winston, Inc., 1973.

————, *Psycholinguistics.* Glenview, Ill.: Scott, Foresman and Company, 1971.

————, *Psycholinguistics* (2nd ed.). Glenview, Ill.: Scott, Foresman and Company, 1979.

————, "Comments on 'Developmental Psycholinguistics,' " in *The Genesis of Language: A Psycholinguistic Approach,* eds. F. Smith and G. Miller. Cambridge, Mass.: The MIT Press, 1966.

————, and C. A. WELSH, "Elicited Imitation as a Research Tool in Developmental Psycholinguistics," in *Studies of Child Language Development,* eds. C. A. Ferguson and D. I. Slobin. New York: Holt, Rinehart and Winston, Inc., 1973.

SMITH, FRANK, *Comprehension and Learning: A Conceptual Framework for Teachers.* New York: Holt, Rinehart and Winston, Inc., 1975.

————, "Twelve Easy Ways to Make Learning to Read Difficult* (*and One Difficult Way to Make it Easy)," in *Psycholinguistics and Reading,* ed. Frank Smith. New York: Holt, Rinehart and Winston, Inc., 1973.

SNOW, C. E., "The Development of Conversation Between Mothers and Babies," *Journal of Child Language,* 4 (1977)a. Published by Cambridge University Press.

————, "Mothers' Speech Research: From Input to Interaction," in *Talking to Children,* eds. C. E. Snow and C. A. Ferguson. Cambridge, England: Cambridge University Press, 1977b.

————, "Mothers' Speech to Children Learning Language," *Child Development,* 43 (1972), 549–65.

Southwest Educational Development Laboratory. *Oral Language Development Bilingual Educational Program.* Austin, Texas, 1971–72.

STAATS, A. W., "Linguistic-Mentalistic Theory versus an Explanatory S-R Learning Theory of Language Development," in *The Ontogenesis of Grammar,* ed. D. Slobin. New York: Academic Press, Inc., 1971.

STEPTOE, J., *Stevie.* New York: Harper & Row Publishers, Inc., 1969.

Teachers and Writers Collaborative. c/o P.S. 3, 490 Hudson Street, New York, N.Y. 10014.

THOMAS, D., "Fern Hill," in *The Collected Poems of Dylan Thomas.* Philadelphia: J. B. Lippincott Company, 1953 & London: J.M. Dent & Sons.

THURBER, J., *The 13 Clocks.* New York: Harcourt Brace Jovanovich, 1950.

TORRANCE, E. PAUL, "Influence of Alternate Approaches to Pre-Primary Educational Stimulation and Question-Asking Skills," *Journal of Educational Research,* 65, no. 5 (January 1972), 204–6.

―――, "Freedom to Manipulate Objects and Question-Asking Performance of Six-Year-Olds," *Young Children,* 26 (1970), 93–97.

TOUGH, JOAN, *The Development of Meaning.* London: George Allen & Unwin Ltd., 1977.

―――, *Focus on Meaning.* London: George Allen & Unwin Ltd., 1974.

URZÚA, CAROLE, "A Sociolinguistic Analysis of the Requests of Mothers to Their Two-Year-Old Daughters," unpublished doctoral dissertation, The University of Texas at Austin, 1977.

VIORST, J., *Alexander and the Terrible, Horrible No Good Very Bad Day.* New York: Atheneum Publishers, 1972.

WARD, M. C., *Them Children: A Study in Language Learning.* New York: Holt, Rinehart and Winston, Inc., 1971

WHITE, E. B., *Charlotte's Web.* New York: Harper & Row, Publishers, Inc., 1952.

WHORF, B., *Language, Thought, and Reality,* ed. J. Carroll. Cambridge, Mass.: The MIT Press, 1956.

WILLIAMS, F., R. HOPPER, and D. NATALICIO, *The Sounds of Children.* Englewood Cliffs, N.J.: Prentice-Hall, Inc., 1977.

ZAHORIK, JOHN A., "Questioning in the Classroom," *Education,* 91 (April 1971), 358–63.

INDEX